State Practices and Zionist Images

For Ellen,
In friendship
and with gratitude
for your activity
With good hopes,
David
April 2009

State Practices and Zionist Images

Shaping Economic Development in Arab Towns in Israel

David A. Wesley

Berghahn Books
NEW YORK • OXFORD

Published in 2006 by
Berghahn Books

www.berghahnbooks.com

First paperback edition published in 2009

Library of Congress Cataloging-in-Publication Data

Wesley, David A.
State practices and Zionist images : shaping economic development in Arab towns in Israel / David A. Wesley.
p. cm.
Includes bibliographical references and index.
ISBN 978-1-84545-058-8 (hbk) -- 978-1-84545-356-5 (pbk)
1. Israel—Economic conditions—Case studies. 2. Palestinian Arabs—Israel—Economic conditions—Case studies. 3. Israel—Ethnic relations—Case studies. 4. Bureaucracy—Israel—Case studies. 5. Power (Social sciences)—Israel—Case studies. 6. Social integration—Israel—Case studies. 7. Social planning—Israel—Case studies. I. Title.

HC415.25.W473 2006
338.9569400917'4927—dc22

2006040747

British Library Cataloguing in Publication Data

A catalogue record for this book is available from
the British Library.

Printed on acid-free paper

Contents

Illustrations

Figures

Tables

Foreword

Max Weber took a deep and lasting interest in the workings of organizations (*Verbände*). While he wrote long essays on the stock exchange, the calling of politics, the industrial worker, and protestant sects, his favorite theme was the administration of states. He studied the running of both historical states, such as traditional China, and contemporary states, such as the Germany of his time, in intimate detail. Analyses of government, power, and authority crop up in all his works. Yet none of these profound and learned studies made an impact equal to that of the relatively concise and highly abstract discussion of the ideal-type of bureaucracy in his posthumous *Wirtschaft und Gesellschaft* ([1921] 1956). Although its limitations were obvious from the outset, these ideas—as interpreted in a partial English translation (Weber 1947)—were taken up with alacrity by students of organizational sociology and management and have continued to dominate their thinking. What was wrong with Weber's ideal type? First, as Albrow (1970: 50) points out, the conception was derived from German administrative ideals and not from observed bureaucratic practice. Second, it gave such salience to force as the root of all power, that the endless variety of powers and their situational contingency were totally obscured. Therefore, any student of an actual bureaucracy could easily refute one aspect or another of the ideal-type of bureaucracy. For almost a century now, scholars have criticized and amended it, but no one has ever come up with an alternative general theory of bureaucracy.

At the same time, scholars of many countries have continued the other Weberian tradition, the study of concrete bureaucratic systems. They have given us a series of insightful and innovative works which, taken together, amount to a complex theory of bureaucratic praxis. My personal favorites are *The Dynamics of Bureaucracy* (Blau 1963), *The Bureaucratic Phenomenon* (Crozier 1964), *Manufacturing Consent* (Burawoy 1979), and *Engineering Culture* (Kunda 1992). While each of these studies deals with a specific social world, they all grapple with Weber's work and seek to refine it, without bothering with ideal-types. There are some other things they have in common: they provide richly detailed ethnographies of living organizations; they break down conceptual and organizational boundaries and treat the outside world as an integral part of the organization; they are alert to the continuous adaptations of organizations to a changing environment; and they offer a sophisticated and nuanced view of power relations. While some scholars still treat bureaucracies as bounded timeless systems, these studies, between them, have transformed the anthropology of bureaucratic organizations.

I believe that there are good reasons for adding Dr. David A. Wesley's study to this illustrious series of books. First, it broaches an unusual theme. It deals with the planning and implementation (or perhaps delayed implementation) of an industrial park for Arab towns in Galilee, a complex process that involves in its course a large number of state agencies and local authorities. It shows how numerous agencies of the State interpret the laws and regulations and prescribed procedures in order to delay the establishment of an industrial park for Arab citizens of Galilee, while permitting legal shortcuts and devising special procedures to set up another industrial park intended for the Jewish town of Upper Nazareth

Second, Wesley devised field methods that were suited to his theme. Instead of observing the workings of an organization, he concentrated on a case and followed the intricate meanderings of official and unrecorded acts connected with it. He attended meetings, followed face-to-face interactions between clients and officials in various agencies, interviewed the participants in negotiations that went on behind the scenes, and accumulated a small mountain of documents and got the authors and recipients to gloss and interpret them. The term "participant observation" may be too narrow for this research procedure, but Wesley certainly has done anthropological fieldwork in the fullest sense of the term.

Third, in his attempt to understand the story of the industrial park, Wesley has identified the numerous forces affecting the understandings and behavior of the participants, such as the laws that bound them (but often only as the occasion suited), the personal networks of politicians and community leaders that often facilitated and speeded up negotiations, and the invisible hands of the Israel Lands Administration that controls 93 percent of all the land in the country and makes rules whose application results in separate outcomes for Arabs and for Jews. All these activities were carried out by officials and clients, each of whom brought into the situation a personal interpretation of rules and interjected personal concerns. He has broken through all the conventional organizational and geographical boundaries and, no less important, he has also overcome the common distinction between text and context. Because the context was reflected in the behavior of actors, it had to be integral to the "text" and not an external force impinging on it.

Fourth, Wesley makes a special effort to point out the various means by which discriminatory practices are made to disappear from view. He shows that secrecy and dissimulation are essential elements in bureaucratic behavior.

Instead of admitting to discriminatory practices, officials promulgate theories showing that the victims are to blame. Thus, Arabs are presented as lacking industrial entrepreneurship, while the authorities block private Arab development initiatives. Even when the State allocates land for industrial development to Arabs, they are made to pay higher prices than their Jewish neighbors. Although the State confiscated much Arab land and few Arabs make a living as farmers, the Arab towns are still left in the backwaters of regional industrial development. Lacking local employment opportunities, most townspeople work as labor migrants.

Fifth, Wesley takes a good look at the perennial and inexhaustible problem of power. It is the theoretical thread that runs through and enlivens the whole argument. He makes it quite clear that violence plays only a limited role in the transactions he describes, and that it certainly does not underlie the countless other forms of power. In every situation, these forms of power are freshly created and molded; they may gain or lose value in a moment, and actors may devise ingenious ways to combine various forms of power to considerable effect.

The shift in focus from State to state practices allows Wesley to produce what he refers to as an ethnography of the macro-order. Of added interest here is his innovative adaptation of Foucault's discourse theory to his own actor-oriented socio-anthropological analysis, enabling him to show how the actors are caught in the nets of their own contextualizing discourse.

Appalled by the systematic discriminatory results of state practices, the author takes a moral stand. Yet he works by understating his case and allowing the reader to draw his own conclusions. At the same time, Wesley points to the possibility of challenging the complex existing configuration of power.

— *Emanuel Marx*

References

Albrow, Martin. 1970. *Bureaucracy*. London: Macmillan.

Blau, Peter M. 1963. *The Dynamics of Bureaucracy: A Study of Interpersonal Relations in Two Government Agencies*. Rev. ed. Chicago: University of Chicago Press. [First published 1955.]

Burawoy, Michael. 1979. *Manufacturing Consent: Changes in the Labor Process under Monopoly Capitalism*. Chicago: University of Chicago Press.

Crozier, Michel. 1964. *The Bureaucratic Phenomenon*. Chicago: University of Chicago Press.

Kunda, Gideon. 1992. *Engineering Culture: Control and Commitment in a High-Tech Corporation*. Philadelphia: Temple University Press.

Weber, Max. [1921] 1956. *Wirtschaft und Gesellschaft*. 2 vols. Cologne: Kiepenheuer & Witsch.

______. 1947. *The Theory of Social and Economic Organization, Being Part I of "Wirtschaft und Gesellschaft."* Trans. A. R. Henderson and Talcott Parsons. London: William Hodge.

Acknowledgments

The anthropological endeavor takes as its point of departure that the researcher will be dependent on others in the attempt to gain an understanding of the world he or she is studying. It starts out with a debt already presumed. In the present case, that debt is so large and extends to so many people that I can only begin to try to acknowledge it here. I thank, first of all, all those people in the field—participants, officials, planners, researchers—who unstintingly shared their knowledge and experience with me and who put whatever material they could at my disposal. Most of them will not be mentioned by name here, but I have attempted to put their contributions to honest use; it is my hope that the pages that follow will reflect the seriousness, commitment, and passion of those who welcomed me into their world.

Awny Zreikat and Yusef Darawshe were ever responsive to my requests to know more about what was going on. Rassem Khamaisi, a planner and encourager of development who has also established himself in the domain of academic analysis, was at the center of events having to do with planning Zipporit D–E; he opened up this world to me and was generous in sharing both information and understanding.

Yoel Segal, in the field of community development planning, and Uri Pinkerfeld, in the field of land-use issues, made themselves available for numerous sessions in which they proved to be patient educators.

The people of the Center for Jewish-Arab Economic Development—in particular, Sarah Kreimer, Helmi Kittani, Mustafa Abu Roomi, Mohammed Younis, and Manal Bahous—were instrumental in introducing me to this world I wished to study, helping to open some of the doors.

Hubert Law Yone, Michael Meyer-Brodnitz, and Aziz Haidar were also among those who opened their doors to me.

I thank all of these people for the important contributions they made to my knowledge and understanding of the field I was studying and its background.

I owe a special thanks to Izhak Schnell, Michael Sofer, and Israel Drori, who were generous in placing at my disposal some of the responses they collected in their important research on industrial development in the Arab towns.

I turn now to the university and the domain of anthropology and sociology. It was my teachers there who equipped me with the analytic tools I took with me to the field. I thank, in particular, Emanuel Marx, Haim Hazan, Abraham Cordova, Tom Selwyn, and Hanna Herzog. I am also indebted to Henry Rosenfeld for his valuable comments. Emanuel, my supervisor, has stamped himself in my mind as the quintessential educator. His experience and wisdom lit the way for me; with the gentlest of words he kept me on the course I had set until I reached my research goal. Now, Emanuel has provided a generous Foreword for this book, and I thank him again.

I extend thanks also to Haya Stier for her comments on my statistical questions, and to Zvi Ron for assistance with topographical terminology.

Zvi Mednik of the Tel Aviv University Department of Geography and the Human Environment provided great assistance.

I am indebted to Alia Abou Shmeiss, Rania Abou Shmeiss, Hayat Abou Shmeiss, and Salim Shomar for their assistance in translating material from Arabic, saving me long, long hours with an Arabic dictionary in hand.

I am grateful to the librarians at the Tel Aviv University Library for Social Sciences and Management for their unfailing assistance, and particularly to Sarah Levkovitch who, through the interlibrary borrowing service, provided ready access to holdings at other libraries.

Daniel Isaacs was a ready source for the correct English titles of Israeli legislation.

Yakov Dorfman of the Tel Aviv University Department of Geography and the Human Environment did important preliminary work on the maps in figures 1.1 and 7.1. These maps were brought to completion by Menahem Egozy who also did a first version of the maps in figures 1.5, 2.1, 2.2, 3.1, 3.2, 3.3, and 3.4. I wish to extend my appreciation to both of these cartographers for their careful work and their patience with me as I struggled to define what I wanted the maps to accomplish. Avigdor Orgad produced the final (book) version of these maps, and also those in figures 1.4 and 1.6. Avigdor also provided computer-assisted photographic composition for the photographs in figures 1.2, 1.3, and 4.1. I extend my thanks and appreciation to him for his contribution.

Moshe Taub is responsible for the photography in figures 1.2 and 4.1, and together with Sheila Shalhevet for that in figure 1.3. I offer my sincere thanks to these professionals for their committed help.

The aerial photograph in figure 3.5 was supplied by Ofek Aerial Photography (1987) Ltd. Their permission to reproduce it here is acknowledged with appreciation.

I thank Yasmin Alkaly of the Social Science Computer Lab at Tel Aviv University for statistical data processing.

An important part of the fieldwork phase of the research was assisted by a grant from the Israel Science Foundation, for which I express my gratitude.

I extend my greatest appreciation to Marion Berghahn for her commitment and endeavor in bringing about the publication of this book. And I thank Michael Dempsey, production editor, and the rest of the expert staff of Berghahn Books, who have collaborated unreservedly on the project. I owe special thanks to Sue Sakai, whose skillful, devoted, and essential copyediting has contributed to the quality of this book. If quirks or idiosyncrasies of language remain, that is the result of my own stubbornness. I also owe special thanks to Shawn Kendrick, compositor, for her energy and heart in bringing this book to the printed page. Joanna Usherwood designed the cover, and I thank her warmly. And I thank Hanna Fuad Farah, artist-photographer, whose photograph of Galilee oak trees speaks from the cover.

My family comes at the end of this roster, but they know that they are first in my heart. I thank my wife Elana, my partner and friend, whose support and total commitment and backing have provided me with spiritual sustenance, intellectual and moral insight, and no small measure of the strength necessary to carry out this project. I thank my children for both their support and patience. And I thank the other members of my family without whose financial assistance this research would not have come to pass.

Abbreviations

CBS	Israeli Central Bureau of Statistics
CPAL	Committee for the Preservation of Agricultural Land
DPBC	District Planning and Building Commission
EIA	Environmental Impact Assessment
HaPaT	Hevra lePituach Tashti'ot (Infrastructure Development Company)
HCJ	High Court of Justice
ILA	Israel Lands Administration
JNF	Jewish National Fund
KT	*Kovetz HaTaqanot* (Collection of regulations)
LPBC	Local Planning and Building Commission
NBPB	National Board for Planning and Building
NPR	National Priority Region
PBL	Planning and Building Law
PBPL	Planning and Building Procedures (Temporary Provisions) Law
RICC	Residential and Industrial Construction Commission (translation of VaLaL—Va'ada Lebniya Lemegurim ulta'asiya). The PBPL is often referred to as the VaLaL law.
UBP	Urban Building Plan (i.e., detailed plan)
VaLaL	See entry for RICC
WMS	Without Municipal Status

Introduction

An Ethnography of Macro-order Power Relations

The Research Problem

This research monograph offers an analysis of the field of power relations in which Arab economic development in Israel takes place. One striking indicator of stunted economic development is the fact that Arab towns predominate overwhelmingly in the lower rungs of Israel's Central Bureau of Statistics (CBS) ranking of Israeli localities by their populations' socioeconomic level (CBS 1999; Sikkuy 1996; see table 2.1 in chapter 2, this volume).

Here in Israel, the law promises equal access to development; officials deny that there is discrimination and go on to declare that discrimination would be unacceptable. I contend that one needs to be able to explain differential macro-order majority-minority outcomes in just such situations. And one needs to do this without recourse to essentializations that put the actors in the role of Oppressor and Victim. To do this in the case of the Arab population in Israel, I write about struggle and confrontation, and about multiple social-political-historical domains, as well as the synergy between them. This, together with my focus on practice at nodes of official social interaction, provides anthropological access to the macro-order. There is theoretical-methodological innovation here, to be elaborated on in the following pages, that will afford a fresh look at Jewish-Arab relations in Israel (*read:* majority-minority relations in the modern state).

Israel social science research often puts Arab traditionalism as a major cause of economic backwardness (for an example, see Schnell et al. 1995). The present analysis rejects such explanations on the grounds that (a) traditionalism should not be assumed a priori, and (b) elements of tradition, when they do appear to have an impact on economic development, need to be seen in the context of the field of power relations. But the present study also eschews explanation in terms of simple models of domination on the grounds that such models tend to short-circuit analysis: lagging economic development or other circumstances are cited to establish the existence of domination, and this in turn is regarded as an adequate explanation of its effects. Such models tell us little about the "how" of the workings of power relations in the modern state. It is this latter kind of analysis that the present study sets as its goal.

I began my anthropological fieldwork by following events in several Arab towns where Israel's Ministry of Industry, in a new policy initiative, had undertaken the development of local industrial areas. This project brought the Arab towns into contact with various agencies of the national government. As I followed events, I came to see that the question of small local industrial areas could not properly be understood in isolation from the web of relationships between the Arab localities and their Jewish neighbors. I have decided to put one case in which that web of relationships is particularly salient at the center of my ethnography. That is the case of the large Zipporit industrial area in which (Jewish) Upper Nazareth and the nearby Arab towns of Kafar Kanna and Meshhed were caught up in struggle, maneuver, and efforts at cooperation. At the same time, Kafar Kanna was one of the Arab towns where the Ministry of Industry was building a local industrial area. I focus on the events and circumstances in which Upper Nazareth, Kafar Kanna, and Meshhed were involved, but where appropriate, I will draw freely on material I gathered from other sites in the research field. But further, when I come to deal below at greater length with my view of the research field, I will describe how my attention was drawn out from strictly local events and up the administrative hierarchy and outward to collateral domains.

During the period in which my fieldwork took place (1992–1997) the Ministry of Industry's initiative in the Arab towns was complemented by the ministry's new small business program and certain of the latter's instruments that meshed with Ministry of Interior, Jewish Agency, and JDC (Joint Distribution Committee) programs whose stated aim was the encouragement of local initiative for urban economic development. Thus, the policy context at the time of this research was neither blatant "control" (Lustick) nor studied neglect, but rather an active government program with the avowed aim of encouraging economic development in the Arab towns. Coming to the research field armed with Foucault's seminal insight that power is not only inhibiting but also productive in its effect, I found the fact that an active program held sway not inauspicious to a study of power relations. After all, is it not at just such a time that revealing confrontations and transactions take place?

Two comments are in order here. First, the policy departure entailed in the programs I was observing is commonly ascribed to the Labor Party's return to power in 1993. Analysis from the vantage point of power should not be taken to imply a thesis of *plus ça change, plus c'est la même chose*. Nothing could be further from the view of power and structure that will be set out in my discussion on theoretical approach. Second, it should be emphasized that the research problem has to do not with the distinction between "policy" and "implementation"—a distinction that is often misleading (cf. Schaffer 1980)—but rather with the question of how power relations are established, how they develop, and how they become manifest in the social fabric.

Bound up in the development efforts I was observing were such issues as (a) the control of local planning through the centralized statutory planning system, (b) local authority jurisdictional boundaries and struggle over those boundaries, (c) private and state ownership of land and the availability of land for development, (d) the allocation of government budgets, (e) the setting of national priority region status, and (f) conditions impinging on the ability of Arab local authorities to press for their inclusion as joint owners and managers of regional areas. It soon became apparent that the local authorities were themselves, as petitioners, applicants, and competitors, central actors. Early on, I adopted the concept of bureaucratic access (see Schaffer 1977) as an analytic category that would aid in understanding the events of the research field, an analytic category relevant not only to the case of individual applicants for approvals, permits, and allocations, but also to the role that the local authorities were playing.

It was also apparent, both from a reading of the research literature having to do with Arab economic development in Israel and from some of my own observations, that my analysis would have to take into account the influence of the state's Zionist character on that development. Theoretical reflection prompted me to formulate that influence as the contextualizing effect of the representations and images defined in the Zionist discourse. Thus, two important analytic categories of my study would be bureaucratic access (ostensibly an element of inclusion) and the images of the Zionist discourse (an element of exclusion).

But if these were central elements in the constitution of the field of power, it was still necessary to arrive at a conceptualization of that field itself. This was a question with which I wrestled throughout the period of my fieldwork—one aspect of the active reciprocal dialectic between theory, field, and interpretation characteristic of the anthropological endeavor. The next section, on theoretical background and approach, will take up the analytic categories of bureaucratic access and representation in some detail, and will formulate a conceptualization of the field of power.

Theoretical Background and Approach

The research school that locates the source of Arab economic backwardness in the traditionalism and factionalism of Arab society in Israel (Bar-Gal and Soffer 1976; Arnon and Raviv 1980) was first seriously countered by Rosenfeld (1978). Rosenfeld, writing from a class approach, attributed the underdevelopment of the Arab village economy to Israeli state policy, which "fosters a Jewish state-nation ethos and economy … and regards development as relating specifically to Jews" (400). Zureik (1979) argued that the economic situation of the Arabs in Israel is a manifestation of internal colonialism, that is, the domination and exploitation of a native population by a colonial settler society. Lustick (1980) described economic dependence as a major component of the system of control to which the Israeli Arab minority has been subject. One or more of the latter three writers, who posited the link between Arab economic development and state power, has served as an anchor for later and recent investigations of the economic/political status of the Arab population in Israel (see, e.g., R. Khalidi 1988; Yiftachel 1992; Haidar 1995).

The present study pursues the implications of Rosenfeld's 1978 statement cited above, but in positing administrative and representing practices as a locus of power relations, it departs from the binary models of domination employed by Zureik or Lustick. This shift in the focus of analysis from the origin of power to the question of how power works is derived from Foucault (cf. 1982). Foucault, of course, dealt with what he referred to as disciplinary, normalizing power, not the politics of economic exploitation and resource control; nonetheless, on this and two other major points, I found that his thinking provided key insights for my own analysis.

The second point that I construe from Foucauldian elements has to do with the polymorphic nature of what present themselves as great, coherent constellations of power. In a 1977 interview (Foucault 1980, chap. 11), Foucault speaks of an ensemble of power relations as a complex strategic situation, "an open, more-or-less coordinated … cluster of relations" (199), and of what he calls the apparatuses or strategies of power as heterogeneous combinations of discursive and nondiscursive practices (196–197, passim). And in a second interview (Foucault 1981), he advocates historical analysis in terms of multiple, plural causes—a polymorphism of elements, relations, and domains. The third Foucauldian point that I found useful has to do with the conceptualization of the discursive formation not as an emergent cognitive order but as being located in objective, tangible materiality; hence, the idea of the exteriority of discourse (Foucault 1972). How these points contributed to my analysis of the field of power relations will be set out in the appropriate places in the discussion below.

Writers as well as actors in the field often present bureaucratic access as though it were rational and apolitical. But I contend that bureaucratic access and the administrative organization of the world in which it is inseparably lodged are nothing if not political (cf. Schaffer 1977, 1980). Administrative organization begins by dividing the world into separate domains. It may be that these divisions must be and can be overcome or manipulated in the course of pursuing a project. But it also happens that such divisions and the administrative and conceptual boundaries accompanying them impose an order that can be challenged only with great difficulty. One prime example would be the distinction I encountered in the field between local authority jurisdiction, on the one hand, and land ownership, on the other—a distinction having its uses and effects of power in the sphere of planning economic development.

Bureaucratic access proceeds by putting a program into place—deciding that a particular social area requires regulation (e.g., land-use zoning) or support (e.g., government subsidies), or both. The decision to allocate resources to one program and not to another is, of course, a political one. Then, criteria are set: Who will qualify, and how will qualification be determined? Administrative procedures are established: What will be the makeup of the planning and building commission? How will members be appointed? Where will the commission be located? Finally, applications are processed: maneuver and negotiation ensue, discretion is exercised, brokers and consultants intercede (cf. Schaffer and Lamb 1974).

The officials who administer bureaucratic access say, "That point you raise, that is political—don't mix politics into this—stick to the (bureaucratic access) issue (*tihyeh 'inyani*)." But many, perhaps most of those who are caught up in access situations, know that the choice is not between impersonal, evenhanded rationality and the corruption of bureaucratic universalism (as Danet [1989] might have it). They know, whether as losers or gainers, that the access system is breachable, manipulable, political. One need only add that the very distinction between the political, on the one hand, and bureaucratic rationality and fairness, on the other, is itself political in the way it is used.

Bureaucratic access involves questions concerning the circulation of knowledge at the official-client interface and within the system itself. Bureaucratic knowledge, purported to be transparent, readily available to any applicant or to any official, is frequently, even if not always, opaque. Information may be denied, withheld, unavailable, uncertain, and vague, and knowledge may have to be pieced together. This is yet another aspect of the nonrational, political nature of bureaucratic access, and it is undoubtedly part of the reason that it often pays to have a planning consultant, for example, to assist in getting a local development project through the statutory planning system.

It is not monolithic state power expressed hierarchically in policy that one finds here, for bureaucratic access situations provide the opportunity for interagency coalition or strife, for trade-off and linkages—in short, for client-agency maneuver and negotiation (cf. Colebatch 1987; Torgovnik 1990). Nonetheless, these administrative practices generate sovereignty—in part by virtue of the obvious circumstance that even as it divides, the access experience incorporates and thereby establishes the field of power (cf. Schaffer 1980; Mitchell 1991).

The approach adopted here shares with Handelman (1978, 1981) both the sense that bureaucratic access provides the occasion for maneuver and negotiation and that bureaucratic categories are discursively determined. Nonetheless, it is not the phenomenology of bureaucratic transaction, perception, and interpretation that is the object of investigation of the present research, but rather the structural aspects of the bureaucratic access situation; not the production of bureaucratic knowledge per se, but rather the sluggishness and fitfulness of its circulation; not the individual bureaucratic case, but rather the macro-order, political-economic consequences of bureaucratic access.

Now, the administrative practices activated by the pursuit of Arab economic development are shot through with representations and images defined in the Zionist discourse. The reference here is not to the debate on Israel as the state of the Jewish people; that is only a subdivision of what is identified here as the Zionist discourse.[1] The present study concerns itself with the *uses* of the basic terms of the encompassing Zionist discourse, its images and representations. In this discourse, the image of Jewish economic development furthering Zionist settlement aims (see, e.g., Soffer 1986) has its counterimage in that of the threat of Arab economic autonomy and of Arab territorial expansion or moves to break away.[2] Such representations filter through the plans and programs that result in the building of roads, the installation of an electric grid or a sewage system, the levying of taxes, or the expropriation of land (cf. Rabinow 1989). And Arab identity, capabilities, and pursuits are marked out in the images of *hamula*, tradition, and (no less an image) modernization (cf. Asad 1975; Rosenfeld 1978: 392, 400–401; Dominguez 1989; Sa'di 1992, 1997). It should be emphasized that it is not collective identity that concerns me here—neither the mobilization of identity, in the case of the Arabs in Israel, nor the state as an instrument of collective will, in the case of the Jews. The view of representation as exterior to either individual or collective consciousness is one of the conceptual elements that make it possible to sidestep the ultimately futile question, Who is the oppressor? and to focus instead on *how* power relations work themselves out in practice.

Representations and images may inscribe a hierarchical order in a plan or program, or they may be invoked to justify or mobilize support for a decision or a request, or to give impetus to an action. Deployed in social practices (such as the administrative practice being considered here), representation contextualizes action (cf. Andrew Long 1992).[3] It does so not as subjective cognition but by providing the focal object around which practice organizes itself. So long as they are not challenged, the terms of the discourse set the limits of what can be said; yet, when conditions are right and subject to the actors' ability to mobilize the requisite resources, they may be challenged, becoming themselves an object of struggle.

Representation, as stated, may inscribe a hierarchical order (Kapferer 1988; Handelman 1994). Nonetheless, the approach to bureaucratic access and representation adopted here should be distinguished from that which informs Herzfeld's 1993 study of symbolism in Western bureaucracy. Taking as a point of departure that "the internal logic of European national bureaucracy follows from that of nationalism … [which distinguishes] between insiders and outsiders" (174), Herzfeld sees the symbolism of exclusion and identity as intrinsic to the bureaucratic enterprise. The present research, on the other hand, considers bureaucratic access to have regularities and dispositions of its own, independently of representation. The weak and the dispossessed suffer at the hands of the state apparatus by virtue of their weakness, not only because of difference (see, e.g., Marx 1976), and that condition should be a distinct dimension of the inquiry. Again, one needs to attend to state *practices* for an explanation of the emergence and persistence of disadvantage. Moreover, representation is not given a priori; representation itself is a consequence of the power relationship, even as it reinforces that relationship (cf. Dominguez 1987). There is, it is suggested, something to be gained from not conflating the two domains. In a recent study of the disadvantaged position of the Arab population in what he terms a dualistic welfare state, Rosenhek concludes that "the partial exclusion of the Arab population from the Israeli welfare state has been patterned by the interaction between two state logics that are analytically distinct: the Zionist logic of the Israeli state, and the inner logic of the welfare state as a stratification regime in advanced capitalist societies" (Rosenhek 1995: v). An analogous analytic distinction is employed in the present study.

Consider this: In such areas as the statutory planning system, local economic development initiative, and leasing state-owned land to local entrepreneurs, the bureaucratic access apparatuses do not exclude the Arab population in Israel. On the contrary, those apparatuses proclaim themselves as being there for all to avail themselves of, irrespective of so-called national identity.[4] The question, then, is, How does power work *there,* in those spheres where distinctions emerge though none are professed? Or further, How does the very refusal to distinguish between Arab and Jew combine with the divisions of the world imposed by bureaucratic access to forestall attempts to challenge power outcomes?

Certain clarifications may be in order concerning the implications of the shift to a focus on practice. First, one ought, in my view, to refrain from locutions that put the state as an actor, with their connotation of coherent purpose. I would follow Colebatch's suggestion that it would be useful to get rid of the definite article in "the State" and "to speak instead of 'state action' to describe a particular mode of political action" (Colebatch 1987: 17). This does not detract in the least from the concrete reality of government practices such as the expropriating of land, the levying of taxes, the paying out of development funds, or the approval of plans.

Second, if not "the State," then also not a "system of control." There have indisputably been policies directed at control of the Arab population in Israel—the military government to which the Arabs were subject from the advent of the state until 1966 and the monitoring of political activity by the security services are examples of outright control. In other cases, such as the establishment of Jewish *mitzpim* settlements in Galilee,[5] "control" may be invoked as rationale for the program or policy, yet turns out to be only partially relevant and, moreover, to have results that cut both ways (cf. Soffer and Finkel n.d.). But there is also change that works to baffle control—for example, population growth, entrepreneurship, educational attainment, occupational shifts, and economic advance (Rosenfeld 1978; Haidar 1985; Gilbar 1991). If one adheres to the thesis of control, then one is led to describe such developments as the result of "aberrations" in the system of control (Lustick 1980: 238). There would be advantages, I suggest, to an approach that recognizes "control" as one of the discursive statements available to the social actors and, seeing control itself as one, but only one, of the multiple elements of power, is also able to see ceaseless maneuver as one of the characteristics of the interaction that constitutes the field of power relations.

But the idea of maneuver should not be taken to imply that the actors in this field of power relations have equal resources at their command, or that outcomes do not fall into a pattern of structure, for it is indeed a field of *power* relations that I am speaking of. One needs, then, even while turning away from the issue of the origin of power to be able to show how the aspects of local economic development looked at in this study are shaped by and contribute to the broad economic and political subordination of the Arab population in Israel. To this end, I avail myself of Foucault's view of power relations, mentioned earlier, as a heterogeneous ensemble of discursive and nondiscursive elements.

This ensemble would include such diverse historical elements as the military government, extensive expropriation of land during the first three decades following establishment of the state, a dearth of government development budgets for Arab localities, and high-handedness and delay in the preparation and approval of outline plans for Arab towns. Historical elements feed into a present-day strategic situation that includes yet other factors: the involvement of various government ministries and bodies together with the extrastate organizations (the Jewish National Fund [JNF] and the Jewish Agency) in the planning and construction of new towns designed for Jewish settlement; the conception of the "regional council" as a local authority that encompasses a number of rural settlements, mostly Jewish, and that is given jurisdiction over relatively vast stretches of territory. The ensemble of elements would include the multifarious practices of bureaucratic access with their various effects of power, often with their own associated discourses, as in the case of the small-business program and the idea of local authority initiative for economic development, or the discourse of equity and rationality that informs bureaucratic access in general. And then there is the encompassing Zionist discourse, which provides the discursive images (e.g., territorial struggle, Arab traditionalism) that serve, in a variety of ways, those practices and those who engage in them. My focus on discourse and its images led to another layer of analysis. Foucault's insights regarding "the interweaving of the effects of power and knowledge" (1980: 109, 131) led me again and again in the course of my investigations to an awareness of the way in which Israeli discourse produces its peculiar rationality, the peculiar truth that breathes in the regime.

Altogether, what one has in the view of power relations that I present here is the synergy of a multiplicity of overlapping factors, which produces what might be called the effect of structure. Each of the elements in this multiplicity acts to fix social arrangements in place; together, they add up to a strategic disposition of forces. Onlookers who perceive the situation in terms of the origin of power are likely to see the subordination of the Arab population in Israel as a given, in need of no further explanation. For them, differential outcomes in the bureaucratic access system are "predictable results," and in saying that, they suggest, one has said all that needs to be said. But I believe that such reduction to a simplistic binary model misses the complexities revealed by attending to *how* power works.

Now each of these overlapping factors also provides the occasion for tactical maneuver, for making new coalitions, for pressing new arguments and new definitions, for raising new demands, and for shifting the attack to other ground, newly revealed by changing circumstances. I would suggest that this is so even in the case of the irreversibility of events that are by now history (e.g., the expropriation of land, which though it entailed the loss of an important economic resource and the passing of a way of life, also made it necessary to push out in new directions). It is also so even in the case of the discourse, that most intractable and perduring of elements, which seemingly anchors everything else, for here, too, circumstances change and the discursive formation may be outflanked, or challenge is mounted and eventually the terms of discourse may give way. The metaphor, following Foucault, is that of war and battle (1980: 114, 209). I see the field of power relations as the particular configuration of its elements at any given moment; these elements provide the terrain on which the lines of battle shift and re-form.[6]

My approach is basically actor-oriented. But determinism lurks in the Foucauldian view of discourse. Awareness of the contradiction led me to take deliberate steps in the course of presenting my ethnography to offer a conceptualization of discourse whose sensitivity to power is available to social anthropology, but which does not objectify human actors.

One may note that on the view of power relations set out here, no situation should be described as though it were *the* Situation, for that would be to essentialize it, to take it out of Time (cf. Fabian 1983). Also, it should be borne in mind that any cutoff in time, presenting an ethnography as though events had come to a close, runs the risk of just such essentialization.

The Research Field and Macro-order Ethnography

My focus in this study is on what may be thought of as the nodes of activity or interaction that, while specific to particular events, also reveal something about the broader disposition of social forces. The piecing together of the research field in this way may be viewed as an extension of the method outlined by E. Marx (1980: 19–20, 24) as an appropriate strategy for the anthropological study of nations. Indeed, it was precisely Emanuel Marx's anthropological approach, proposing an alternative to conceptualization of the nation as a closed system, which made it possible to arrive, via Foucault, at the idea, used here, of a field of power relations. It should also be noted that the focus, following Marx, on nodes of activity rather than bounded systems, offers a way of breaking away from perceptions of traditional society that cloak the power-laden interactions between agents of the larger political regime and the local population.

It was only natural that as an anthropologist I was looking at local events. But there were two elements in my observations that led me to cast a wider net. The first is this: I was following the maneuver and confrontation in which the heads of local authorities and their officials were struggling to capture resources—such things as territorial jurisdiction, investors, national government classifications and dispensations that would bequeath benefits—and, by the same token, struggling to prevent the loss of such resources or having to share them with others. The interactions involved neighboring localities, but also went up the administrative hierarchy and extended to actors at the level of district and national government. The data/artifacts I was collecting included plans, applications, and appeals in which the political and the economic breathe; government policy decisions that include or leave out, define and redefine; and, through numerous interviews and the study of documents, the rationale and the images of the discourse that inform and shape events.

The second element that led me outward from a strictly local perspective originated directly in the anthropological frame of my investigation. There were things here that were self-evident to anyone immersed in Israeli society, but that from an anthropological view required elucidation: How to explain that Jews and Arabs live, for the most part, in separate towns, and that these are perceived as "Jewish towns" or "Arab towns"? What does it mean to say "the Arab towns are weak" and how did/does that come about? To deal with these questions I was led to extend my inquiry to domains other than the specific development of local or regional industrial areas. It is perhaps characteristic of anthropological investigation that I became deeply aware of the dialectic of fieldwork and theory building. In the present case, the outward-leading element of my inquiry led me to the aptness of the theoretical conceptualization of the field of power relations as a multidimensional disposition of forces. And, in both this and in the upward-reaching element, I found that I had moved away from micro-locale to a macro-order view.

Now, one authority (and no doubt others) posits ethnography as one of the three points of the anthropological triangle, the other two being contextualization and comparison (Sanjek 1996: 193). Clearly, such a model has heuristic value, but, like all models, it is vulnerable to challenge. I submit that by extending my ethnographic net to the macro-order, I have broken down the ethnographic/contextual dichotomy. Indeed, that is the implication of the theoretical position at which I had arrived through my fieldwork—that I was looking at a field of power relations constituted by the disposition of multiple, synergetic forces.

As an ethnography that takes hold of the larger macro-order, this study may be seen as one methodological response to the problematic raised by Marcus (1986) and Marcus and Fischer (1986) of integrating interpretive and political-economic concerns in ethnography. Marcus calls for an ethnography capable of encompassing a *system,* but he writes within the American tradition of cultural anthropology where "political-economic" is seen as the system and "cultural" is identified with the local. Finding an appropriate path to the ethnography of system might be easier for a social-anthropological approach, especially one such as that developed here, in which the discourse and its images are perceived as contextualizing local manifestations of political-economic maneuver and struggle.[7]

The very idea of an ethnographic/contextual dichotomy (as in Sanjek, cited above) implies that there exists a reserve of objective, power-neutral data on which the anthropologist may draw for so-called context. But I found again and again that even (perhaps particularly) the purportedly objective data generated by or for the official government bureaucracy—for example, data on the seemingly simple matter of which towns did or did not have outline plans—were hopelessly shaded by the political interests of social actors. And if one adds to this the view of context emerging from the deployment of discursive images in ongoing maneuver, then surely one has turned away from the ethnographic/contextual dichotomy.

The Plan of the Book

The approach to the research field set out above had direct consequences both for my investigations and for how they would appear in the book. Chapter 2 opens with a brief scene at the Zipporit site, but it turns immediately to the material that serves to introduce the actors and the resources they command. These are the Arab towns in Galilee, the Jewish towns of Upper Nazareth and Karmi'el implanted in the midst of the Arab population, and the Jewish rural community settlements and the regional councils that unite them. Together, chapters 2 and 3 present what I will call *the lay of the land*—the strategic disposition of forces that join in constituting the field of power. These chapters touch on the history of settlement and war, and again settlement, in Galilee; the Jewish perception of territorial and demographic threat; and the disparate experience of the Arab as distinguished from the Jewish localities in gaining approval for outline (i.e., zoning) plans and development plans. They also deal with local government in the Arab towns and relations with the central authorities, municipal budgets and financial weakness, and the elements of lagging local economic development in the Arab towns.

These chapters are the beginning of a response to one of the major questions that arose in the course of following the Zipporit case: What are the lineaments and origins of the weakness of the Arab towns? I draw heavily here on much relevant previous research, but I conjoin to it my own investigations, including interviews and examination of documents and data (including data generated and/or collected specifically for the present study). Thus, in addition to synthesis, the reader will find here fresh insight and interpretation.

Chapter 3 follows the individual strands that are woven together in the Zipporit case: the desire of Israeli development planners to throttle, or at least to counter, the development of the growing Arab conurbation around Arab Nazareth; the political protest of the Arab towns, which led to plans for joint development; and the difficulties encumbering such joint development, including (a) the fact that land in the Arab town jurisdiction contiguous with that in the jurisdiction of (Jewish) Upper Nazareth did not enjoy equal National Priority status and was priced, by the government, at over three times the cost of land within the boundaries of the Jewish town, and (b) the reluctance of Upper Nazareth to give up or share its own development prerogatives. Another strand in the Zipporit story is the government's plan for a small local industrial area in the Arab town of Kafr Kanna, which became an enclave within the larger area. But of looming salience in the Zipporit events was the question of municipal boundaries—jurisdiction over land—and, indeed, of the proper use of state-owned land.

It is particularly in the Zipporit case of chapter 3 that I encountered the kind of ethnographic data on which I commented above, data having to do with plans and their progress through the statutory channels, applications and permits, petitions in the judicial system, agreements, and policy decisions. It is through these that one is able to follow, without giving way to special pleading, the administrative practices through which power relations work themselves out. In my view, the gripping story of the Zipporit case is embedded in these artifacts, but the reader who prefers less detail may find a way to let his or her eyes move more lightly through the account.

Each of the next three chapters engages in greater depth a different aspect of the macro-order power differentials that found expression in the Zipporit case. These chapters may be thought of as growing out of chapter 3; together they flesh out the sketch of the field of power relations begun in chapters 1 and 2. Chapter 4 takes a look at the various elements of Israeli state land policy and the state's relentless pursuit of each and every dunam;[8] it asks the reader to consider these elements as generating the Arab experience of land loss—being surrounded, hedged in, having the very grounding of one's existence inexorably chipped away. This experience underlay the response of the Arab towns to the government's Zipporit plans, and also expressed itself in apprehension that the program to build small local industrial areas in the Arab towns was a new stratagem to expropriate Arab land. Chapter 4 goes on to consider the restrictive setting of Arab town boundaries of jurisdiction both as a result of and as a contributing factor to the weakness of these towns. But beyond this, chapter 4, together with the preceding chapters, brings to light the psychosocial conundrum, pregnant with power, in the meeting of the Arab experience of land loss and constriction with the Jewish perception of Arab territorial threat.

The Arab townsmen asked why the land of the Zipporit project, formerly part of the village lands of Meshhed, could not have served for regional development without being transferred to Upper Nazareth jurisdiction. Part of the answer to their question has to do with the image of Arab traditionalism that is an element in the Zionist discourse of modernization. This image of Arab traditionalism is the focus of chapter 6. The study of Arab industrial entrepreneurship in Israel by Schnell and colleagues (1995) referred to at the start of this introduction asserts that Arab industrial development is held back by the absence of a land market, which is said to derive from Arab traditionalism. Chapter 5 criticizes the conceptual and methodological validity of that assertion, and uses material from my own fieldwork demonstrating Arab land-use initiative at the local level. It shows how the image of Arab traditionalism colors the Ministry of Industry's dealings with Arab entrepreneurs and local authorities. The chapter goes on to argue, on the basis of ethnographic data, that the image of Arab traditionalism erects imaginary boundaries around the Arab localities, making government incursion disappear from view, while underpinning and rationalizing the exclusion of the Arab towns from development planning.

Chapter 6 looks at a carefully thought out planning document for Galilee produced in 1977. One finds in this plan, *Accelerated Urban Development in Galilee* (*AUDG*), the discursive principles that lay at the heart of government development policy in the 1980s and 1990s. It is a matter of regional development meant to establish and consolidate the Jewish hold on Galilee; yet one of its tenets is the integration of the Arab population. The Jewish towns are to develop into vibrant urban centers, while Arab employment needs, as well as needs for commercial and professional services, are *appropriated* to that end. But it is a two-pronged program, providing both for small local industrial areas in the Arab towns and for large regional interurban industrial parks located in the Jewish development centers. Although they are referred to as "regional," the large industrial parks were not conceived of as belonging to the Arab towns in their vicinity.

This chapter argues that the archetypical *AUDG* plan was situated at the discursive intersection of the perception of the growing Arab towns as constituting a territorial threat, on the one hand, and of the image of Arab traditionalism, on the other. Thus, Zipporit (see chapter 3), one of the locations included in the *AUDG* plan, was seen by its planners not in terms of regional development, but rather in those of territorial struggle.

Chapter 6 argues further that the two-pronged program of *AUDG* contributed to the objectification of the Arab/Jewish distinction (see chapter 5), and shifted attention away from the absence of Arab town participation in the regional areas. One aspect of such objectification is that it came to be taken for granted that development to meet Arab town needs could only be accomplished by inserting and developing a Jewish town (viz., Karmi'el and Upper Nazareth). This chapter considers the potential for within-region polarization entailed by the "growth center" strategy of *AUDG*: Has the transfer of resources (such as land; cf. chapter 4) from the Arab hinterland to Jewish centers led to augmented development disparities?

In chapters 4, 5, and 6 the discursive figured prominently, though by no means exclusively. In Chapter 7 the focus shifts back to the realm of contest and maneuver that was paramount, though again, not exclusive, in chapter 3. Chapter 7 looks at a changing constellation over the 1990s and until the present of

Arab town attempts to become a part of development in Galilee and the struggle and maneuver involved in those efforts. This is a confutation of the conceptualization of the macro-order in terms of control. But this chapter is far from being the story of a new age. It is not at all clear how many of the initiatives for Arab-Jewish industrial partnership described here will come into being, nor can there be any conclusions regarding what participation would mean: How much shared control, how much contact, how much tax revenue? Power relations continue to work themselves out in changing and shifting lines of battle. It is perhaps indicative of this that programs of tourism development aimed at the Arab towns and discourses of landscape and environment have appeared on the scene.

Chapter 7 offers a critique of recent (2001) findings by Israeli researchers that there has been meaningful improvement in the receptivity of Israeli planners to needs of the Arab population. This chapter considers the often-neglected distinction between statutory planning and development planning, and argues that the Arabs have to be more than just participants; they must be full, equal partners. It also argues for the necessity and rightness of using state land for the benefit of all citizens, Arabs no less than Jews. Those demands are part of the new activism evinced by Arab officials and planners.

To put the plan of the book into the starkest terms: chapters 3 and 7 tell the story of Arab town struggle for participation, as towns, in economic development; chapters 4, 5, and 6, together with chapters 1 and 2, tell how and why they are unequal contenders in that struggle.

Other Methodological Notes

This is manifestly a study not of Arab society in Israel, but of certain processes in Israeli society. As such, it takes what Nader calls the "vertical slice," and in so doing, it encounters the problems of access connected with "studying up" (Nader 1972). Bureaucratic principles of openness and transparency notwithstanding, it is difficult to observe critical moments in the politics of bureaucratic access—those moments at which a telephone call is placed, a note passed across the table at a meeting, or a sentence or two exchanged before the meeting commences. The secret working of power extends far beyond those areas of information that officials are, by their own admission, reluctant to make public because of what *they* see as the undesirable consequences of doing so.

My way of dealing with this methodological problem had to do with the kind of data I chose, (seemingly) of necessity, to gather. The events in the world of bureaucratic access that I was studying were such things as the submission of a plan, approval of an application, publication of a decision. These had dates and signatures, and were recorded in print. To them I would add many overlapping accounts of how such events came to pass; to these, testimony offered at commission and court hearings (and accounts of such proceedings); and to this swelling material I would conjoin plans, regulations, laws, and, further, accounts of procedure. Acquisition of documents was interspersed with interviews, and this worked in a cumulative way, with one interview feeding on the other and on newly uncovered documents to take me back and around one event or another, and further back to what had preceded it—but not only back, for having in my possession documents and accounts having to do with the past also worked to my advantage in gaining current access. Coming to an interview equipped with already acquired knowledge served to elicit still more information. Using this data collection procedure, I was able to build up a picture of the administrative practice that was at the heart of the events I was observing.

In carrying out interviews, I made no attempt to produce a verbatim record of what was said, whether by recording or by writing with my nose in my field journal. I would take notes—closer or not so close. At times, I would interrupt the interviewee to double-check what I had understood and noted; at times, I would lay down my pen altogether in order to let the response of the interviewee flow. As soon as possible after the meeting I would rewrite/write up the interview, giving my best efforts to recall accurately the sense of what was said, and making use, of course, of the fragmentary notes I had recorded. Thus, in the ethnography that follows, a quotation from an interview is actually a reconstruction of what was said, even where quotation marks or block extracts are employed. I believe that the reports of interviews, as well as the material presented as direct quotation, are good and faithful representations of what I heard. There were a few occasions where I had an opportunity to check this in conversation with one or another of the people with whom I spoke, and these occasions served to confirm my confidence in the reliability of my method.

I should mention that I am responsible for the translation to English of all quotations from source material and secondary material that appeared originally in Hebrew. I had the assistance of others, as indicated in the acknowledgments section, for the translation of material from the Arabic press. Transliteration has been a matter of compromise. Place names, in most cases, follow the Ministry of Interior and CBS usage for English. Thus, "Tiberias" and, also, inconsistently, "Akko." Thus, also, "Zipporit" (*Z* for the initial *tzadi*). But I could not bring myself to follow Ministry of Interior–CBS usage on "Nazerat Illit" and have used "Upper Nazareth" throughout. Generally, I have used *K* for *Kaf* and *Q* for *Quf*, but even so, I have used *Kovetz HaTaqanot* (*KT*) rather than *Qovetz HaTaqanot*. Where appropriate, both Hebrew *Aleph* and Arabic *Alif* and *Hamza* are marked by ('); *'Ayin* in both Arabic and Hebrew is marked by ('). I have used *h* for *het* as well as *heh; kh* for *khaf*. Names of authors follow the Latin spelling that appeared in their publications. Where this was not available, I made a point of checking with the author wherever possible. I must ask the reader to be forbearing with regard to variations in the spelling of place names in the maps. Such variation is a remnant of the diverse sources from which the maps were derived.

The question of the proper designation for the Arabs in Israel is a vexatious one. There is no doubt in my mind concerning the validity of Sa'di's contention (1992) that the identity of "Palestinian" has been denied them through government policy and practice, as well as through the agency of Israeli social science research (see also Rabinowitz 1993, 1997). I have no difficulty in acknowledging the rightness of the appellation "Palestinian citizens of Israel." Nonetheless, I feel that to adopt it here would be to sidetrack and confuse the main thrust of the study, which, it will be recalled, brackets the issue of identity. The terms "Israeli Arabs," "Arabs in Israel," and "Arab population in Israel" are those that are currently used by both Jews and Arabs, particularly in reference to the domain of administrative practice that I am studying. I choose to use these, while suggesting that it be borne in mind that they are, indeed, terms of power; they reflect the circumstance that the experience of being an Arab in Israel has been in part produced and certainly shaped by Israeli government action, constraints, and intervention. It may be observed that in the realm of bureaucratic access, the Arabs in Israel struggle and negotiate for the equitable share that is their due as citizens of the state, however problematic and anomaly-ridden the concept of "Israeli" might be. But this is simply evidence of incorporation—one of the prime power effects of bureaucratic access.

I do not use such items of government officialese as "the Arab sector," "the minorities," "the minority population." I avoid, where possible, the term "non-Jews," which is what the government and the Central Bureau of Statistics use in presenting data. I also avoid the distinction between "the Arab sector" and "the Druze sector," which is commonly made by government bodies (unless, of course, I am dealing with a program to which that distinction is integral). Altogether, these distinctions, starting from that between Jew/Arab or Jew/non-Jew, are what Appadurai has referred to as "state-imposed categories." The problematics of using them in research will be dealt with in chapter 1.

Chapters 1 and 2 will introduce the social actors who took part in the events I deal with, as well as the official setting in which they interact. Chapter 2 will close with a consideration of the field of power relations in light of the material assembled in it and in chapter 1. These chapters set out the elements composing what I referred to above as the strategic disposition of forces. Handler (1985: 180) points out the danger of essentialization that lurks in beginning an account of contested matters with a presentation of historical background. But I argue that it is precisely the conceptualization of a fluid disposition of forces that counters the danger of such essentialization.

CHAPTER 1

The Lay of the Land (I)

The Territorial Demon

New Sights in Kafar Kanna

On a December day in 1993, I stood at the second-story window of the offices of the Center for Strategic Planning in the Arab Municipalities in Kafar Kanna, looking west toward the Phoenicia glass factory under construction in Zipporit, Upper Nazareth's large new industrial park. The center of Upper Nazareth lay about 6 km to the south, but that city had recently been reaching out with a new industrial area and a new residential development at Har Yona to its northeast. Now, it had leapfrogged due north over the territory of its Arab neighbors—Reine, Meshhed, and Kafar Kanna—to establish Zipporit, in what might easily be thought of as the backyard of the latter two towns (see figure 1.1). Zipporit was located on land that had lain, during British times, within the village boundaries of Meshhed (but those were not jurisdictional boundaries; the Meshhed local authority only came into being in 1960, and then this land was not included in its jurisdictional boundaries). In anticipation of the construction of the industrial park, most of the land for Zipporit A had been transferred to Upper Nazareth in 1991. Kafar Kanna and Meshhed protests during the early stages of park construction and following the laying of the Phoenicia cornerstone in September 1992 led to proposals to expand the industrial park to include a large contiguous area in the jurisdictions of the two Arab towns, and to admit them to the municipal industrial park authority as joint owners and managers.

Standing at the window in the offices of the Center for Strategic Planning in the Arab Municipalities, I gazed out over the houses of Kafar Kanna and the olive trees at the new glass factory, just 1,700 meters away,[1] its tall chimney pointing skyward in its red-striped splendor (see figure 1.2). Now, it is not unusual for cities to have industrial areas located in such proximity or

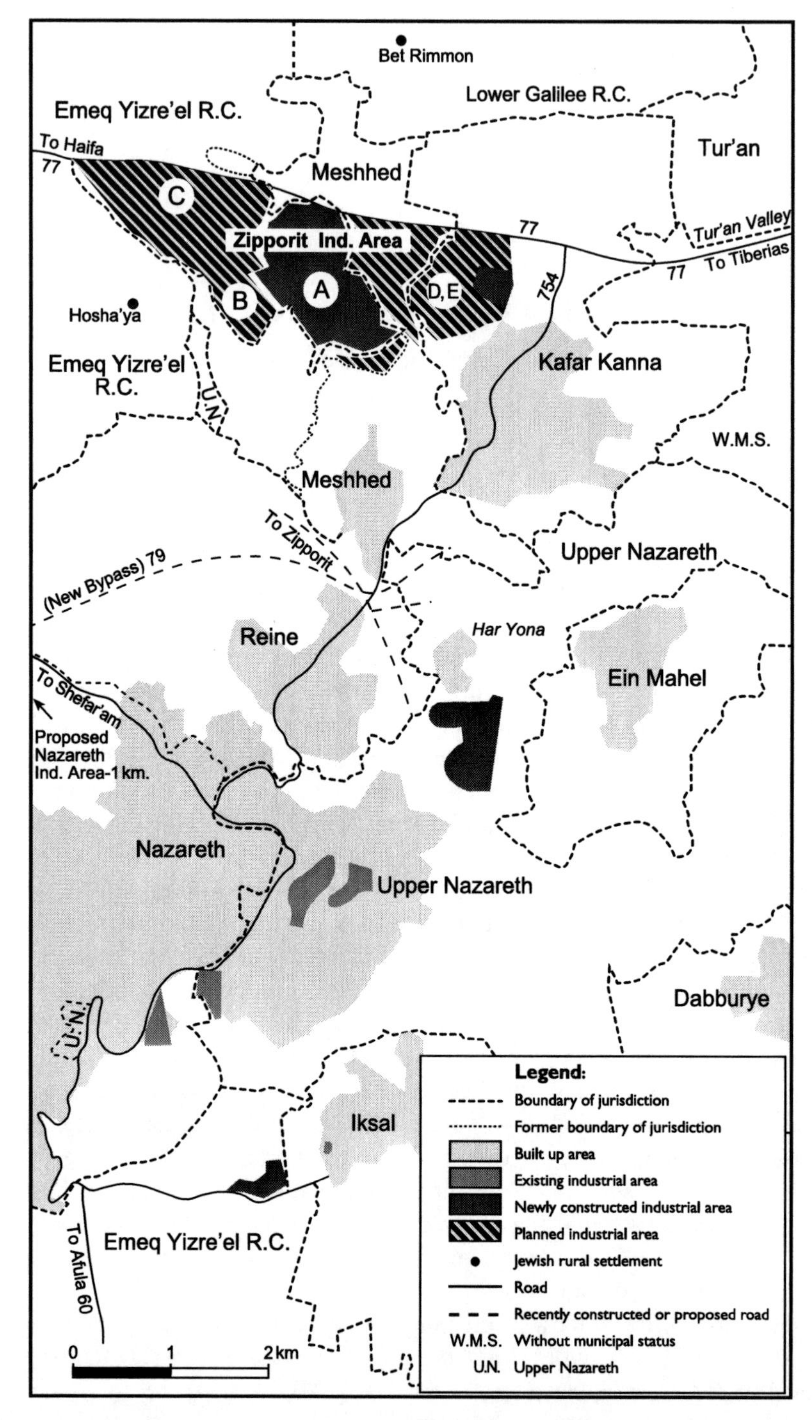

Figure 1.1 Nazareth Area. *Sources and notes:* Based on Ministry of Interior sources for boundaries of jurisdiction and on specific urban building plans, as well as municipal sources for industrial areas. Built-up areas are adapted from the 1:50,000 series of trip and paths maps edited by Ori Dvir (printed by Survey of Israel). Except for the city of Upper Nazareth, all of the local authorities shown in figure 1.1 are Arab localities. Jewish rural settlements in regional councils (such settlements are localities but not local authorities) are marked by a small dot.

Figure 1.2 Phoenicia and the Zipporit Industrial Area, Seen from the Main Road in Kafar Kanna (2000)

closer to residential quarters—indeed, Upper Nazareth itself had until now constructed its industrial areas in the main part of town, and at Har Yona, in just that kind of proximity. But now Zipporit A was being located well away (by several kilometers) from Upper Nazareth residential areas. Kafar Kanna and Meshhed were relatively small towns (populations of 12.8 and 5.2 thousand, respectively); they were not used to such sights. Moreover, the glass factory, which would burn sulphur-rich heavy fuel oil to heat its furnace to temperatures of 1500° to 1600° C, would produce poisonous sulphur dioxide and nitrous oxide. Unless controlled, these would spew out into the prevailing westerly wind. Thus, here in the backyard of the Arab towns, Phoenicia's chimney loomed as an ominous intruder. This had figured prominently in the then-current struggle and negotiation over the control of factory emissions.

Rassem Khamaisi, the director of the center, who had been talking to me about the events of the past year, also directed my attention to where the bulldozer, between there and where we stood, was working on a 157-dunam industrial area in Kafar Kanna's jurisdiction (the solid dark gray area in what is designated as Zipporit D and E in figure 1.1. This was part of the Ministry of Industry's then current industrial area project in several Arab localities. Work had begun just the month before. (See figure 1.3 for the view southward across the Tur'an Valley toward Kafar Kanna, Meshhed, and Zipporit. In this photo, not taken until the early summer of 2000, the factories going up in the Kafar Kanna industrial area are visible, as is further development in Zipporit A.)

Chapter 3 will return to the events of the Zipporit industrial area involving Upper Nazareth and its Arab neighbors. But in the remainder of this chapter and in chapter 2, I would like to set out something about the lay of the land. I mean this not only in the geographic sense, but also in the sense of who the actors are and what resources they command in the complex relations and interactions that were shaping the landscape I saw before me on that December day.

The Territorial Demon

Land, Numbers, and Jewish Settlement

The case to be considered takes place in the Northern District, one of the Ministry of Interior's six administrative districts in the state of Israel. This district more or less overlays what is known as the geographical region of Galilee.

Galilee is mountainous.[2] Peaks in Lower Galilee reach an altitude of 550 to 600 meters above sea level; those in Upper Galilee rise to double that height. Lower Galilee is separated from Upper Galilee by Biq'at Bet Hakerem, the northernmost of four geological valleys or basins that lie parallel to the Lower Galilean mountain ranges, running in a general east-west direction (see figure 1.4). The southernmost of the basins—formed by the Yizre'el and Harod valleys—separates the Galilee from the mountainous region of Samaria, a north-south formation.

Figure 1.3 Looking Southward across the Tur'an Valley toward Kafar Kanna, Meshhed, and Zipporit (2000)

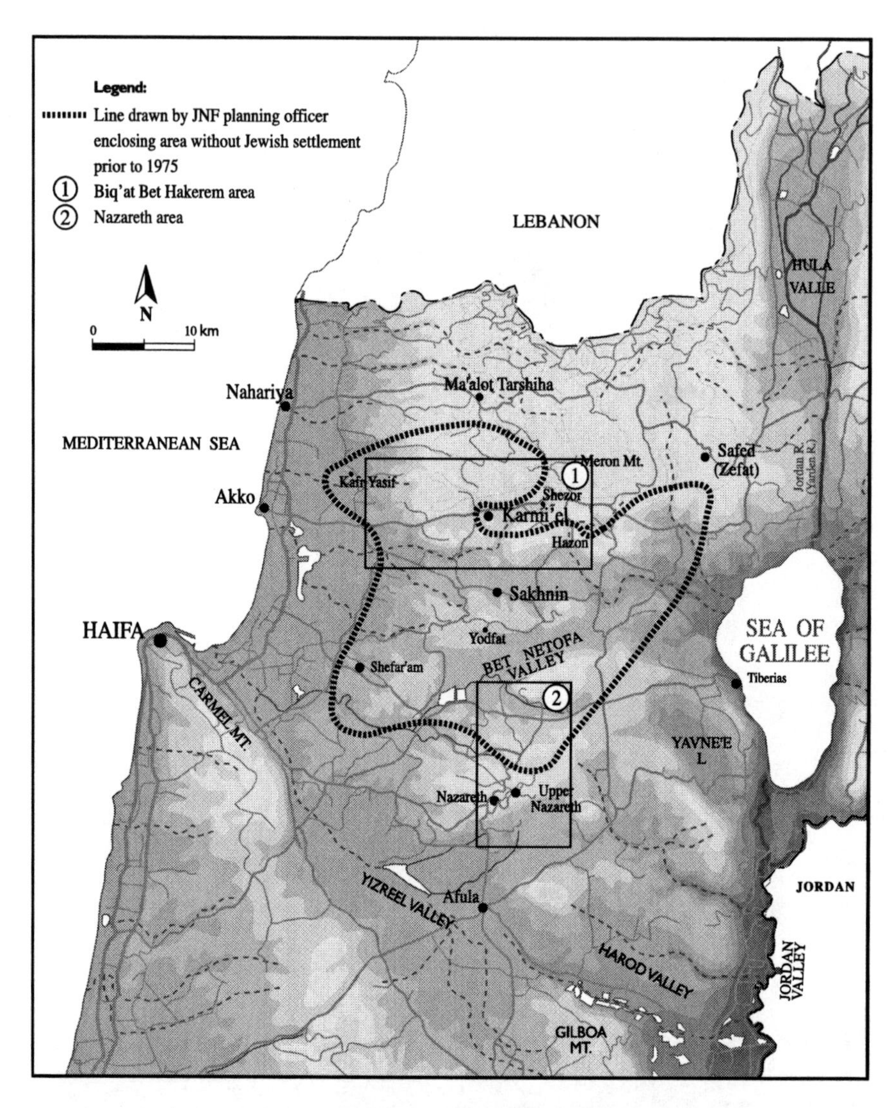

Figure 1.4 Northern Israel Physical Map. *Notes:* The broken line indicating a line drawn by a JNF planning officer is from Muvhar 1983. Detail of Rectangle 1, the Biq'at Bet Hakerem area, is found in figure 7.1; detail of Rectangle 2, the Nazareth area, is found in figure 1.1.

Upper Galilee does not have the regular transverse east-west lines characteristic of central Lower Galilee; rather, it is dominated by the Meron mountains (1,208 meters)—the highest elevation inside Israel's former borders—which rise just to the north of Biq'at Bet Hakerem. The mountainous formations of Upper Galilee extend to the north and northeast of Meron as far as the Litani River, some 22 km into Lebanon (from the western portion of Israel's northern border), becoming gradually gentler as one proceeds northwest from Meron.

The mountainous topography of Galilee expresses itself in high rainfall levels and other climatic features, in relatively abundant water sources, and in characteristic vegetation. So central are the mountains to the sense of what Galilee is that the most prevalent geographical definitions of Galilee exclude the coastal plain on the west, the Yizre'el and Harod valleys in the south, and the Huleh Basin in the Jordan Rift on the east, as well as the area around and to the east of Lake Kinneret. Yet some geographers do include these areas, and popular usage certainly does, at least as far as the coastal plain and the northern part of the Jordan Rift are concerned. The administrative lexicon of the state is even more inclusive; for example, the Galilee Development Authority includes in its mandate the Yizre'el and Harod valleys, the Bet She'an Basin, the area around and to the east of the Kinneret, as well as the Golan Heights to the east of the Jordan Rift (this latter occupied by Israel in the 1967 war and outside the geomorphological bounds of Galilee). This makes the referent of the term "Galilee" coextensive with the Northern District of the Ministry of the Interior.[3] Unlike the geographers, both popular and state usage draw the northern border of Galilee at the Lebanese frontier.

Geographers point out that the inaccessibility of the mountainous terrain and the possibilities for protection afforded by it have made Galilee, over the centuries, a region of refuge for minorities. Ziv (1970) and Kliot (1983) cite the reference to "Galilee of the Nations" (i.e., of peoples other than the ancient Israelites) that appears in Isaiah 8:23.[4] This is an image entirely congruent with the perception of Galilee entertained by national planners and administrators over the past five decades.

This is the point at which geography shades off into demography. Table 1.2 gives the 1995 Census figures for the Jewish and Arab population in the Northern District in the geographical areas that the Central Bureau of Statistics refers to as "natural regions."[5] The natural regions and the percentage of Arabs in the population of each are shown in figure 1.5. I have drawn a line to indicate the areas in which the Arabs constituted more than 50 percent of the population, designated as "Area A" in figure 1.5. Altogether, in that central area of the Galilee, reaching up to the northern border, Arabs were then 73.7 percent of the total population (see tables 1.1 and 1.2).[6] As tables 1.1 and 1.3 show, of the 453.7 thousand Arabs living in Galilee in 1995, 429.5 thousand lived in Arab towns. There were about 4.6 thousand Bedouin in unrecognized hamlets. The rest of the Arabs in Galilee resided in the "Jewish and mixed" localities.[7]

Now even a cursory glance at the data published by the CBS reveals that the distinction between Jew and Arab is the linchpin of the bureau's population statistics, inevitably present as the chief organizing element in the endless permutations of those data. The language employed adopts a certain deliberate indirection: the data speak of religion, the main ones among the Arab population being Muslim, Christian, and Druze. Until 1995, CBS publications would sum up the members of these categories as "non-Jews," that is, as distinguished from Jews. The benefits of this language in terms of control are clear. Focusing

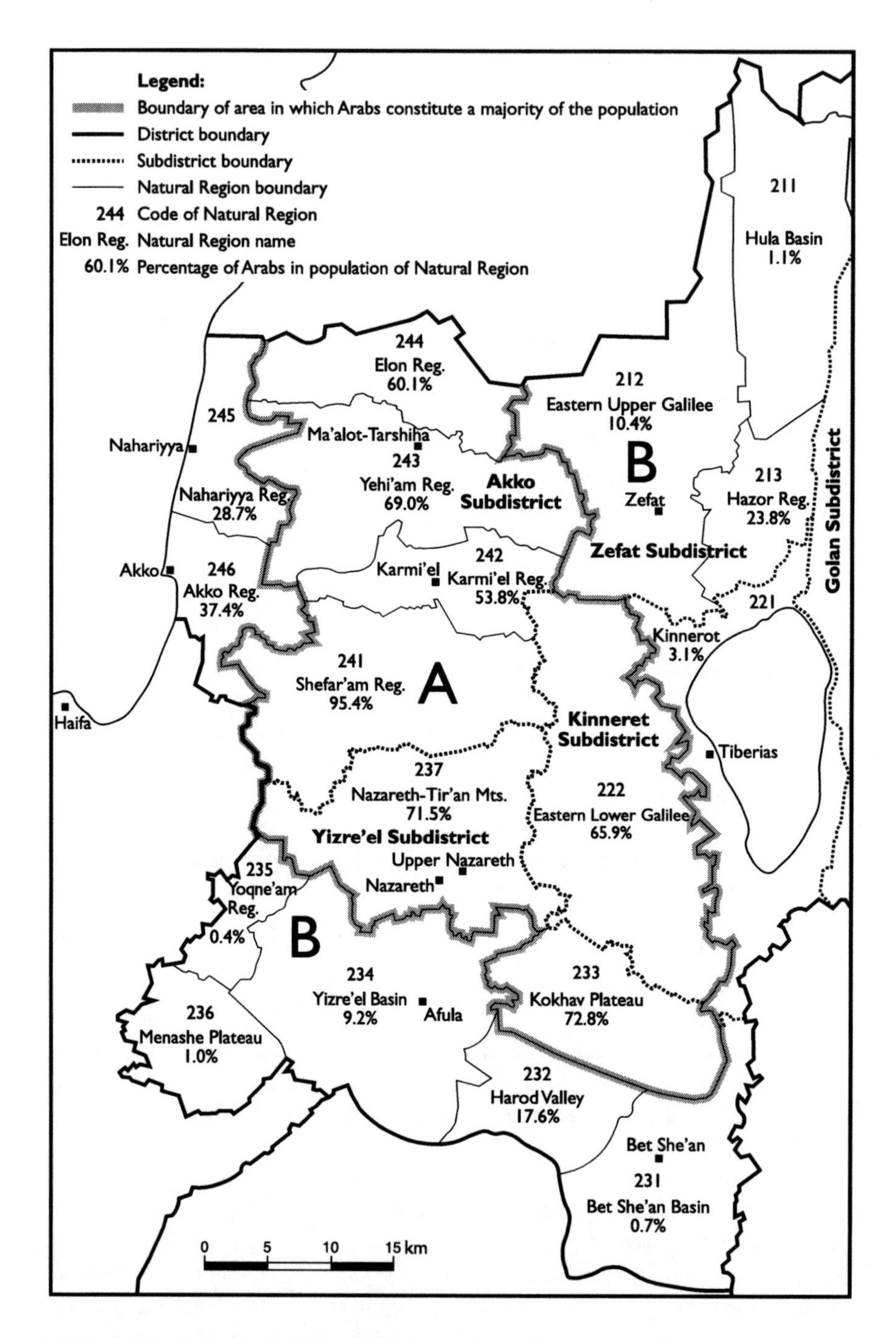

Figure 1.5 Northern District Natural Regions. *Sources and notes:* Redrawn from map provided by the CBS in its 1995 Census Publication No. 3 (1998b). Population data are extracted from the 1995 Census.

Table 1.1 Population in the Northern District (Excluding the Golan Subdistrict) in 1995 by Area A/Area B and Population Group

		Jews	Arabs	Ratio Arabs/Jews	Unclassified[2]	Total
Area A	1,000s	138.0	396.2		3.2	537.4
(Arab majority; 1,484 sq km[1])			(73.7%)	2.872		(100%)
	Persons per sq km	93.0	267.0			362.1[3]
Area B	1,000s	301.6	57.5		4.5	363.6
(Jewish majority; 1,841 sq km)			(15.8%)	0.191		(100%)
	Persons per sq km	163.8	31.2			197.5
Total	1,000s	439.6	453.7		7.7	901.0
(3,325 sq km)			(50.4%)	1.032		(100%)
	Persons per sq km	132.2	136.5			271.0

Notes: 1. One sq km = 0.3861 sq miles = 247.1 acres.

2. Includes (a) non-Jews who are not classified as Arabs; (b) ostensibly Jewish immigrants from the former Soviet Union and from Ethiopia whose Jewish identity is not recognized by the Ministry of the Interior; and (c) foreign workers who had been in the country for more than a year at the time of the census.

3. Note that Area A, despite its mountainous nature, is much more densely populated than Area B. This is a function of (a) the relatively small population in the Jewish rural localities, and (b) the larger number of Arab towns.

Source: Population figures (including those who do not reside in localities) based on 1995 Census data supplied courtesy of the CBS for the present study for the natural regions that make up Area A and Area B.

attention on sectarian divisions among the Arab population facilitates myriad comparisons between them on such topics as education, fertility, natural increase, and so forth; it avoids having to refer to the Arabs in national terms, such as the "Palestinian citizens of Israel." Indeed, these classifications enable the regime to refer to the Arab population as "the minorities [*sic!*]"—a common locution in the official lexicon of Israel.[8]

One anthropological approach to official record keeping concerns itself with the way in which that activity essentializes, hammers human material into regime-inspired categories, and brings the subjects of the state into being (cf. Appadurai 1996; see also Anderson 1991). These effects are all present in the official statistical undertaking in Israel, and although they are not the main concern of the present study, they inspire caution against allowing oneself to be seduced into thinking of statistical categories as a priori givens.

The statistics I present on Jewish/Arab populations, and later on natural increase, are cited by virtue of their connection to the Zionist imagination, and

Table 1.2 Population in the Northern District (Excluding the Golan Subdistrict) in 1995 by Area A/Area B, Natural Region, and Population Group

Code of natural region	Natural region	Jews	Arabs	Total	Ratio Arabs/ Jews	Per-cent Arab	Unclas-sified and others	Total
Area A								
222	East Lower Galilee	10,686	20,832	31,518	1.949	65.9	74	31,592
233	Kochav Plateau	2,206	5,944	8,150	2.694	72.8	13	8,163
237	Nazareth-Tir'an Mts	61,962	157,334	219,296	2.539	71.5	862	220,158
241	Shefar'am Region	5,770	120,627	126,397	20.906	95.4	91	126,488
242	Karmi'el Region	33,952	41,012	74,964	1.208	53.8	1,263	76,227
243	Yehi'am Region	18,359	42,814	61,173	2.332	69.0	900	62,073
244	Elon Region	5,040	7,663	12,703	1.520	60.1	37	12,740
	Total (Area A)	137,975	396,226	534,201	2.872	73.7	3,240	537,441
Area B								
211	Hula Basin	29,503	329	29,832	0.011	1.1	613	30,445
212	East Upper Galilee	30,077	3,539	33,616	0.118	10.4	488	34,104
213	Hazor Region	12,230	3,874	16,104	0.317	23.8	170	16,274
221	Kinnerot	47,892	1,553	49,445	0.032	3.1	593	50,038
231	Bet She'an Basin	23,604	164	23,768	0.007	0.7	78	23,846
232	Harod Valley	6,771	1,458	8,229	0.215	17.6	76	8,305
234	Yizre'el Basin	46,830	4,778	51,608	0.102	9.2	510	52,118
235	Yokne'am Region	17,235	76	17,311	0.004	0.4	188	17,499
236	Menashe Plateau	3,943	40	3,983	0.010	1.0	45	4,028
245	Nahariyya Region	46,448	19,024	65,472	0.410	28.7	874	66,346
246	Akko Region	37,111	22,647	59,758	0.610	37.4	837	60,595
	Total (Area B)	301,644	57,482	359,126	0.191	15.8	4,472	363,598
	Total (Both)	439,619	453,708	893,327	1.032	50.4	7,712	901,039

Source: Population figures (including those who do not reside in localities) based on 1995 Census data supplied courtesy of the CBS for the present study for the natural regions that make up Area A and Area B.

through it, to the struggle for territorial control as that struggle is constructed in the Zionist discourse. Striving for Jewish demographic superiority in the Galilee, or at least for checking Arab numerical domination there, has been a main theme in Israeli policy in the north of the country. It should perhaps be pointed out that the numerical relation of majority and minority, a key trope in the Zionist discourse, is a function of power, of being able to set oneself up as majority and draw the social or geographical boundaries required to make the definition hold (cf. Soffer 1983b). As a statistical aside, one may note that in the case of Galilee, the deliberate demographic homogeneity of the natural regions is countered by the manner of their aggregation into subdistricts. Three of the four Galilee subdistricts each take over a chunk of the Arab-dominated (numerically) heartland, attaching it to an area of Jewish numerical

Table 1.3 Localities and Total Population in Localities in the Northern District (Excluding the Golan Subdistrict) in 1995 by Area A/Area B and Population Group

Type of locality by Area A/Area B	Area (sq km)	Number of localities	Population in localities[3]	Population per locality
Area A (Arab majority)	1,484			
Jewish				
Urban[1]		5		
Rural		99		
Arab[2]		60		
Area B (Jewish majority)	1,841			
Jewish				
Urban[1]		11		
Rural		190		
Arab[2]		12		
Total	3,325			
Jewish				
Urban[1]		16	339,096	21,194
Rural		289	126,324	437
Arab[2]		72	429,490	5,965

Notes: 1. According to CBS classification, urban localities are those with a population of 2,000 and above. Jewish urban localities include mixed localities, notably Akko and Ma'alot-Tarshiha, the latter a case of a new Jewish immigrant town having been grafted onto an Arab town. Some Arabs live in other towns known as Jewish towns. Of the total population of 339,096 in the towns classified as Jewish and mixed, about 24,906 are "Arabs and others." The CBS added data on religion to the information present in the Census' long questionnaire—a 20 percemt sample. The distribution of religion obtained from this source for each of the Jewish and mixed towns was applied to the Census population results for each town to arrive at the figure of 24,906.

2. Jewish rural localities are composed overwhelmingly of three types: (a) the collective, (b) the cooperative, and (c) the so-called community settlements. None of these have shown any indication over the years of urbanizing or growing beyond the 2,000 mark. Arab localities do not have this distinction: smaller localities have grown larger over the years, and it is difficult to see those that are currently under 2,000 in population as different in kind from those that have already grown beyond this point.

3. Of the 901,000 Census population in the Northern District (excluding the Golan), only 894,910 persons reside in localities. Of those living outside localities, about 4,600 are Bedouin who reside in unrecognized hamlets.

Source: Localities and population in localities extracted from CBS 1998b, Publication no. 3 of the 1995 Census of Population and Housing.

superiority (see figure 1.5). Curiously, these subdistricts are themselves little more than statistical creatures, at least as far as the Ministry of the Interior is concerned (cf. Newman 1984: 145). That ministry, one of the few government or government-affiliated units to declare its adherence to the official division of the Northern District into subdistricts, maintains no administrative apparatus or functions at the subdistrict level.

One might also note that the 1995 Census divided what had until then been the Western Lower Galilee Natural Region into two: the Shefar'am Region and the Karmi'el Region. The Arabs constitute 79.7 percent of the population of these two regions taken together, but their separation enables showing an area (the Karmi'el Region) in the very center of the Arab heartland in which Arabs are only 53.8 percent of the population (at the cost of having the Shefar'am Region with a population that was 95.4 percent Arab). Of the 34.0 thousand Jews in the Karmi'el Region, 33.1 thousand live in the city of Karmi'el (see below on the establishment of Karmi'el).

The concomitant of the struggle for Jewish numerical superiority in the Galilee has been settlement. During the period prior to the establishment of the state, Jewish agricultural settlement naturally followed the lines of Zionist land purchases. Both were carried out, particularly during the latter years of the British Mandate, with an eye to the geostrategic considerations of establishing territorial claims (see, e.g., Kimmerling 1983; Stein 1984). By 1947, there were ninety-three Jewish rural settlements in Area B (figure 1.5).[9] Most of these were spread through the Yizre'el, Harod, Bet She'an, Jordan, Kinneret, and Hula basins, that is, outside the southern and eastern perimeter of mountainous Galilee, but four of these were in Upper Eastern Galilee, and six were in the Coastal Plain. Also, Jews lived in Zefat, Tiberias, in the new small town of Nahariyya on the coast, and in two new rural towns in the Yizre'el Valley. On the other hand, there were, by that time, only sixteen Jewish rural settlements in Area A (figure 1.5). Of these, nine were in the southern portion of Lower East Galilee, and four were in the Elon and Yehi'am regions, mostly near what would become Israel's northwestern frontier.

Israel's war of independence brought about a radical change in the distribution of Arab localities in the area of the Northern District. Altogether, about 158 Arab towns and villages were destroyed there (Morris 1987).[10] Most of these were from the southern valleys of the district, and from its entire eastern half (i.e., the Kinneret and Zefat subdistricts and the Kochav Plateau). Eleven were from the coastal area, and another eight were from the Elon Natural Region; "only" about nine were from the central portion of Area A. The subsequent distribution of Arab localities and Arab population in the Northern District was a direct result of this destruction (in 1995, there were sixty Arab localities in Area A, and only twelve in Area B [see table 1.3]).[11]

National policy regarding settlement of the mass immigration arriving in Israel during and following the war brought large numbers of Jews to Akko, Tiberias, Zefat (the last two now completely devoid of their former Arab population), and to seven new towns that were set up on the site of former Galilean Arab towns. Moreover, a concerted settlement effort saw the establishment of numerous new rural localities in the Northern District, seventy-nine in the four years alone from 1948 to 1951, all or nearly all on land that had been taken over from its former Arab inhabitants. Thus, this settlement did not touch the center of what is indicated on figure 1.5 as Area A.

In 1953, Yosef Nahmani, a veteran Zionist activist famous for his long years of purchasing land from the Arabs, wrote to Ben Gurion about the western half of Galilee, with Nazareth at its heart and the Arab presence there. His letter included the following lines (Weitz 1969: 118):[12]

> The Arabs, in particular the Muslims, have not come to terms in their hearts or in their thoughts with the establishment of the Israeli state, and they entertain the hope that one day its existence will come to an end, or at least that the Galilee will be annexed to Lebanon. The fact that four years have passed since the conquest and no serious settlement activities have been carried out within this Arab bloc encourages them to believe that the Jews themselves are doubtful and uncertain as to whether the Galilee will remain in their state.

Nahmani's sentiments on the threat of Arab irredentism were regularly echoed in the Israeli policy discourse on what was and is referred to as the Judaization of the Galilee.[13] In his letter, Nahmani urged that particular attention be addressed to settling Jews in the city of Nazareth.

Upper Nazareth, a Jewish town, was established in 1957 on land expropriated from Arabs of the region. One newspaper correspondent (Hare'uveni 1965) reports the government's decision to set up the new town thus:

> [a decision] to impose on Arab Nazareth a Jewish town ... whose purpose—whose basic, primary, and even sole purpose is "to break" Arab autonomy in the region and in this city, and later, to create a Jewish majority.[14]

The establishment of Karmi'el followed in 1964, again on land expropriated from Arab villagers in the vicinity. From the beginning, the settlement of the new towns and then Upper Nazareth and Karmi'el was seen as the primary means of bringing about change in the demographic balance in the north (Kipnis 1984, 1987). But as the early waves of immigration to Israel waned, so too did the growth rate of the Jewish population in Galilee (Kipnis 1983). At the same time, the Arab population was growing rapidly through natural increase. During the late 1950s, the 1960s, and 1970s, and on into the 1980s, the annual rate of natural increase among the Arabs of Israel ranged from just below to well over forty per thousand (CBS 1973, 1997b). The outcome was that the Jews declined from 57.6 percent of the population of the Northern District in 1961 to 53.9 percent in 1972 and further to 50.3 percent in 1983 (data are for the Northern District, minus the Golan). This decline, as well as comparative rates of natural increase, was closely monitored year by year by the official record keepers of the state. High-level planning efforts during the 1970s were directed toward developing a strategy that would be conducive to greater growth of the Jewish urban population in the north (Kipnis 1983).

But, in the Zionist view, numerical superiority was only one aspect of establishing sovereignty. The other was the exercise of jurisdiction over territory in some concrete way; thus, the emphasis on Jewish rural settlement in tandem with growth of the urban population. Settlement was seen as one of the main ways of protecting endangered territory (Jewish Agency 1974; Kipnis 1984, 1987).

The phenomenon of "illegal building" among the Arab population was frequently invoked to fuel the perception not only of the danger of future irredentism, but also of the existence of an immediate tangible threat to state sovereignty. One aspect of this was the growing incidence of residential building in the officially recognized Arab towns outside the bounds of the "blue line," a line that had been drawn on Ministry of Interior maps in lieu of proper outline plans[15] for these localities (see further discussion of the planning experience below). Strictly speaking, this was illegal building, even when situated on land owned by the builders, and the authorities issued demolition orders. It may be noted, in passing, that the vast majority of the structures involved later became legal when the "blue lines" were redrawn in recognition of the facts on the ground and the needs of the burgeoning population in the Arab towns and villages.[16]

The other manifestation of illegal building was associated with the Bedouin population in the north. Various Bedouin tribes had come to Galilee as early as the sixteenth century, and others continued to come throughout the remainder of Ottoman rule and the British Mandate.[17] Bedouin settlement took place on land acquired by purchase, lease, or squatting. Ottoman land law, continued first by the British, and again under Israeli law, had provided for the acquisition of property rights on state land by means of a period of uninterrupted occupancy and cultivation. But wherever it could, the Israeli state contested claims based on that principle (see discussion in chapter 4). The image of Bedouin incursion into state land was a factor, in addition to illegal building, compounding the public perception of endangered territory.

The building of permanent dwellings by the Bedouin began toward the end of the Ottoman period. Between 1963 and 1973, the Israeli state had accorded recognition to or made plans for the recognition of some ten Bedouin settlements in the north. Some of these were located in the vicinity of areas in which spontaneous settlement in hamlets had taken place; others were a matter of post-facto government recognition of spontaneous villages by stages. But there were at that time six other villages that would only later be recognized, and in addition, some twelve tribes living in numerous dispersed hamlets.[18] Needless to say, all structures erected in such unrecognized or not-yet-recognized settlements, whether dwellings or lightly constructed farm shacks, were ipso facto classified as illegal. Again, this was the case even when they were located on land owned by the builder.[19]

From the mid 1970s, the Jewish Agency entered the scene as the driving force behind a push to establish new Jewish rural settlements in Galilee.[20] The two major studies of this settlement drive (Soffer and Finkel n.d.; Carmon et al. 1990) both show how Arab illegal building and incursion into state lands and the concomitant image of threatened territory figured in the planning discourse that gave rise to the settlements. Indeed, these settlements became known as "outlook posts" (*mitzpim*), an allusion to the expectation that the settlers would monitor and somehow deter the perceived land takeover.[21]

Another researcher (Kipnis 1987: 134) refers to the protection and preservation of national land as the "pretext" for the settlement initiative.

Reporting on the planning efforts that preceded the establishment of the *mitzpim*, one Jewish Agency official presents a map featuring a line circumscribing the area in mountainous Galilee in which there had been no Jewish settlement prior to 1975 (Muvhar 1983: 707, 709). I reproduce this line in figure 1.4.[22] The Jewish Agency planning documents that preceded the settlement drive spoke of the need to deploy Jewish rural settlement in the large areas still without a Jewish presence (Jewish Agency 1974: 8). Between 1975 and 1987, forty-four Jewish rural settlements were established in the area delineated by Muvhar's line, thirty-one of them in the four-year period from 1979 to 1982. The settlements are dispersed throughout this area, with most falling into four major clusters, while about eight follow the area's southern margin.

Twenty-three of the forty-four settlements had a population of under two hundred in 1995. Three of these were down to zero population at that time, while the average population of the next twenty was 139 (CBS 1998b). Though dispersed and small, the settlements are connected to the power, water, and telephone grids; they have good access roads, and their children are regularly bussed to school. These are among the things that distinguish them from the Bedouin hamlets, which are similar in size or larger, but are denied recognition by the Ministry of the Interior on the grounds that providing such infrastructure to small and scattered settlements would be prohibitively expensive.

The deployment of the settlements was such as to insinuate barriers in the spaces between a number of clusters of Arab towns. The growth of these towns was beginning to bring them into physical contact with one another within each cluster, and was seen as threatening regional takeover. Jewish Agency planning documents at the time spoke of the need for creating such barriers (see, e.g., Jewish Agency 1975: 7). By 1977, Arnon Soffer (a geographer with connections to the national planning establishment) was writing of the emergence of an urban cluster or conurbation around Nazareth, and concluded with a warning about similar developments in four other Galilee areas: around Shefar'am, Sakhnin, Kafar Yasif, and the Bet Hakerem Valley (Soffer 1977; see also Bar-Gal and Soffer 1981). Later, in their evaluation of the *mitzpim* project, Soffer and Finkel (n.d.: 35–36) describe the deployment of the new Jewish settlements as the driving of wedges (a concept with military implications) between emerging blocs of Arab settlement in the Galilee. They refer to this as a process of "deterritorialization" of the Arab population in Galilee, calling this an implicit aim of the project, and one of its accomplishments.

The Misgav Regional Council, which would eventually include thirty settlements, was established in Central Galilee in 1982 on land that, until then, had been without municipal status. Misgav's jurisdiction extended at that time to an area of about 170,000 dunam.[23]

Regional councils are a contrivance in the domain of local government unique to Israel. They are regional in the sense that they unite geographically dispersed small rural settlements and have jurisdiction over the entire territorial expanse that surrounds and includes those settlements, although the presence of other local authorities sometimes results in the regional council having expanses of territory that are not contiguous (see figure 1.6). But they are local authorities, not counties, functioning vis-à-vis their residents and the national government as any local authority would. The individual settlements within their boundaries do not have local authority status (see Local Councils Ordinance [Regional Councils] 1958, in "Legislation Cited"; I. Peled 1988: 191–194).

Now, parallel to the local authority in Israel is the Local Planning and Building Commission (LPBC), a body established by the minister of the interior under the Planning and Building Law (PBL 1965) independently of the local authority. In the case of large Jewish municipalities, the LPBC is closely associated with the local authority: aside from technical staff and the representatives of government ministries who participate in an advisory capacity, the membership of such commissions is identical with that of the local or municipal council (PBL 1965; I. Peled 1988: 184–186). It should be noted that this is not so for many smaller Jewish localities, nor for nearly all of the Arab localities; these are combined in local planning and building commissions that include several or many localities, with the attendant absence of direct local control.[24]

In the case of the regional councils, the territorially defined jurisdiction of the council and the writ of the Local Planning and Building Commission combine to establish effective spatial control. Kipnis (1987: 135) observes that regional councils are set up to cover all territory outside existing Arab municipalities, "thus helping to freeze Arab spatial sprawl to the boundaries of their existing settlements." Kipnis is referring here to the establishment of Jewish regional councils in the West Bank and Gaza, but it would be reasonable to impute the same rationale to the setting up of at least some of the regional councils within Israel's boundaries, particularly in the case of Misgav. The planning documents dealing with the establishment of Misgav (see, e.g., Kipnis 1982) and Ministry of Interior officials who served at the time (Interviews) focus on the need to provide municipal services to the residents of the rural settlements. But the element of territorial control is manifest in the sprawling contours of Misgav boundaries, and in the fact that the way in which these were originally set had the effect of choking off the possibility of responding affirmatively to the then-pending requests of neighboring Arab towns for expansion of their municipal boundaries. Some modification, both of Misgav boundaries and those of the Arab towns, was achieved subsequently in response to vociferous Arab protest (Yiftachel 1992: 174–180; Interviews; see figure 1.6). Soffer (1998) described the establishment of the Misgav Regional Council as a move in the deliberate and successful policy of "deterritorializing" the Arab population in Galilee (he had previously used this term with regard to the establishment of the *mitzpim* settlements themselves).

That territorial control is a dimension of the regional council is underscored by the case of the rural councils (*mo'etzah kafrit,* sing.). When the Ministry

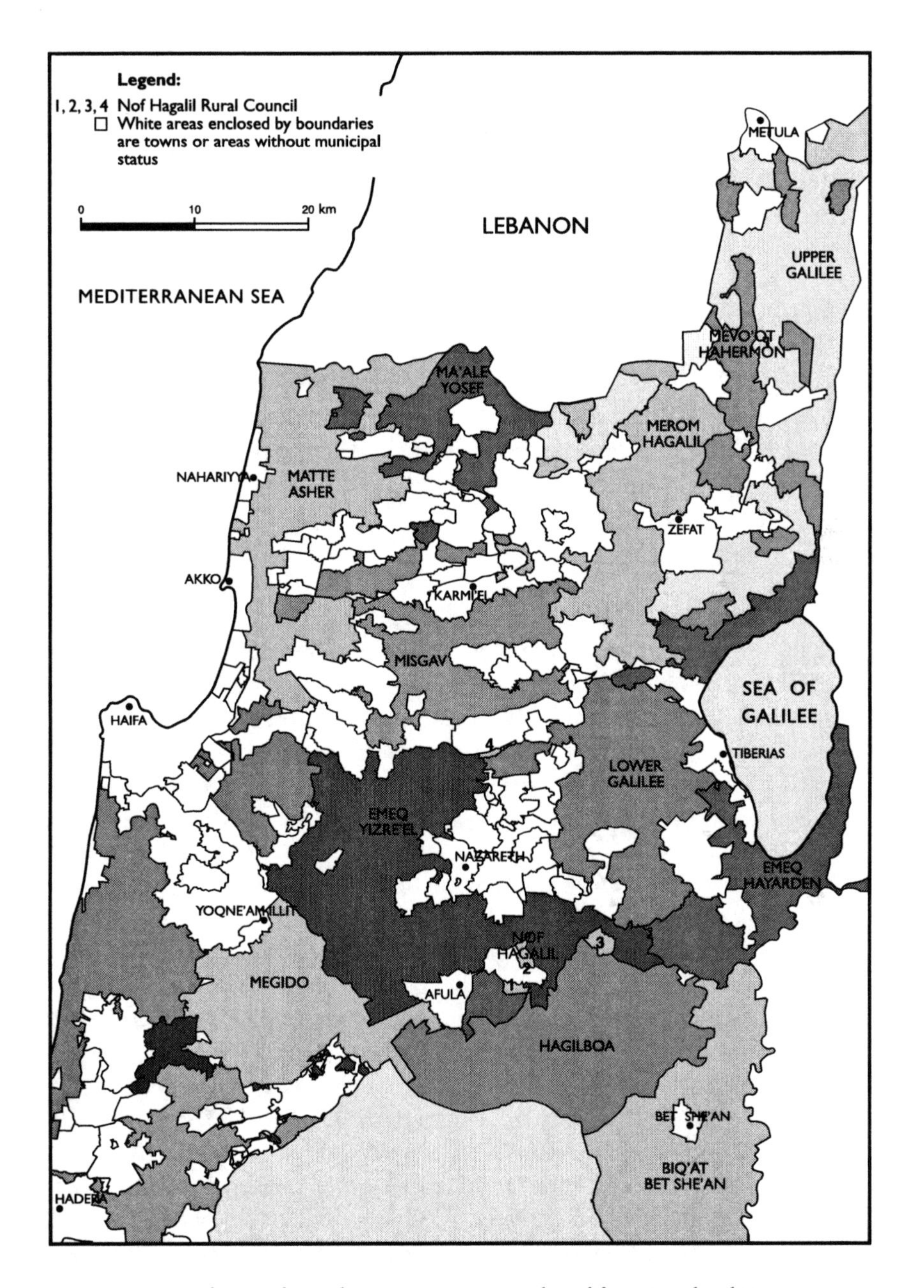

Figure 1.6 Regional Councils Northern District. *Source:* Adapted from Orgad and Newman 1991

of the Interior came around to establishing a municipal framework for some small, scattered Arab villages (Bedouin or other Arab), it united them in rural councils, similar in conception to the regional councils, with the exception that the rural councils do not have jurisdiction over any territory beyond the limits of the individual settlements (Nof Hagalil Rural Council in the Northern District is an example; see figure 1.6).[25]

It may be noted that several regional councils (mostly in the Northern District) have recognized Bedouin or other Arab settlements among their members (see, e.g., Abu Raya 1995). In 1993, Bedouin constituted about one-third of the population of 30,000 in the Emeq Yizre'el Regional Council (Jewish Agency 1994: 18, 66–71). In Misgav Regional Council, there were in 1995 two recognized Bedouin settlements with a combined population of 1,377. In addition, there were seven Bedouin hamlets, some of them on the way to being recognized, with a population of about 2,700.

Disparate Planning Experiences

The establishment of Jewish rural and urban settlements in Galilee was directly linked to initiatory, activist planning and infrastructure development on the part of various national government and quasi-government bodies. In a major study on land-use planning and its functions in controlling the Arab population of Galilee, Yiftachel (1992: 88) refers to such activist policy as developmental planning, and distinguishes it from the operation of the statutory planning system, which is generally regulatory in its effect (see also Carmon et al. 1990: 54–56).

The statutory planning system may be thought of as a two-stage process. A proposed local outline plan or urban building plan is sent by the LPBC to the District Planning and Building Commission (DPBC).[26] The latter body may at that point request that changes be made by the plan's originators. If the DPBC is satisfied, it awards preliminary acceptance to the plan, approving it for public deposit. This is the end of the first stage. During the deposit period, objections to the plan may be lodged by persons affected by the plan, the local planning commission (the body that sent it to the DPBC) itself, local authorities, or public bodies. A successful plan, amended if necessary in response to those objections accepted by the DPBC, receives final approval (*ishur letoqef*) as the culmination of the second stage.

In the case of the *mitzpim* settlement project, the interested authorities were able to circumvent the requirement of plan deposit (and consequent exposure to public objection), as well as the lengthy statutory process, by invoking only the provisions of the British 1946 Regional Planning Outline Scheme (RP/50/42) still in force at the time. Under that outline plan, the district commissioner had discretionary power to issue permits for building on land zoned for agriculture. It was under that regional plan that *building permits* for the *mitzpim* were issued, this in the absence of approved statutory outline plans for the settlements themselves (Soffer and Finkel n.d.: 96–101; Carmon et al. 1990: 45–50, 56; Yiftachel 1992: 244–246).[27] Yiftachel points out that over twenty years earlier, the Northern District Planning and Building Commission had disallowed the relevance of these discretionary provisions to Arab building on agricultural land, thus rendering questionable their invocation in the case of the *mitzpim*.

With the qualified exception of the new towns for the Bedouin,[28] it was not the initiatory face of development planning that the Arab population encountered, but rather the constraining and limiting side of the statutory planning system. The authorities had originally conceived the "blue line" as an interim measure that would be a basis for the issuing of building permits until outline plans could be prepared. But that preparation, beset by difficulties, dragged on. Factors that impinged on the planning process included the following: (a) these were outline plans for large, already settled populations, involving numerous landowners and a constraining social and geophysical layout of land ownership; and (b) the planning initiative and execution came from outside (recall that the LPBCs in the Arab sector were, despite their name, not under local control), and they met with wariness and suspicion on the part of the local population, whose interests, at the immediate individual level, were often jeopardized by the proposed plans. Moreover, the LPBCs demanded that the outline plans for the Arab localities be prepared at a scale of 1:2,500 or even 1:1,250, rather than at the scale of 1:10,000 or 1:5,000 stipulated by the customary planning regulations. Meyer-Brodnitz (1994: 172) explains that the local commissions were afraid that it would not be possible to finance the preparation of the detailed plans (at the larger scale) that would ordinarily come after the outline plans and that would serve as a basis for the issuing of building permits by the commission. The demand that outline plans be prepared at the larger scale imposed additional difficulties, and apparently contributed markedly to drawing out the length of the planning process. Altogether, the result was that the outline plans prepared for the Arab localities were generally outmoded before they were approved, overtaken by events on the ground (Khamaisi 1986, 1993; Meyer-Brodnitz 1994; for a detailed consideration of the events and relations of the planning process in a single locality set in the overall planning context, see also Yiftachel 1997: 47–61).

Yiftachel (1992: 238–240) assembles comparative data on the duration of the outline plan approval process for Arab and Jewish settlements in the Yehi'am natural region, the area of his study in the Galilee. According to these data, outline plan preparation and approval took an average of over twenty years per Arab settlement, and seven years per Jewish settlement. These figures probably understate the length of time required for approval of plans for the Arab sector as compared with the Jewish sector, since Yiftachel counts only the period until 1988, even for plans that were then in process but not yet approved. The bare figures also fail to convey the relative severity of the consequences of not having an approved outline plan, since nearly all of the Jewish settlements in Yiftachel's study are small collective, cooperative, or community settlements. These have little difficulty in availing themselves of the provisions in the Planning and Building Law (§68), according to which the Planning and Building Commission will, as mentioned above, treat proposed detailed plans (for residences, industry, etc.) relating to areas without outline plans as though they were themselves proposed outline plans.

For all their restraint, Yiftachel's data, particularly in conjunction with his 1997 description of planning events in a single locality, point clearly to the comparative gloom of the experience of the Arab towns with the planning process. On the other hand, government statistics may be organized in such a way as to make the differences between the Arab and Jewish localities in this regard disappear from view. A case in point is a national survey prepared by the Ministry of Interior (1997c) dealing with the preparation and status of master plans, outline plans, and development plans at the level of the local authority.[29] According to this survey, the average duration of the statutory process for outline plans in the Arab localities of the Northern District has been under 4.5 years, not different from that for non-Arab localities (181–188). But the government survey defines the duration of the statutory process as the time elapsed from the time that deposit of the plan is announced, to the time that final approval is announced (230). It will be recalled that this is really the second stage in the statutory planning process. Although the PBL sets limits to the duration of the approval process (§62c), these limits are generally exceeded. In particular, the first stage—from the time that preparation of the outline plan is initiated, until the decision of the DPBC on preliminary approval and deposit—may drag out inordinately, and, indeed, it was here that Yiftachel found extremely long durations in the case of the Arab localities. The government survey simply ignores this period.

It should be observed that failure to consider the entire length of the approval process (both first and second stages) leads to distortion in the interpretation of data on the comparative *age* of outline plans. According to the government survey, many of the Arab localities have recently approved outline plans, and the implication is that recency of approval entails being up to date. But surely plans that have been in the works for twenty years or longer would be prone to lack the current validity of plans formulated more recently.

The same government survey (1997c: 195) asserts that 45 percent of the Jewish and mixed localities in the Northern District did not have an approved outline plan as of 1996, while that was the case for only 25 percent of the Arab localities. But of the sixteen Jewish local authorities that did not have approved outline plans (the 45 percent), thirteen are regional councils (p. 194) (these, it will be recalled, are local authorities in the Israeli scheme of local government). Now, it is hard to imagine that the lack of an outline plan for the regional council would hinder the approval of plans and building permits for the rural Jewish collective, cooperative, and communal settlements that make up the council.[30] Thus, it must be with a considerable degree of disingenuousness that the minister of the interior refers obliquely to such data when he suggests, as he has done, that the situation regarding outline plans in the Jewish sector may be worse than in the Arab sector (Knesset debate 17 July 1996).

By 1996, 75 percent of the Arab local authorities in the Northern District[31] did finally have approved outline plans, but the circumstances of their preparation make them largely inadequate even for present needs, let alone for the future urban development of the Arab towns. It is against this background that Arab leaders assert that, for the most part, the Arab localities do not have current valid outline plans (Knesset debate 17 July 1996; Interviews).

The experience of the Arab localities with the statutory planning system was shaped by the response of the authorities and of public discourse to illegal building; the difficulties of gaining approved and adequate outline plans; the sometimes arbitrary stringency of the Committee for the Preservation of Agricultural Land (CPAL); and an administrative organization that, in effect, kept control of local planning out of the hands of the localities themselves. This experience contrasted starkly with what the Arabs in Galilee could see going on around them with regard to Jewish settlement. There, the initiatory planning entailed by the establishment of new towns and new rural settlements was the order of the day. And it was clear to all that settlement activity was carried out with "demographic balance" and "'deterritorialization' of the Arab population" inscribed on its banner.

The Perception of Threat

For all the settlement activity that has taken place over the years, and despite other far-reaching changes, the perception of threat posed by an Arab majority in the central portion of Galilee and the image of endangered territory have persisted into the 1990s and beyond with unabated fervor. Four examples will be adduced:

1. In 1990, the National Board for Planning and Building (NBPB) decided to initiate the preparation of a development plan for the Galilee that would be framed and processed as an amendment (no. 9) to the Northern District Outline Plan. The NBPB asked the planners to address eleven problems that it saw as relevant to planning for the Galilee. The first three, in order, were (a) a marked Jewish minority in many parts of Galilee, (b) the territorial contiguity of Arab towns, and (c) the takeover of state land and illegal building (by implication, by the Arabs). The other points did not single out the Arabs in Galilee; they had to do with such things as level of income, employment opportunities, and social services as compared with the center of the country; out-migration of Jews from the region; keeping the Galilee green. But the Arab presence in Galilee provided the top three problems that the NBPB put to the planners (Shefer et al. 1992: 3–4).

2. In 1993, the Jewish Agency authored a plan for the establishment of twenty-six new community settlements, twenty-three of them in Galilee, and

three in Wadi 'Ara. The third major point in the plan's rationale is the geopolitical change expected to ensue from the pending peace arrangements with the Palestinians and Israel's other neighbors.[32] Nevertheless, the two main elements in the program remain demography and the control of state land (Sorojun and Arrarat 1993; Bendar 1994).

3. In 1996, the Ministry of Construction and Housing gave preliminary consideration to a draft proposal for housing objectives for the year 2020. The draft proposal was called "Magen David 2020." The term *Magen David* refers to the six-pointed star that is generally rendered in translation as the "Star of David," but literally means "David's Shield." The map accompanying the proposal superimposes a six-pointed star on the area of central Galilee: Jewish urban settlement and development are to be concentrated at the star's points. The center portion of the star contains a heart shape, labeled as "the Green Heart," projected as a rural area of Jewish-Arab coexistence. The account of the draft proposal that reached the Hebrew daily press was couched in terms of "the fear of an Arab majority in Galilee," "control of Galilee by the Arab towns," and "the aim of preventing the spread of the Arab population in Galilee and its control of territory" (Petersburg 1996). Such language makes evident the implications of the term "David's Shield."

I was not allowed to see the draft proposal, since it has apparently been shelved. According to a ministry official, it had been inadvertently leaked to the press. One should note that the language of the newspaper account probably reflects a blatancy more typical of press conferences and what the press makes of them than of official documents, the language of the latter generally being more circumspect.

The public discourse is not devoid of critical voices, but criticism is easily absorbed or contained. Thus, in the case of the 1993 Jewish Agency plan for twenty-six new settlements, Agency officials may downplay the importance of demographics and control of state land as the rationale of their program, even though these are clearly there in the plan itself and are prominently displayed in Bendar's 1994 press account. Agency officials say that they are content to carry out the plan a little at a time, thus avoiding the political response that a concentrated campaign would elicit.

Something similar may be at work in the case of Amendment 9 to the Northern District Outline Plan. Despite having been presented by the planners in 1992, the plan had still not, as of 1999, been accepted for deposit by the NBPB. There are those who suggest that the planning authorities fear that the plan will be seen as a proposal for Judaization of the Galilee and would be vulnerable to public criticism on that ground. Such criticism can be shrugged off so long as the plan has not been deposited for public scrutiny and objections (Interviews). Meanwhile, the perception of territorial and demographic threat as the paramount concern of the NBPB is a matter of record.[33]

4. The fourth example of the persistence of the perception of endangered territory is found in the practice of awarding large tracts of land (several thousand

dunam each) to individuals (Jews) who establish private ranches in the Galilee and the Negev. This has been carried out since 1997 by the Ministry of Agriculture, the ILA, and the Jewish Agency, aided by the JNF, in direct contravention of national and district outline plans, and in many cases, without regard for statutory approval. As of December 1999, the practice was being challenged in a suit brought before the High Court of Justice. According to a newspaper account of the suit and its background (Shehori 1999b), insider informants relate that "the real, but unacknowledged, reason for government support given to [such] individual settlement is the view that it constitutes a barrier to Bedouin and Arab expansion in the Negev and in Galilee." It is alleged that the land is awarded without following the mandatory procedures of public tender, and at just 5 percent of the regular land-lease fees. One might reflect on how curious it is that this practice is represented to the public as a way of "protecting state land."

The image of territorial threat is conspicuously present in the broad ground where national planning policy and the academic discipline of geography meet. For a particularly outspoken partisan presentation, see, for example, A. Sofer 1997[34] in the distinctly right-wing *Nativ.*

So pervasive is the discourse of exclusion that even analysis written from the critical perspective of sociology must come to terms with it. Thus, Kimmerling, whose *Zionism and Territory* (1983; see also Kimmerling 1979) speaks of *presence, ownership,* and *sovereignty* as the three types of control over territory. If this, in the manner of any discursive formation one inhabits, seems less than remarkable, I would offer for consideration the statement of Meyer-Brodnitz, a prominent Israeli planner who said at a 1998 university-sponsored conference: "I believe that many populations may live in one territory, all with a sense of rootedness, possession, and control, without pushing out the others … just as every child sees its mother as its only mother, while his/her mother may have many children and love them all" (Jewish-Arab Center 1998: 42). That statement offers a way of looking at the discourse on territorial threat from a position outside its bounds.

Thus far, in describing the lay of the land in Galilee, I have touched on the elements of (a) Jewish land purchase and settlement during the pre-state period; (b) the destruction of Arab towns and villages and Arab population loss and dislocation; (c) Bedouin settlement; (d) major Jewish urban and rural settlement projects involving expropriation of Arab land and consolidation of Jewish landholdings; (e) the Israeli innovation of constituting the regional council as a local authority, one suited to controlling territory; (f) disparate Jewish and Arab experiences with the initiatory and regulatory planning systems; and (g) the salience of images of minority/majority demographics and of territorial threat in most of the above, images that have fuelled the drive of the land authorities and planning institutions to secure control of the land in the name of the Jewish people. The result of all these has been to create a checkered map of Arab/Jewish population dispersal in the Northern District, one strongly suggestive of a played-out board of the Japanese game of *Go* (although games, unlike the case of Galilee, tend to be played between contenders who are quite evenly matched). As a senior official in one of the Jewish local authorities put it to me, speaking of the Arabs, "They live among us." He was explaining to me why the needs and interests of the Arab localities (as he understood them, of course) had to be taken into account. But, depending on the point of view and where in the expanse of Galilee one stood, that statement could just as well be uttered by an Arab speaker.

Looking at the workings of Israeli land-use planning in Galilee solely through the lens of control, Yiftachel (1992) hypothesizes increasing interethnic political instability in Galilee. Yet consider as an alternative the recent statement of the Israeli planner that attachment to the land need not be exclusionary. One should be careful, though, of reading too much into that statement; it may merely signal diminished discursive relevance in some quarters rather than. outright discursive break. And it may be precisely the mosaic of Jewish/Arab population dispersal in Galilee, the fact that "they" live among "us"—"we" among "them"—that makes such a statement possible. Perhaps the territorial demon in Galilee looms less large than it once did. Indeed, this might be construed from Soffer's contention in a 1998 paper that the Jews have by now won the battle for territorial control in Galilee.

CHAPTER 2

The Lay of the Land (II)

Urban Drive and the Arab Towns

Urban Drive

Chapter 2 will take up the elements having to do with municipal authorities and their budgets and infrastructure, and with local economic development. It will be shown how these elements form a second dimension (in addition to the geographic dispositions dealt with in the preceding chapter) of the position of the Arab towns in the field of power relations. Chapter 1 dealt with Galilee; the present chapter relates to the Arab local authorities throughout Israel.[1] The chapter will conclude with a brief consideration of some theoretical aspects of the concept of the disposition of forces and its ability to handle complex relations of power without oversimplification.

Socioeconomic Rank

At this point, I would like to introduce data on the socioeconomic ranking of local authorities in 1995 prepared by the CBS (CBS 1999).[2] This ranking lies on the border between the economics of population and the economics of place. The ranking is commissioned by the Ministry of the Interior, one of its purposes being its use as an indicator for distributing budgetary grants to local authorities (to be dealt with below) (CBS 1999: xvii, 9, 16–17). The sixteen variables used to construct the index of rank have to do with demography (dependency ratio, median age, persons per household), standard of living (including per capita income, as well as other variables), education, and employment. These are all measures of the economic and social well-being of the population. The sixteen variables of the index were selected by factor analysis, and these were then used to assign a rank to each of the localities. Following this, the localities were grouped by cluster analysis into ten clusters in ascending order of rank.[3]

The distribution of Arab local authorities in the clusters is shown in table 2.1, together with the average per capita income for each cluster.

Table 2.1 Local Authorities and Average Per Capita Income by Socioeconomic Cluster

	Local authorities			
	Total	Arab	% Arab in cluster	Average per capita income (NIS)[1]
Cluster 1	9	9	100.0	704
Cluster 2	26	23	88.5	968
Cluster 3	44	30	68.2	1,140
Cluster 4	24	12	50.0	1,359
Cluster 5	16	1		1,591
Cluster 6	22	2		1,816
Cluster 7	19	—		2,161
Cluster 8	9	—		2,415
Cluster 9	18	—		2,733
Cluster 10	16	—		3,653

Notes: 1. Including transfer payments.
Source: CBS 1999, Publication no. 1118.

It will be seen that the Arab localities are concentrated in the four lower-rank clusters. Six of the nine Arab localities in Cluster 1 are Bedouin towns in the Negev; two of the twenty-three Arab localities in Cluster 2 are Druze villages in the Golan. Of the remaining sixty-six Arab localities in the bottom four clusters, forty-nine are in Galilee. Seven of the Jewish localities in the bottom four clusters are in Galilee or the Northern District. Of the three Arab localities in Clusters 5 and 6, two are in Galilee.

Conceived and organized, as it is, on a locality by locality basis, this ranking has direct implications regarding the ability to levy and collect local taxes, local infrastructure, and the attractiveness of place in terms of urban development and the reciprocal relations between these elements. I turn now to a consideration of these dimensions of the lay of the land.

Early Development Plans

From the beginning, new Jewish settlement, rural or urban, meant the planning and construction of the requisite physical infrastructure for housing, education, transportation, and economic development. The attendant planning and public discourse, at least from the 1960s, contained the element of calls for the inclusion of the Arab population in such development. One example is found in an article by Yehuda Shaari (1963), a Liberal Party MK, that spoke in terms of coordinated Jewish-Arab development of the Galilee; nonetheless, the article does little more than assert that Jewish settlement benefits the local

Arab population by providing employment and services. Others (see, e.g., Flapan 1963) called for government development efforts to be channeled directly to the Arab towns and villages.

Indeed, that is what was proposed by a Five Year Program prepared in 1962 by the Bureau of the Adviser on Arab Affairs of the Prime Minister's Office (*New Outlook* 1962). A second five-year program was prepared for the years 1967/68 to 1971/72 (PMO, Bureau of the Adviser on Arab Affairs and the Economic Planning Authority 1967). These plans addressed the development of local physical infrastructure, education and health services, as well as agriculture and industrial production. Lustick (1980: 192) compiles figures according to which annual expenditure on development in the Arab towns was 1.5 percent of the total development budget expenditure in the years 1962/63 to 1966/67, and 1.3 percent of the total expenditure in the period from 1967/68 to 1971/72. It should be noted that in 1961, the Arabs residing outside the mixed Jewish-Arab towns were 9.5 percent of the total population of the country (CBS 1998b and the 1961 Census). But then, only a minor portion of the plans' goals was accomplished. Since then, until new development allocations in recent years (to be dealt with below), there were no further special efforts on the part of the government.

The 1974 proposal for mountainous Galilee prepared by the Settlement Department of the Jewish Agency dealt mainly with the development of Jewish urban and rural settlements, in which great sums were to be invested. The first to benefit, it was averred, would be the region's veteran, mostly Arab population. But the proposal also called for direct investment in planning, infrastructure, and services for the Arab localities (Jewish Agency 1974: 9–10, 22). The proposal was submitted to the "Inter-institutional Committee for Settlement," which in all likelihood would have included not only the Jewish Agency and the JNF, but also relevant government ministries and the Israel Lands Administration (ILA). For the Jewish Agency Settlement Department, the proposal to invest in Arab towns was easy enough, since it, as the representative of the Jewish people, not of the citizenry of Israel, would never be called on to actually carry out such a proposal. At the same time, the absence of real interest within the government—that is, someone to push—on the one hand, and the Arabs' lack of political clout, on the other, meant that such proposals would remain in the realm of pious intention.

Arab Local Government

One dimension of the lack of political potency had to do with the establishment and functioning of Arab local government. The Ottoman ruler had established municipal councils in the larger centers, but these began to function properly only during the period of the British Mandate. The British also began to promote the establishment of Arab local government in the rural areas (Government of Palestine 1946). But, as Miller (1985: 71–76) relates, the villagers regarded British intentions, as they had those of the latter's Ottoman predecessors, with suspicion. For their part, the British proceeded with caution: they established Arab councils with "limited franchise, restricted prerogatives, and carefully controlled access to office" (ibid.). The (British) district commissioners had supervisory powers which deprived the councils of full responsibility for their actions, hindering the emergence of local policy based on village-wide rather than narrow *hamula* (agnatic descent group, pl. *hama'il*) interests. Miller describes the way in which the arrangements encouraged manipulation and the persistence of the traditional role of village leaders as mediators between local *hama'il* and superior authorities. Moreover, according to one account (S. Shamir 1962: 103), the British also gave support to the institution of the *mukhtar*, a henchman selected locally to represent the central government, as "a counter-balance to the local councils in order to facilitate their [i.e., British] rule over the village" (also, cf. Miller: 54–62). In any event, a number of the local councils were abolished after varying periods, "owing to dissension and quarrels amongst the members of the various families" (quoted by Miller: 73, from Mandate sources). The British then attempted to introduce a more flexible form, which they called "village council." By the end of 1945, there were in the Arab localities in Mandatory Palestine eighteen municipal councils, eleven local councils, and twenty-four village councils (Government of Palestine 1946) (at least some of the latter category were located in places where a local council had previously been established and then abolished).

Miller argues (1985: 75) that "the new structure [of local council] could not be successful without a concurrent reformulation of its social and cultural base." But this is not, as might initially appear, a simple essentialist argument of "Arab traditionalism," for one of the main conclusions of Miller's study is that "the British administration used its position to try to control and limit changes in the Arab countryside ... with the intention of protecting [what they, i.e., the British, perceived as, DW] a traditional native community" (164).

In any event, the position of the Arab local authority vis-à-vis the central government did not change for the better with the advent of the Israeli regime in 1948. It is true that the Israeli government continued to promote the establishment of Arab municipal authorities. One former Ministry of Interior official explained to me that the localities where local councils were first set up were selected carefully: places were chosen where the population was thought to be not hostile to the new Jewish state and where there were strong Jewish local authorities nearby (Interviews). By 1968, there were forty-four Arab local authorities (municipal councils and local councils), thirty-nine of which had been set up after 1948.[4] It is also true that the office of *mukhtar* as local representative of the national government was gradually being phased out (S. Shamir 1962: 103–104).

However, the pattern of intervention and manipulation persisted; indeed, it grew in intensity. A salient element was the military government, which was imposed on Arab towns and villages with the advent of the state of Israel and which continued until 1966 (although it was gradually phased out during the early 1960s). Prominent among the oppressive regulations enforced by the military government were a series of closure orders, applied only to Arabs, making it necessary for the latter to obtain permits for travel outside their own villages and forbidding entry to various areas altogether, thus denying them access to their own lands, and the imposition of curfews. These restrictions, and others, harshly curtailed personal freedom and had serious economic ramifications, and it is often this aspect that seems to stand out in treatments of the military government in the literature (see, e.g., Jiryis 1976; Kretzmer 1990). But the fact of intervention in the area of local government may have been of even greater consequence. Jiryis (39–40, 248), al Haj and Rosenfeld (1988: 37), and Lustick (1980: 204–208) all deal with this intervention and the prizes that it held out in return for loyalty and submission—prizes in the form of permits, licenses, jobs and teaching positions, opportunities for higher education, funding, and representation on the local council. Together with the military government, the various government ministries dealing with the Arab local authorities all played their part. Local social and political activity was organized on traditional *hamula* lines, and competition among the leaders of the different *hama'il* for the favors controlled by the national authorities was the natural outcome of the situation; indeed it was a state of affairs actively encouraged by the latter.

Various other studies, anthropological in bent, also deal with this intervention. Nakhleh (1975) shows how the intrusion of national political parties and the long-range policies of the (Israeli) regime combined with and exploited the social structure of the Arab village to produce local political factionalism and impede the development of a higher level of political consciousness. A. Cohen (1965) describes the dependent response and strengthening of the *hamula* organization in the Arab village he studied ensuing from regime intervention, patronage, and manipulation of resources. Asad (1975), who offers a critique of Cohen, makes explicit the way in which the Israeli regime made use of what he calls the "*hamula* ideology" to control the Arab population.

Like the British before them, the Israeli authorities had no difficulty in attributing the resulting dissension and factionalism to the persistence of the traditional *hamula* social organization, cast as inimical to the requirements of modern municipal government (Interviews; also cf. Reuveny 1988: 245–246).[5] But, of course, it was a bow from outside and above that was being drawn across the strings of traditional forms. Undoubtedly, one may tell the story of Arab local government in Israel with varying emphases on the diverse elements that enter into the picture. Among these are the apprehension of villagers regarding the intentions of the central regime (Ottoman, British, Israeli), traditional social organization and interclan rivalry, and absence of modern education. But one ought to be wary of establishment-oriented treatments that ignore the element of regime intervention. I will have occasion to return to the uses of the image of tradition as applied to the Arab population.

In general, local authorities in Israel—Arab or Jewish—find themselves dependent on the national government for budgets and approvals. But the special dependence of the Arab local authorities was not particularly alleviated with the dismantling of the military government in 1966. The contacts of the Arab councils with the various ministries and national agencies were channeled through the "minorities departments" or the officers for Arab affairs of each body. One former Ministry of Interior official described to me the discretionary and filtering power of these officials, exercised outside regular procedures of the government administration (Interviews). The effect would certainly have been to curtail the ability of the Arab local authorities to initiate development projects; it would have also exacerbated dependence and manipulation.

In 1974, the Arabs in Israel established the National Committee of Chairmen of the Arab Local Authorities. Al Haj and Rosenfeld (1988) describe the way in which this organization grew in strength and purposefulness during the 1970s, and the vicissitudes of its struggle for recognition by the national government during the 1980s. The National Committee was a key factor in the growing awareness of the rights of Arab local authorities, and in the greater assertiveness of the Arab leadership in pressing their demands.

In 1990 (or thereabouts), the Ministry of the Interior did away with the position of "National Officer for Druze and Arab Local Councils." What remained of the former special administrative apparatus was the Adviser on Arab Affairs in the Prime Minister's Office. Over the years, a younger generation of university-trained personnel had been taking over from the older *hamula* leaders as elected and administrative officials in the Arab local councils. *Hamula* affiliation remained an important organizing element in Arab local politics, but nonetheless, university-trained local officials speak to the national government in a different voice. Secret service surveillance of the population of the Arab towns, with its attendant manipulation and enlisting of informers, continued and continues (Interviews; also cf. Algazi 1998), yet today, the Arab local authorities, as such, are better able to work within the government system to protest against discrimination and advance their interests. In addition to the evidence available in al Haj and Rosenfeld (1988), this was manifest in events I followed during my fieldwork. For all that, the position of the Arab local authorities in the structure of regional relations is such as to make competitive urban development exceedingly difficult, and they remain the weaker party, vulnerable to government pressure. These too are things I learned in the course of my fieldwork.

Municipal Budgets

As suggested above, the relative weakness of the Arab local authorities was manifested directly in their municipal budgets, and through these, in their prospects for local development. To deal with this subject properly, it will be necessary to put it into the perspective of the relations of the local authority in Israel (whether Jewish or Arab) with the national government regarding municipal finance. I turn to this topic now.

In general, local authority budgets are divided into two: the current budget and the noncurrent or development budget. The current budget covers four main categories of expenditure: (a) administration, (b) local services, (c) state services, and (d) municipal works. Local services include such items as sanitation, security, management and maintenance of public buildings, zoning, building permits, and business licensing and inspection. The main items in the so-called state services are education, welfare, and culture. Municipal works include water supply, sewage, and abattoirs. The current budget also covers long-term debt service.[6]

The current budget is financed primarily by locally generated revenue, directed or earmarked transfers from the central government, and the general grant from the Ministry of the Interior. Locally generated revenue includes residents' payments for water and services, license fees, levies and development charges, and local property tax. Earmarked transfers come from the various ministries and are meant to cover part of the expenditures in the so-called state services. The general grant, known also as the "balancing grant," is allocated (or not allocated) to each local authority to close the gap between its ability to generate municipal income from the other sources and the cost of a minimal level of services to its residents. In addition to the socioeconomic level of the local authority, calculation of the grant due each locality also takes into account population (returns to scale), distance to be traversed in providing services, location in a national priority region (see below) or in a border area. There are also special Ministry of Interior grants for the purpose of dealing with unmanageable debt.

The development budget covers development projects in the various areas of municipal activity. It is principally financed by central government participation, by treasury and bank loans, by transfers from the current budget, and by the participation of property owners.[7] It should be pointed out that the distinction between the current budget and the development budget is far from rigid. Capital acquisitions may be approved in either budget; as noted above, the current budget may allocate funds for transfer to the development budget; and development projects may be carried out under the current budget itself. Also, as noted, repayment of loans (principal and interest) taken to finance the development budget appears as an expenditure in the current budget. All this gives well-to-do local authorities, as well as more daring or reckless ones (those able to raise capital in the banking system), considerable room for maneuver in pushing for local development.

It will be apparent that the system provides ample opportunity for confrontation between the local authorities and the national government. One such area is that of the financing of the state services. The Ministry of Education, for example, recognizes certain items in the education budget and sets regulation prices at which it finances them. It is generally accepted that Ministry of Education transfers will cover about 75 percent of the local authority education budget (Soari 1993: 24). But regulation prices are not generally free market prices and do not allow for variation in quality. Moreover, the local authority may wish or need to go beyond the basket of educational services of which the recognized items constitute 75 percent, or, indeed, may be urged to do so (at their own expense) by the government. Then there is the whole area of the general grant. Just what *are* the minimal service needs of the individual local authority, and what *is* its ability to raise locally generated municipal income? And just how much of the difference between the cost of needs and the available resources is the Ministry of the Interior willing or able to shoulder?

Since about 1985, national law has severely controlled the amount by which local property rates may be raised from one year to the next. The squeeze on the local authorities is exacerbated when the national government decides, as it often does, to cut back on spending. Local authorities, advised to cut back themselves, find that costs are downwardly rigid, both for political reasons and because there are long-term commitments involved. But the system has been kept going by the ability of the local authorities to mobilize bank credit. Periodically, however, this breaks down, and at such points, the national government has stepped in to bail out the local authorities, no matter what the mix of current expenditures or development projects that contributed to their financial distress. The Soari Commission report (1993) provides details on four such nationwide interventions between 1980 and 1992. In addition, solutions have been provided for numerous ad hoc local financial emergencies. The management of each crisis leads to a new agreement between the national government and the local authorities, but each side later asserts that these have been adhered to only in part. One such breakdown occurred in the first half of 1997, and was finally resolved by negotiations with the heads of the local authorities who, together with their municipalities, had been on strike for nearly a month. Reporting on these events, Lahav (1997) observes that this pattern of municipal finances compels the local authorities to incur a deficit, which is convenient for both sides: convenient for the national government because it enjoys the power that accrues to it by virtue of being able to dispense budgetary additions at its discretion, and convenient for the local authorities because the system releases them from responsibility for the proper management of fiscal affairs.

It is in this general financial setting that the Arab local authorities provide services to their residents and pursue local development. Reuveny (1988: 248) points out that the narrow scope of services in Arab towns is the *cause* of lower government participation in Arab local authority budgets. The Ministry of the Interior, he writes, attributes this to the "underdeveloped infrastructure," which is "related to local demand and the attitudes of the local leadership." There is, at least on the surface, a certain logic to this position. Government participation is, indeed, a function of the services the local authority has undertaken to provide. Earmarked transfers are allocated only for items that are part of the local budget. Also, the general grant (figured on a per capita basis), while not linked to a locality-specific set of services, was at one time explicitly lower for Arab localities than for Jewish local authorities on the grounds that, on the average, the former provided their residents with a smaller "basket of services." One former Interior Ministry official explained the obvious to me: if the municipality does not have a sewage system, it does not need government assistance for maintenance and operation. Although the grant is no longer calculated in this way, I discovered in the course of my investigation that this historic difference carries over to the present day (see below).

From the start, however, the experience of the Arab local authorities was more charged than the sanitized formulas "government participation as a function of services provided" or "absence of local demand as the cause of inferior services" would suggest. Former Ministry of Interior officials described the beginnings to me thus: "In the early years, most local development was financed by loans. But the Arab localities refused to take loans—they were afraid they would be required to mortgage their village lands, afraid that [in the case of foreclosure] the government would throw them across the border." And again: "In the 1960s, the Arab local authorities didn't ask for much—it was possible to buy quiet with 500 meters of road." Furthermore,

> if Arab demands were different, then that was because of lower development—meeting Jewish demands in that circumstance was not discrimination, it was simply a matter of different levels of needs.
>
> But then a new generation of young Arab leaders arose—the result of having been educated by the Jews—and they began to demand. But they would demand everything all at once—because those things hadn't existed before—and that would require great outlays. So we said to them: "Do these things, but do them slowly, a little at a time [*l'at l'at*]."

Al Haj and Rosenfeld (1988) recount the struggle of the Arab local authorities vis-à-vis the central government for proper funding of their current budgets and development budgets.[8] The mayor of Shefar'am is quoted to the effect that until 1976, the Arab local authorities "almost never received development budgets" (138). And the head of the Jatt Local Council speaks of special development budgets and a special credit line for development in the early 1980s, attributing these achievements to the pressure exerted by the National Committee of Chairmen of the Arab Local Authorities (122).

But then came the retrenchment of the 1980s in government public sector activity as part of the attempt to control hyperinflation (Hecht 1988: 358–359). Despite occasional statements recognizing development needs of the Arab municipalities, little was actually done. Strikes mounted by the Arab local authorities followed in the 1990s, and, coupled with greater receptiveness on the part of the government (linked, at least in part, to the dependency of the flimsy Rabin coalition government on the tacit support of the Arab parties in the Knesset), they resulted in new commitments.

In June 1995, the government signed an agreement with representatives of the Druze and Circassian local authorities that provided for a development budget of 1,190 million NIS for those localities (according to prices of the 1995 budget), to be spread over the five-year period ending in 1999, with the local authorities to raise about 10 percent of that sum themselves (Agreement, 1 June 1995; see also Government Decision 5880, 16 July 1995).

The discussion here on government decisions and special agreements with the heads of the local authorities reflects the distinction between *Druze and Circassian* local authorities, on the one hand, and *Arab* local authorities, on the other, made by the government, and sometimes by the local authorities themselves.[9] It may be noted that the fact that the Druze and Circassians, unlike Muslim (except for the Bedouin) and Christian Arabs, serve in the Israeli armed forces gives them a card to play in their negotiations with the government. Nonetheless, the data I will present include them as part of the general Arab population in Israel. It is generally accepted that, at least until very recently, the Druze towns and villages have not enjoyed greater local development than the other Arab localities; the present study does not investigate the possible differential effects of separate treatment by the government. If there are such differential effects, they may well even out over the long run, inasmuch as the so-called *Arab* local authorities, in their struggle with the government, are able to take advantage of Druze groundbreaking. To avoid confusion, *Druze and Circassian* and *Arab* will appear here in italics to denote the government's reference to one of these groups.

The 1995 agreement came about thus: in the course of striking in 1994, the heads of the *Druze and Circassian* local authorities presented the Ministry of the Interior with a two-page document stating the need for a 1.5 billion NIS development program.[10] The government, thinking the demand exaggerated, said that was no way to request such a large sum of money and proposed setting up a commission, including representatives of the government ministries, to prepare a proper assessment of infrastructure development needs. The Hevra Lemesheq Ulekalkala Economic Corporation, a subsidiary of the Union of Local Authorities in Israel, carried out the evaluation for the commission without undue delay, and arrived at a figure of 2.5 billion NIS as the investment required to close the gap between the *Druze and Circassian* localities and their Jewish neighbors. It was on the basis of this assessment that the government and the *Druze and Circassian* local authorities signed the agreement of June 1995, which provided for 1.07 billion NIS of funding (90 percent of 1.190 billion NIS).

Toward the end of 1996, I was told by a prominent member of the Committee of the Chairmen of Druze and Circassian Local Authorities that the government was, indeed, carrying out the agreement, and that the local authorities were raising their 10 percent share through local levies and taxes. As for the discrepancy between 2.5 and 1.190 billion NIS, the member stated, "Well, the program that was agreed upon is not a bad one, and it would not be realistic to try to do more at one shot." But by 1999, the representatives of the *Druze and Circassian* local authorities were claiming that the government was 120 million NIS in arrears as of 1998, with an additional 190 million NIS due for 1999 according to the five-year development program (i.e., nearly a third of the original program was still pending in its fifth and final year) (Algazi 1999).

Actually, the 1994 agreement with the *Druze* to set up the commission that would assess development needs came in December, after a similar agreement with the *Arab* local authorities in August of that year. But the commission to assess the development needs of the latter localities never really got started on carrying out its mandate (although it was, according to one source, instrumental in at least getting the socioeconomic ranking carried out by the Ministry of Interior and the CBS reformulated in a single unified list, thus making it possible to speak of Jewish and Arab localities comparatively in that regard). One local council head recounted that around that time, there had been a constant turnover in the position of minister of the interior: "Just when the new minister would tell us he was going to act, he would be replaced. But then one of the later appointees told us the real reason—'the needs are so great that too much money would be required, and so the Treasury is stalling.'" It may be observed, of course, that it is convenient for the government to have the Treasury as "the bad cop"; it should not be forgotten that the Treasury is *made* to come through with funds when coalition politics require it.

In the fall of 1996, a senior official in the Ministry of the Interior explained to me:

> There will be another strike, and then finally the government will set up the commission to carry out the survey of infrastructure needs in the *Arab* local authorities. What holds it up is apprehension over the vast sums that are involved; once the survey is made, then there will be expectations and it will be absolutely necessary to do something
>
> The whole idea ought to be to make progress—not necessarily everything all at once—but fast enough to enable people to feel that things are moving ahead, that there is hope. The alternative is despair and radicalization.

A new agreement was signed with the *Arab* local authorities in January 1997 after a further strike and demonstrations. The agreement this time spoke about interim funding until the size of the development budgets was finally determined. According to the agreement, the minister of the interior was to discuss with the minister of finance the setting of a definitive timetable for advancing development in the *Arab* local authorities (Ministry of Interior 1997a).

Now, as one person with whom I spoke put it, a survey of needs is not really necessary: it is obvious that the *Arab* localities are no better off than the *Druze*; all one has to do is take the programs approved for the *Druze* and pro rate them on a per capita basis. According to figures I base on the 1995 Census, the population in the *Arab* local authorities was then 6.4 times that in the *Druze and Circassian* ones.

The Office of the Prime Minister's Adviser for Arab Affairs[11] occasionally publishes figures on government investment in infrastructure in the Arab localities (e.g., 1998; these figures do not distinguish between *Druze and Circassian* and *Arab* localities). I reproduce these figures in column 2 of table 2.2. Note that they are given in current prices. Column 3 gives the figures for 1995 and onward in 1995 prices (current prices corrected by the price index of inputs in residential building). Column 4 gives cumulative figures for 1995 and on in 1995 prices (the 1995 agreement with the *Druze and Circassian* local authorities specified that it was speaking of 1995 prices).

Table 2.2 Government Development Budget Allocations to Arab Local Authorities

(1)	(2) Allocation (million NIS) (current prices)	(3) Annual allocation (since 1995, in 1995 prices)	(4) Cumulative (from 1995, in 1995 prices)
1992	159.9		
1993	338.4		
1994	404.6		
1995	458.8	458.8	458.8
1996	432.4	400.7	859.5
1997	503.9	432.2	1,291.7
1998	592.1	482.2	1,773.9
1999	703.7	554.1	2,328.0

Source: Figures in column 2 are from Israel's Prime Minister's Office (PMO), Office of the Adviser for Arab Affairs 1998.

One may get a rough measure of what the government has done against what would be required to close the gap between the Arab and Jewish localities by means of the following relatively simple calculation:

> 7.4 (i.e., 1.0 [the *Druze*] + 6.4 [the *Arabs*]) times 2.25 billion NIS (i.e., 90 percent of 2.5 billion) = 16.65 billion NIS in the *Druze and Circassian* and in the *Arab* localities together

By that calculation, the sums invested from 1995 through 1999 may have closed 14 percent of the gap as it very likely was in 1995.

In January 1999, the government publicly announced new commitments regarding development budgets for the Bedouin localities in the north (Gal 1999a, 1999b).

The government often adopts an upbeat self-congratulatory tone in reporting the progress that has been made in infrastructure development in the Arab localities. But it may be asked whether progress geared to the time horizon of a generation (14 percent of the 1995 gap in five years) can reasonably be expected ever to close the gap.

I turn now to a more specific consideration of the current budget of the Arab local authorities, beginning with a brief look at the situation in 1972 and earlier. In 1972, the per capita locally generated revenue in the average Arab local authority was 26.7 percent of what it was in the average Jewish urban locality (0.20/0.75, where 1.00 = the per capita figure for all local authorities together; Razin 1998: 35, table 3).[12] But this lower value constituted a greater proportion of the total budget than in the Jewish urban localities (49 percent compared to 35 percent; see table 2.3 for selected years from 1972 to 1995; cf. Razin 1998). The two corollaries are that (a) government participation per capita in the Jewish localities was much greater than in the Arab ones, and (b) the total per capita budget in the Arab localities was extremely small. In 1972, the per capita current budget expenditure in the average Jewish urban locality was 6.5 times what it was in the average Arab local authority (1.11/0.17, where 1.00 = the per capita figure for all local authorities together; Razin: 36, table 4).

Table 2.3 Government Participation as a Percentage of Total Revenue in Local Authority Budgets for Selected Years

	1972	1982	1988	1993	1995
Jewish and mixed cities and local councils	65	72	49	49	50
Arab cities and local councils	51	77	64	75	77

Source: Data adapted from Razin 1998: 32, table 1. (Razin's figures include the four Arab rural councils among the Arab cities and local councils.)

This had been the case from the beginning of the state through the 1970s (see al Haj and Rosenfeld 1988). Since then, however, government per capita participation in the Arab local authorities has constituted a greater proportion of the current budget than in the Jewish ones (see table 2.3). Also, the per capita general grant for the Arab local authorities has increased significantly over the years (see table 2.4, which relates the average for the localities of each sector to the overall per capita grant). In 1991, responding to recurrent fiscal crises, the government decided to increase the grant to the *Druze and Circassian* local authorities by a factor of 2.7 over a three-year period and that to the *Arab* local authorities by a factor of nearly 2.4 over a four-year period (Government Decisions 21 May 1991 and 26 August 1991, reviewed in Ministry of Finance 1991: 81–82; 1994). The results are evident in the jump that table 2.4 shows from 1988 to 1993 (but see discussion below on measures of the convergence in the per capita grants between Arab and Jewish local authorities).

The government decisions on increasing the grant were couched in the rhetoric of bringing the per capita expenditure in the Arab municipal budgets to a level equal to that in the Jewish ones. But in 1994, in response to continuing

Table 2.4 Government General Grant Per Capita for Selected Years

	1972	1982	1988	1993	1995
Jewish and mixed cities and local councils	1.81	2.34	3.63	3.00	2.31
Arab cities and local councils	0.21	0.49	1.17	2.18	2.07

Notes: 1.00 = general grant per capita in all local authorities, including regional councils (the latter constitute a third category that is not shown here). Per capita value for each local authority is not weighted for size of population in computing the average for each group of local authorities.

Source: Data extracted from Razin 1998: 37, table 5. (Razin's figures include the four Arab rural councils among the Arab cities and local councils.)

crisis, the government agreed to an additional increase in the grant to the *Arab* local authorities over a three-year period. Again, in January 1997, the government stated that it recognized a gap in the allocation of the general grant to the *Arab* local authorities and agreed to another increase over an additional three-year period (Ministry of the Interior 1997a).[13]

Why would the disparity between the per capita grant in the Arab and Jewish local authorities persist despite repeated large increases in the allocation to the former made for the declared purpose of equalization? I found this hard to understand until I got more detailed information from the Ministry of the Interior on the way in which the grant is calculated (Ministry of the Interior n.d. [c. 1998]). Since 1994, it has been the practice to calculate for each local authority what is known as its "model grant" for the coming year. The model carries out the recommendations made by the Soari Commission (1993), and is known as the Soari Model. Model per capita expenses are figured according to formulas that give higher values for smaller population, lower socioeconomic ranking of the locality, location in a national priority region, and location in a border area. Model per capita revenue takes into account, among other things, lower per capita property tax collection rate and lower locally generated revenue from other sources for localities of lower socioeconomic rank. Essentially, expected model per capita revenue is subtracted from expected model per capita expenses, and the result is multiplied by the population of the locality.

At this point, the local authority is referred to a table ranked according to the ratio of the grant actually received in the current year to the model grant figured for that year. For each rank, the corresponding column in the table gives the maximum addition to the current year's actual grant that will be allowed for the coming year's actual grant (but totaling not more than the computed model grant). The table is set up so as to give greater increases to localities with lower "actual grant to model grant" ratios; thus, a Jewish locality whose grant in 1998 was only, say, 72 percent of its model grant had its grant for 1999 increased by a maximum of 12 percent over the current actual grant, whereas a locality with a ratio of, say, 82 percent had its current grant increased by a maximum of 9 percent.[14] The idea here is this: government fiscal policy is bound by constraints and does not allow for full implementation of the normative Soari Model, but preference is given to those localities furthest away from the normative values. Provision is also made for those localities with an actual-grant to model-grant ratio of over 100 percent—their grant is reduced, again by a percentage graduated according to distance from the model.

Notwithstanding the incommensurability of the grant in the various sectors due to adventitious modifications, the Soari Model itself is applied equally, without distinction, to Arab and Jewish local authorities.[15] The Ministry of the Interior is able to assert that since the system's initiation in 1994, local authorities have been treated equally without regard to sector, and, moreover, that despite constraints in the national budget, affirmative action is being taken to advance those furthest away from the normative model more rapidly. Nonetheless, with implementation tied to historic levels, which at one time openly differentiated between Arab and Jewish localities, it is certain that closing the gap will not be accomplished over anything less than a good number of years. On average, Jewish local authorities get less than the model grant: it is reported that in 1997 they received only 70 percent of the model. But Arab local authorities got less than that: in 1997, they received only 55 percent of the model (Lahav 1998). It might also be mentioned that the national budget places at the disposal of the minister of the interior a fund that he is able to allocate at his discretion to meet specific local needs or crisis situations. While this fund might conceivably be used to achieve greater equality, there is nothing to prevent its being used with the opposite effect.[16]

It should be observed that the figures in table 2.4 tend to overstate the convergence in the per capita grant for the Arab and Jewish local authorities. As indicated earlier, this table relates the average for the localities of each sector to the overall per capita grant. But this does not take into account the greater allocation that the model makes available for smaller population and lower socioeconomic rank. Razin carried out multiple regression on variables influencing the level of the per capita grant. He found that controlling for size of population, socioeconomic rank, and location in the periphery, the per capita grant for the Arab localities in 1995 was still influenced negatively by a factor of 0.31 (i.e., $1 - e^{-0.37}$; Razin 1998: 46, table 6), despite whatever convergence between Jewish and Arab localities had taken place up to that time. He also found, in a similar analysis, that for 1996 there was still a negative factor of 0.21 (i.e., $1 - e^{-0.23}$; Razin 1999: 22, table 3).

All in all, it is not surprising that despite the moves in the direction of equalizing the grant, per capita expenditure in the current budget remains unequal. In 1995, it was in Jewish urban localities still 1.5 times what it was in the Arab local authorities (see tables 2.5 and 2.6).[17] Note that due to the effect of returns to scale, this figure can only be a stand-in for basket of services. Since the Arab localities are on average one-fourth the size of the Jewish ones, an equal basket of services would cost them more; hence, the figures in tables 2.5 and 2.6 understate the disadvantage of the Arab local authorities.

Table 2.5 Total and Selected Per Capita Expenditures in the Local Authority Current Budget and Government Participation in 1995 (NIS)

	Arab cities and local councils	Jewish and mixed cities and local councils	Jewish/Arab
Total expenditure	2,182	3,269	1.50
Local services	370	718	1.94
State services	1,037	1,542	1.49
Total government participation	1,484	1,003	0.68
Government participation as percentage of total expenditure	68.0	30.7	—

Sources: Financial data extracted from CBS 1998d, Publication no. 1095; population data taken from the 1995 Census.

Table 2.6 Expenditure on Education Services in 1995 and Government Participation per Child Aged 3 to 17 (in Local Authorities of Population 2,000 and Above; NIS)

	Arab cities and local councils	Jewish and mixed cities and local councils	Jewish/Arab
Expenditure on education	1,882	3,165	1.68
Government participation in education	1,519	1,578	1.04

Sources: Financial data extracted from CBS 1998d, Publication no. 1095. This publication gives data for all local authorities, including seventeen Jewish and three Arab local councils with populations under 2,000. These were excluded from the computation inasmuch as data on age were not available for them. Population by age taken from CBS 1998a, Current Briefings in Statistics no. 11. Ages 3 to 4 were estimated by taking 40 percent of the 0 to 4 age group.

Razin found that of the forty local authorities with the lowest per capita expenditure in the current budget in 1995, thirty-seven were Arab (Razin 1998: 87). In reading these tables, it should be recalled that state services are financed by earmarked participation of the relevant government ministries, the general grant, resident payments for services, and local taxes.

It will be seen that, on the average, government participation in the current budget did not, in 1995, disfavor the Arab population. This statement must be qualified immediately by the observation that here, too, one would need a comparison stratified for both size and affluence of locality in order to reach definitive conclusions concerning comparative per capita government participation in the current budget.

Nonetheless, the figures on government participation presented here are helpful if merely because they indicate that one must look elsewhere for the origin of the significantly smaller scope of services provided by the Arab local authorities. It emerges that this is to be attributed to two major factors. The first of these, as discussed earlier, is the vastly deficient municipal infrastructure in these localities; the second is the paucity of locally generated revenue (see table 2.7). The various government decisions regarding raising allocations to the Arab (*Druze and Circassian* and *Arab*) local authorities, and the agreements with the representatives of those authorities, are replete with exhortations and solemn declarations to the effect that increased allocations are to be accompanied by increases in locally generated revenue. In some cases, this general term is the one adopted; in others, the property tax is singled out.

Table 2.7 Per Capita Locally Generated Revenue in the Local Authority Current Budget in 1995 (NIS)

	Arab cities and local councils	Jewish and mixed cities and local councils	Jewish/Arab
Property tax	277	1,204	4.35
Other locally generated revenue	274	769	2.81
Total	551	1,973	3.58

Sources: Financial data extracted from CBS 1998d, Publication no. 1095; population data from the 1995 Census.

The portion of locally generated revenue that does *not* come from the property tax ought to be a direct function of municipal activity (with some link to socioeconomic level). More developed infrastructure would increase the scope of this, and would also elicit greater earmarked participation on the part of the government. There are two main dimensions to consider regarding increasing per capita property tax revenue, which, it may be noted, was, in 1995, 4.35 times larger in the Jewish urban localities than in the Arab local authorities. The first of these has to do with deepening the collection of the assessed tax, the second with increasing the tax base.

The Arab local authorities have, in general, not done well in collecting the assessed property tax. In 1995, the average collection rate in the Arab localities was 68.1 percent of the current tax assessment, compared with 88.8 percent for the Jewish localities in the lower six socioeconomic clusters. This is not to say that there were not a few Jewish local authorities that did poorly on tax collection, nor that there were not several Arab localities that did well (Ministry of Interior 1997b).[18]

Speakers with an establishment perspective are prone to fault the Arab population for delinquent tax payment ethic, attributable, they say, both to antagonism toward the Israeli regime and the political price of enforcing collection in a milieu where traditional rather than civic loyalty prevails. But the local citizens say: "Look at the roads, the sewage, the water pressure—you want us to pay taxes? Supply infrastructure!" Moreover, in addition to the low socioeconomic rank of the Arab localities involving, first and foremost, low per capita income, there are other bona fide economic factors that come into play. Property tax is levied per square meter of structure. Now, for one thing, in Jewish urban localities with populations over 2,000, children aged 0 to17 constituted 32 percent of the population in 1995; in the Arab localities, they were 46 percent of the population.[19] Children require space, that is, square meters, but do not contribute significantly (at least not in an urban setting) to defraying the family's expenses. As a result, the property tax weighs more heavily on Arab families. And secondly, the Arabs are accustomed to building their own homes, rather than relying on building contractors, as the Jewish population does. Their building costs per square meter are therefore significantly lower. Residential space is a function of family income, but the scale for the Arabs, by virtue of the cheaper costs, shifts upward, leading to higher tax assessments.

I was told in regard to the municipal budget situation that "the main problem is that the Arab local authorities don't collect the property tax; the fact that they don't collect means that it's hard for them to expand services—the result of that is low budgets—and the end result is *an image of discrimination*." As with all such statements, and disregarding for the moment the final trope (in italics), there is a certain element of truth here. Better collection could be used as leverage, and together with other sources, might make some difference. But it should be borne in mind that municipal activity, like much else, is characterized by a lumpiness of expenses: for additional educational services, for example, one needs not only more teachers, but also classrooms, janitors, watchmen, electricity, and so forth. And, after all is said, the addition to the local budget that is to be gained from deepening property tax collection is of limited scope: to have increased collection to the average that obtained in the Jewish urban localities in the six lower socioeconomic clusters in 1995 would have added 84 NIS per capita to the Arab local authority budgets, whereas the average per capita difference in expenditure between the two groups was 1087 NIS ($[88.8-68.1] \div 68.1 \times 277 = 84$; see data cited above and tables 2.5 and 2.7). Nonetheless, the depth of property tax collection provides a convenient stick with which to beat the Arab local authorities. For example, in January 1999 the minister of the interior let it be known that the ministry would distribute the conditional portion of the grant[20] only to those local authorities that had collected at least 50 to 60 percent of the property tax (of the total owed, not just of the current year's account) (Shehori 1999a). Responding to criticism that this would discriminate against the Arab towns, the ministry spokesperson observed that "the government has transferred large sums of money for development in the Arab towns, and there is no reason why they shouldn't collect taxes like everyone else." The earlier discussion, in the present work, of development budgets may put such Ministry of Interior assertions into some perspective.

Despite vociferous remonstrations over the depth of property tax collection, however, it is clear that a major change in property tax revenue in the Arab local authorities would have to come as the result of increasing the local tax base, or, alternatively, from some kind of regional, interlocality tax base sharing. Increasing the local tax base is primarily a matter of increasing land uses for business activity. Commercial enterprises may pay property tax at as much as 3.2 times the rate for residential use; industry and workshops may pay, respectively, as much as 1.4 and 1.9 times the residential rate (see State Budgetary Arrangements Regulations 1997, in "Legislation Cited"). Both Hecht (1997: 25–26, 45) and Razin (1998: 8–9, 58) point out the great disparity between the weaker local authorities and the stronger ones with regard to the presence of local business activity as a source of local tax revenue. Razin makes a direct connection between this factor and the fiscal situation of the Arab local authorities in particular, observing that the socioeconomic level of the population is also relevant in attracting nonresidential land uses. He also notes that there is growing fiscal inequality between localities in the center of the country and those in the periphery, which results from the proportionately greater nonresidential tax base enjoyed by the former. The periphery of the country is exactly where a good portion of the Arab local authorities are situated.

Some comparative data on land use are presented in table 2.8. These data are for nine Arab cities and forty-nine Jewish and mixed cities. Note that these are cities only. In smaller Arab local authorities (i.e., local councils), reported nonresidential land use drops to negligible proportions. Fuller, more accurate and current data, including for the smaller localities, could probably be drawn from local authority tax assessment records, were such a study to be undertaken. But in discussing economic development in the Arab towns below, I will have occasion to suggest that comparative data on employee posts may serve as a proxy indicator for nonresidential land use, and hence for the extent of the local tax base.

Table 2.8 Land Use in Nine Arab Cities and Forty-nine Jewish and Mixed Cities

	Arab cities		Jewish and mixed cities	
	Total area (dunam)	Dunam per 1,000 population	Total area (dunam)	Dunam per 1,000 population
Industry	754	3.1	63,261	15.8
Mixed (offices, commerce, residence)	326	1.4	19,560	4.9
Hotels and tourism	71	0.3	7,802	2.0
Total	1,151	4.8	90,623	22.7

Source: Data are drawn from CBS 1998c, Publication no. 1082, which bases them on the 1983 Census, with updates to varying times up to 1990.

It was the cutback in central government participation in municipal budgets in the mid 1980s (linked to the government's attempts to control runaway inflation) that led to the growing weight of locally generated revenue in those budgets and to efforts by the local authorities in general to increase commercial and industrial land uses (see, e.g., Hecht 1997: 33–34; Razin 1998: 30). By 1992, the Ministry of the Interior had become a participant in the swelling discourse on local economic development and local strategic planning as instruments for strengthening municipal government (see Ministry of the Interior 1992; also Interviews). The active interest of the Arab local authorities in developing industrial infrastructure for their towns and in participating in regional industrial parks was, and is, part of this overall picture (see Khamaisi 1994: 27).

It would seem, in sum, that the critical elements in the municipal budgetary disadvantage of the Arab local authorities are the deficiency of municipal infrastructure and the paucity of locally generated revenue, linked particularly to the absence of nonresidential land use. Action on both counts would be required if there is to be any chance of arriving at an equal basket of municipal services for the residents of the Arab towns.

Now this, I suggest, is merely where the lines of struggle are currently drawn. Over the years, the Arab towns and villages have had to contend with the British colonial administration, the upheaval wrought by the Israeli war of independence, the looming presence of the military government, the filtering powers of the district commissioner and the Arab affairs officers of the various ministries, the use of the statutory planning system to curb local development, and general indifference to their development needs. As always, even when its personnel are genuinely concerned, the government apparatus is forthcoming to the extent made necessary by the perceived social or political costs of not being so. This is evident here from "do these things, but do them slowly" of the early years, to the stillborn commission of the mid 1990s that was to have assessed the municipal infrastructure needs of the so-called Arab local authorities. But establishment personnel would have it otherwise; in their view, all progress is attributable to the beneficent modernizing influence of the state of Israel. The picture of traditional society that is invoked, whether in current statements on the depth of tax collection, in justifications of differential government allocations for municipal services, or in historical accounts to the effect that "they didn't ask for much" helps to deny the presence of conflict and the forces with which Arab society has had to contend. And the locution of an "*image* of discrimination" in reference to the implicit charge that rouses those personnel to defend themselves skirts recognition of the fact that just what constitutes discrimination is a matter of contest, so that the definition of discriminatory action or policy varies from one place to another and from one time to another.

Local Economic Development

In theory, the municipal administration I have been discussing has to do with the development of infrastructure, the provision of services, zoning, licensing, taxation. These are instruments that promote and regulate the growth of nonagricultural economic activity. Such activity entails the emergence of market centers and a proliferation of enterprises and places of employment. It is one important element in urbanization—that process by which a locality is transformed, or transforms itself, into a place that draws people to it, growing in density of population and in built-up area, a place where life is no longer village life.

Writing some twenty years after the establishment of the state of Israel, Meyer-Brodnitz (1969) coined the term *latent urbanization* to describe what had been going on in the Arab towns and villages. This involved, among other things, a doubling of the population in those localities during the two preceding decades (resulting from natural increase of the local population, along with the relocation of refugees displaced by the war of independence, but without other internal migration); the absence of migration from the towns to metropolitan areas; decline in agriculture as a source of income; failure of local economic development to keep pace with the burgeoning population; and, in consequence of all these, economic dependence on employment outside the towns, through commuting. Nearly two decades later, Gonen and Khamaisi (1993: 10) state that "of all the Arab towns in Israel, only Nazareth [has] developed as an economic and administrative center, attracting residents from other areas."[21]

A caveat is, I believe, in order here. One needs to avoid the essentialized image of "the traditional Arab village" that lurks in the term "urbanization" and in the appellation "village." Meyer-Brodnitz himself, writing in 1986, took pains to counter oversimplification in the use of those and related terms. That urbanization and economic development occur in some localities but not in others is not a matter merely of internal processes, without regard to exogenous forces. Important correctives in spelling out such forces that were at work in the case of the Arab towns in Israel are found in Rosenfeld 1978, Lustick 1980, Carmi and Rosenfeld 1992, and Haidar 1995. But there is another important thing, one that should not be obscured by the fact of constrained economic development. It is the vitality and drive that characterize the lives of residents of the Arab towns, perhaps in part due to the need to deal with and overcome the obstacles that confront them. Even the smaller Arab towns are no longer villages. A resident of Upper Nazareth, who was among those interviewed by Rabinowitz, described Nazareth and the Arab towns around it as "bursting and bubbling with development" (1997: 58).

Now, theorists and planners often perceive industrial activity as a key engine for local or subnational (i.e., regional) economic development.[22] It should be pointed out that sectors other than industry (commerce, services, tourism) may have a share in local economic development, and diverse studies of Arab economic development and entrepreneurship in Israel (Lewin-Epstein and

Semyonov 1993; Falah 1993; Abo Sharkia 1998) cast their nets accordingly. Nonetheless, and understandably, an important body of research in Israel has focused explicitly on manufacturing activity in the Arab towns (Meyer-Brodnitz and Czamanski 1986; Atrash 1992; Schnell et al. 1995). It is, of course, a focus particularly apt for the present study of events having to do with attempts by Arab towns to set up their own industrial areas or to join regional or interurban parks. It may be mentioned that the term *industry* covers a wide range of activity: from small workshops or manufacturing activity to large enterprises, from "traditional" branches (such as manufacture of clothing or food and beverages) to hi-tech and so-called growth branches—but, then too, one needs to be careful, for such simple classifications may turn out to be misleading. They do not, for example, account for the crosscutting dimensions of technological sophistication and product innovation.

The three works cited above surveyed manufacturing firms in Arab towns in 1983, 1990, and 1992, respectively. Firms were defined as manufacturing enterprises employing three or more workers, although there were some discrepancies between 1983 and 1990 in the definition of what kind of enterprise would be included (see Atrash 1992: 113–114; Schnell et al. 1995: 43).

These surveys listed 415 firms in 1983; 829 in 1990; and 900 in 1992. Just under one-fifth of the firms manufactured food and beverages; textiles and clothing accounted for 36 percent of the firms in 1983, going down to just over one-quarter in the later surveys; construction materials and iron works were 42 percent in 1983, and returned to this proportion in 1992, after rising to 47 percent in 1990; and the remainder of the firms were in the residual category, "others." The latter category includes jewelry, electricity, electronics, chemicals, and machinery.

According to data presented by Schnell and colleagues (1995: 48, 50),[23] firms in the textile and clothing branch employed an average of 36.7 employees per plant, 86 percent of them women. From the data of these authors, it is possible to determine that the firms in the other branches employed an average of under seven employees each, 95 percent of them men. Atrash (1992: 117–118; his table 4) assembles figures providing a rough sense of the place of Arab town industry in the Israeli industrial sector. He found that the manufacturing firms employing at least five workers in the Arab towns constituted about 7.2 percent of such enterprises nationally, and employed about 3.5 percent of all workers in Israeli industry. Large plants employing hundreds of workers each do not exist in the Arab towns, with the modest exception of the Kadmani metal works in Yirka.

Meyer-Brodnitz and Czamanski (1986: 540; their table 4) found that 84 percent of the plants in their survey were locally owned. It should be pointed out that most of the textile and clothing firms are either (a) branches or subsidiaries of national Jewish parent concerns, or (b) locally constituted subcontractors to such parent outfits. In either case, these firms are, for the most part, totally dependent for marketing of their output on the national (Jewish) parent company (Schnell et al. 1995: 112–115). In general, the locally owned firms of smaller size are financed by family capital, employ members of the *hamula*, and are simple in organization.

Schnell and colleagues (1995: 128; their table 9) found, in their sample of industrial plants, that 8.9 percent of them were located at the outskirts of the town, while another 10.5 percent were located in an industrial area. The rest of the firms (over 80 percent of the total) were located at family dwellings (a common location is on the ground floor, i.e., "between the pillars") or in rented quarters in the residential area of town. In particular, marble cutting plants, cement block manufacture, or large metal construction frame operations are likely to be located outside of the residential area due to dust, noise, and the need for the maneuver of large transport vehicles. Still, that is often not the case, and the presence of most of the enterprises in the residential area of town is a source of environmental nuisance. Such location has certain advantages, to be sure: (a) space for industrial activity is available without heavy investments in land and infrastructure, and (b) it skirts the vexatious problem of rezoning land for industry through the statutory planning authorities. But the advantages come with a price besides the nuisance factor: there is constraint on the scope of operations and on access of heavy transportation for delivery and shipment, as well as the curtailment of potential expansion imposed by the residential setting. Now, the general situation is that industrial areas with developed infrastructure have been generally nonexistent in Arab towns. Schnell and colleagues (81) find that such absence is one of the three primary factors "impeding the incorporation of modern methods and therefore the rise to higher levels of [industrial] entrepreneurship" in the Arab towns.

The terminology of the industrial area lexicon can be misleading. The fact that land is zoned for industry in an outline plan does not necessarily imply that infrastructure has been developed there. The tract of land so zoned may be without hookup to the electric grid or to a central water supply, without access roads, without grading, not to mention such finer points as drainage, sewage, paved roads, street lighting, and telephones. Yet if the land is privately owned, that is, it is not state land, one may find a limited number of plants located in just such areas, perhaps with rough, minimal connections made by the owners. This situation—of land zoned for industry but without infrastructure development—sometimes continues for many years. To avoid confusion with land that is zoned for industry but is still undeveloped, I would prefer to use *industrial area* in reference to a tract of land in which infrastructure is available. Yet one often encounters the term *industrial zone* applied to both cases. If the process of development is already or soon to be underway, even as early as the stage of preparing detailed site plans, then it would be quite usual to refer to the particular tract of land as an *industrial area*. The term *industrial park* is often used to denote a modern, aesthetically appointed industrial area, one that is well maintained—perhaps by a special *municipal industrial authority* or by a *municipal economic corporation*, possibly with additional services offered by the industrial area management to the area's occupants.[24] Similarly, the term *industrial park* may carry connotations of an industrial area housing a high proportion of hi-tech industry, or one that serves a large region.[25]

Actually, none of the industrial areas in existence in the Arab towns as of 1992 could ever begin to be thought of under the category of industrial park. In table 2.9, I present data on industrial area development in the Arab towns as of 1992. Generally, where the outline plan is not yet approved, infrastructure would not yet be developed, although one may note the single exception appearing in the table in that category. Also, the Arab local authorities have found it virtually impossible to raise the funds, whether from private owners with land in the area zoned for industry or from the government, for developing infrastructure on their own. In Jewish towns, such as Karmi'el and Upper Nazareth, or the other so-called (Jewish) development towns in the periphery—that is,

Table 2.9 Industrial Area Development in the Arab Localities as of 1992

	Land zoned for industry in an approved outline plan			Land zoned for industry in an outline plan on deposit		
	Number of areas	Size (dunam)	Infrastructure	Number of areas	Size (dunam)	Infrastructure
Center and north of country	1	150	The local authority reported connection to electricity, water, access road, telephones, and sewage. Land is owned privately.	1	100	In 1998, this industrial area area had still not been approved, and the local authority had an industrial area of 15 dunam, without infrastructure.
	6	4–60	According to reports of the local authorities, one of these had connections to electricity, water, and access road.	4	30–65	According to reports of the local authorities, one of these, on privately owned land, had connections to electricity, water, access road, and telephones.
Bedouin towns in Negev	2	150; 340				

Notes: These data do not reflect a few cases of state-owned land zoned for industry in outline plans prepared for Arab localities by the ILA (this subject will be treated in chapter 3). As of 1992, however, these had not yet been developed, and it is my opinion that the data presented in this table represent fairly the picture of industrial area development in the Arab towns as of 1992.

Sources: Compiled from data collected by Sofer et al. for their 1994 publication. Questionnaires were completed by twenty-seven local councils (out of the sixty localities in which at least one industrial plant was found). The material in the above-cited publication served as the basis for the discussion on land and infrastructure in the 1995 volume by Schnell et al. (125–131). The authors generously put these responses at my disposal for purposes of compiling the table presented here. I have made use here of some additional information made available by the Municipal Unit of the Center for Jewish-Arab Economic Development and that unit's director, Mohammed Younis.

in regions or localities classified as national priority regions (formerly known as "development areas"; see figure 2.1 for national priority regions in the Galilee in 1995)—the government offered grants, loans, and tax relief to investors (through provisions of the Encouragement of Capital Investment Law), in part for the development of industrial infrastructure. The government also carried out such development directly through its own or affiliated agencies (on the absence of government participation in developing such infrastructure in the

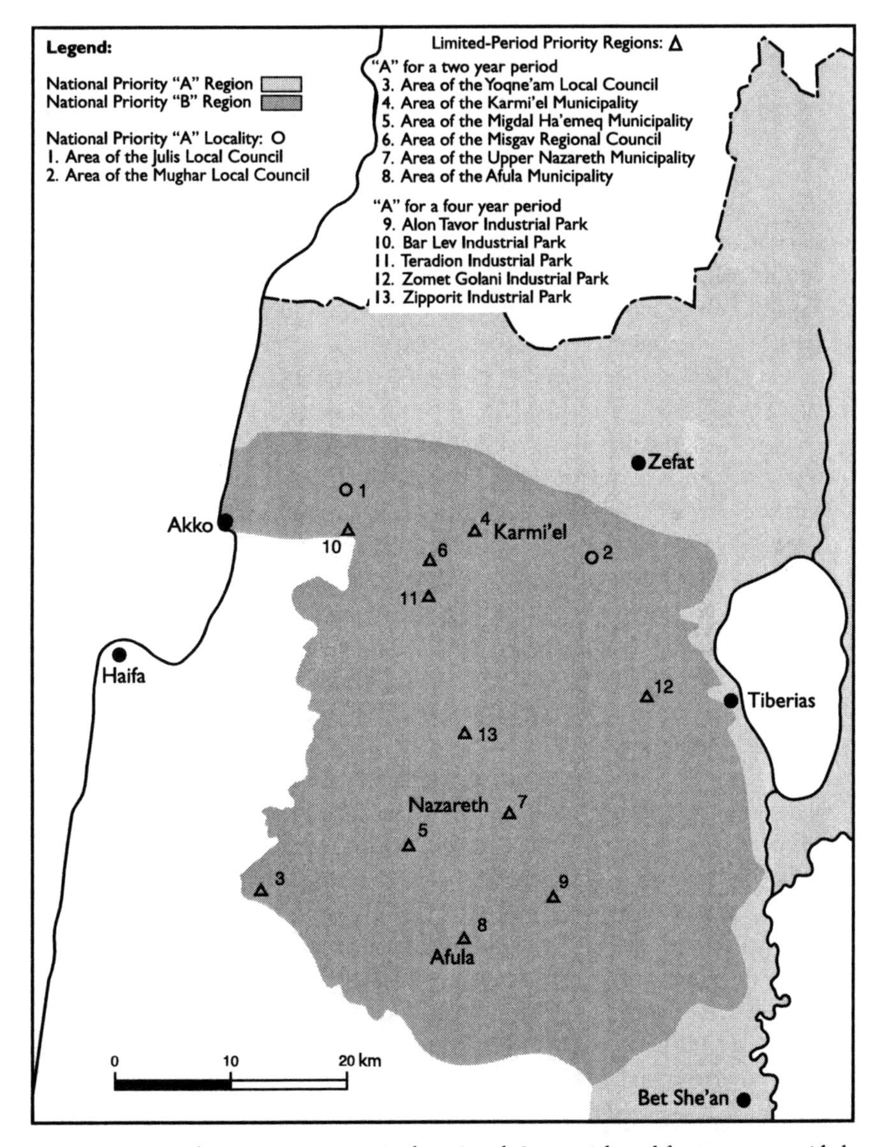

Figure 2.1 National Priority Regions—Northern Israel. *Source:* Adapted from a map provided courtesy of Israel's Ministry of Industry.

Arab towns, cf. Carmi and Rosenfeld 1992: 50; also Bar-El 1993). In the early 1990s, when the government began to apply itself in earnest to its program of developing industrial infrastructure in the Arab localities, it did so only in towns located in the national priority regions, and only on tracts of land in which at least most of the land was owned not privately but by the ILA. Thus, financing industrial infrastructure on privately owned land, problematic at the time covered by table 2.9, remains so to this day. Although, again, it may be noted that two of the four localities that reported at least some infrastructure development in their industrial areas in 1992 are exceptions in this regard. (See figure 2.2, drawn from a Ministry of Industry map published in 1997, for the Arab localities in Galilee included in the government's program of the 1990s; see also the notes to that figure.) It should be pointed out that having land zoned for industry in an outline plan on deposit is no guarantee that the plan will be approved as deposited or that infrastructure will be developed. For example, the locality that in 1992 reported an area of 100 dunam zoned for industry in an outline plan on deposit had, in 1998, an industrial area of just fifteen dunam, and that, without infrastructure.

The size of the industrial area is also a constraining factor as far as local industrial development is concerned. When the area required for infrastructure and other, auxiliary, uses is deducted, an industrial area of, say, sixty dunam would be left with only about thirty dunam net for industrial use.[26] While a tract of that size might suffice to absorb a modest number of a small town's currently existing enterprises, it would be extremely limited in its ability to offer land for expansion or for new industrial initiatives, whether by local townspeople or by outside investors (see, e.g., Schnell et al. 1995: 129).

A comparative figure is in order here. Of the industrial areas with approved outline plans reported by Arab localities in 1992, 355 dunam were located in Galilee; of the industrial areas reported to have infrastructure connections, 271 dunam were located in Galilee. But there were at the time about 11,800 dunam net developed for industry in the Jewish localities in Galilee (Shefer et al. 1992: 141–142; based on a report submitted in 1991). That this figure relates to net dunam available for industry means that it represents industrial areas probably totaling well over 20,000 dunam (see note above). These comparative figures need to be seen against the simple fact that of the population of 901,000 in Galilee in 1995, 429,000 lived in the Arab towns (from data compiled for tables 1.1 and 1.3).

In discussing the development of industrial areas above, I have mentioned the Encouragement of Capital Investment Law (1959) (in the pages that follow, this will be cited as "the Law") and the national priority regions. These too were part of the lay of the land. To investors in industrial plants that meet relevant criteria (mainly the export of a minimal percentage of output), the Law gives grants, subsidized loans, and provides tax allowances. These benefits vary according to national priority regions, whose determination is provided for by the Law (see, for example, Ministry of Industry 1997).

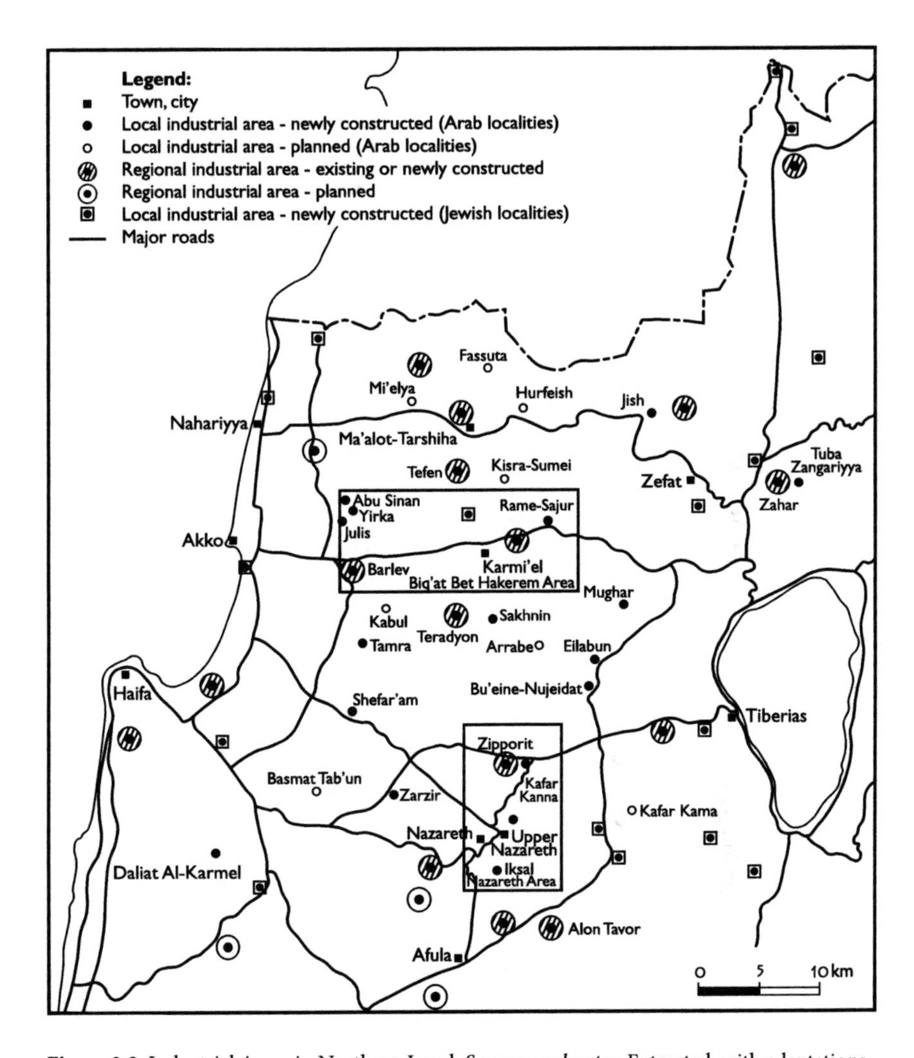

Figure 2.2 Industrial Areas in Northern Israel. *Sources and notes:* Extracted, with adaptations, from a 1997 Ministry of Industry map. Two of the industrial areas shown on the 1997 Ministry of Industry map as existing are shown here, as of 2000, as planned—in the case of Kabul, work had been held up; in the case of Basmat Tab'un, plans were never approved. The area in Jish, according to the municipal engineer, is a mere ten dunam, and although it was constructed in 1996, even that was only partially occupied in 2000. The 1997 Ministry map indicates that work had also been carried out or was planned at five Arab localities in the south. Ministry lists of industrial areas in Arab localities sometimes include other localities where plans were being considered (see, e.g., Ministry of Industry 1995: 19). The fluidity of the planning and construction processes undoubtedly leaves room for a certain amount of imprecision.

Figure 2.1 shows the boundaries of the national priority regions in effect in the northern part of Israel in 1995. These boundaries were the result of changes made in 1993 (see PMO 1993); they were subsequently altered again in 1998 to reflect changes in government policy. It will be seen that certain municipalities or industrial areas are given exceptional status, raised by one degree above that of the geographic area in which they are situated. Thus, Karmi'el, Upper Nazareth (and its exclave industrial area Zipporit), Afula, Migdal Ha'emeq, Misgav Regional Council and its industrial area Teradyon (Jewish localities all), and other large industrial areas in Galilee have all been accorded such exceptional Priority Region A status. Government speakers would often explain that the intention was not to discriminate against Arab localities in the area, but merely to advance the development and demographic growth of the relevant Jewish localities. This was in accordance with one of the Law's primary purposes, which was to promote the national goal of population dispersal (that is, the augmentation of the Jewish population in the country's peripheral areas), in part by attracting investment, and thus expanding employment opportunities. (The other two purposes of the Law are increasing exports and attracting foreign investment.) The differential conditions for Arab and Jewish towns in National Priority Region B (where most of the Arab towns of any appreciable size in the north are located) combined with the absence of local industrial infrastructure development to ensure that Arab entrepreneurs whose projects qualified for benefits under the Law would be drawn away and attempt to locate in the industrial areas of the Jewish towns. Even when industrial areas were constructed in the Arab towns, costs of land and investment were higher for the local residents than for their neighbors in the Jewish towns, and the new industrial areas in the Arab towns could not compete with those of the neighboring Jewish towns in attracting outside investors. Successful efforts to equalize these conditions were undertaken during the period of my fieldwork, and they will be described in chapter 3.

As a historical note, it might be mentioned that the government's 1967 Proposed Development Program for the Minority Population (PMO, Bureau of the Adviser on Arab Affairs, and the Economic Planning Authority, p. 33) raised the idea of giving such benefits under the Law to the Arab towns, but rejected it on the grounds that this would enable unfair competition with the Jewish development towns, particularly on the part of Arab towns close to the center of the country (a convenient, but illogical juxtaposition inasmuch as the latter would, in any case, not have received more benefits under the Law than Jewish localities in the center of the country).

The Law also gives benefits to investment in tourism, according to a different map of priority regions. Another law, working on the same principle, extends benefits to investment in agriculture. It will be recalled that the Ministry of Interior grant to the budgets of the local authorities is also graded by Priority Region. And various orders and regulations decree a host of other benefits in the realms of housing, education, welfare, labor, and income tax, all following a third map of national priority regions. That map is somewhat different from the one used regarding investment in industry under the Encouragement of Capital Investment Law, but it is similar in structure, and in this case, Karmi'el and Upper Nazareth are raised one degree above that of the surrounding region (PMO 1993).

I turn now to a consideration of the subject of commuting to work for the light it may shed on local economic development. R. Khalidi (1988: 141–145) and Haidar (1995: 110–112) find that such commuting, or labor force mobility as it is also known, is higher in the Arab sector than in the Jewish sector. It has fluctuated over the years in response to swings in the economy, ranging from as low as 40 percent of employed persons to 54 or even 60 percent. Arab labor force commuting, it is argued, is the result of dependency on jobs outside the Arab towns, and thus its contraction during periods of recession is a source of hardship for the Arab population.[27] It should be noted that the absence of local employment opportunities impinges directly on the participation of Arab women in the labor force (12 percent in 1990, compared with 46 percent for Jewish women; Lewin-Epstein and Semyonov 1993: 87–89).

In his 1993 study, Bar-El develops a typology of Arab towns with regard to their pattern of economic development. I would like to make use of an idea that Bar-El sets forth in his introductory material (24–25), that of the ratio of the number of employed persons working in localities of a particular size (without regard to where those persons reside) to the number of employed persons who reside in localities of that size. This ratio can be expected to be greater than one for large localities that provide employment not only for their own residents but also for those who commute from outside, and to decrease gradually as the size of the locality goes down—to values below one for smaller towns whose residents are compelled to seek employment in the larger centers. Bar-El connects this to the circumstance of high labor commuting in the Arab towns.[28]

Seeing that it held the potential for shedding greater analytic light on the comparative scope of local economic development in the Arab towns, I chose to pursue this matter further. The results, based on data from the 20 percent sample enumeration of the 1995 Census, supplied especially for the present purpose by the CBS, are given in table 2.10 (see the notes to the table for a discussion of the problem of "unknowns" in the census responses and their treatment here, as well as for an explanation of the decision to use census rather than Labor Force Survey data). The table may be read as follows: Columns 2 and 5 represent the number of local employee posts available per employed person residing in the average town of that size and that population group; columns 3 and 6 represent the part of those available local employee posts filled by local residents in the average town of that size and that population group; columns 4 and 7 represent the part of the available local employee posts filled by persons who commute to work from outside the locality in the average town of that size and that population group. Columns 8 and 9 give the difference between Jewish/mixed localities and Arab localities (column 8 with regard to the number of local employee posts available per employed resident, and column 9 with regard to the part of the local employee posts filled by nonresidents).

Table 2.10 Employees' Locality of Work and Locality of Residence by Type of Locality (Size and Population Group) in 1995

	Jewish and mixed localities			Arab localities			Jewish and mixed, minus Arab	
1	2	3	4 (2) minus (3)	5	6	7 (5) minus (6)	8 (2) minus (5)	9 (4) minus (7)
Locality or locality group by size	L of W / L of R	W in L of R / L of R	Difference	L of W / L of R	W in L of R / L of R	Difference	L of W / L of R	Difference
Jerusalem	1.037	.904	0.133					
Tel Aviv-Yaffo	2.095	.720	1.375					
Haifa	1.428	.798	0.630					
100,000–199,000	0.802	.451	0.351					
50,000–99,999	0.760	.443	0.317	0.942	.601	0.341	–.182	–.024
20,000–49,999	0.752	.428	0.324	0.438	.357	0.081	.314	.243
10,000–19,999	0.614	.358	0.256	0.453	.369	0.084	.161	.172
5,000–9,999	0.870	.298	0.572	0.496	.367	0.129	.374	.443
2,000–4,999	0.253	.213	0.040	0.358	.312	0.046	–.105	–.006

Notes: L of W = number of employed persons (without reference to the size of their locality of residence) working in localities of this size. L of R = number of employed persons residing in localities of this size. W in L of R = number of persons who work in their own locality of residence in localities of this size. Column 8: Difference between Jewish/mixed localities and Arab localities in number of local employee posts available per employed resident. Column 9: Difference between Jewish/mixed localities and Arab localities in part of local employee posts filled by nonresidents.

I call attention to the particularly high rate of "locality of work unknown" responses in the census data drawn on in compiling this table: 16.7 percent on average for the five groups of Jewish localities from 2,000 to 100,000 population, ranging from 14.6 percent to 23.4 percent for the individual groups; 18.3 percent on average for the five parallel groups of Arab localities, ranging from 17.5 percent to 20.2 percent for the individual groups. The census questionnaire collected information on locality of work by asking respondents to list the address of their place of employment—the only question that required more than a number or an X mark as its response. I was told that this led to difficulties during the coding of responses. I considered the possibility of using data from the CBS Labor Force Surveys, but these are based on a sample of 0.7 percent of households, and I decided to use the census data despite the high rate of "unknowns" in view of the size of the sample and its geographic comprehensiveness.

"Locality of work unknown" responses were handled here by subtracting them from the denominators of both the "L of W"/"L of R" ratio and the "W in L of R"/"L of R" ratio. The assumption here, in the case of the second ratio, is, of course, that "unknowns" are distributed between "work in the locality of residence" and "work outside" it in the same way as are the "knowns," in the case of the first ratio, it is that "unknowns" are distributed between types of locality of work (size and population group) in the same way as are the "knowns." I examined two extreme alternatives to these assumptions: (a) using gross rather than net values for the denominators—that is, assuming that all "unknowns" work in a locality of a type unlike that in which they live, and ipso facto work outside their locality of residence; (b) adding the "unknowns" to the numerators of both ratios—that is, assuming that all "unknowns" work in their locality of residence and ipso facto work in the type of locality to which their locality of residence belongs. The results corresponding to those in column 9 of table 2.10, reading from largest group to smallest, were as follows: (a) –.009, .204, .148, .332, –.006; (b) –.010, .207, .149, .332, –.004. It will be seen that both series follow the same pattern as that presented by column 9, both shift similarly in direction and distance from column 9, and the values for the Jewish localities in the three 5,000 to 49,999 population groups are still strikingly higher than those for the Arab localities in those groups. Thus, the interpretation of the data would not change in the event of either of the extreme assumptions. It seems reasonable, therefore, to proceed as though the "unknowns" are distributed similarly to the "knowns."

"W in L of R" is net of those who work in agriculture, on the grounds that that category is not an indicator of the kind of economic development being considered here. However, the number of those who reported working in agriculture in their locality of residence was extremely low: 1.5 percent for the Jewish localities from 2,000 to 99,999 population, and 3.5 percent for the Arab localities.

Sources: Data are from the 20 percent sample enumeration of the 1995 Census. Data on "work in locality of residence" and "work in agriculture" were compiled from census data provided by the Social Science Data Archive at the Hebrew University, Jerusalem, with the patient assistance of Yasmin Alkaly at the Social Sciences Computer Lab at Tel Aviv University. Data on "locality of work" were provided especially for the present study by the CBS.

Higher labor mobility for Arab localities (values in column 6 subtracted from 1) than that reported by Haidar and Khalidi is probably due to the fact that the data here are for localities, not for Arab population as distinguished from Jewish population. The latter categories naturally include among the Arabs those Arabs who reside in the large, mixed localities, which are par excellence the place *to which* mobile labor commutes.

One surprising result emerging from the table, however, is that only for localities in the 20,000 to 49,999 population range is the population of those who work in their locality of residence greater in the Jewish towns than in the Arab ones (columns 3 and 6). There is only one city in the 50,000 to 99,999 range in the Arab sector, and that is Nazareth. Evidently, Nazareth does serve somewhat as a center, both with regard to providing employee posts (i.e., jobs) for its residents and with regard to the "work in locality" to "reside in locality" ratio (column 5), which is also higher than for Jewish localities of that size. One may suggest two possible factors in explanation of the unexpected direction of the results for the towns smaller than 20,000. First, the Arab towns in the two smallest ranges may be on average further removed geographically from population centers than Jewish towns of the same size, thus dampening the pull of those centers. Further disaggregation of the data or multiple regression procedures would be required to check this possibility.

Second, it should be observed that commuting to work is not necessarily a negative thing. It may take place because of the utter absence of a local alternative (Haidar's and Khalidi's point), and perhaps then it would more properly be referred to as labor migration (see E. Marx 1987; Rosenfeld 1978);[29] but it may also be a move to economic optimization, acting to upgrade income and increase the opportunities for obtaining good work commensurate with one's training. This would be just as true for Jews as for Arabs. And, over the years, improving transportation—roads, cars, public transportation—would have facilitated increasing commuting on the part of Jews, raising the value of that variable to a level similar to that which had prevailed earlier in the Arab sector due to lack of local opportunity.

The interesting result, I suggest, emerging from the data has to do with the higher number of jobs available in Jewish towns in the ranges between 5,000 and 49,999 (columns 2 and 5, and the difference between them in column 8), and the ensuing higher number of local jobs filled by those who come in from outside (columns 4 and 7, and the difference between them in column 9). These differences are large, and apparently, systematic. I will spell out two of the three cases. In the case of the 10,000 to 19,999 population range, there are for each thousand locally resident employed persons 161 more jobs available locally in the Jewish towns than in the Arab ones (614 minus 453) and 172 more jobs filled by outsiders (256 minus 84). Of the three groups of localities by size that exhibit greater labor in-migration in the Jewish towns than in the Arab ones, this population range (10,000 to 19,999) has the smallest difference. The largest difference is found in the 5,000 to 9,999 population range. There, for each thousand locally resident employed persons, there are 374 more jobs available locally in the Jewish towns than in the Arab ones (870 minus 496) and 443 more jobs filled by outsiders (572 minus 129). The difference in the 20,000 to 49,999 population group falls between the other two. The problem in the Arab towns is thus not so much that so many leave town to work, as it is the dearth of those who come from outside to work there;[30] *that* is one significant way in which the lagging economic development of the Arab towns manifests itself.

Now, if one posits a direct relationship between the number of employee posts and the area of floor space given over to economic activity of one sort or another, then the difference values shown in column 8 of table 2.10 are a striking indicator of the lower tax base in the Arab towns. And one should bear in mind that the denominator for the ratios presented here is the number of employed persons who reside in the town. If one takes into account both the much higher proportion of children in the population of the Arab towns and the much lower labor force participation rate of Arab women compared with Jewish women, then *per capita* employee post values (rather than the "per employed person" values used here) would show an even greater difference to the disadvantage of the Arab towns. The implications for the issue of low per capita municipal property tax revenue in the Arab towns are straightforward.

I commented earlier about statistics, and I will say here again, in the present regard, that one needs to be wary of the essentialized images to which statistics give rise. There are great differences among the Jewish towns themselves: there are well-established small towns that have stayed with agriculture, others that are affluent bedroom communities; there are once dusty, stagnant so-called development towns that have taken off, and towns that have, with the inflow of development funds, industry, and new population, turned one-time standstill around.

There are differences among the Arab towns, too, although in their case, the element of the inflow of outside resources has been absent. The head of the local council of one Arab town explained to me the need for a local industrial area by pointing to the situation he wanted to change: "During the day, the town is empty," he said. But recall the observation quoted by Rabinowitz to the effect that Nazareth and the Arab towns around it were "bursting and bubbling with development" (cited earlier). There are surely differences between towns that are swallowed up by the statistics, but one needs to add that, just as surely, what one sees and says—whether one sees or calls attention to the undisturbed dust or to local urban drive—changes with where one stands, whom one addresses, and one's political objectives in the current exchange.

An economist of neoclassical, liberal bent, listening on one occasion to recommendations for developing industrial infrastructure in the Arab towns, stated that, in his opinion, people, not towns, ought to be the objective of government policy—that the aim should be to provide better education opportunities and, in addition, good roads so that people could travel to where the work is. But an analyst of development and policy replied, in essence: "There's a great difference between Karmi'el and Sakhnin [an Arab town of 18,000, 6 km nearly

Table 2.11 Local Authorities in the Nazareth and Biq'at Bet Hakerem Areas by Population, Year of Settlement or Year Local Authority Established, Year Connected to Electric Grid, Socioeconomic Rank, and Employee Posts

Locality	Population (1995)	Settlement or local authority established		Connected to electric grid	Socioeconomic rank		Employee posts		
1	2	3	4	5	6	7	8	9	10
Nazareth Area									
Tur'an	8,330		1959	1965	45	3	.464	.423	.041
Ein Mahel	7,722		1964	1972	69	3	.282	.237	.045
Dabburye	6,092		1961	1973	62	3	.631	.517	.114
Iksal	8,097		1962	1971	78	3	.434	.326	.108
Yafi'	12,116		1960	1962	71	3	.327	.255	.072
Nazareth	51,946		1877	1935	74	3	.958	.601	.357
Upper Nazareth	37,271	1957			116	5	.858	.599	.259
Reine	11,689		1968	1975	52	3	.313	.213	.100
Meshhed	5,187		1960	1973	15	2	.411	.330	.081
Kafar Kanna	12,775		1968	1974	11	2	.412	.303	.109
'Ilut	4,708		1991	1980	27	2	—	—	—
Biq'at Bet Hakerem Area									
Majd Al-Kurum	9,118		1964	1975	22	2	.412	.342	.070
Bi'ne	5,456		1976	1977	37	3	.367	.310	.057
Deir Al Asad	6,485		1975	1976	48	3	.433	.328	.105
Nahef	7,152		1968	1976	23	2	.357	.301	.056
Sajur	2,722		1992	1976	47	3	.600	.394	.206
Rame	6,685		1954	1964	99	4	.485	.396	.089
Karmi'el	33,145	1964			136	6	.915	.602	.313

Notes and sources: Column 1: Localities in the Nazareth area are listed in general clockwise direction, starting with Tur'an in the northeast (see figure 1.1). Localities in the Biq'at Bet Hakerem area are listed in a west to east direction. Yafi' is contiguous with Nazareth at the latter's southwestern corner. It lies just beyond the western edge of the map of the Nazareth area. 'Ilut is a town located 2 km outside Nazareth to the northwest. It had been a part of the Nazareth municipality, but sought independence and was recognized as a local council in 1991. 'Ilut does not appear on the map of the Nazareth area, lying about 2 km beyond the western edge of the map.

Column 2: Data extracted from CBS 1998b; 1995 Census.

Column 3: Year of settlement for Jewish localities; from CBS 1998b.

Column 4: Year local authority established for Arab towns. These towns themselves were, of course, in existence for hundreds of years or longer. Data from CBS 1998c. Ghanem 1993 gives slightly different data for a number of these localities (with a large discrepancy in the case of the year Kafar Kanna Local Council was established). CBS publications (1998c and others in this series) do not give date of establishment of the Iksal Local Council; the date shown here is taken from Ghanem 1993. Rame had local council status for a period during the British Mandate.

Column 5: Year the town was connected to the electric grid. Data extracted from Jaffa Research Center 1991. Jewish towns were connected at the time of their settlement.

Column 6: Socioeconomic rank of locality among 203 local authorities in ascending order from one. Data from CBS 1999.

Column 7: In this cluster, out of ten clusters of socioeconomically ranked localities in ascending order from one. Data from CBS 1999.

Column 8: "L of W"/ "L of R", where "L of W" = number of employed persons working in this locality, without regard to their locality of residence, and "L of R" = number of employed persons residing in this locality.

Column 9: "W in L of R"/ "L of R", where "W in L of R" = number of persons working in their own locality of residence; "L of R" as in column 8.

Column 10: Column 8 minus column 9; number of employee posts in locality (per employed person residing in this locality) filled by persons who do not reside in this locality. Sources for columns 8, 9, and 10 explained in notes to table 2.10. Also, see there for treatment of "locality of work unknown" responses. There is no data for 'Ilut in these columns (I failed to include 'Ilut in the list of localities for which I requested the basic data from the CBS).

due south of Karmi'el, but nearly 13 km by the new road, which needs to find its way across a network of deep-lying streams and abrupt hills] that is plain to see—and it is well known that government policy toward the two places has not been equal" (Field Journal). It is, I suggest, merely this "plain-to-see difference" that comes across in the statistics.

Now, one of the attributes of a vital, living town is local economic activity. Going to work outside one's town does not fuel the spiraling dynamic of urban development. I encountered the drive to promote local economic development in one after another of the Arab towns to which my fieldwork took me. As the strategic development officer of one Arab town put it, "Karmi'el does not worry about the needs of my town—it concerns itself with the needs of its own population. But my town is today already a city; it too can pursue a program of developing local employment for its residents" (Interviews).

It will be seen that I have, by just the slightest turn, brought the focus of my discussion back to the more specific geographic space of my fieldwork. Before going on to sum up what I have been about in this and the preceding chapter, I wish to press further the present turn to introduce here some relevant statistics on the two groups of towns that were the general locale of the events I studied: the Nazareth area and the Biq'at Bet Hakerem area (see figures 1.1 and 7.1, respectively; the locations of these areas are indicated both in figure 1.4 and in figure 2.2). In the Nazareth area, Upper Nazareth and the Emeq Yizre'el and the Galil HaTahton regional councils are Jewish; the rest of the local authorities are Arab. In the Biq'at Bet Hakerem area, Karmi'el and the various regional councils appearing on the map are Jewish local authorities; the other local authorities are Arab. Data concerning these local authorities are presented in table 2.11.

The Lay of the Land

Perhaps it is time to be explicit about an ambiguity that has thus far been allowed to stand without remark. The *lay of the land* has, of course, a simple geographic meaning. It refers here to geographic dispositions: such things as the results of war and of land purchases and settlement, the constraint of urban expansion through the statutory planning system, the establishment of regional councils. But I have used it also in the sense of an abstract topology—the disposition of forces in a field of battle (a metaphorical *field,* although one with concrete effects of power). Yet the distinction between geography and topology is merely an analytic one; now that I have taken note of it, it might just as well be set aside. For surely the obviously geographic elements I have enumerated, and others as well, are part and parcel of the disposition of forces. As for the other elements in that disposition of forces—such things as the ability of local government to press its cause vis-à-vis the national government, to develop local infrastructure and promote local economic development—in the end, they come down to quintessentially spatial flows of labor and taxes and urban vitality. One needs, then, to acknowledge Harvey's seminal insight to the effect that social interactions take place and have outcomes in space as well as in time, and that the spatial dimension ought to be a part of social analysis (Harvey 1996). Surely that is so in the present instance, where territorial images and territorial aims figure prominently, and where the landscape itself is, indeed, a "landscape of power" (Zukin 1991).

Thus, by *lay of the land* I refer to the complex disposition of multiple forces (and hence, I use the two terms, *disposition of forces* and *lay of the land,* interchangeably—they stand for a particular configuration of forces in the field of power relations). Some of these forces (those having to do with issues of land ownership and municipal jurisdiction) I have touched on only in passing, preferring to deal with them at greater length where they are most salient in the ethnography and analysis to follow. Others, such as the uses to which the image of traditionalism is put, will come up again where attention to them can, I feel, shed light on one aspect or another of the analysis. As observed in the introduction, and as should be apparent from the material set forth in chapters 1 and 2, the elements of the field of power relations are diverse in nature, ranging from war and settlement and demography to administrative practices and discursive images and distinctions. Any of them may be discerned at any level of detail on which the analysis chooses to focus.

The great advantage, in my view, of this analytic image of the disposition of forces lies in its ability to handle complex relations of power without oversimplification. In the particular instance under examination, one is able to see how, in one dimension after another, the Arab towns are at a disadvantage—a state of affairs generally perceived as macrostructure. Yet at the same time, it can be seen that the field is dynamic and that the lines of battle are constantly shifting terrain and reforming. This is a conceptualization capable of countering the essentialization implicit in statements asserting that *the Arab village* has (or has not) brought forth out of itself one manifestation or another of modernity. By the same token, it is able to counter the equally essentialized image of a monolithic tyrant in unmitigated control of all, an image which assigns to the Arab population the role of passive subservience. Importantly, the lines of battle in the field of power relations I have described have not been fixed: they are subject to challenge at any moment, the forces deployed at any point may stir and rally to any new or ongoing engagement.

The picture painted here may appear more smooth, more seamless than is justified. That is the danger of a unified account, written from too broad a perspective; to escape that danger, one needs to get closer, as I will do in the coming chapters. On the other hand, the picture may seem forced and disjointed. If that is the case, I hasten to add that for the participants as well as for the observer, the terrain is often rough, and connections are not so easily made. Certainly the edges of the picture are jagged, for the subjects I am dealing with have been ripped out of the fabric of life. And when it comes down to events in the field, it will be seen that there are internal holes, events that pass through the net of my ethnographic account. As for the geographic boundaries of what my maps call the Nazareth area or the Biq'at Bet Hakerem area, nothing could be more arbitrary, for there are a host of threads that run across them. In short, although I have attempted to begin the description of the multiple dimensions of the lay of the land, this is not, nor could it ever be, a totality.

As suggested in the introduction, I found that the bureaucratic access situations I observed were imbued with an intrinsically political dimension. That dimension is a feature of the regulation of Arab participation in the planning process; it lurks in the discretion and the room for maneuver granted to official bodies, and it is nourished by the opaqueness of knowledge and the fitfulness of its circulation in the bureaucratic system. I also found, in the course of my study, that the obverse of such politicism is what I would call normalization—one thinks of Weber's concept of routinization, with the qualification that the word "normalization," at least since Foucault, can not be used without reference to the aspect of control. Once such places as Upper Nazareth and Karmi'el are established, normalization takes over from the drive for territorial control and reduces it to the quotidian: urban development measured in residences, schools, and places of employment. At the same time, this normalization both channels Arab development endeavors and serves to deny and obscure the political nature of administrative practice, thus deflecting challenge to the interests of power.[31]

To attend to an analysis of the Zipporit industrial area case is merely to add another level—one of finer resolution—to the picture of the disposition of forces, the lay of the land. Chapter 3 returns, as indicated, to Galilee and the events involving Upper Nazareth, Kafar Kanna, and Meshhed.

CHAPTER 3

The Zipporit Industrial Area

I turn now to the case of the Zipporit industrial area. As set out in the brief scene that opened chapter 1 (the reader may care to glance again at the opening pages of that chapter [see figure 1.1]), Upper Nazareth had leapfrogged over the territory of the Arab towns to its north to establish in 1992 that expansive industrial area, virtually in the backyard of its Arab neighbors and on land that had served the Arab townspeople in earlier times.

The establishment of Zipporit was the result of development planning[1] by national bodies and the vigorous pursuit of urban development by the mayor of Upper Nazareth. One part of a preliminary plan broke off and was absorbed by the Ministry of Industry program of establishing small local industrial areas in Arab localities. But there was also Arab protest, driven both by a sense of being besieged and by a desire to have a share in the fruits of development planning. Arab planners and local leaders who subscribed to the latter aim fanned the regional connection and kept it burning during the 1990s and beyond. Thus, the account that follows will reflect separation, forking, but also coalescence and coming together. In the fabric of these events are woven the uses of the statutory planning system and the comparative abilities of local authorities to make things happen, as well as the images of territorial conflict and Arab traditionalism.

Early Moves

The area that would eventually be known as Zipporit had been the subject of planning activity for many years. In the latter half of the 1970s, the ILA prepared a map that showed 4,235 dunam of ILA-owned land to be zoned for industry and "allocated to Mivnei Ta'asiya" for infrastructure planning and development (see figure 3.1; see also the chronology of events following the main body of the text).[2] During the early 1980s, planners proposed new Jewish settlement here that would integrate residences, commerce, and industry. A 1983 team including representatives of the ILA, the Ministry of Commerce and Industry, the Jewish Agency, the Ministry of the Interior, and the Upper Nazareth municipality formulated a program that allocated 1,800 dunam to residence and services, 1,400 for hi-tech industry and R&D, and, in addition, 1,000 dunam for conventional industry. The latter was referred to as "a complete solution for the industrial needs of Nazareth and its satellites [*benoteha*]."[3] The planners suggested that the ILA give immediate authorization for detailed planning of the area earmarked for conventional industry.

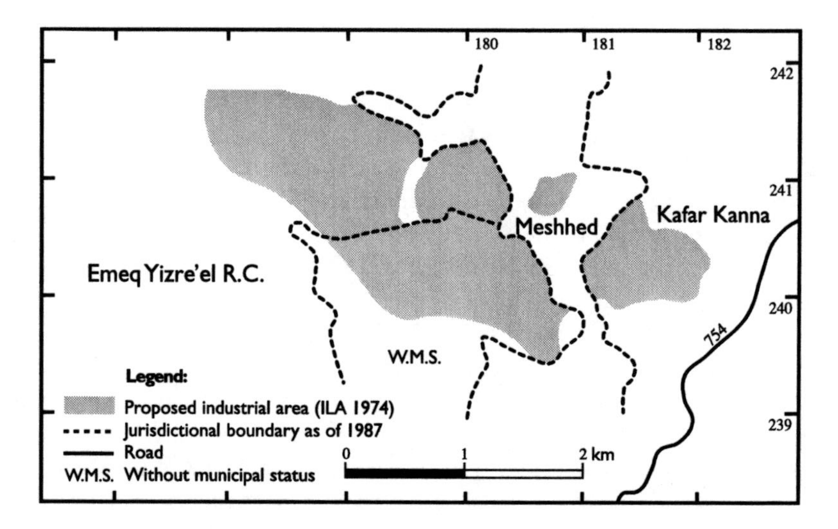

Figure 3.1 ILA Industrial Area Proposal, 1974. *Sources:* The industrial area proposal is from a map provided courtesy of the ILA. Jurisdictional boundaries and municipal status are adapted from the Ministry of the Interior.

It will be observed that the area indicated for industry by the 1974 ILA plan (figure 3.1) included 615 dunam in Kafar Kanna's jurisdiction, and about 100 dunam in Meshhed's jurisdiction. Furthermore, a 1985 ILA document specified that of the 1000 dunam then being planned for conventional industry, 615 dunam were located in Kafar Kanna (i.e., the same area shown in Kafar Kanna's jurisdiction in figure 3.1). Prompted by its shape, planners at the time referred to this area as "Australia."

Looking back, officials and planners who began to take part in events in the early 1990s explained to me that planning new Jewish settlement in the Zipporit area was inspired by "an ostensibly objective perception of the threat of Arab irredentism and demography." Jewish development in the Galilee was perceived by the planners in militant terms—as the mirror image of Islam as a religion of territorial conquest and expansion. The intention was explicitly

"Judaization of Galilee." At the same time, it was understood that "Australia" would be developed for Kafar Kanna: "You can't do this large industrial area without doing something for the Arab towns—otherwise you just invite hostility and objections. One shouldn't go straight up against the wall with one's head [*lo holchim im harosh bakir*]." And one of the planners with whom I spoke added: "To succeed in development, you need development for the Arabs too—to reduce conflict. People [i.e., new Jewish settlers in Galilee, DW] won't come to or stay in a place where there's hostility." In any event, by the late 1980s, "Australia" was being planned for Kafar Kanna by the ILA's Planning and Development Division in Jerusalem.[4] I will return below to this strand of events.

During 1991, a new planning team in which the Ministry of Construction and Housing, the ILA, and Upper Nazareth took part, headed by Mivnei Ta'asiya, returned to active planning of a new functionally integrated settlement in the area just south of Highway 77 and west of Meshhed (see figure 1.1; see also figure 3.1). At a planning meeting on 25 August 1991, it was declared that (a) the new quarter (*rova'*), now being referred to as "Zipporit," would be part of Upper Nazareth (a matter that had until then been left open), and (b) the residential portion and the industrial area portion would be treated as separate entities (Mivnei Ta'asiya 1992: 71, 72). The record of the August planning meeting reveals the urgency now attached to developing the industrial area. Menachem Ariav, mayor of Upper Nazareth, declared that it was his city's burning need, and the director of the Galilee District of the Ministry of Construction and Housing asserted that the intention was to begin work on the industrial area by 1 December 1991.

Whether it was being thought of as a large industrial area or as a functionally integrated settlement, the area slated for Zipporit was in part in the jurisdiction of the Emeq Yizre'el Regional Council and in part without municipal status (WMS; i.e., did not fall into the jurisdiction of any local authority) (see figure 3.1). In 1981, Upper Nazareth had requested that the minister of the interior transfer to its jurisdiction about 3,500 dunam for industry (more or less, but not entirely, congruent with the area being planned in 1991). The request was taken up by a boundary commission appointed by the minister, headed eventually by Moshe Glazner.[5]

It may be noted that the team engaged in planning the functionally integrated settlement in 1983 recommended transferring the area for that settlement to Upper Nazareth (August 1983), but the idea of a functionally integrated settlement was never put to the boundary commission by Upper Nazareth. Rather, the matter before the commission was formulated exclusively in terms of a large industrial area for that city. The commission's final report in about 1989[6] recommended transferring to Upper Nazareth only about 500 dunam that had been without municipal status; it was felt that the city would be overextending itself if it attempted to develop a larger tract. In March 1991, the minister of the interior transferred about 740 dunam to Upper Nazareth's jurisdiction (577 dunam from the area without municipal status and 164 dunam from

Emeq Yizre'el Regional Council) (*Kovetz HaTaqanot* [*KT*] 5342, 752, 21 March 1991). This was just a few months before the Mivnei Ta'asiya planning team moved ahead decisively on the industrial area part of the functionally integrated settlement proposal.

The Zipporit Industrial Area: Stage A

The events recounted thus far may be thought of as the preliminaries to the rise of the Zipporit industrial area. In November 1991, following through on the August planning decisions, Mivnei Ta'asiya submitted a detailed plan for Zipporit A to the Northern District's Residential and Industrial Construction Commission (RICC).[7]

After modification in response to objections, the plan covered an area of about 1,340 dunam.[8] It may be noted that the plan extended south of the tract transferred to Upper Nazareth in March (740 dunam) into an area without municipal status, and northwest into Emeq Yizre'el's jurisdiction. During December 1991, the RICC dealt with the plan and decided to approve it for deposit.

The former head of the Meshhed Local Council told me how just shortly before, on 26 November, the Upper Nazareth municipal engineer had paid a visit to Meshhed:

> He came and spread the plans for Zipporit on the table and said, "We need to be able to have an access road from Highway 77 at the northeast corner of the industrial area [Zipporit A]—it would cut through Meshhed jurisdiction and over privately owned land. We need it temporarily—can you give your agreement and help convince the landowners?" (See figure 1.1)

According to the head of the local council, this was the first that Meshhed had heard of the plan.

Meshhed (the head of the local council and at least eleven private landowners) submitted objections to the RICC. The local council's deposition argued:

1. Contrary to the provisions of the PBL, Meshhed representatives had not been included in deliberation as members of the RICC dealing with a plan pertaining to its jurisdiction.
2. Not only did the proposed access road from the northeast cut across Meshhed lands, but the road at the southern end of the tract was designed to provide access from Highway 754 [see figure 1.1] and would cut a wide swath across Meshhed lands, cutting off access to Meshhed's fields to the north. Other roads in the plan also threatened Meshhed's lands.
3. The southern portion of the plan related to territory not in Upper Nazareth's jurisdiction, and, indeed, this land (without municipal status) was needed by Meshhed for its own urban development, including a high school, football field and sports center, a cemetery, and an area for light industry. (The deposition noted that Upper Nazareth already had several industrial areas [see figure 1.1],

while Meshhed had none. It also noted that a Meshhed request for this area [still WMS] had long since been submitted to the Ministry of the Interior, and that whereas it was difficult to carry out such development on Meshhed's land since nearly all of it was privately owned, this area that Meshhed had requested and that now appeared in the Zipporit A plan was ILA-owned.)

4. The proposed industrial area not include environmentally polluting factories.

The RICC responded to Meshhed's contention that they should by rights have been represented *on*, as distinguished from *at*, the commission that dealt with the plan by assuring the head of the local council that Meshhed would participate in the meeting to be devoted to hearing objections with status as fully fledged members of the commission. I was told, though, that Meshhed representatives were not present for the deliberations that followed the presentation of their objections on 23 March 1992.

In any event, the RICC decided that the southern access road and southernmost parcels were not, for the moment, essential to the program, and that the blue line[9] would be redrawn to exclude them, thus obviating the necessity of dealing with the substance of Meshhed objections concerning them for the time being.[10] The RICC also reiterated that the access road from the northeast would serve for only two and one-half years, following which the land would be returned to its former state.

The RICC did not address other aspects of the objections raised by Meshhed. After all, it had before it a concrete urban building plan (UBP)[11] for Upper Nazareth; urban development for Meshhed was not on its agenda. And objections from threatened Meshhed landowners could be deflected by the simple expedient of redrawing the blue line, thus putting the threat on hold; when the industrial area became an accomplished fact, the logic of further development steps would have a life of its own. Consider also the fate of Meshhed's contention that, by rights, its representatives ought to have been part of the commission. One may suggest that the RICC's patronizing response to this contention merely underscores the fact that Meshhed's objections were those of the weak, not the strong. The statutory planning system, in which public participation is conceived in adversarial terms, reinforces confrontation and works to make an appeal on the broader grounds of exclusion from the planning process inconceivable. Indeed, neither Meshhed nor the other Arab towns in the vicinity had a share in the development planning that led to the Zipporit A UBP. Exclusionary practices and what I will refer to as the appropriation of Arab development needs by Jewish localities in their midst are themes that will recur in the course of the present ethnography.

But it should also be reported that Zipporit A was established without the temporary access road from the northeast and that, in an attempt to minimize incursions into Meshhed land, the road to the planned water towers in the southwest (not mentioned hitherto) was rerouted from what originally appeared in the plan.

The outcome of the RICC's meeting of 23 March 1992 was a decision to give final approval to the Zipporit A plan (labeled G/IC/125 in the DPBC), subject to certain modifications, including the ones mentioned with regard to Meshhed objections. It would be a full eleven months, however, before G/IC/125 would actually become valid (*ishur letoqef*). For one thing, the RICC made final approval conditional on submission of a detailed plan regarding treatment of sewage. But there was also something else delaying validation of the industrial area plan. Early on, following the RICC's decision to *deposit* the plan at the beginning of 1992, the minister of the interior had ruled that the plan would require his approval.[12] The plan was finally actually referred to the minister of the interior on 12 November 1992, and ten days later it was decided, in light of a recommendation by the ministry's Planning Administration, not to approve it until the plan's instructions regarding the environment were acceptably formulated.

At any rate, following RICC's March 1992 decision to grant final approval, the Upper Nazareth Planning and Building Commission issued a building permit for earthwork operations as a first step in installation of the industrial area infrastructure (29 April 1992). On 4 June 1992, the same local planning and building commission issued a building permit to the Phoenicia America-Israel Float Glass Company, the firm that was to be the "anchor" for the new industrial area. The LPBC permit included conditions, among them, that Phoenicia fulfill the requirements that would be stipulated by the Ministry of the Environment. Now, paragraph 97a of the PBL authorizes the *District* Planning and Building Commission to grant building permits in accordance with plans that have been approved for deposit; it is only when the plan is finally approved (*ishur letoqef*) that the LPBC is able to issue permits on its own. It is true that the RICC had decided to give final approval to the industrial area plan, but the minister's approval was still pending (and the plan, it will be recalled, would not actually become valid until the following February). Thus, it is arguable that the two permits issued by the Upper Nazareth LPBC were not (at least, not yet) valid.

The Phoenicia plant had been located in the Haifa Bay area. During the previous six years it had undergone reorganization, leading to a doubling of the turnover per employee; now it had been purchased by American investors who were moving it to the Zipporit industrial area at a cost of $87 million. It expected to have an annual turnover of $60 million, with two-thirds of the output slated for export. It would employ four hundred workers (Brenner 1992; Interviews).

Work on the industrial area and/or on the Phoenicia factory proceeded apace. There was a lot of blasting involved; during the month of July, the residents of Kafar Kanna and Meshhed felt the earth tremble and said that they couldn't sleep at night due to the explosions—that it was like being at the battlefront. The work continued day and night, even on Saturday. Newspaper accounts report that the blasting was so severe as to cause damage to the houses in Kafar Kanna and Meshhed (according to one report, sixty-five houses in the former and thirty-five in the latter) (W. Awawdy 1992, 1993a; A.

Shehada 1992c, 1992d; Interviews).[13] Later, when the Arab towns instituted High Court of Justice legal proceedings against establishment of the factory and cited the earthwork outfit among the respondents, the latter organization replied that it should not have been named as a respondent, inasmuch as it was working only on the earthwork for the industrial area infrastructure and not on the factory. But that reply was surely disingenuous; after all, blasting was being done exactly where the factory was to be erected, as a precursor to building at that spot.[14]

Over the summer, particularly in July, a public campaign took shape against incursion of the Phoenicia factory into the area. One two-part article in the Arabic press (W. Awawdy 1992) spoke of the twin dangers of expropriation and pollution. The expropriation of Arab land was a grievance of long standing: this included the state takeover of absentee lands and the later establishment of Jewish rural settlements in those areas; the confiscation of land from local owners for the establishment and then, later, the expansion of Upper Nazareth; the current (1992) takeover of private land in Reine and Meshhed for the construction of Bypass Road 79 (see figure 1.1); and, now, the appearance of the Phoenicia factory. The land on which the Zipporit A industrial area was being developed had been registered as state land during the land settlement of title campaign undertaken by the British Mandate government, and, although Mandate maps showed it as being within what were called the village boundaries of Meshhed, it had not been included in the Meshhed boundaries of jurisdiction when the local council was established in 1960 (see figure 3.2).

The heads of the two local councils acknowledged publicly at the time that the land on which Zipporit was being built had been registered as state-owned by the Mandate government, and also that it had never been in Meshhed jurisdiction, but they also called attention to the fact that it had served as grazing land for the farmers of Meshhed and Kafar Kanna. Certainly it was right there in the backyard of the two towns, as the destructive effects of the blasting made clear. And now, Upper Nazareth was to reap the tax benefits and employment benefits of the new industrial area, while the Arab towns were being exposed to the dangers of pollution. The perception was that these two dangers were joining forces to threaten the very existence of the Arabs in the region. This was not development of the Galilee but rather Judaization, the article stated.

The proclamation issued jointly during this period by the Kafar Kanna Local Council and the Public Committee against the Establishment of the Phoenicia Factory gave expression to these themes and spelled out the idea of Arab exclusion: government policy was eating up the land reserves that could be used for the possible industrial development of the Arab towns and annexing these lands to the Jewish ones, all under the false cover of declarations about developing the Galilee. One article (R. Awawdeh and Isa 1992) points out that Arab requests for development have been answered negatively, while the government proceeds with development for Upper Nazareth (on Arab exclusion, see also A. Shehada 1992a; and on the public campaign, see

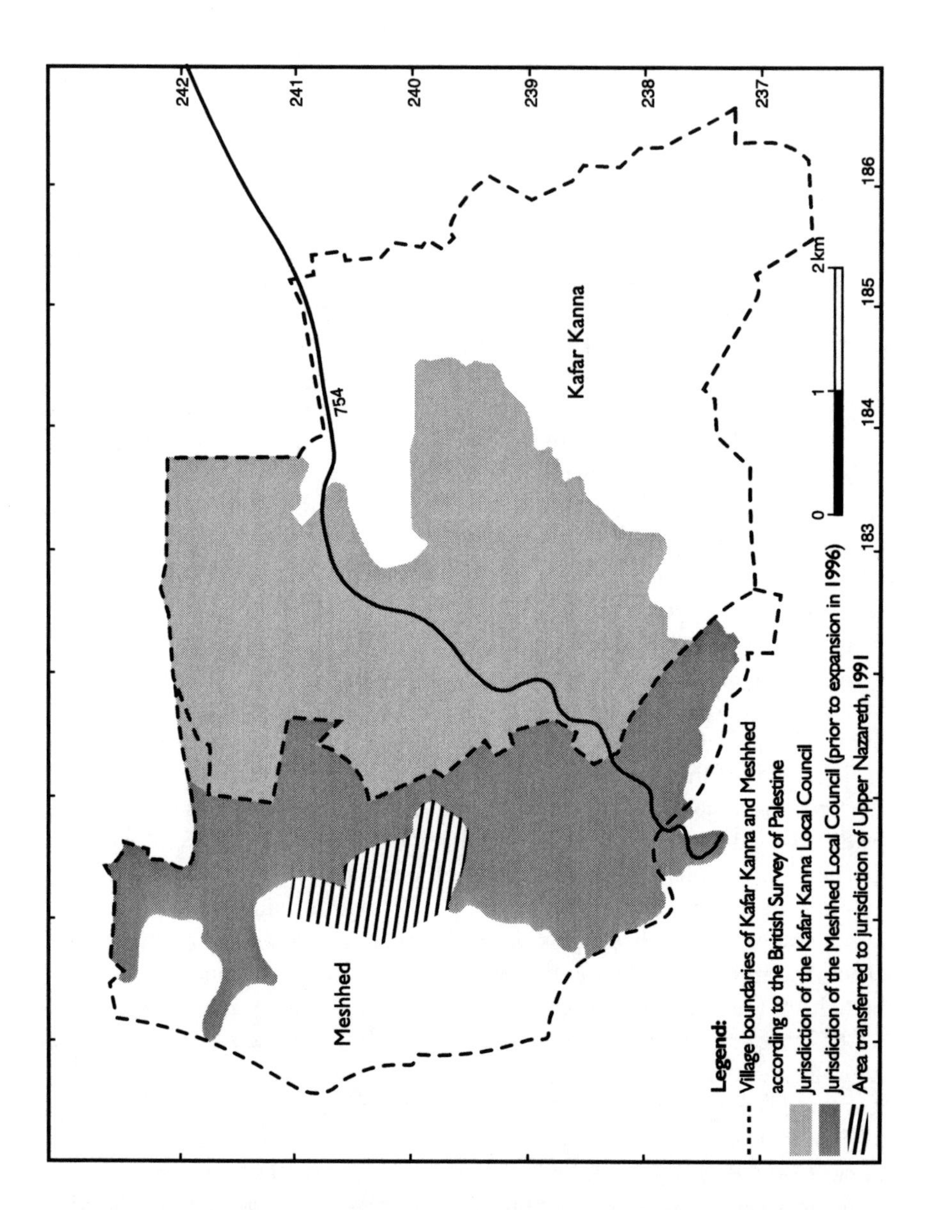

Figure 3.2 Village Boundaries and Boundaries of Jurisdiction—Meshhed and Kafar Kanna.
Sources: Village boundaries are from a 1941 1:20,000 Survey of Palestine map based on a 1:10,000 Topocadastral Survey map of 1932. Boundaries of jurisdiction are from the Ministry of the Interior.

also Shehada 1992b, *Al Ittichad* 1992, Abu Basel 1992, W. Awawdy 1992). I will return at later points in this study both to the subject of land and to that of development for the region's inhabitants.

A formal cornerstone-laying ceremony for the Phoenicia factory was held on 22 September 1992. The festivities took place in a large tent erected for the occasion, and, among others, the prime minister, the minister of industry, the mayor of Upper Nazareth, senior officers of the firm, and the American investors were present. The heads of the Kafar Kanna and Meshhed local councils had also been invited, but they remained outside, at the head of a protest demonstration of residents and high school students of the towns (according to Brenner 1992, there were several hundred participants). The protestors carried signs saying, "We Want Industry for Our Towns, But We Do Not Want Death for Our Children," and "We Want Land for Development, Not Factories of Devastation" (Shehada 1992e).

It was about this time that the idea of a joint industrial area, one that would include Meshhed and Kafar Kanna along with Upper Nazareth, began to take shape. By mid October, the heads of the two Arab local councils, along with Rassem Khamaisi (head of the Center for Strategic Planning in the Arab Municipalities located in Kafar Kanna) had met on the subject with representatives of the infrastructure development companies working for the Ministry of Industry. They also participated in high-level meetings at the Ministry of the Interior and the Ministry of Industry in Jerusalem. The discussion at the Ministry of the Interior opened with the issue of pollution, but the head of the Kafar Kanna Local Council recounted to me that then the thrust of the discussion shifted:

> If you want a fight, we'll give you a fight (whole page ads in newspapers, New York, London; lawsuits at the High Court of Justice)—you'll never open. The alternative is to include us—these were the grazing lands of the people of Meshhed and Kafar Kanna, and now you go ahead and do this without including us?! As for the pollution, we'll overcome it—for the sake of the people of Upper Nazareth and of Kafar Kanna and Meshhed.

It should be pointed out that this is how this person composed the elements of the situation for me a few years after the event.

By mid November, the head of the Meshhed Local Council was already stating publicly that the idea of a joint industrial area was supported by the minister of the interior, the minister of industry, and the Prime Minister's Office (Bsool 1992).

At the same time, a petition to the High Court of Justice (HCJ) was being organized in the name of the Kafar Kanna and Meshhed local councils, primarily against the municipality of Upper Nazareth, the DPBC, and the Ministry of Environment, asking that a building permit be withheld from Phoenicia, or rescinded if it had already been issued, on the grounds that an EIA (Environmental Impact Assessment) acceptable to the second respondent had not yet been carried out, and arguing that the third respondent was not fulfilling its obligation to investigate and to set standards for the control of pollution (HCJ [*BaGaTZ*] 6221/92).[15]

Just as the petition reached the HCJ at the end of December 1992, the DPBC, citing paragraph 97a of the PBL, hastened to ratify (28 December) the building permit that had been issued to Phoenicia by the LPBC about seven months before; this was tantamount to admitting that the earlier permit had not been valid. But as will be seen below, the government itself soon had recourse to arguing in its own defense in the HCJ suit regarding Phoenicia that this DPBC building permit to Phoenicia was not valid either.

In Jerusalem on 12 January 1993, the Ministry of the Interior held a meeting regarding the acceptable formulation of the environmental protection provisions of G/IC/125 (the Zipporit industrial area plan). It will be recalled that two months earlier, the Interior Ministry's Planning Authority had recommended that the plan not be granted final approval until this had been accomplished. At the January meeting, the representative of the Infrastructure Development Company stated that the government had already invested 12.5 million NIS in the industrial area. The CEO of Phoenicia spoke of the $17 million that had already been invested in foundations for the plant's furnace; he also pointed out that Phoenicia was working against the clock, and that each day's delay in construction of the factory would cost $40 thousand. It may be observed that until G/IC/125's environmental protection provisions (i.e., those of the industrial area) were in place, there was no way to specify the environmental requirements in a building permit to Phoenicia. The participants I mentioned above, together with other Ministry of Industry representatives, the head of the DPBC, and Menachem Ariav, mayor of Upper Nazareth, argued that setting standards might turn out to be time consuming and that, due to the urgency of the project, it would be best to approve the G/IC/125 as it was; it would be possible to settle with the Ministry of the Environment later on, they said, and they reiterated their commitment to protecting the environment. But the Ministry of Interior Planning Authority officer pointed out that if the plan were approved as it was, it would be vulnerable to appeals to the HCJ on environmental grounds. At this January meeting, Ariav mentioned the HCJ suit brought by the two Arab towns against the municipality, the DPBC, and the Ministry of the Environment with regard to the building permit that had been issued to Phoenicia—"the subject of the suit is the environment," he said, "but in actuality, the subject is political."

The 12 January meeting set up a special committee to make recommendations to the RICC. Things moved quickly in response to the sense of urgency that was now being expressed. By 21 January, the RICC had already received the recommendations of the special committee and adopted them all. This cleared the way for the signature of the head of the Ministry of Interior Planning Authority (acting for the minister) on 9 February 1993, and publication of G/IC/125's approval (*ishur letoqef*) in the press by the end of that month (see also *Yalqut Hapirsumim* 4092, 1960, 18 March 1993).

The HCJ had set 2 February 1993 for hearing Kafar Kanna's and Meshhed's suit regarding Phoenicia. In the joint response they had submitted, the DPBC and the Ministry of the Environment argued that the Phoenicia building permit approved by the DPBC on 28 December had been issued by mistake and was not valid because the Ministry of the Environment had not been asked for its approval. The Ministry of the Environment would only give its approval after it had evaluated Phoenicia's Environmental Impact Assessment (EIA), they said, and only then would a valid permit be issued by the DPBC. Inasmuch as no valid permit had yet been issued, the respondents argued, the suit against the DPBC and the Ministry of the Environment was premature and should be dismissed.

On 1 February, Kafar Kanna and Meshhed announced that they were suspending their suit. According to press accounts (W. Awawdy 1993b; Shehada 1993), the heads of the local councils had been convinced that their chances of winning the suit were slim and that their aim of having Phoenicia pollution controlled would be better served if the suit were withdrawn. The accounts emphasized the commitment of the Ministry of the Interior, the Ministry of Industry, and the Prime Minister's Office to turning Zipporit into a joint industrial area in which the two Arab towns would have a say in the control of pollution and a share of the municipal tax proceeds.

It would seem clear that the HCJ suit, though formulated only in terms of the threat of pollution, had become tied up with the question of Kafar Kanna's and Meshhed's participation in the tax revenues of industrial development. In that sense, it was indeed political, as Ariav had asserted. In January, the chairman of RICC stated that he had been led to understand that the Arab towns would withdraw their suit in return for being included in a joint industrial area. But there were also suggestions made by members of the Public Committee against the Establishment of the Phoenicia Factory that the heads of the local councils had been told by government representatives that if they did not withdraw the suit, their municipal budget allocations would "dry up," although this was denied by the local council chairmen (Rozen 1996; Interviews).

The question arose as to whether Meshhed and Kafar Kanna would be taken in immediately as partners in the Zipporit A industrial area that Upper Nazareth was constructing on land that had recently been transferred to its jurisdiction. Reports in the press were ambiguous on this point. Some of the participants in these events were clear that this is what they thought should happen. Rassem Khamaisi made this point in my presence back in October 1992, and others did so in the course of interviews later on. One of them pointed out that if the idea were that the Arab towns ought to have a degree of control over Phoenicia pollution, then logic had it that they should have a say in managing the industrial area from the start.

But Menachem Ariav easily deflected the demand by arguing that it was Upper Nazareth that had carried out the statutory process that had paved the way to G/IC/125 and Phoenicia, that it was not his intention to give these up, and that he could not give up land. Ariav's position was that Kafar Kanna and Meshhed should develop industrial infrastructure on adjoining land in their own jurisdictions, and this would become part of an expanded joint industrial area. The Arab towns did not contest this.

This is a key question that goes to issues of land, jurisdiction, and participation in regional development. It will be brought to the fore again by later events. At this point, it is enough to observe that, considered only in terms of the map of local authority jurisdiction abstracted from relations of power, this land could just as well, indeed, could more reasonably have been placed in Meshhed's jurisdiction.

Although the Kafar Kanna and Meshhed local authorities had, apparently at least, used up the pollution card in gaining the promise of a share in the Zipporit industrial area, there were alternative actors present on the local scene able to take over the fight to control Phoenicia pollution. During February and March, the Tur'an Local Council (just across the valley and east of Kafar Kanna), the Galilee Society for Health Research and Services, and the two chairmen of the local public committees against pollution in Kafar Kanna and Meshhed expressed to the Ministry of the Environment their opposition to and protest against the leniency of the environmental protection conditions that the ministry was now engaged in setting. On 16 March, a new, this time valid, permit was issued to Phoenicia (one should not imagine that work on erecting the factory had been halted when the government admitted in court that the earlier building permit had not been valid). Unsatisfied, the new environmental activists submitted a new petition to the HCJ on 1 April 1993. On the 20th of that month, one day before the scheduled hearing, the court was informed that the petitioners and Phoenicia were discussing practical proposals for pollution control. There were hard-fought discussions leading to Phoenicia's agreement to set up and finance a regional air-monitoring system and to install, by a reasonable date, electrostatic precipitators that would clean up the plant's atmospheric emissions. Eventually, the agreement was given the status of a court judgment (August 1994); Phoenicia lived up to the terms of the agreement, and made other provisions in constructing and operating the plant that seemed to demonstrate reasonable concern on its part for environmental protection. On 1 November 1993, the Phoenicia furnace was fired, and on 11 January of the following year, plant operations were inaugurated.

For an account that deals with the plan for Zipporit—Zipporit A, B, and C in Upper Nazareth jurisdiction, and Zipporit D and E in Kafar Kanna and Meshhed jurisdiction (over 5,000 dunam altogether)—see Rozen 1996. Rozen juxtaposes these plans with environmental concerns relating to the nearby presence of the National Water Carrier (an open canal in the Bet Netofa Valley, together with open reservoirs near the Movil Junction), vulnerable underground water, and preservation and development of the region's tourism potential. He quotes Amiram Derman, an urban planner: "The entire region was once virgin, but already today the most prominent feature in it is Phoenicia's chimney."[16, 17]

In May 1993, a meeting of the representatives of the local authorities and of the Ministry of Industry, together with the Ministry of Interior Northern District Commissioner, decided to prepare detailed plans for stage D and E (*daleth* and *heh*),[18] and to work through the RICC. Khamaisi told me that the aim was to have an *approved* plan by November (the intention was in all likelihood "November 1994"; Rassem was telling me this in December 1993). Planning would be done by the same architect who had planned Zipporit A, and who would continue on planning Zipporit B and C as extensions of the Upper Nazareth industrial area; HaPaT (Infrastructure Development Company), which was handling the Upper Nazareth industrial project, would also handle this. It was also decided that, in parallel with the detailed plans, it would be necessary to work on creating a joint municipal industrial authority for the industrial area. The division between Zipporit D and Zipporit E was made according to land ownership: Zipporit D was the area of ILA-owned land; Zipporit E was privately owned land. The understanding was that plans for privately owned land would entail reparcellation, and that this and the zoning change would probably prompt (at least some) objections by the landowners, thus slowing progress, whereas the statutory process for ILA-owned land would be able to proceed unhindered.

During the same month, a plan submitted by Mivnei Ta'asiya for what was still being thought of as the residential portion of Zipporit (to the west of Zipporit A) showed planning for industry in the larger area in Meshhed and Kafar Kanna that would figure in the Zipporit D–E plans, that is, an area that was much more extensive than the 629 dunam area that early ILA plans had proposed for industry (the area that had been known as "Australia"). In other words, it was obvious that planning for Zipporit D–E, which included privately owned as well as state-owned land, was already being taken into account by those involved in the overall project (see figures 1.1, 3.1, 3.3, and 3.4).[19]

During the next month, representatives of Kafar Kanna, Meshhed, and Upper Nazareth met to discuss the principles of the joint industrial area. In August, a program for Zipporit D–E prepared by Khamaisi was conveyed to the architect who was planning the site. In February 1944, HaPaT informed the architect that the Ministry of Industry had authorized planning (at ministry expense) for the part that was privately owned as well. It was unusual for a government body, whether the ILA or the Ministry of Industry, to undertake planning for privately owned land, let alone to bear the cost. But advocates of the departure in this case argued that this could be seen as an opportunity to plan a region, to take advantage of returns to scale, and to provide the impetus for change. The head of the Ministry of Industry's Development Areas Unit,[20] who had been taking an active part in moves to advance the joint industrial area project, had been instrumental in effecting this step.

By May, the architect had produced a preliminary plan showing land uses in Zipporit D–E. Actually, the first detailed plan for Zipporit D–E was not dealt with by the Mevo Ha'amaqim Planning and Building Commission (the

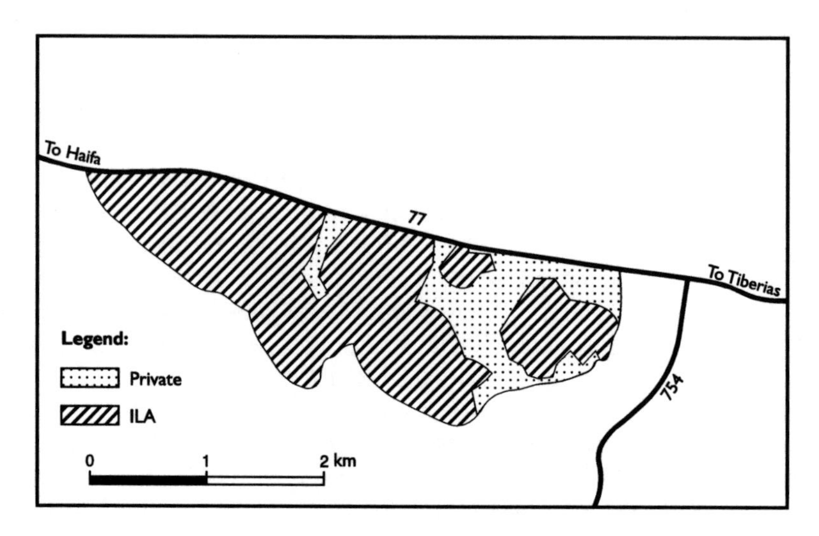

Figure 3.3 Land Ownership in the Zipporit Industrial Area. *Sources:* Adapted from Mivnei Ta'asiya 1992, with some details of Zipporit D–E provided by local planners/officials.

LPBC with planning jurisdiction for Kafar Kanna, Meshhed, and *eight* other towns) until September 1995 (so much for that brave goal early on of having an approved plan by November 1994). The statutory process was still far from conclusion as of the year 2000. Before attending to these later events, however, it will be appropriate to take up the story of G/7088, the 157-dunam industrial area in Kafar Kanna's jurisdiction where I had seen the bulldozer doing land grading in December 1993. This, it will be recalled, was being done in the framework of the Ministry of Industry's then-current industrial area project in sixteen Arab localities in the north.

G/7088

As mentioned near the beginning of this chapter, the area known as "Australia" was by the late 1980s being planned as an industrial area for Kafar Kanna by the ILA's Planning and Development Division in Jerusalem. This resulted in a 629-dunam plan, of which 370 dunam were zoned for industry. In May 1990, the ILA Northern District forwarded the plan to the Mevo Ha'amaqim Planning and Building Commission. The latter sent it up to the DPBC the following month with a recommendation for deposit.

In October that year a DPBC subcommittee approved the plan, now designated G/7088, for deposit, but to a limited extent (*beheqef metzumtzam*) and on condition of approval by the CPAL. The plan had been cut back to 278 dunam, with 90 of them slated for industry.[21] In April 1991, CPAL approved the downwardly revised plan.

I found nothing in the records to indicate what considerations had led to its being reduced so drastically (the area zoned for industry had been slashed by 75 percent) or whether the change had originated in the DPBC or perhaps in some exchange between that body and the CPAL. The engineer of the LPBC explained to me that it was their policy to push programs ahead by sending them up to the DPBC: "The LPBC can approve a large program, knowing it will be cut down in the DPBC—that various considerations will be brought into play there—but our approach is to let the statutory process get under way." "Perhaps," speculated one of the planning officials with whom I spoke, "it was cut back because it was too big, too grandiose, too daring—'better to do one part at a time' may have been the view." And indeed, 370 dunam net for industry was an area far beyond the scope of what was being planned at the time for Arab localities; 90 dunam was more in keeping with what was then being planned in the ILA Northern District. (See figure 3.4 for the planning stages of G/7088.)

Public notice of deposit of the plan was given in May 1992, that is, a year later. In July 1992, the Kafar Kanna Local Council lodged an objection to the plan at the DPBC: "Only now did we find out that the ILA has made this plan for an industrial area in Kafar Kanna—we were not consulted by the ILA, and the plan does not address the public needs of the locality." The local council submitted an alternative proposal. This proposal deleted the southernmost tier of industrial plots and allocated greater area to sport and educational facilities. This was the proper place for these functions, the local council argued. The alternative plan encompassed 106 dunam, 70 of them for industry. In May 1993, the DPBC decided to accept the local authority's objections and, because of the serious change, to redeposit the plan (*lehafqid mehadash*).

That the ILA would have planned this industrial area without consulting the local authority may seem curious; yet that is consistent with what is known about ILA planning in other localities. A senior Northern District Ministry of Interior planning official told me that it was entirely conceivable that the ILA would have planned for Kafar Kanna without including them in the process and without their knowledge. The PBL accords landowners the right to initiate statutory planning for the land they own. As landowners, the ILA could indeed undertake planning without consulting the local authority.

It was at about this point that G/7088 became part of the broader Ministry of Industry program for building industrial areas in a large number of Arab towns. First, however, I turn back briefly to the late 1970s and the 1980s when the ILA Northern District had begun to prepare detailed plans for industrial areas in several Arab localities. It was done, I was told, out of a sense of filling a need that no one else was attending to at the time. These tended to be quite small (most well under 100 dunam), but the plan for Sakhnin (planning begun in 1987) called for 159 dunam net for industry, and for Tamra (planning begun in 1976), 226 dunam net. Thus, the 370 dunam planned in Jerusalem for Kafar Kanna, a town whose population was two-thirds that of Tamra,

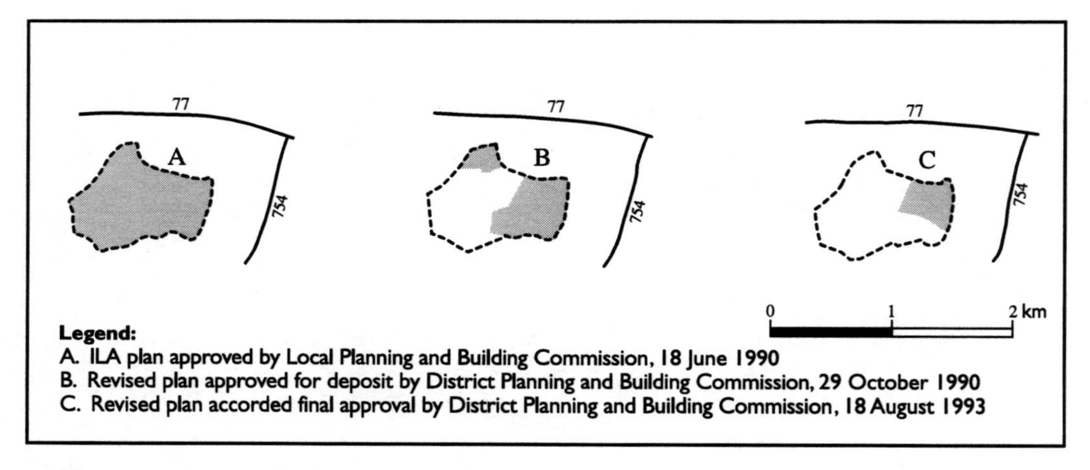

Figure 3.4 Planning Stages—Kafar Kanna Industrial Area (G/7088). *Note:* Extracted from urban building plans submitted to the DPBC.

does appear to have been exceptional. Now, planning alone, though crucial, is not enough—the ILA is, after all, an administrative body, not an implementing one, as ILA personnel explained to me. No one took up these plans for implementation until 1992, when the Ministry of Industry, under the Likud government, following through on the then-current trend of privatization of functions hitherto carried out directly by the government or its subsidiaries (e.g., Mivnei Ta'asiya), engaged the Yoram Gadish project management firm to carry out the construction of industrial infrastructure in several Arab towns in northern Israel. The project included bringing plans up to date and getting statutory approval finalized. In July 1992, a new, Labor-led government took office, and the Ministry of Industry pushed the project of industrial areas for the Arab towns vigorously.[22]

The local industrial area in Kafar Kanna was incorporated in this project. In August 1993, the DPBC gave final approval to the industrial area part of the G/7088 plan (70 dunam for industry) without its having been redeposited—after all, it was now being pushed by the Yoram Gadish firm with the latter's unmediated concern for earnings. The area shown as Stage C in figure 3.4 is about 106 dunam (70 dunam net for industry, 11 dunam for open public area, and 25 dunam for roads); this is the dark gray area in figure 1.1 in Kafar Kanna jurisdiction within Zipporit D–E. It might be mentioned parenthetically that the industrial areas actually built in this same project in Sakhnin and Tamra were each 120 dunam net, not 159 in the case of Sakhnin, and not 226 in the case of Tamra.

As I have related, earthwork on this industrial area began in November 1993. The aerial photo presented in figure 3.5 looks southward across the industrial area. It was taken in August 1994. At the time it was taken, earthwork had already been done, that is, plots were leveled and roadways were broken through. By the beginning of 1996, sewage, drainage, water, telephone, and electric systems had been installed, and asphalt had been laid on the roads.

This was the stage when what is known as "marketing" becomes serious, that is, soliciting and processing requests for leasing the industrial area's parcels. An applicant has his or her request for a plot approved, and pays a leasing fee to the ILA, and part of the cost of infrastructure development to the Ministry of Industry. Then he or she prepares plans and applies to the LPBC for a building permit. When erection of factories is complete, which can take several years, the Ministry of Industry comes back into the picture to complete the second stage of development: sidewalks, street lighting, landscaping, signs (were these things to be done earlier, they would be torn up in the course of construction of the area's enterprises). In G/7088, there were thirty-seven parcels and over one hundred applicants.

Altogether, the local Kafar Kanna industrial area, represented by G/7088, had become an already accomplished enclave, around which planning for Zipporit D–E continued.

Figure 3.5 Aerial Photo of Kafar Kanna Industrial Area during Construction (1994)

Zipporit D–E

The Joint Municipal Industrial Authority

I turn now to the strand of events in connection with efforts by Kafar Kanna, Meshhed, and Upper Nazareth to set up a municipal industrial authority through which joint control and management and tax revenue sharing were to be effected. It will be recalled that a decision on this had been taken early on, in May 1993.

At first, the Ministry of Industry, acting through HaPaT, had set this as a condition for proceeding with statutory planning. There were some meetings on the subject, but efforts soon fizzled out. As one person with whom I spoke put it, once Meshhed and Kafar Kanna protest had been disarmed, the joint authority no longer seemed pressing to Upper Nazareth. Rassem Khamaisi was apparently one of those instrumental in convincing HaPaT to relax the requirement of a joint authority before submission of detailed plans. The statutory process was important, he argued for it would entail an official change of land-use zoning from agriculture to industry, and the two Arab local councils would come to negotiations with something in their hands, some resources that would make them desirable partners. The head of the Upper Nazareth Economic Development Unit, directly involved in the establishment and marketing of Zipporit A, also took the position that it would be best to delay attempts to set up the joint industrial authority until after Kafar Kanna and Meshhed each had their own industrial area in place (he referred to the larger Zipporit D–E and not to Kafar Kanna's 70 dunam G/7088).

But there were also objective circumstances complicating efforts to set up the joint authority. For one thing, the Upper Nazareth industrial area, like Upper Nazareth itself, enjoyed National Priority Region (NPR) A status, while Kafar Kanna and Meshhed, like the region in general, had B status (see chapter 2 for an account of how such differential classification had come into being). Investments located in NPR A would be entitled to significantly higher government benefits. Second the ILA charged lessees of state-owned land in Kafar Kanna and Meshhed jurisdiction considerably more than it did leasers of land in Upper Nazareth's Zipporit. This stemmed in part directly from the NPR classification.

The ILA had set its land-lease fees for industrial developers at 31 percent of the locally obtaining price for land between willing buyers and willing sellers in the open market in NPR A and at 51 percent of that price in NPR B.[23] The "locally obtaining price of land," however, was itself a source of difference between new (Jewish) regional industrial areas and those in immediately adjacent Arab localities. The government Appraiser, an official within the Treasury, set the locally obtaining price for land between willing buyers and willing sellers in the new regional industrial areas at a low rate because these were places where there had been no demand for land previously, and the government and the local authority were attempting to attract investors. In the Arab towns, there had previously been no land available for industry, and therefore no market, so the government Appraiser made do with taking the price that had obtained locally for residential land. Inasmuch as the demand for such land in the Arab towns was high and the supply was limited (due to Ministry of Interior restraints on updating outline plans to keep pace with growing needs and the absence of state land within the outline plan), the open market price for residential land was high. Thus, for Upper Nazareth's Zipporit, 31 percent (NPR A status) x NIS 77 thousand (low open market price set by the Appraiser) gave a price of NIS 23.87 thousand per dunam for the industrial investor. For Kafar Kanna and Meshhed, 51 percent (NPR B status) x NIS 154 thousand (high open market price set by the Appraiser) gave a price of NIS 78.54 thousand for the industrial investor (3.29 times what the investor in Zipporit A was required to pay). Similar systematic comparative differences were found throughout Galilee (with the ratio of the price for industrial land in the Arab towns to that in the Jewish town/regional industrial area ranging from 2.15 to 3.5). The differences between Kafar Kanna and Meshhed, on the one hand, and Upper Nazareth's Zipporit A, on the other, in (a) benefits under the Encouragement of Capital Investment Law (NPR classification), and in (b) the price of land charged by the ILA to industrial investors, were undoubtedly an impediment to setting up a joint industrial authority.

When the new Rabin government took office in 1992, it committed itself to equalizing NPR status for industrial areas in Arab towns in Galilee to that of neighboring regional industrial areas. It took quite awhile to accomplish this, for the government had set itself to revamping the entire NPR map, and the Arab industrial areas were only a small element of the change. During the time that making the change was in process, Arab national and local leaders would use what occasions they could to keep the issue alive politically. Rassem Khamaisi explained to me:

> The appeal was to the principles of justice and equality—principles to which the Labor government was committed. The threat of an appeal to the High Court of Justice on the basis of those principles always lurked in the background (although of course, it never came to that). And, then, we mobilized supporting forces such as the Association for Civil Liberties.... I would show maps to people, point out the different status of the Upper Nazareth industrial area as distinguished from the Meshhed-Kafar Kanna area. People were simply not aware—"It can't be that there would be discrimination like that," they would say. And then I would show them the map—a matter of overcoming unawareness—then, all of a sudden, everyone saw that the situation was not right and needed correction.

In August 1995, the status of the area of Zipporit D–E (including G/7088) was equalized with Zipporit A–B–C. In this particular case, the Ministry of Industry followed the simple procedure of referring to the entire area as Zipporit and extending the NPR boundaries to include it all (Amendment 2 to the Encouragement of Capital Investment Order 1995; see "Legislation Cited"). At the same time, industrial areas in other Arab towns in Galilee were brought up to the preferred NPR A status hitherto enjoyed only by the nearby Jewish localities (Amendment 3 to the Encouragement of Capital Investment Order 1995; see "Legislation Cited"). This was in addition to two towns whose status had been raised nine months earlier. It may be pointed out that, at least in the case of Kafar Kanna, it was only the status of the industrial area that was changed and not that of the area of the town proper, and only regarding benefits for industry and not other benefits (housing, education, welfare, labor, and income tax), benefits that residents of Jewish towns with NPR A status did enjoy.

One month later, the Israel Lands Council decided to equalize land prices for industry in Arab localities to those in effect in neighboring regional industrial areas. The equal prices were to be in effect for a period of two years, in each case beginning with the date that allocation of plots to investors would begin (Decision 736, Israel Lands Council, 28 September 1995). Treasury officials had fought this decision with tenacity, and, indeed, continued to do so even after the council's decision. During this period, council decisions that had the effect of lowering ILA income required the countersignature of the minister of finance before they would become effective. The minister of finance did not sign the decision until May 1996.

One Treasury official explained to me that it was not good to meddle with the principle of free market prices. But the fact that an industrial investor would have to pay over three times as much for a plot in Kafar Kanna, just a few hundred meters away from Zipporit A,[24] was a function of where jurisdictional boundaries ran, zoning restrictions/permissions, and whether the ILA made land available or not. Governments in this age are constantly intervening in market processes. In the present case, the Encouragement of Capital Investment Law and the ILA land-pricing practices were interventions that had made it worthwhile for Phoenicia to build a new plant in Zipporit A. For that matter, the very construction of the industrial area by the government, not to mention the establishment of Upper Nazareth itself, was an intervention. When the government chooses, it intervenes.

There was, in addition to NPR status and differential land prices, another objective factor holding back progress on the joint industrial authority. This had to do with Emeq Yizre'el Regional Council objections to the transfer of about 2,783 dunam to Upper Nazareth, 2,261 from its jurisdiction and 522 dunam of land without municipal status, for the construction of Zipporit B and Zipporit C (see figure 1.1) (*KT* 5692, 1653, 13 July 1995).[25]

The request for this land transfer had first gone to the Barzilai Boundary Commission in March 1992. It will be recalled that at that time, the Mivnei Ta'asiya program for Zipporit had called for residential construction in Zipporit B and C. Emeq Yizre'el had agreed to the transfer, knowing that Upper Nazareth, the city, was capable of absorbing large numbers of new residents and providing them municipal services, whereas Emeq Yizre'el itself was not. In September of that year, the boundary commission submitted an interim report recommending the transfer. One year later there was an exchange of letters between Upper Nazareth and the regional council recording the understanding that if the requested territory were to be rezoned for uses other than residential, arrangements for joint operation (Upper Nazareth–Emeq Yizre'el) would be considered. But eventually the regional council reversed its earlier acquiescence, and in April 1994, it asked the boundary commission, which had not yet submitted a final report, to reconsider. It was clear by this time that the residential program for the area had been shelved and that Upper Nazareth intended to develop industry there. In January 1995, the boundary commission submitted its final report and upheld its earlier interim recommendation. In June, the minister of the interior signed the order giving Upper Nazareth jurisdiction over the area (*KT* 5692, 1653, 13 July 1995), and in July, the Hoshaya moshav, a member settlement of Emeq Yizre'el Regional Council, petitioned the HCJ against the manner in which the boundary commission had performed its task and the minister's adoption of that body's recommendation (Bagatz [High Court of Justice] 4522/95; see also related Bagatz 4767/95 and Bagatz 4824/95).

In an expert opinion submitted on Hoshaya's behalf, it was argued that the Emeq Yizre'el Regional Council too was capable of developing industry, and were it to do so, it would be more responsive to the environmental concerns of its member settlements than would Upper Nazareth, while there was no reason for the regional council to forgo for Upper Nazareth's sake the tax and levy income from such an industrial area (Derman 1995).

So long as the HCJ case was pending, there was a possibility that plans for Zipporit B and C would be aborted, or that Upper Nazareth would have to share with the Emeq Yizre'el Regional Council in developing the industrial area. Indeed, in December 1994 and January 1995 (prior to the minister's order transferring jurisdiction), the regional council and Upper Nazareth exchanged counter drafts of an agreement between them on partnership. Either outcome (abortion of the expansion or Upper Nazareth–Emeq Yizre'el partnership) would have direct ramifications for the partnership arrangement that could be made with the two Arab towns. It might be pointed out that in the first case, Meshhed and Kafar Kanna together might end up with an industrial area (net) nearly twice the size of the area zoned for industry in Upper Nazareth's Zipporit A. It is likely that the latter town would be reluctant to enter an arrangement in which it was not the major partner. In any event, the HCJ suit against the transfer of jurisdiction to Upper Nazareth was another factor obstructing progress on a joint Upper Nazareth–Kafar Kanna–Meshhed municipal industrial authority.

On 19 February 1996, the HCJ dismissed Hoshaya's suit (and the other associated suits) against the transfer of jurisdiction. Given Emeq Yizre'el's determined fight against the transfer and its unambiguous defeat in the court, Menahem Ariav now declared that the possibility of Emeq Yizre'el–Upper Nazareth cooperation on the industrial area was a dead letter. With the equalization of NPR status for Zipporit D–E with that of Upper Nazareth several months earlier, and the equalization of land prices that was now awaiting the signature of the minister of finance, the way was now cleared for the active pursuit of a joint industrial authority that would include Meshhed and Kafar Kanna.

The Ministry of Industry (the unit in charge of industrial development in national priority regions) was interested in promoting the establishment of joint municipal industrial authorities in all of the several cases where industrial areas involving more than one local authority were being established, and particularly in this one, both because it entailed cooperation between Jewish and Arab towns and because of its scope. "Think of the size of it," one HaPaT agent said to me, "this is an area in which one hundred thousand people will come to work—that's more than most cities in Israel. It *has* to have an industrial authority."

At this time, the Ministry of Industry had engaged outside project management consultants to assist in several places where more than one local authority was attempting to set up joint industrial parks. One of these was the Upper Nazareth–Kafar Kanna–Meshhed project. During 1996 there were a number of meetings devoted to this. Among the questions being dealt with was the basis for division of the tax revenue. One Upper Nazareth representative explained to me:

> The simplest and most straightforward way might be according to area—but then, the matter of occupancy ought to be a factor. What if 90 percent of my area is occupied and only 10 percent of Kafar Kanna's is? Also, what *kind* of occupation of territory? A marble plant might have only a small area covered and then have a large outside area. Maybe the key ought to be the number of workers in each locality's portion, or perhaps even where the workers come from—it's a complex issue.

It would seem clear that the "complex issue" of how to divide the tax revenue would be a central feature of any agreement. But one of those involved in the process thought that the parties were getting bogged down in detail (not the manner of dividing the tax revenue), rather than pushing to reach an agreement and actually set up the joint authority. "Menahem Ariav is lukewarm," reported another of those with whom I spoke, "he agrees to the joint industrial authority, but he holds back." One government official involved in trying to advance the process thought that "Ariav is not interested—I tell him about the advantages of control inherent in doing it together, but he tells me in return that the presence of Arabs will deter Jewish investors." But there was also another matter exercising the mayor of Upper Nazareth. Now that attempts at the HCJ to prevent the transfer of land for the expansion of the industrial area westward had been set aside, the DPBC was handling the statutory process for Zipporit B. I was told that hundreds of objections had been lodged, many of them on the part of residents of Kafar Kanna and Meshhed. "I am not running ahead with the joint project," declared Menahem Ariav, "until all those objections are removed." Early in 1996 he had already told the Arab towns, "When you have an industrial area, that's when we'll work together."

There were financial considerations also. A municipal industrial authority cannot set itself up and function during an initial period without a budgetary source outside the industrial area itself. In 1996, those in the Ministry of Industry who were pushing for the establishment of the joint authority were attempting to secure an allocation for that purpose. Had they been successful in this, it might well have given the additional leverage required to make the joint authority come into being.

All in all, the assessment of one source close to the scene was that "the local authorities are apprehensive about a body like the joint authority—it would be a competing center of power, and mayors are in no hurry to give up power and control." And it was possible to fall back on the idea that each town would simply administer on its own the industrial area that would be established in its territory; these would simply be independent but adjacent areas.

It may be pointed out that Upper Nazareth already enjoyed a measure of control without the price of having to *share* control in a joint authority. Plans for Zipporit D–E were being submitted for approval not only to the Mevo Ha'amaqim Local Planning and Building Commission (which was invested with planning jurisdiction there), but also to the Upper Nazareth Local Planning and Building Commission. That was only natural and desirable, it was explained to me, in order to make sure that plans were consistent with Zipporit A.

The Statutory Process

Meanwhile, on the statutory process front, there had been (as mentioned earlier) a preliminary hearing on plans for Zipporit D–E at the Mevo Ha'amaqim Planning and Building Commission in September 1995. The original plan called for 1,035 dunam net for industry in a total area of 1,956 dunam. In February 1996, the LPBC recommended that the DPBC deposit the plan, subject to conditions.

One of the conditions was that tables of adjusted land rights (*tavla'ot 'izun*) ensuing from reparcellation be drawn up. This was particularly demanding in view of the circumstance that about 60 percent of the land was privately owned. Privately owned land in the Arab towns means small parcels, generally with each of them having multiple owners. Now development projects entail the planning of infrastructure and allocation of land for other public purposes. The PBL (§§188–196) empowers the LPBC to expropriate up to 40 percent of an owner's land for such purposes without paying compensation. The PBL (§§120–128) also makes provision for the procedure known as reparcellation (*'ichud vehaluqa mehadash*), in which multiple parcels are combined and then repartitioned in a manner congruent with the demands of the land use and infrastructure being planned. The law requires (a) that each owner receive in return a parcel of land as close as possible to the location of his or her original plot, and (b) that the share of his or her new parcel in the totality of land being reassigned be proportionately equal to the share of his or her old parcel in the combined tract. The law further provides that when deviations from such proportionality are unavoidable, the owner affected will pay/receive compensation. The table of adjusted land rights is meant to serve the reparcellation process. It should be mentioned that when agricultural land is rezoned for other uses (residence, commerce, industry) and detailed plans are prepared, the value of an owner's land increases far beyond what he or she has lost to the requirements of infrastructure and other public uses.

In response to the LPBC February 1996 condition, HaPaT began work on the tables of adjusted land rights. This, I was told, was more difficult in Meshhed because of the disposition of the private holdings there in relation to where the roads and other infrastructure systems would have to pass. It didn't help things that about 87 percent of the land slated for the industrial area in Meshhed was privately owned (compared with only about 40 percent in Kafar Kanna). In any event, sometime around April 1996, Meshhed, prompted by the private landowners, asked that planning be halted in its jurisdiction. It appears that Meshhed landowners were opposed to the reparcellation and the proposed rezoning. They were apparently motivated by considerations other than the increase in value that, at least in theory, would accrue to their land. In chapter 5, I shall return to this subject in the course of dealing with the image of traditionalism.

This turn of events was an opportunity for Meshhed to return to the idea that it could be and ought to be a partner in the joint industrial area, even without contributing land from its own jurisdiction. It will be recalled that this idea had been broached by the two Arab towns back in 1992/93, at which time it had simply been ignored by government figures dealing with proposals for a joint industrial area, and had been deflected by Menahem Ariav on the grounds that it was Upper Nazareth that had done the work enabling Zipporit A to come into being.

Now, in 1996, Menahem Ariav declared: "Kafar Kanna will be a part—they have a dowry to contribute. But Meshhed? They can't be part only on Upper Nazareth land." A former senior district official explained to me that one of Ariav's concerns was not to be perceived by the voters in his city as giving away land to the Arabs. As in 1992/93, Meshhed's position and Ariav's response go straight to the key issues of territory and jurisdiction.

By October 1996, plans for Zipporit D–E were ready to go from the LPBC to the DPBC. At a meeting at the DPBC on 24 December, the district planner conveyed to those involved in the planning the requests for changes and additions arising from his preliminary examination of the plan.[26] Planners were asked to (a) take the privately owned Meshhed land out of the plan, with the exception of the roads required by the plan; (b) provide tables of adjusted land rights; (c) provide a programmatic analysis giving the number of workers to be employed in the industrial area compared with a demographic analysis of the entire region for which the plan was relevant, including a juxtaposition of future needs with the existing situation; (d) show stages of implementation in accordance with conclusions of the programmatic analysis; and (e) add environmental protection provisions. It was stipulated that the planners were to have the amended plan and the additions back for consideration by the DPBC by the middle of February. It was also stipulated that the plan would be divided into two: Zipporit D (state land) and Zipporit E (private land). That way, in case of delay due to objections regarding the privately owned land, it would be possible to go ahead with approval of the portion on state land.

I was told that at the meeting of 24 December, the district planner had suggested that there really was no need for Zipporit D–E, and this is what lay behind the demand for a programmatic analysis. He apparently also asked for an assessment of the effect of the 450 or so dunam slated for industry in Kafar Kanna's portion of Zipporit D–E on transportation in the entire Northern District (although this latter request is not on record). The sense of the meeting, in the eyes of one of the participants, was that the district planner and Upper Nazareth did not want Kafar Kanna to have an industrial area that might compete with Zipporit A, and that they were going to see to it that the proposal did not get approved. Perhaps there were tears lurking behind the eyes and the voice of the person who told me this—I cannot say for sure. But his frustration was evident.

The municipal engineer of Kafar Kanna, also, was dismayed at the prospect that his town would be left with only the 70 dunam of G/7088, which was already all marketed, while there was a long list of further applicants—and not only from Kafar Kanna. "Don't forget," he pointed out, "the effect of G/7088 now being classed as National Priority Region A."[27]

During the summer of 1996, I had had occasion to ask the district planner about Zipporit D–E. "It's not necessary that every town have an industrial area of its own," he told me, "rather, there should be large, joint regional industrial areas.... [W]hat the Arab towns need locally are small areas of 30 to 40 dunam for manufacture—to get the workshops out from under the houses ... but there's no reason why a large Arab entrepreneur can't apply for a spot in the regional industrial area." I had the impression, though I am not able to say with certainty, that he saw the plans for Zipporit D–E not as a stepping stone toward bringing a large, joint regional industrial area into being, but rather, as the unnecessary result of a narrow localistic vision. In this view of things, Zipporit A already served as a large regional industrial area, even though Upper Nazareth alone controlled and managed it, and was the sole beneficiary of the municipal revenue it might generate.

Recall that in 1993 those involved in planning Zipporit D–E had foreseen final approval by November 1994. That kind of timetable would have been consistent with the thrust and drive that had characterized the statutory process in getting G/IC/125 (Zipporit A) approved and its anchor plant Phoenicia into place. But progress on G/9155 (Zipporit D–E) was turning out to be far different. "There have been changes all through the process," I was told, "and alternative solutions—everyone finds his own solutions." Some suggested that the architect was slow, but another of the planners with whom I spoke said that wasn't really what was holding things up: "It's entirely natural, even desirable, for the planning process on something this big to take four years." In addition, this plan, unlike G/IC/125, was not being handled through the expeditious

RICC. For one thing, the large proportion of privately owned land meant that a great number of objections might be expected; and second, the availability of the PBPL had lapsed for plans not already in process under it.

Moreover, there were the stages in the statutory process that could stretch out, seemingly forever. Regarding the first of these—the recommendation or decision to approve for deposit "subject to conditions"—one DPBC official explained to me that "it sometimes takes years to meet the conditions." The second was the preliminary examination, a point at which the district planner was able to stipulate that changes be made or other supporting material be provided before the submitted plan would ever be placed on the DPBC agenda. "There is actually no limit to the length of time that this can drag out—[it is] a way of choking a plan," another official told me. Thus, I discovered that the statements "the plan is ready to go up to the DPBC" or "the plan will go to the DPBC tomorrow"—statements I heard on more than one occasion in reference to G/9155—were slippery indeed.

Was it the intention in this case to choke the plan? "One can't say that," I was told by one of the planners. "The things the district planner requested were within the realm of professional warrant. Part of the problem is that there is no overarching master policy for the Arab population—policy principles that could be appealed to in order to get things moving." Rassem Khamaisi, head of the Strategic Planning Center in Kafar Kanna, put it this way:

> The district planner can logically require demonstration of demand—but it's hard to demonstrate demand for something that doesn't exist. How do you demonstrate a changed future, how do you prove the future? And then, not to approve the industrial area acts as the first block that keeps a changed future from coming into being. Activist development means to *create* demand.

One may consider, by contrast, the establishment of Upper Nazareth's industrial area, Zipporit A. In that case, the policy of Judaizing Galilee gave sense and direction to development planning that originated, as it were, *outside* the statutory planning system and provided thrust for the statutory process. Ultimately, it was this too that enabled activists to push on ahead of proper statutory approval and licensing—steps that in turn were used to apply pressure on the authorities ("now that we have invested so much, it would be too costly to stop").

But plans for Zipporit D–E were caught up in the practices of the domain of the statutory process. There may have been nothing untoward in this of itself, but there was nothing to grab on to for support in the domain of development planning. One should not underestimate the burden of that situation. Back in the summer of 1997, with plans still not ready to go back to the DPBC with the requested additions, one might have legitimately wondered whether Zipporit D–E, even in Kafar Kanna's jurisdiction alone, would ever come to pass. By the same token, it seemed remote, indeed, that any kind of Jewish-Arab partnership in a municipal industrial authority would eventually arise.

A qualification is in order here regarding the distinction between development planning and the statutory planning system. Policymakers interested in promoting the Judaization of Galilee were able to harness the statutory system to their ends, something that those who sought to advance the idea of a large *joint* industrial area were not. But the flow from policy to statutory planning spotlighted here should not be allowed to obscure the fact that the statutory system does not lie *outside* of policy—neither in regard to Judaization of Galilee nor with regard to development for the Arab towns. As in all bureaucratic access, here too the political is part and parcel of the domain. The point is that plans for Zipporit D–E languished in the very same system that moved Zipporit A ahead with all dispatch.

At the end of 2001, the case of Zipporit D–E and the joint industrial authority with Upper Nazareth was still pending. The programmatic analysis requested by the DPBC was prepared in June 1997. In May 1999, the Ministry of the Environment demanded an EIA. In January 2000, a DPBC subcommittee divided the plan into two, according to the division between ILA-owned and privately owned land, to facilitate expediting the ILA-owned part. Also, the Ministry of the Environment declared that it was willing to accept an environmental survey that would be less detailed than the EIA, and it was decided to deposit both plans on condition. In September 2000, the CPAL gave its conditional approval to the plan for the ILA-owned land. As of May 2001, however, not all the DPBC conditions had been met for that part of the plan, and a DPBC planning official issued a letter itemizing the changes that still had to be made and the approvals that still had to be secured.

In August 2000, Kafar Kanna and Upper Nazareth signed a declaration of principles regarding the establishment of a joint industrial authority. A meeting in June 2001 set out the principles for the inclusion of Meshhed in the joint authority. Apparently, Meshhed had also requested that planning be resumed on the privately owned land in its jurisdiction—it would have something to bring to the future joint industrial area. Meanwhile, in 2001, Upper Nazareth's Zipporit B was being developed, and planning for Zipporit C was getting underway.

I should like, at this point, to step away somewhat from the flow of events in order to consider three subjects: (a) territory and jurisdiction; (b) the image of Arab traditionalism, which I will argue is a mediating factor in the exclusion of the Arab towns from regional development; and (c) the appropriation of Arab town development needs and potential by the implanted Jewish settlements of Upper Nazareth and Karmi'el. But this, of course, is merely to gain other perspectives on the events I have been describing, part of my attempt to understand the way in which power works to shape the economic development of the Arab towns in Galilee. Chapter 7 will return to the maneuver and engagement involved in concrete cases in which Arab towns have come to challenge the Arab/Jewish divide in regional development.

CHAPTER 4

Land, Territory, and Jurisdiction

The Experience of Land Loss

It will be recalled that in the course of protesting against the establishment of the Phoenicia glass factory and negotiating with Upper Nazareth and representatives of the national government, Kafar Kanna and Meshhed entertained expectations that they would be admitted to Zipporit as partners right from the beginning. The best-case scenario for the Arab representatives was that Zipporit A would be reconstituted as a joint industrial park without waiting for the later stage at which the two Arab towns would have statutory plans and development on land in their own jurisdictions to contribute to the joint park.

But Menahem Ariav, the mayor of Upper Nazareth, had deflected this demand by declaring that having brought the planning and marketing of Zipporit A to its current state, it was not his intention to give them up. For their part, national officials simply avoided giving a clear response to these expectations of the Arab towns. Their evasiveness found expression in the ambiguous, equivocal wording in the press reports at the time and probably in the statements by the Arab leaders that occasioned those reports (see, e.g., A. Shehada 1993). It is likely, though, that having the aspiration for immediate partnership shunted aside was made easier to accept by the other expectations then current that the statutory process for Zipporit D–E would be nearly as swift as had been that for Zipporit A (expectations that were, as has been seen, not borne out by events). As for the government officials, the expectations of rapid progress, whether promoted cynically by them or not, would have made it easier for them to ignore the demand for immediate partnership.

Subsequently, Meshhed residents who owned land in the Meshhed area slated for inclusion in Zipporit D–E demanded that planning for industry on their land be halted. Meshhed officials took the position that the town could be and ought to be a partner in the joint industrial area, even without contributing land from its own jurisdiction, but this was met by a firm declaration of the Upper Nazareth mayor that Meshhed could not be a part only on Upper Nazareth land. The question as to whether Meshhed and Kafar Kanna *could* be part of a joint industrial area without putting in land from their own jurisdiction was answered by events and actors in the field. But one ought, I suggest, to interrogate the self-evident nature of that answer. After all, the land on which Upper Nazareth was developing Zipporit A had been until just then without municipal jurisdiction; it lay alongside Meshhed, not Upper Nazareth, and it was only through a decision of the minister of the interior that Upper Nazareth had gained jurisdiction over it. This, on the one hand. On the other hand, there was the sense of injury expressed by the Arab townsmen and by Arab leaders that this piece of land, which had been part of the village lands of Meshhed and was within the village boundaries set by the Mandate government, and which had in former times served as grazing land for the local herders, had been plucked up, as it were, and awarded to Upper Nazareth. And more: there was the sense, on the part of the Arab inhabitants of the region, of being squeezed and closed in upon, and closely associated with that, an awareness of being excluded from development (see, e.g., Awawdy 1992; Farhi Hassan interviewed in Rozen 1996; other articles in the Arab press cited in the previous chapter; also, Interviews).

These are the subjects I wish to address at this point. I will summon here the experience of land loss through state takeover by various methods of land formerly owned and used by the Arab inhabitants, the shortage of land in Arab localities, and the effect of the Jewish settlements established in the midst of Arab territory. These are elements that feed the sense of being hedged in. I will then return to more immediate ethnographic material to show how the conception of Zipporit in terms of militant struggle had direct territorial implications. But long before the plan for Zipporit was formulated as a wedge—a Jewish salient intended to break up Arab territory—this land had been left without municipal status. I will discuss the nature of the village boundaries recorded in the British Survey of Palestine and suggest that the land left without municipal status when the state established Arab local authorities and set their boundaries of jurisdiction may be seen as a measure of the weakness of the Arab towns. I will conclude this chapter by arguing that questions of power and the ability to press one's claims further express themselves in the interlocality dispute over land for development in the arena provided by the boundary investigation commission.

All these are the *territorial* aspects of Zipporit's having been established in Kafar Kanna's and Meshhed's backyard with only a promise of future participation by the Arab towns—and that only on condition that they would add land from their own jurisdictions to the industrial area, and only from the time they would do so. These will be the subject of the present chapter. Chapter 5, focusing on the image of Arab traditionalism that informs academic studies of Arab entrepreneurship as well as official dealings with the Arab towns, will discuss, inter alia, the Meshhed landowners' demand that planning for industrial development for their land be halted, and will present the objective factors that lay behind that demand.

But first, to the matters of land and jurisdiction. One needs to begin with a consideration of Arab land loss during and in the wake of the Israel war of independence. The problem of the Palestinian refugees and appropriate compensation is, of course, a serious issue in its own right. That is not my subject, however. I refer, rather, to loss of land by Arabs who remained in Israel. This took place in the setting of general wartime dislocation; yet there were certain distinctive state actions and practices that were crucial in determining the extent and impact of that dislocation on those who became the Arab citizens of Israel.

The Experience of Land Loss

The Definition of "Absentee" and Its Uses Vis-à-Vis the Land of Those Who Remained

In October 1948, the Cultivation of Waste Land Regulations (see "Legislation Cited" 1948a) empowered the minister of agriculture to take over for a period not to exceed two years and eleven months the extensive areas of abandoned Arab agricultural land and to assign them to (Jewish) cultivators. In January 1949, the maximum period of occupation by the minister of agriculture was extended to five years. However, the Custodian of Absentee Property, under the Absentee Property Regulations of 1948 (see "Legislation Cited" 1948b), remained the ultimate legal authority. His function was to protect and preserve absentee property, but he had not received the legal right to dispose of it (Peretz 1958: 149–161).[1]

In March 1950, the Absentee Property Law (which replaced the earlier Absentee Property Regulations) enabled the Custodian to sell land to a development authority when such a body would be established by the Knesset; any other sale or transfer of ownership was prohibited (see "Legislation Cited" 1950a, §19(a)(1)). The Development Authority was indeed established in August that year ("Legislation Cited" 1950b). The law (§3(4)(a)) permitted the Development Authority to sell land only to the state, the JNF, a municipal authority, or to an institution for the resettlement of landless Arabs. In September 1953, the Custodian sold all of the property in his possession to the Development Authority. According to a review of activities in the *Israel Government Yearbook* (1959: 75), the JNF purchased 2,324,000 dunam from the Development Authority.

Now, the Custodian of Absentee Property stated in January 1953 that 2.5 million of the 4 million dunam of Arab land then held by him were cultivated (Peretz 1958: 144, 165, 181). Jewish agriculture had encompassed just 700,000 dunam on the eve of the 1948 war; by 1950/51, this had grown to 3.3 million dunam (*Israel Government Yearbook* 1959: 241). The inconsistency in dates in these data is only apparent. Land had been occupied by Jewish cultivators under the Cultivation of Waste Land Regulations even before the formal takeover by the Custodian of Absentee Property. The Development Authority's purchase of the land from the Custodian was a second step in legalizing the occupation and did not disturb the actual occupiers. The same process was repeated when the Development Authority sold the land to the JNF (see Peretz 1958: 180–181). Despite its name and the authority to carry out development activity provided by the law, the Development Authority was actually circumscribed in its activity to effecting these transfers of property. As the intervening step between the Custodian and the JNF, it was a legal fiction, and that is how one of my ILA sources described it to me.

Writing of the Development Authority in 1955 (English translation, 1956), Avraham Granott, chairman of the JNF Board of Directors in the 1950s, used the term "legal fiction" in reference to another aspect of that institution. He described the Development Authority Law as "based upon a sort of legal fiction. It was not desired to transfer abandoned land to government ownership, as this would be interpreted as confiscation of the abandoned property."[2]

Many of those who were defined as absentee and whose property had been taken over by the Custodian were actually present in Israel at the time. These are the people who became known as the "present absentees." The Absentee Property Law includes in its definition of an absentee owner of property in Israel any individual who at any time subsequent to 29 November 1947 (the date of the United Nations [UN] Partition Resolution) was outside the area that later became Israel or who left his regular place of residence for a place that was held at the time he was there by forces that tried to prevent the establishment of the state or who fought against it after its establishment.

The application of the law was nothing if not activist. Anyone who simply went on a business trip or family visit to neighboring countries in the months between November 1947 and May 1948 was an absentee. All those who sought refuge from the fighting in a neighboring or distant village or town, so long as that place had not yet been conquered by the Israelis, became absentees, including the many who fled at that time to Nazareth (H. Cohen 2000: 68–69). Cohen (71) reports on the case in which the Custodian argued that the Arab residents of Bet Shean who had been transferred to Nazareth by the Haganah itself were to be classified as refugees and their property seized. The Custodian cited the clause in the law that states that a person could not maintain that he was not an absentee merely because he was not responsible for the circumstances that led him to leave his home. Even the residents of the villages of the Triangle who never left their homes were classified as absentees. In this case, Transjordan held the villages at the end of the fighting, but not their farmland to the west, which was under Israeli control. The villages were transferred to Israel by the Rhodes Armistice Agreement of 1949, and the villagers were ostensibly reunited with their lands. Although they had not left their homes, they had been in an area controlled by the Transjordanian Legion and separated from their land, and that was now taken as absentee property (Kislev 1976: 23–24; Cohen 2000: 69).

Through the years, the Custodian has been unflagging in his pursuit of land. Thus, where land is held in shares (a common state of affairs among the Arab population) and some of those shares belong to absentees, or, by virtue of inheritance laws, will belong to absentees, the Custodian takes advantage of suitable opportunities (development, sale, death) to claim his due (Interviews). As a result of the Custodian's activity immediately following the war and since then, the state owns parcels and shares of parcels interspersed among the land owned by the local Arabs throughout their towns and villages.

Closed Areas, Security Zones, and the Manufacture of Waste Land

There were other avenues by which Arabs who remained in Israel lost their land in the period following hostilities or in the lulls between them in 1948/49. These had to do with the uses of Regulation 125 of the British Defense (Emergency) Regulations (see "Legislation Cited" 1945: 1055) and the Security Zones Regulations ("Legislation Cited" 1949), in conjunction with the Cultivation of Waste Land Regulations ("Legislation Cited" 1948a). Military commanders were empowered by Regulation 125 to declare an area closed. This could be applied to the area of a village's land or to the entire village. Cohen (2000: 68) found that forty-three villages were declared closed areas after they had been taken over by the military. Unable to work their land, the villagers then lost it under the Waste Land regulations. As an example of the blatant cooperation between the IDF (Israel Defense Forces) and the JNF in such matters, Cohen (67) relates how the townspeople of Yafi' near Nazareth lost their most fertile lands in the Jezre'el Valley by such means.

The Security Zones Regulations empowered the minister of defense to clear wide expanses along the borders, not only by closing an area to entry, but also by ordering residents within it to leave. Iqrit and Kafr Bir'im near the Lebanese border were among the places cleared in this way. In this particularly well-known case, the villagers were *asked* to leave and were told that they would soon be allowed to return. Once they were gone, the air force reduced the buildings to rubble. Although the undertaking to allow the villagers to return (which has not been honored to this day, despite HCJ rulings) may have been unique, these were but two of the four hundred or more Palestinian villages taken over during the 1947–1949 period and later destroyed; there are indications (based on General Security Forces statements) that as many as 150 of these, among them Iqrit and Bir'im, were cleared of their population *after* the fighting had subsided (Rabinowitz 1994). Some of the people moved under the Security Zones regulations were transferred across the borders, but many remained in Israel in other locations. In any case, they too lost their land under the Waste Land regulations (Kano 1992: 80–84).[3] It will be recalled that the Cultivation of Waste Land Regulations were promulgated early on, in October 1948. The minister of agriculture accompanied publication of the regulations with an explanation to the effect that the conditions of war had led to the abandonment of lands by their owners. "The good of the state requires," the explanation went on, "that without prejudicing land ownership rights or other property rights, it is necessary to maintain and expand agricultural production as much as possible ("Legislation Cited" 1948a: 8). But obviously, the drive to take over land led well beyond the land that had been abandoned (or cleared) in the heat of battle. It may be observed that considerable overlap between the mandate of the Absentee Property Law and that of the Cultivation of Waste Land Regulations obtained (see Kislev 1976). Kano (1992: 84) cites a statement at a meeting held in 1949 at the Ministry of Agriculture: "It does not matter under which [of the two laws] the land is leased [to Jewish farmers].... [T]he important thing is that these lands will, in the end, belong to the state." So much for the minister's pious declaration concerning property rights. As for those who lost their land, even when they were not strictly absentees under the definition of the Absentee Property Law (e.g., when they had been moved off their land by the army to a location in Israel and were never in a place controlled by hostile forces), so long as they were still in Israel, they joined the ranks of the internal refugees and the present absentees.

The Absentee Property Law did make provision for revocation of absentee status under certain conditions. But the appeal process dragged on interminably, and while some urban property was released to its original owners in this way, very little rural property was (Cohen 2000: 69–70). According to Cohen, government agencies used the process as an opportunity to recruit collaborators. As for the provisions in the Development Authority Law that some of the Authority's land might be used to resettle landless Arabs, Cohen reports (88) that by 1954, 72,500 dunam had been leased to about 3,747 individuals.[4] It should be pointed out, though, that this was neither restoration of the confiscated land nor compensation for it, but rather leasehold, generally for a period of one year at a time.

In 1953, the Knesset enacted the Land Acquisition (Validation of Acts and Compensation) Law (see "Legislation Cited"). The twofold intention was (a) to bolster the legality of the takeover of land under the Absentee Property Law and the Cultivation of Waste Land Regulations, and (b) to finally provide compensation for former owners who were present in Israel (Peretz 1958: 184–187). Jiryis (1976: 96) points out that the earlier laws and regulations had been temporary in nature and linked to the emergency security situation, and that they had been phrased in terms of seizing possession, not ownership, from the original Arab owners. The Land Acquisition Law was intended to take legal *ownership*. According to the new law, a government minister would issue a certificate to the effect that the property in question (a) had not been in the possession of its owner as of 1 April 1952; (b) had been used or allocated between 14 May 1948 and 1 April 1952 for vital development purposes, settlement, or security; and (c) was still needed for one of those purposes. Such property would become the legal possession of the Development Authority. The former owner would receive compensation in cash or, if agriculture was his chief source of income and he had no other land, the Development Authority was required, at his request, to offer other property.

Cohen (2000: 84) gives information based on state archives indicating that over 1.2 million dunam were transferred to the Development Authority under this law; of these, 704,000 had already been given to the Authority under the Absentee Property Law. Only a small part of the latter belonged to present absentees, but altogether, according to Cohen's sources, of the land dealt with by the Land Acquisition Law, 325,000 dunam had been the property of Arabs still living in Israel. It may be inferred that the part of these 325,000 dunam not taken under the Absentee Property Law had been taken under the Cultivation of Waste Land Regulations.[5] Peretz (1958: 185) estimates that immediately after the war there were thirty thousand internal refugees in Israel. Cohen (2000: 22) puts the figure at over twenty-three thousand or about 15 percent of the Arab population that remained under Israeli control.

Purchase of land under the Land Acquisition Law progressed more slowly than the authorities would have liked (ILA Report for 1964/65 [no 4], 167–168; State Comptroller's Report for 1966 [no 17]: 291–294). One factor was the low compensation being offered. The law, promulgated in 1953, set prices at those that had prevailed in 1950, with the addition of 3 percent interest per year. Due to inflation, however, land prices in 1953 were fourteen to sixteen times what they had been three years earlier (Peretz 1958: 84). And when alternative land was offered in compensation, the land offered was often of inferior quality to that which had been taken (Cohen [2000: 87] cites to this effect Ministry of Agriculture officials speaking in closed forums). On the other hand, the Arab dispossessed were often reluctant to give up their claim to the land that had been theirs, as accepting compensation entailed; similarly, they were reluctant to take in return land that had belonged to fellow Arabs who were now beyond the borders. A third factor delaying the progress of compensation was the fact that registration of land ownership (a process known as "settlement of title") was still pending for considerable portions of the land in question. In its settlement of title campaign, the state was challenging the claims of many who sought to have land registered in their name, and was pressing its own claims (see discussion below). The framers of the Land Acquisition Law had been careful to specify (§ 2(d)) that issuance of a certificate for any parcel of land, as the law provided, would not constitute admission that the state did not already have rights to it.

The reluctance of the Arabs to sign away their claims was countered by certain measures. By 1956, the government made the leasing of land (generally for one year at a time, as noted above) to farmers who had been left without land conditional on making progress in accepting compensation under the Land Acquisition Law (Cohen 2000: 88–89). In 1958, the government began a bona fide rehabilitation program involving loans and grants for the construction of housing where the refugees and present absentees had resettled. In this case, too, the assistance was made conditional on the settlement of claims for confiscated property (91–98). On the other hand, building permits were denied to those who refused to relinquish their claims.[6]

By 1962, 8,310 claims had been settled under the Land Acquisition Law, involving 132,036 dunam (ILA Report for 1961/62: 36). Subsequently, a small number of claims were settled each year. By 1999, a total of 15,922 claims had been settled, involving 205,416 dunam (ILA Report for 1999: 83). It should be noted that in 1973, the Absentee Property (Compensation) Law was enacted (see "Legislation Cited"). Also, in 1989, the ILA decided to increase compensation under both the Absentee Property Law and the Land Acquisition Law (ILA Report for 1999).

Obviously, the government has long desired to have done with this matter. For their part, many Arabs, by now constituting a second generation since the original events, express a desire to simply get on with their affairs. But even when compensation is accepted—and not all have accepted—the past continues to rankle. The wresting of land by arbitrary seizure from those Arab citizens of Israel who by and large had merely been trying to survive the war remains the underlying stratum on which subsequent land relations have played themselves out.

Settlement of Title: Shifting Land Rights

The state's drive to complete registration of title, mentioned above, was the occasion for further land loss among the Arabs of Israel. The Ottoman Land Code of 1858 had made the registration of arable land compulsory, and the keeping of land records was initiated. However, plans in 1912–1913 to carry out a systematic cadastral survey as the basis for registration of title were interrupted by World War I (Gavish and Kark 1993). The British, after some earlier fumbling, began again in 1928 with the Land Settlement Ordinance. This provided for a cadastral survey, producing provisional maps of parcels grouped in blocks which were then used by settlement officers to record and adjudicate claims and to register title (Government of Palestine 1946, vol. 1, chap. 8, sections 2–3: 233–245).

The Ottoman Land Code, which provided the legal basis for claim to title, was continued in force by the British, and subsequently by the Israeli state.[7] The three legal categories of land under the code relevant to the present discussion were *mulk* (land held in absolute freehold); *miri* (state land, usufruct rights to which were granted to any private interest); and *mewat* (waste and unused land). *Mulk* land was restricted to the built-up areas of the villages and towns, and the orchards adjacent to them. *Miri* (usufruct) land was equivalent to the outlying arable land. *Mewat* lands were defined as those situated at a distance from the nearest inhabited place at which a loud human voice could not make itself heard, that is, a mile and a half.

The grant of usufruct rights (*miri* land) was subject to payment of an entrance consideration to the state and an annual tithe. These rights were transferable by inheritance (but not by bequest) and by purchase. They could also be established by undisputed possession and cultivation for a period of ten years (par 78 of the Land Code). *Mewat* land could be granted to usufructuaries (i.e., converted to *miri*) if it were developed or revived with state permission. In keeping with the Ottoman desire to stimulate cultivation and engender tax revenue, such grant of *mewat* land to a reviver was free of the initial entrance payment (Goadby and Doukhan 1935: 17–51; Granott 1952: 85–94; Ben Shemesh 1953: 131–134; Gerber 1987: 69).[8] It is important to note, however, that in 1921 the British enacted the Mewat Land Ordinance (see "Legislation Cited"), which made it illegal henceforth to revive *mewat* land without first obtaining permission from the Lands Department.

As indicated above, the Ottoman Land Code provided the legal basis on which the British carried out settlement of title. By 1948, the British had completed such land settlement in the coastal area of Palestine, including a narrow strip along the coast of Western Galilee; the Yizre'el, Bet She'an, and Jordan valleys; areas currently occupied by the Galil HaTachton Regional Council; eastern Upper Galilee; and most of the area of the Nazareth-Tur'an mountains (but land title had not yet been settled in a relatively small area just to the east of Nazareth). It will be seen that the area completed did not include central Galilee, although preliminary surveys had been carried out in part of Biq'at Bet Hakerem (see Gavish and Kark 1993: 79 and map on page 77).

The Israeli state took up the task of completing registration of title in its territory, with the bulk of the process taking place between the end of the 1950s and the end of the 1960s. It was a project perceived as urgent, since it impinged on the state takeover of land under the Absentee Property Law, the Development Authority Law, and the Land Acquisition Law. Moreover, as will be noted below, Israeli legislative and juridical practices having to do with private claims of title under the provisions of the Ottoman Land Code impelled the state to move quickly during the 1960s.

The Israeli state saw registration of title as a way of establishing state ownership, as distinguished from and opposed to private ownership, in the lands it claimed—a way to prevent the takeover and alienation of state land by elements defined as hostile.[9] This was, it would appear, a twist introduced into land relations by the perception of struggle over land defined in national-ethnic terms.

Writing in 1983, Hilleli[10] stated that over thousands of years, the successive rulers had always seen the land as belonging to the sovereign, and, indeed, that the Ottomans saw this as a condition for the survival of the regime (576–577). However, during Ottoman times, Hilleli goes on, "hundreds of thousands of dunam of *miri* and *mewat* land passed from state to private ownership via the channel provided by paragraph 78 of the Ottoman Land Code, that is, by possession [occupation]" (580).

But it should be observed that although under the Ottomans the *ultimate* ownership of *miri* land resided in the state, the arrangement of usufruct was the primary system by which land rights were allocated to individuals (see

Kedar 1998: 668; see also R. Shehadeh 1982, who is cited by Kedar). Thus, Goadby and Doukhan (1935: 60–61) include *miri* as state-domain public lands (i.e., land subject to the control of the government of Palestine) only where the *miri* usufruct has lapsed (*mahlul*). Although Granott (1952) classifies *miri* as state land, he is careful to specify that by 1912, the rights of the owners of *miri* land were "on the same footing as those of an owner subject to no restriction" (89). And, continues Granott regarding the Ottoman land system, so long as the land is used by individuals "for agricultural cultivation, for building, or for some other useful purpose ... the State does not assert any claim to it while the owners occupying it can do with it what they please" (90). Granott also notes that even under the Ottomans, the *mahlul*, by which owners forfeited their claim to the land if they did not cultivate it, had fallen into desuetude.

Altogether, the picture of Ottoman land tenure that emerges with regard to *miri* is that of a variable bundle of property rights. Conceptually, this is entirely consistent both with anthropological treatments of the subject of land rights (see entries on land, land ownership, and property in Hunter and Whitten 1976 and Seymour-Smith 1986) and, for example, with Alterman's 1999 analysis of the subject in present-day Israel itself. Notwithstanding the Ottoman concept of *raqaba* (ultimate residual ownership), the category of *miri* was not a means by which the state guarded its land, but rather, an instrument by which the population had access to and control of the land for its own use.

Now Gerber (1987: 68–71) is unequivocal in arguing that registration of title as provided for by the Ottoman land laws was in no way an attempt to prevent state lands from gradually falling into private hands. Rather, registration of title had to do with encouraging land use and the orderly collection of taxes. According to Gerber, the most significant change brought about by the 1858 law was that from that point on, the state could now issue title deeds to unoccupied and formerly unclaimed land (72). By contrast, settlement of title under the Israeli regime turns out to have been a way of severing, or at least curtailing, the hitherto taken-for-granted connection between the local Arab population and the land they occupied and cultivated. This was a new use of the conceptualization of *miri* as state land. It emerges that Hilleli (1983: 576–577, quoted above) has merely projected the Zionist preoccupation with establishing sovereignty backward in time.[11] It would be in place to take note here of the point made by Alterman (1999: 9–11ff.) that Israel is unique among the Western states (including those of eastern Europe) in having so much of its land owned by the state.

The Prescription Law of 1958 (see "Legislation Cited") extended the period of possession required to establish title from the ten years that had been prescribed by the Ottoman Land Code to fifteen years. Moreover, the law determined that the five years beginning in April 1958 would not be taken into account. Thus, for a person who came into possession of land after March 1943, the period was in fact extended to twenty years. The provisions of the Prescription Law were retroactive; the new prescriptive periods were to apply even if the claimant could show possession for ten years prior to 1958 (see Jiryis

1976: 111–115; Kretzmer 1990: 52–53). Kedar (1998) provides an exhaustive study of Israeli juridical practice in the application of the Prescription Law in the course of carrying out settlement of title. He shows how the courts moved in the direction of greater stringency in insisting that the claimant prove both possession and cultivation (708–709), and how they established a formal criterion for cultivation (712–718). Unlike the Mandatory courts, which had demanded "such regular cultivation as is reasonably possible having regard to the nature of the land and the crops for which it is suitable," the Israeli courts came to insist on cultivation of at least 50 percent of the parcel. In arguing the government's case, the land settlement officer of the Justice Ministry made use of a set of aerial photographs that had been taken by the British in 1944 and 1945. These photographs made it possible to establish whether 50 percent of the land in question had indeed been cultivated at that time. Kedar (719–720) shows how there had been room within the Israeli juristic system for a more flexible interpretation of "cultivation" had the courts so desired, and argues that the social and ideological context of "redemption of the land" played a part, beyond mere legal formalism, in shaping the 50 percent rule.

The availability of the 1944–1945 British aerial photographs explains the selection (in 1958) of 1943 as the year after which the law would require establishing possession and cultivation for twenty years. The courts interpreted the initiation of settlement of title procedures in a given area as stopping the flow of prescription time (Kedar 1998: 697; see also Jiryis 1976: 113–114). A claim to land 50 percent of which had not been cultivated according to the 1944–1945 photographs would have to depend on showing cultivation during a subsequent twenty-year period. But if the state initiated registration procedures before 1965 or 1966, it would become impossible for a claimant of such land ever to meet the twenty-year requirement. It was this which impelled the state to move quickly during the 1960s in carrying out the settlement of title project (see ILA 1965: 66).

Kedar (1998: 690–691n89) calls attention to the fact that in settlement of title litigation in the Israeli courts, arguing the intent and applicability of paragraph 78 of the Ottoman Land Code (the prescriptive period) was only one of three main courses taken by the state. The other two were (a) arguing in the name of an absentee by the Custodian of Absentee Property against a present claimant, and (b) arguing that the land was *mewat*. To establish a claim to *mewat* land, a possessor would have to prove that he had taken possession and revived the land prior to the British Mewat Land Ordinance of 1921. The courts made this virtually impossible to do. Thus, the state only had to show that land was *mewat* and not *miri* to gain title at the expense of Arab possessors, who at times had cultivated the land in question for generations.

In a subsequent article, Kedar (2001) shows how the Israeli Supreme Court introduced new rules that expanded the category of *mewat* land. Article 6 of the Ottoman Land Code had defined *mewat* land as land that "lies at such a distance from a village or town from which a loud human voice cannot make itself heard at the nearest point where there are inhabited places, that is, a mile and a half, or about half an hour's distance from it" (Goadby and Doukhan 1935: 44). The Ottoman definition is not unequivocal. Kedar traces the juridical path by which (a) the mile-and-a-half criterion of distance became the exclusive measure, (b) inhabited places or settlements that were not fully fledged villages or towns were disqualified as points from which to measure, and (c) "villages and towns" were themselves redefined to exclude places not already recognized as such at the time of the promulgation of the Land Code in 1858. This disqualified as points from which to measure settlements of Arab nomads who had gradually moved into permanent dwellings at the end of the nineteenth century and the beginning of the twentieth. Kedar observes (2001: 953–954) that expanding the category of *mewat* "restricted the ability of Arab land possessors to acquire prescriptive rights to land that they had at times cultivated for several generations."

Hilleli (1983: 585) argues that the readiness of an individual to accept land rights under the Ottoman Land Code also obliges him or her to accept the verdict of a statutory or legal authority denying such rights under the provisions of the code. But Kedar's analyses reveal just how tendentious and disingenuous Hilleli's contention is.

As Kedar points out (1998: 688), the land laws involved in settlement of title were shaped juridically by litigation that in the main put Arab possessors against the state—a process of manifestly ethnic dimensions. Kedar goes on to show how, while juridical practices have resulted in a contraction of rights for Arab occupiers and cultivators, there has been, as a result of a different set of practices, an expansion of rights for Jewish settlers who make the transition from cultivation to such land uses as commerce and residential building (Kedar 1998: 734–744; see also Alterman 1999: 20–22 on "creeping privatization" in agricultural land).

Now, the assertion of land ownership by the state paved the way to continuation of the Zionist settlement project. In relatively vast areas, the Jewish settlers had moved onto the land taken over from Arabs. The arrangements under which they were settled on state land were not much different in principle from those of *miri* in the Ottoman land regime (see Alterman 1999 for a description of the variable bundle of property rights that currently obtain for Jewish occupiers of state land). Thus, I would suggest that the argument that the Ottoman system was archaic and feudal and that the Israeli state replaced it with a system based on modern capitalist conceptions of ownership merely invokes the image of *modernization*, a companion image to that of Arab *traditionalism* in the Zionist discourse, to cloak the ethnic displacement that has occurred.

How much land did the Arabs lose as a result of changes in settlement of title practices under the state of Israel? The question, it seems to me, is hypothetical. To answer it, one would have to have some idea of what the results of registration would have been had Israel continued the process as it had been carried out by the British. The difference is not simply a matter of the effect of the five or ten years added to the prescription period by Israeli lawmakers, but has been very much determined, as Kedar has shown, by Israeli juridical practice.

Nevertheless, some indication of the possible scope of the loss, at least in the sense of establishing outer limits, may be gained from data published by the ILA. The ILA report for 1964/65 (ILA 1965: 65–68, 236–240) deals with settlement of title in what it refers to as the "special area," a group of forty-two towns and villages (most of these are in the north, with a few located in the Triangle). What made these a special area is the fact that land settlement had not yet been carried out there, but the Arab population remained. Thus, it was here that the clock of the prescriptive period was ticking. Altogether, the area of these localities totaled 702,000 dunam. Of these, the state was claiming title to 276,000 dunam, while the Custodian of Absentee Property and the Development Authority were claiming another 124,000. There were, in addition, another fifty villages in the north with an area of 620,000 dunam, but these were classified in the main as abandoned, and the settlement of title project was able to proceed with less urgency (ILA 1965: 68–69). Outside of the north, there were another 6.2 million dunam, mostly in the Negev, where settlement of title was underway or in the offing.[12]

In the special area, of the 400,000 dunam claimed by the state, the Custodian of Absentee Property, and the Development Authority, 212,000 were registered in the name of the state "without challenge," while registration of another 126,000 was still being disputed. The report indicates that the state had won nearly 3,000 of the 4,022 cases regarding nearly 53,000 dunam that had gone to court, and that another 425 suits (of the 4,022) had been cancelled. Such cancellations may have been the result of compromise. The dry statistics of the ILA do not reveal the factors that moderated challenge to the state's claims and led to compromise, but one must have been the burden of long and expensive litigation that would have been entailed by such challenge (see, e.g., Jiryis 1976: 116).

It should be noted that land claimed by the Custodian of Absentee Property and the Development Authority in the so-called special area, as well as most of the land claimed by the state in the fifty abandoned villages, would probably have been included in data on land losses under headings other than the settlement of title process. But whatever the difference might have been between Israeli practice and that of the British, there seems little question that settlement of title after 1948, in large part because of the purpose and spirit with which it was pursued by the Israeli state, was another of the elements that contributed to the bitterness of the experience of land loss among the Arabs.

The Zionist Development Drive and Further Land Loss

Land taken over through the Absentee Property Law, the Land Acquisition Law, and the settlement of title process provided the space for the first surge of Jewish settlement in Galilee immediately following the 1948 war. The subsequent drive to Judaize Galilee was the next phase in Arab loss of land and territorial constriction. Land was expropriated for Upper Nazareth in the mid 1950s and in 1963, and for Karmi'el in 1961. Then, in 1976, large expropriations, chiefly for the expansion of Upper Nazareth and Karmi'el, were announced. The latter event took place during the same period in which land was being located and taken over for the establishment of the *mitzpim* settlements. The 1976 expropriation announcement was one of the direct triggers of Arab demonstrations in which six demonstrators were killed by the police and which became known as Land Day (on Land Day, see Yiftachel 1999b; see also discussion on the settlement of Upper Nazareth, Karmi'el, and the *mitzpim* settlements in chapter 1 of the present study).

The expropriations for Upper Nazareth and Karmi'el were carried out under the Land Ordinance (Acquisition for Public Purposes) of 1943 (see "Legislation Cited"). Under this law, the minister of finance was empowered to expropriate land for whatever use he would define to be a public purpose. Now one might expropriate land to meet local needs—infrastructure, schools, hospitals—or to meet needs defined on a nationwide scale—transportation, power lines, water carriers, defense. In the case of Upper Nazareth, establishment of a military school and government offices were adduced as the purposes of the expropriation, but what was built there extensively were residences and factories—the real purpose of the expropriation was to settle Jews in the region as a way of countering the threat perceived to inhere in the very existence of the Arab towns and villages. By the time of the expropriation for Karmi'el, authorities were arguing outright that such settlement was a security need (see, e.g., Oded 1964).

In addition to Oded (1964), those who have written on this subject include Jiryis (1976), Rosenfeld (1988), Falah (1992), and Rabinowitz (1997). It appears that many of the studies of expropriation for the purpose of Jewish settlement find it difficult to distinguish unequivocally between expropriation, the transfer of municipal jurisdiction from existing Arab local authorities to new Jewish settlements, and/or the absorption by the new settlement of land that would otherwise have served for the future growth of the Arab locality but that until then did not have municipal status. Obviously, the categories overlap—much land is owned by Arab farmers outside the current municipal boundaries of their locality. Despite the inadequate distinctions between such categories, the Arab loss of land is manifest. As one official at the Northern District Settlement of Title offices told me in response to my attempts to get some historical data on the routes by which the state acquired the land on which Upper Nazareth was established (Absentee Property Law/Land Acquisition Law/settlement of title/Land Ordinance [Acquisition for Public Purposes]):

> As a rule, all of Upper Nazareth is built on expropriated land—whether this way or that—and the original owners are still here. Just the other day, one came here and cried about his eighteen dunam that the new hotel is built on. The idea was Judaization of Galilee—and that means taking land. There was no land that wasn't cultivated or that wasn't claimed.

Rabinowitz (1997) makes use of the vivid personal testimony of Nazareth residents who lost their land.

Announcement of expropriation did not always result in immediate implementation of the order. In such circumstances, many of the erstwhile Arab owners would go on to "their" land to plant olive orchards in the hopes that this might forestall the actual takeover, but it was actually one of my Jewish sources who stated:

> It's the Jews who during the 1970s began a campaign of "political plantings"—planting a forest was an easy way to establish your control over land, and a lot of the JNF plantings were carried out with that in mind. So the Arabs would interpret that as a move that threatened further expropriation of Arab-owned land, and they would plant olives on their own land in response. Also, there was the case of Area 9, a large area near Sakhnin that, ostensibly for army maneuvers, was closed by the military to the Arabs who owned land there (but not to the Jewish settlers in the settlements established there). The Arabs interpreted the closure as a prelude to further expropriation and planted olives.

Such olive plantings were described in the Hebrew press as the Arab invasion and takeover of state land (see, e.g., Ariel 1977). In contrast, Soffer and Finkel (n.d.: 34) are aware that planting could be a defensive move in the face of perceived threat. See also Doron 1988 (45) regarding plantings in the area slated for the expansion of Upper Nazareth. But as of the amendment of the property tax law in 1981 (Amendment 16; see "Legislation Cited"), there was also a straightforward economic reason for planting olives. That amendment left only vacant land that was not agricultural land subject to the tax. To qualify as agricultural land and the exemption, however, the land had to be either cultivated or unworthy of cultivation (§2(4)). Olive trees could be tended with little investment of time, effort, and water, and planting them was an easy way to escape the tax (Soffer and Finkel also cite this factor [n.d.: 34]).

The consolidation of land for the *mitzpim* settlements encountered difficulty that was often solved by means other than expropriation. As I was told, "No matter where you mark out a stretch of land, no matter where you draw a circle in Israel, you will find there a mosaic of ILA and private land" (cf. Hilleli 1983: 595; Soffer and Finkel n.d.: 30). The islands of Arab-owned land abutted the new settlements, or even lay within them, and the ILA and the JNF were hard at work buying or exchanging land in order to eliminate them (see Hilleli).

The parcels of Arab-owned land in question fall outside the jurisdictional boundaries of the Arab town in which the land owners reside. Land for residential building inside the towns is at a premium due to the general circumscription of the outline plans and the fact that many villagers/townspeople do not own land within that area. But the state does own land there due to takeovers from the war refugees ("present-absentees" or not). The ILA offers such land in exchange for that held by the landowner, but at a rate that it argues reflects the value of land on which it is possible to build as compared with that of agricultural land. Yiftachel

(1997: 43–45) describes this process and gives data for the rate of exchange over the period from 1965 to 1980 in the town of Majd al Kurum. The average rate during that period was 5.3 dunam of agricultural land for 1.0 dunam of land on which it was possible to build. It may be observed that very often the land that the state acquires in this way is not intended to remain agricultural land but, instead will be planned for intensive development (e.g., residence, industry). The Arab townspeople have generally lacked the strength to hold out for an exchange rate that takes into account the increase in value to be expected as soon as development plans are made.[13] One person involved on the part of the JNF/the state in pushing the project of land exchange (or sale) to eliminate such Arab holdings described to me some of the tactics employed:

> During the course of events we would do things to make things difficult for the owner—clip off a corner of his field, uproot a tree, put a water line through his property (which is something that's legal to do)—to chip away at his resolve to hold on. It costs money to go to court, and it's not easy to hang on in the face of the planning institutions. Anyway, that's all part of the game.

Hilleli described the ongoing land consolidation project in 1983. That project continues until the present day. Yiftachel (1997) points out that it is yet another move in the drive to deterritorialize the Arab population in Galilee.

Arabs in central Galilee saw the establishment of the Misgav Regional Council in 1982 as a further territorial move against them. Much of the regional council's jurisdiction included land that had previously been in the Mandatory village boundaries of the Arab towns, and it used up the land reserves that might have served for the expansion of those towns. But further: Misgav contains within its jurisdiction considerable land *owned* by residents of the Arab towns in the area. Yiftachel (1994: 78) asserts that fully 100,000 dunam of Misgav land is owned by Arabs.[14] He bases this on information he acquired in the Arab towns (personal communication). This may be an overestimate. The discussion above on settlement of title suggests that there may be considerable difference between ownership claims and actual ownership. The municipal engineer of the Misgav Regional Council told me that the regional council does not maintain data on land ownership, but that he would estimate that 20 to 30 percent of Misgav land is owned by Arabs. Even that would be from about 35,000 to over 50,000 dunam, a serious enough matter—especially for the very many small landowners involved.

In 1995, Misgav tabled an outline plan proposal at the DPBC and set out to work on a master or development plan. The thing is that the Arab landowners are not involved in such planning. And once there is an outline plan, it becomes possible for the local authority (in this case the regional council) to expropriate land (cf. Hussein and Adiv 1997; Hussein 1998).[15]

It is characteristic of administrative practice to split domains; in this case, ownership and jurisdiction have been set off as separate things. One hears from the administrators: "What do the Arab landowners in the area of the regional council have to complain about? Their situation is no different than that of, say, a resident of Tel Aviv who owns land in Haifa—*he* doesn't argue that his land ought to be placed under Tel Aviv jurisdiction." But the effect of the separation of domains is not the same for that hypothetical Tel Aviv resident as for the residents of Arab towns who now find their land in the jurisdiction of the regional council. Haifa, after all, did not come into being as part of an effort to deterritorialize the residents of Tel Aviv and to keep the latter town from developing. And the Arabs who own land in Misgav are not consulted and do not participate in formulation of the regional council's outline and development plans. The Jewish/Arab distinction was very salient in the establishment of the outlook settlements, and again in the establishment of the regional council—and now again in the planning of development. But those who hold the upper hand are able to deflect challenge by asserting that these matters of ownership and jurisdiction now belong to the ostensibly power-neutral realm of administrative practice.

In 1962, the state and the JNF owned 92.6 percent of Israel's pre-1967 area of 20,255,000 dunam.[16] There were about 1.4 million dunam of land owned privately by Jews and Arabs. In 1999, the JNF owned 2.5 million dunam (ILA 1962: 6–7; ILA 2000: 48; see also Lehn and Davis 1988). Current estimates put Arab-owned land at 713,000 dunam (not including land where ownership is disputed) or about 3.5 percent of the pre-1967 area of the state.[17]

JNF land is administered, along with state-owned land, by the ILA. Neither category of land may be sold. JNF land, owned as it were in the name of the Jewish people and not by the state, may be leased only to Jews. The leasing of state-owned land to Arabs, although possible within the land laws of the state, has been extremely limited (see Lehn and Davis 1988). Thus, the development of industrial areas in Arab towns on ILA land and the possible development of Zipporit D (the ILA-owned part of Zipporit D-E), taken up in the present study, may be considered to be a new departure in ILA land practices. Yiftachel (1999a) coins the term *ethnocracy* in reference to the Israeli power structure, and describes the ownership and spatial distribution of Israeli land, the takeover of Arab land that produced it, and the legal encumbrances on its use as the territorial aspect of the Israeli ethnocratic regime.[18] His is a broadly focused analysis of political-historical processes. But what is of interest for the present study of how power works is the Arab *experience* of land loss. This is intimately connected to the *practices* by which that loss came about. It is in order to convey something of the palpability of the experience that I have devoted so many pages to setting out, in as orderly a fashion as I could, the unfolding of those practices.

Beyond the bare facts of dislocation and dispossession, the experience of land loss—the relentless drive of the state regarding land—has led the Arab population in Galilee to a sense of being throttled, encircled, subject to constant surveillance. It will be argued in chapter 5 that this experience and this condition play a significant role in Arab relations to land. Certainly, they found expression in the Arab response to the Zipporit industrial area plan. It may be noted that Land Day continues to be observed, an annual institutionalized occasion for the expression of Arab anger and grievance and demands for corrective action.

Could This Have Been Meshhed Land?

Zipporit and Jewish-Arab Territorial Struggle

It will be recalled that Zipporit had been planned explicitly as part of the Zionist drive to fill up territory and create wedges between areas of Arab settlement. Ministry of Construction and Housing planning orientation documents on the proposed functionally integrated settlement at Zipporit referred to the growth of Arab towns in the area as "development [that] has taken place along main transportation arteries and intersections of strategic importance in the north of the country" (documents; also reproduced in Mivnei Ta'asiya 1992: 7). As people involved in planning during the early 1990s put it, the plan for Zipporit had been conceived in terms of militant Jewish development acting against militant Islam. I received a variety of answers to my attempts to discover what had led to the abandonment of the plan for a functionally integrated Jewish settlement here and the switch to a plan for industry only. One suggested that Menahem Ariav, mayor of Upper Nazareth, did not want there to be a new, high-quality residential area competing with the marketing of Upper Nazareth's new neighborhood at Har Yona; another elaborated to the effect that given the existence of the new neighborhood at Har Yona, Ariav's main concern was providing employment for the growing population of his city—it was this he was pushing for—and that without someone to adopt the settlement plan and shepherd it through the administrative system, it would not materialize.

But the most definitive explanation for the shift was that when the new Rabin government took office in July 1992, it gave the order to put the settlement plan on hold. The jurisdictional boundaries of Upper Nazareth had already completely encircled the town of Ein Mahel (see figure 1.1), and the building of the Har Yona industrial area and residential neighborhood on land expropriated in 1976 was in full swing. The new government's perception was that it would not be politic vis-à-vis the Arab population to push out at the same time to the north-northwest. Nonetheless, the Zipporit A industrial plan on its own produced the immediate response on the part of the local Arab population of being further surrounded and squeezed, of its very existence being threatened (see chapter 3). Awawdy's 1992 two-part article gave eloquent expression to this, and one of its subtitles declared: "Upper Nazareth is a city that devours its neighbors."

I suggest that the response of the Arab towns to the Upper Nazareth Zipporit plan can only be understood if it is seen in the context of both the territorial struggle as waged by the state and the Arab experience of land loss dealt with in the present chapter. In this connection, see figure 4.1. In this photograph,

Figure 4.1 Meshhed and the Residential High-Rises of Upper Nazareth, as Seen from Kafar Kanna (2000)

taken from the parking lot of the Kafar Kanna Local Council, one sees to the left the high-rise apartment buildings of Upper Nazareth on Har Yona and the houses of Meshhed to the right, keeping close to the ground as they ascend the lower hill on which Meshhed is built. The Phoenicia chimney towers to the right and rear of the spot from which the photograph was taken.

But it should be noted that the inhabitants of the Jewish town, inserted into the midst of the Arab population, are themselves painfully aware of the territorial struggle that has been thrust on them. See Rabinowitz 1997 (33, 57–59, 72–81) for ethnographic material and analysis on the Jewish sense of territorial insecurity in Upper Nazareth and of *settlement* as that which finalizes the Judaization of territory. Planners of the Zipporit industrial area, as well as officials concerned with Upper Nazareth as a whole, express a sense of siege that focuses on the need for access to Zipporit that does not have to pass through the Arab towns and for bypass roads that circumvent the critical points where the population of Nazareth and the surrounding towns threatens access to the city of Upper Nazareth itself. This latter need was explained to me emphatically by one planner who described the new bypass of Highway 79 in these terms. The main thing about Bypass Highway 79 (see figure 1.1) is not that it enables traffic on the east-west axis to bypass Nazareth and Upper Nazareth—such routes already existed—but rather that it eases the flow of traffic into and out of Upper Nazareth by avoiding densely populated built-up Arab territory. The images that arose from the explanation proffered to me were those of enabling the unhindered provisioning of and evacuation from the Jewish city. Note that this new highway and new roads providing a direct link between Har Yona and Zipporit A (the beginning section of one such proposal is marked in figure 1.1) cut through Arab land, severing access and possible future contiguity of built-up areas. It is, after all, in the nature of roads that they have both linking and severance effects (see, e.g., OECD 1973).

The point to be made is that the planning of Zipporit was unequivocally a move by national planners in the arena of Jewish-Arab territorial struggle. The accounts in the Arab press expressed the understanding that this was a plan for the Judaization of Galilee, not for development for the region's inhabitants. The policy of Judaization made it untenable that the land on which Zipporit A was built might have been allocated to the development of Meshhed rather than that of Upper Nazareth. The transfer of land for Zipporit A took place in 1991. It should be noted that Meshhed's petitions, struggle, and perhaps its cooperation were not unrewarded. In 1996, the minister of the interior transferred about 950 dunam from land that had been without municipal status to Meshhed (*KT* 5744, 755, 18 April 1996; see figure 1.1).[19]

The Setting of Boundaries of Jurisdiction

I turn now to consider the circumstance that the land of Zipporit A had been without municipal status even though it had lain within the village boundaries of Meshhed as recorded in maps prepared by the Mandate government. The reader may care to refer again to figure 3.2. In that figure, the heavy dashed line delineates the boundaries of Meshhed and Kafar Kanna according to the British Survey of Palestine. The lighter gray area, in the case of Kafar Kanna, and the darker gray, in the case of Meshhed, is that which was included in the jurisdictions of the two local councils established by the Israeli government.[20] The transverse parallel lines indicate the area transferred to Upper Nazareth for Zipporit A in 1991. The large discrepancy in area between that included in the village boundaries and that included in local council jurisdiction is typical of most (but not all) of the Arab localities in Israel.

The village boundaries shown here are reproduced from a 1941 1:20,000 Survey of Palestine map based on a 1:10,000 Topocadastral Survey map of 1932. The topocadastral survey had served as a basis for maps for the British land registration process and for fiscal property tax maps (see Gavish 1991: 165–177). Personnel at the Survey of Israel offices carried out inquiries for me as to how the village boundaries came to be recorded as they appear in the British maps. The received wisdom among mapmakers appears to be that a mapmaking team would go out to the field, and the *mukhtar*s of the villages and the landowners would gather at that place and say to the surveyors "that plot is so-and-so's, from this village, and that is so-and-so's; starting from there is so-and-so's from the neighboring village." The impression one gets from this account is that the village boundaries were recorded by the British in an amorphous, discretionary manner, quite unlike the legal precision with which the state was later to set local authority boundaries of jurisdiction. Indeed, one Israeli town planner put it thus: "These lands would be set down to a certain village, and afterwards, people would claim that this was the land of the village" (Jewish-Arab Center 1998: 62).

But there are two main reasons to think that there was considerable substance to the British-recorded village boundaries. The first has to do with records that do exist of a series of Ottoman land surveys in Palestine. Kark (1997: 57–62) relates how in a survey carried out between 1869 and 1873, land registration commissions of inquiry (*yoklama* or census) proceeded from village to village, issuing title deeds and recording "the area, boundaries, and proprietorship of all land in private ownership or private tenure." The survey for each place began by describing the village as a whole, including its boundaries and area. Although the commission was assisted by a land surveyor, no maps were attached to its reports. Then, in 1872 and from 1878 to 1879, two successive commissions (the *shemsiye* commissions), were appointed to examine and propose the disposition of unclaimed lands. The second commission revisited the same settlements, detailing the boundaries and area of all sites, and, of interest here, found that "the area of the settlements was identical to that found by the previous commission." Kark goes on to cite an inspection of the *shemsiye* records regarding the village of Shatta in Emeq Yizre'el and a new survey of the village lands, both carried out in 1931 by the Mandatory Acting Director of Lands pursuant to the projected sale of part of the lands to the JNF. The inspection was carried out in the presence of the *mukhtar,* notables of Shatta and two neighboring villages, and a considerable number of Shatta villagers. According to Kark (62), "The 1931 report concluded that 'the boundaries of the village as a whole are correct and in accordance with the description made by the Shemsieh Commission [1870].'"

Schechter (1987), making use of a registry book produced by one of the *shemsiye* commissions, provides a description of the work of those commissions and their findings, including translation of several of the registry book's pages into Hebrew. Schechter relates how the boundaries of the village were given by noting "objects in the field such as roadways, ruins, streams, cliffs, special plantings.... When the boundary between villages was a winding one, each change of direction was given, and even its length.... Where there was no identifying object, it was stated that this point was reached when a well-known peak, or [perhaps a] bridge, at a distance of several kilometers, first came into view" (147).

The point I would like to suggest is that when the British collected information from the villagers on the village boundaries, what they then set down was in no way arbitrary; rather, it would have been tangible, substantive local knowledge—knowledge that may have already been recorded in the past, perhaps more than once. The British maps may simply have been a repository for such local knowledge.

One needs to exercise caution, no doubt. Schechter provides a translation of the list of *shemsiye* villages in the Acre sanjak that appeared in the registry book to which he had access. Kafar Kanna and Meshhed were not among them. Thus, there is no direct evidence that the village boundaries of Kafar Kanna and Meshhed were surveyed in Ottoman times. But I would like to also cite Carmon and colleagues (1992), who state in their study of the town of Iksal that the boundaries recognized today between Iksal, Ein Mahel, Dabburye, and Yafi were set in Ottoman times (11).[21] Jacob Yonish, the researcher who did the fieldwork on which that study is based, described to me the same sort of boundary-setting procedures, using objects and local landmarks, as that reported by Schechter on the basis of Ottoman documents. Furthermore, Yonish recalls that he was told by the village elders (who were told by their parents) that there are Ottoman documents on the village boundaries (personal communication). These towns (which were villages then) do not appear in the list translated by Schechter either. They are very close geographically to Kafar Kanna and Meshhed. In any case, the material I have cited from Kark and Schechter is certainly evidence for Ottoman practices, and it is reasonable to infer that the British-recorded village boundaries of the latter two localities also represent the solidness of local knowledge.

The second reason to reject the contention that the British-recorded village boundaries were haphazardly or lightly drawn is found in the few cases where the Mandate government set up local councils in the Arab villages. There were three such places in Galilee: Rame (in 1922), Kafar Yasif (1925), and Jish (1931). The orders establishing the local councils would naturally have to specify boundaries of jurisdiction. The formula adopted by the British was this: "The area of jurisdiction of the Council shall extend to the limits of the village lands" (see, e.g., par. 7 of the order establishing the local council in Rame, *Official Gazette of the Government of Palestine*, no. 77, 15 October 1922, 4–5). It is clear that this referred to the area enclosed by the Survey of Palestine village boundaries. An inspection I carried out on the Mandate maps for three localities establishes that this is the area that appears again in the Mandate government's *Village Statistics* (Government of Palestine, Office of Statistics 1946).

Consider now the setting of boundaries of jurisdiction when the Israeli state came to establishing local government in the Arab towns, mostly in the 1950s and 1960s, but in some instances, later than that. As one of my sources conversant with Ministry of Interior practice put it: "The boundaries of jurisdiction in Arab localities were set in a confining manner—according to the historical nucleus of the village plus a certain addition—not much.... This was different from the approach to setting the boundaries of the Jewish towns." It is possible to compare the areas within the British-recorded village boundaries and those within the Israeli-set boundaries of jurisdiction. I give figures here for three places: [22]

	Mandate Village Boundaries (dunam)	**Area of Jurisdiction (dunam)**
Rame	24,516	6,084
Kafar Kanna	19,455	9,835
Meshhed	11,067	5,751

There are a few places where the area of jurisdiction did not diverge so widely from that of the village boundaries, but the data presented here are indicative of the overall picture.

It should be observed that the boundaries of jurisdiction of most of the Arab local authorities in Israel were set during the time of the military government, or just toward or after its end. The still-weak Arab population was not in a position to stand up for its interests against the dictates of the Ministry of the Interior (see chapter 2). At a 1998 conference (Dayan Center for Middle Eastern and African Studies), Rassem Khamaisi commented that at that time, some of the traditional leadership saw the establishment of the local authorities as a "plot" designed to replace local leadership and constrict the territory of the Arab localities. In light of the balance of power that prevailed at that time, it should not be surprising that the new local councils were perceived as a move toward tightening state control over the local Arab population and, with the boundaries of jurisdiction set as they were, alienating village lands.

The boundaries of jurisdiction, lines newly drawn on the map, made it clear that the excluded land could no longer be thought of as a reserve for future development. More than that, apparently where there were large tracts of state-owned land, these were generally left outside the boundaries when it was possible to do so. Narrowly drawn boundaries of jurisdiction contributed to limiting the extent of outline plans, and the exclusion of ILA land from the jurisdiction of the towns further exacerbated the problem of finding land for public purposes such as schools, or for industrial areas supported by the Ministry of Industry, or even for new residential building that would ease the housing shortage for those who did not happen to own land *within* the area of the outline plan. And of course, setting restrictive jurisdictional boundaries also created space for Jewish settlement and its expansion; Upper Nazareth and its reaching out first to surround Ein Mahel, and then to establish a bridgehead to the north at Zipporit A (see figure 1.1) is a case in point.

In 1996, the head of the Meshhed Local Council said to me: "The land of Zipporit A was ours until 1964; in 1964 it was taken away." Although he was mistaken about the date, the head of the local council was alluding to the jurisdictional boundaries set at the time the local authority was established.[23] Now the land of Zipporit A was never in Meshhed's jurisdiction at any date. But I have also heard other Arab political figures assert that this land was taken from Meshhed. Such a statement, as well as others to the effect that the Arab towns lost land when the state set up the local authorities, is countered by establishment-oriented speakers. The latter explain that *jurisdiction* is a term that comes from another domain—it is not, nor does it have to be, equivalent to *village lands*. It is at this point in the exchange that these speakers are likely to add that, in any case, the British drew the village boundaries arbitrarily and for their own administrative purposes, and it is suggested that to conflate boundaries of jurisdiction with village boundaries results in distortion of the truth. But I have attempted to show that, to the contrary, the village boundaries as recorded by the British were well grounded in Ottoman practice and local knowledge, and moreover, were acknowledged as such by the British when they did establish local councils in the Arab towns.

Yet there is something more. There *is*, after all, a distinction to be made between village lands and their boundaries, on the one hand, and jurisdiction, on the other. Anderson (1991: 172), writing of the colonial determination of Thai borders, refers to the lines on a map as a new phenomenon, "demarcating an exclusive sovereignty wedged between other sovereignties." One might conjure up an imaginary conversation in which the head of an Arab local council in Israel, speaking of the loss of land associated with the establishment of the local authority, would say to the minister of the interior:

> You set me up with something you call "jurisdiction," and you elaborated the municipal context in which I can only function by having such "jurisdiction"—and in so doing, you took away what was my natural jurisdiction.

The world created by Israeli administrative practice has won out. Its power effects of categorization and organization determine the things that can or cannot be said. If one would speak the truth in the conceptual world that has come into being, one cannot confuse jurisdictional boundaries with the village boundaries of the past—not, that is, without challenging the present order.

Even so, *within* the system of municipal jurisdiction, it is possible to contest whatever happens to be the current division of jurisdiction. Such contest formed part of the events dealt with in chapter 3. There is much interlocality conflict over land for development, and, indeed, boundary disputes are a general condition of the municipal system in Israel. In broad terms, this is a conflict of cities (i.e., urban areas) against regional councils (agriculturalists). The cities argue that the regional councils have all the land and very little population: the city has much greater need for municipal income and is starved for land on which to generate such income. A number of articles deal with principles and boundary dispute cases in the macro-sociopolitical Israeli context (Hasson and Razin 1990; Razin et al. 1994; Razin and Hazan 1994b, 2001).

Among the several boundary-change requests dealt with by the Barzilai Boundary Commission (the one that dealt with and recommended the transfer of land from Emeq Yizre'el Regional Council and of WMS land to Upper Nazareth; final report, 1995) were two requests submitted by Iksal. The person who had been telling me about the manner in which boundaries of jurisdiction had been set for the Arab towns (see above) was responding to my surprise as to how it had come about that the northernmost row of houses in Iksal was in Upper Nazareth rather than Iksal jurisdiction (see figure 1.1). Those houses, an extension of Iksal's built-up area, are separated from the built-up area of Upper Nazareth by quite a distance and the steep, rugged ascent of the Nazareth mountain. They are not joined to Upper Nazareth in any way, nor were they served by the Upper Nazareth municipality. The first Iksal boundary-change application before the commission was a request to have Iksal jurisdiction extended to include that row of houses. The commission made its recommendation to that effect, and the change was made.

The second Iksal boundary change request had to do with its new industrial area. This was one of the several small local industrial areas being constructed by the Ministry of Industry for Arab localities in the years 1993 and onward. In this case, the site selected lay just outside the town's jurisdiction, to the west, in the jurisdiction of the Emeq Yizre'el Regional Council (see figure 1.1). The location of the 125-dunam industrial area (75 dunam net for industry) reflected the fact that no large enough tract of ILA-owned land was available for this purpose inside the then-current boundaries of Iksal. Iksal had requested that the industrial area be transferred to its jurisdiction, but the boundary commission, in line with Ministry of Interior attempts to promote interlocality cooperation, encouraged Iksal and Emeq Yizre'el to see if it were possible instead to reach an agreement on joint management of the area. It will be recalled that this was the same boundary commission that recommended transferring over 3,100 dunam to Upper Nazareth jurisdiction, 2,500 of these to be taken from the jurisdiction of the Emeq Yizre'el Regional Council. Upper Nazareth, it turns out, was more effective than Iksal in pressing its claims and making its arguments stick.

The same system that established jurisdictions and put their boundaries in place also made provisions for having them changed. The Arab localities have found that it is possible to get such egregious malarrangements as that of the Iksal houses in Upper Nazareth jurisdiction rectified. But the transfer of a large tract of land for development purposes has been, so far as I have been able to discover, an unusual occurrence (cf. Razin and Hazan 2001). As indicated above, 950 dunam were transferred to Meshhed in 1996, and at the same time, on the recommendation of the same boundary commission, a large tract of land was transferred from Emeq Yizre'el jurisdiction to the Arab city of Nazareth. These transfers took place toward the end of the incumbency of a government coalition that was making what it thought of as special efforts to be responsive to Arab demands and needs. Other projected transfers, the result of increased activity on the part of the Arab localities in recent years in the political arena and in the HCJ, have so far not come to pass (cf. Razin and Hazan 2001).

It should be mentioned, though, that in May 2005 the minister of the interior did finally sign orders transferring an area reportedly totaling over 10,000 dunam to the jurisdictions of a number of Arab towns in Wadi 'Ara (not in Galilee; rather, to the southwest of Afula; see figure 1.4). This came as a resolution of conflict that welled up in 1998 when the Israeli army tried to take over large tracts of Arab-owned land in the area for training purposes. Arab demonstrations that ensued were forcibly put down, but these were followed by negotiations and subsequently by a Ministry of Interior–appointed boundary commission. It has taken well over six years (with the eruption of other Arab protests along the way) for this transfer of jurisdiction to materialize.

In general, despite the fact that boundaries can be changed, they are not changed easily. Once set, they acquire a being of their own (see Razin and Hazan 2001: 18). The jurisdictional boundaries of the Arab towns, having been set at a time when the towns and their populations were particularly weak, carried over and projected that weakness into the years that followed. On these grounds too, it would have been unthinkable in 1991 that the land on which Zipporit A was to have been built might have been transferred to Meshhed instead.

This chapter opened with a somewhat detailed consideration of the state practices resulting in the Arab experience of land loss, an experience that fed directly into the Arab response to plans for the Zipporit industrial area, and, as will be argued in chapter 5, into Arab attitudes toward land in general. The chapter then took up the question of jurisdiction, showing first that since

Zipporit was conceived by its planners not in terms of regional development but rather in those of territorial struggle, there was no chance that the land on which it was built might have been assigned to Meshhed's jurisdiction instead. The second aspect of jurisdiction considered had to do with state practices in setting boundaries of jurisdiction when local authorities were established in the Arab towns. It was argued that the fact that the land on which Zipporit A was built had been left outside Meshhed's boundaries without municipal status was a measure of the impuissance of the Arab town.

CHAPTER 5

The Image of Arab Traditionalism

I turn now to a consideration of the discursive image of Arab traditionalism as it is applied to and impacts on economic development. The image of Arab tradition finds its way into scholarly studies of Arab entrepreneurship; it pervades and shapes Ministry of Industry perceptions of Arab actors on the local scene; it equips the actors themselves with a ready formulaic interpretation of events such as the request by Meshhed landowners that planning for an industrial area on their land be halted. I will attempt to show how multiple, complex, real factors rather than "cultural traits" or "cultural identity" lay behind the actions and responses of the Arab townspeople, and to this end, I will draw on Bourdieu's concept of habitus, privileging practice as it does, as an apt explanatory concept (Bourdieu 1979, 1990). Further, I will suggest that one of the effects of the image of traditional Arab society is to feed back into the exclusion of the Arab population in Galilee from regional development. This may be seen as one of the concrete outcomes of the discourse that objectifies the traditional Arab village and establishes Zionism as an agent of modernization vis-à-vis the native population (cf. Eyal 1993; Sa'di 1997; Rabinowitz 1998).

A Study of Arab Entrepreneurship

It will be useful to focus for a moment on Schnell and colleagues' 1995 study, *Arab Industrialization in Israel* (hereinafter *AII*). This volume assembles a great quantity of valuable data, and using the topological approach of q-analysis,[1] reveals structural relations between the various elements that further (or inhibit) the development of local manufacturing enterprises in the Arab towns. I have had occasion to cite it in earlier sections of the present work. I suggest here that it may be instructive to see how the image of "traditionalism" creeps into and imposes itself on the analysis presented in *AII*.

Curiously, *AII* excludes from its study population those Arab entrepreneurs (admittedly not many) who have established their enterprises in Jewish localities to take advantage of the benefits under the Encouragement of Capital Investment Law available in the Jewish towns and not in the neighboring Arab ones due to differential national priority region status (see chapter 2 in the present study). Thus, Schnell and colleagues create the impression that the subject of their study is local industrial development in the Arab towns. It may be suggested, however, that taking account of the differential availability of such benefits might have contributed to their topological analysis. And surely those who established their enterprises in the Upper Nazareth or Karmi'el industrial areas are to be considered as exhibiting the qualities of entrepreneurship. Yet despite the exclusion of such Arab entrepreneurs from the study, it turns out that the qualities of entrepreneurship serve as a central component of the *AII* analysis (as indicated in the subtitle of the work). The authors of *AII* argue that as a result of marginalization in Israeli society and in its economy, Arab entrepreneurs are compelled to rely on traditional institutions as support mechanisms (*AII*: 166). These institutions include ownership of enterprises based on kinship relations, management in the hands of the owners, employment generally restricted to *hamula* members, capital raised from the family rather than from financial institutions, and location on family-owned land (primarily in residential areas). The authors find that these have been "sufficient for promoting entrepreneurship up to the third level [out of four,[2] measured in terms of total investment in plant].... [B]eyond this, they are incapable of providing additional support for further industrial growth and highlight the internal forces which promote underdevelopment" (166).

At first perusal, the argument seems acceptable—that is, until the final clause in the quoted passage with its reference to "internal forces." These, in the authors' presentation, are the forces of tradition, to which they refer as the "cultural features" of Arab society, and which they distinguish from what they call "the structure of opportunities" available to Arab entrepreneurs (162, passim).

Now, among the elements one finds in the data subjected to q-analysis (the core of *AII*, chapter 6 there),[3] are those (as mentioned above) that the authors refer to as traditional institutions, such elements as family ownership, employment of *hamula* members, family as a source of capital, and so forth. But there is no element that may be identified as *tradition* per se, only data as to who the owners are, who is employed, and where capital is raised. It is the authors who, looking at their data, supply the term "tradition." This observation is in keeping with theoretical writing on the methodology of q-analysis and the "vernacular" interpretation given to technical computer output (Johnson 1990: 278): "In all cases the interpreters bring some new information or expectation to the q-analysis output" (281). It is an "evocative procedure" that draws on the "researcher's experience, intelligence, and intuition" (282). According to another writer on q-analysis, "one of the most difficult tasks in any research program is to choose well-defined words for the elements of our sets" (Gould

1980: 174). Another q-analysis theoretician deals with the problem of defining what he refers to as the "cover set" (Johnson 1983). Both problems seem to be comparable to the problem of naming common factors in the more familiar statistical procedure of factor analysis; thus, according to one text on multivariate analysis, the researcher attempts "to assign some meaning to the pattern of factor loadings," assigning "a name or label that reflects, to the greatest extent possible, the combined meaning of the variables." But "labeling the common factors is more an art than a science and depends, in large part, on the researcher's expertise and knowledge of what is being investigated" (Dillon and Goldstein 1984: 69, 94).

Thus, the interpretation of data in an analysis such as that in *AII* draws on what is already known. The authors of *AII* import into their work theoretical constructs from the domain of entrepreneurship studies among ethnic minorities, constructs such as *cultural traits, normative patterns of traditions and behavior,* and, altogether, *cultural identity* (139–140). The concept of *traditional institutions* comes from this discourse.

The idea that traditional institutions support the early stages of Arab entrepreneurship might seem unexceptionable. Yet the grounds for suggesting that these involve "cultural traits " (or, as the authors of *AII* also put it, "internal forces") which promote underdevelopment, that is, which inhibit development, are problematic, to say the least. That is, unless the authors are suggesting that Arab entrepreneurs are, for example, so immersed in the practice of turning to their families as a source of finance that they refuse to accept bank credit when it is offered. They do not say this, however; on the contrary, they assert that their analysis "reveals that when alternative institutions in the modern economy are offered them, Arab entrepreneurs are soon able to adapt to them" (*AII,* 88).

On the other hand, the authors of *AII do* say that Arab entrepreneurs are reluctant to take bank credit due to an overcautious and suspicious attitude (134)—these are, after all, the cultural traits of tradition. But the authors also mention the lack of risk-reducing mechanisms, the high costs of bank financing, and the high collateral demanded (92, 94, 143). Thus, the Arab entrepreneurs' perception of risk, on evidence reported by the authors of *AII* themselves, is situationally grounded.

With regard to land and the availability of developed industrial areas, the authors of *AII* have this to say (136):

> The model [their analysis] suggests that the marginalization processes influence entrepreneurial culture, which in turn affects industrialization processes. Hence, there is no specific procedure in Arab society for the allocation of land for industrial zones, and thus, no opportunity for the allocation of industrial zones to encourage potential entrepreneurs to invest in industry.

The authors refer to this as a striking failure of Arab society. They connect this to traditional attitudes toward land, an approach that "prevents the emergence of a sophisticated land market and limits the extent of trade in land, thus curtailing the potential land reserves available for industrial use" (*AII*, 134).

I find these to be amazing statements. For one thing, the overwhelming majority of land in Israel is owned by the JNF and the state. The JNF explicitly excludes non-Jews from occupying its land; the ILA has not been forthcoming, to say the least, in making state land available to Arabs. The principle of not selling JNF or state land has been enshrined as canon, and the Arabs come up against this principle. The realities of their experience and their situation teach Arabs in Israel that land has more than mere economic value; it constitutes security and the basis for continued presence and existence. Before linking the alleged absence of a land market to traditional attitudes, it would be well to consider Kimmerling's incisive historical observation (1983: 14): "The Zionist strategy of assigning only an economic value to every resource controlled by others (as much as this was possible), while according national significance to the very same resource when it was in Jewish hands, was formulated with reference to land from almost the very beginning of settlement in Palestine."

Now, the discourse of Zionist modernization finds it convenient to fault Arab society for allegedly failing to perceive and act on the economic value of land. But the supposed absence of a land market among the Arabs may not be borne out on the ground. In the course of my own fieldwork, I encountered enough evidence regarding the purchase or leasing of land from other landowners for agricultural or commercial purposes to suggest that the allegation of such absence may be something of a canard.

Moreover, one set of events I observed directly contradicts the description of the absence of industrial areas as "a failure of Arab society." Next to the industrial area being developed by the Ministry of Industry on ILA land for Iksal just outside that town's jurisdiction (see discussion in chapter 4) lay a parcel of 125 dunam just inside Iksal's boundary that was owned by a resident of Nazareth. This parcel lay at some distance outside the town's outline plan (see the built-up area marked on figure 1.1). It had been the experience of Iksal landowners that the CPAL would deny approval even for already existing buildings situated just a few meters from those within the outline plan. Now that the new industrial area was being built by the Ministry of Industry, the owner of the adjoining parcel realized that the development of his own land, hitherto something that would not be countenanced by the Ministry of the Interior and the CPAL, was now a possibility.[4] He submitted plans to the LPBC for reparceling his land and developing it for industry. His idea was that sale of about half of the area to potential investors would finance the cost of infrastructure development for the entire parcel, leaving him with a smaller area in his own possession, but one worth more than his former holding due to its development and rezoning.

As of 1997, marketing of the Ministry of Industry–ILA 75-dunam industrial area (begun in 1996) was not progressing well. The head of the Iksal Local Council thought that the owner of the private parcel would do better: "Investors will prefer to buy a plot from him even though the cost of development is not being subsidized by the Ministry of Industry; taking a plot from the ILA gives them only a leasehold, but they can register the one they buy from the private owner as their own private property." But the DPBC held up approval of this plan. "We want to see the industrial area in Emeq Yizre'el marketed first," one of the DPBC planners told me in April 1997. The implication was that there was no sense in allowing competition with the marketing of ILA land in which the Ministry of Industry had invested in development. But the head of the Iksal Local Council suggested that successful marketing of the privately owned parcel, were its development to be allowed, would attract investors to the state-owned area as well. "The current [state-owned] area is just so small by itself that it can't attract investors from outside Iksal," he said.

In this case, a private Arab landowner did not succeed in developing land for industry, but it was not tradition that held him back, neither in the earlier stages when practices of the planning authorities thwarted the very possibility of thinking seriously about development for his land at a distance of some 300 meters outside the existing outline plan, nor in the later stages when those authorities were acting (perhaps not wisely, even if merely in terms of their own concerns) to protect the government's investment. Toward the end of this chapter, in discussing the reluctance of Meshhed landowners to have an industrial area planned on their land, I shall have occasion to return to the allegations that traditional attitudes toward land prevent the emergence of a land market.

It may be suggested that the very term "traditional institutions," which is seemingly innocuous because it is so taken for granted in the discourse on modernization, is unwarranted. One has only to consider the non-Arab part of the Israeli economy and the innumerable examples of large, thriving family-based concerns found there in practically all economic fields. In their case, too, there are instances where the presence of family members among the owners or managers seems to interfere with rational decision making. But even in such instances, one would not think of describing these family enterprises in terms of "traditional institutions." Such concepts only seem to be in place with regard to the objects of the modernization discourse: the Third World, colonized peoples, the Arabs in Israel.

Now, on the one hand, the authors of *AII* do attempt to stay close to their data and to analysis in terms of situation. Immediately after introducing the idea of cultural identity, they return to "the structure of opportunities, the capability of competing in the market, and to accessibility of resources" (140). But no amount of weight given to structure and situation can prevent the overriding return of the elements of the discourse of modernization. In large measure, this is due to the fact that "traditional institutions" is the name given by the authors of *AII* to one major subset in the set of elements that promote, are needed for, and constrain Arab industrial development. Indeed, given the hegemony of the discourse of modernization, how could they do otherwise.

And that discourse ensures that the elements of tradition are never considered only as enabling factors, but also as constraining ones.

The analysis of *AII* is one that government officials can easily live with. For all that such analyses expose the limiting conditions in which Arab economic development takes place, they also, through the element of tradition, make the Arabs themselves responsible for their own predicament. Moreover, beyond being shaped by the discourse of modernization, such analyses become new bricks in the entrenchment of the discourse. And, following Foucault (1982), one notes how in the field of power constituted by the discourse, its objects transform themselves into subjects: "That is the way we are," I have heard Arabs say. And the authors of *AII* quote two of their respondents thus: "That's the way things are with us"; "that's how it is with us" (151, 152).

Ministry of Industry Perceptions

Ministry of Industry personnel and those associated with them entertained their own notions of Arab traditionalism. It was expressed in various asides and comments, mostly along the lines of "they aren't serious" in reference to the officials and potential entrepreneurs in the Arab towns. Such comments figured particularly with regard to what turned out to be two problematic situations. One of these had to do with getting private landowners to agree to the construction of the new industrial areas financed by the Ministry of Industry; the other concerned marketing the new industrial areas once the appropriate stage for that had been reached.

The need for agreement by private landowners was a result of the circumstance that just about any stretch of ILA land in Galilee has privately owned parcels lying within it or adjacent to it. This had been (and still is) a problem for state planners in consolidating land for the *mitzpim* settlements (see chapter 4); it was a problem in the case of Teradyon, the large Misgav Regional Council industrial area (see figure 2.2); and it turned out to be a problem in many of the industrial areas planned as part of the Ministry of Industry's project in the Arab localities. In the latter case, owners of in-lying parcels could have their land developed along with the rest of the area if they were willing to pay the costs. Planners would try to leave such parcels intact, as well as those lying at the edges of or along the approaches to the area. Still, the laying of roads and other infrastructure systems generally meant that there would be some incursion into and some expropriation of privately owned property. In the case of the small Kafar Kanna industrial area (G/7088), there were such parcels at the southeast and northeast corners of the ILA tract (see the aerial photo, figure 3.5).[5]

In some localities, such as Sakhnin and Tamra, work on the industrial area was held up considerably before things were worked out with the private owners. The compromise in Sakhnin involved making narrower roads and doing without a sidewalk. Still, in the new Sakhnin industrial area, there is a privately owned olive orchard in the middle of the area. The owner claimed a much larger area and used to farm it, but he lost in court registration of title proceedings. "The owner carried on a struggle for years," I was told. "The sense is that after all those years of struggle, this is what he's left with—and he's going to hold on to it—in his way. That means olive trees, not giving in to the industrial area (were he to accept the rezoning of his land for industry, he would have to pay land betterment tax, development costs, and then perhaps have to sell because he can't develop manufacturing on his own)" (Interviews).

In the year 2000, private owners along the edge of the industrial area in Sakhnin were building residences on their land even though it was zoned for industry. "But," I was told, "the owners have no alternative for building a home except on their own land" (Interviews).

In Kafar Kanna, a strip of land thirty-five meters wide located to the east of the road at the eastern edge of the industrial area (see aerial photo, figure 3.5; road is seen at the left with the right-hand edge of the page as the bottom of the photo) was included by the outline plan (but not by detailed plan G/7088) in the area zoned for industry. The Kafar Kanna municipal engineer explained the planning logic to me: that way, it is possible to charge the owners for part of the costs of constructing the road. In this case, the owners welcomed having their land zoned for industry in the outline plan, or at least they did not object. But the road itself turned out to be a source of contention.

An official of the development company engaged by the Ministry of Industry told me that in this case, the private owners had moved the boundary of their parcels to encroach on ILA land—the landowner had planted a hedgerow, which he said had been there since his grandfather's time, where the road was supposed to go. But the Kafar Kanna municipal engineer rounded out the story for me. The idea was that the road would be laid half on state land (westward) and half on the private land (eastward). Now, the industrial area and the road lay at a higher elevation than that of the adjoining land to the east (something of this is suggested in the aerial photo). The original plan was to have a sloped embankment at the east edge of the road joining the two levels. The infrastructure development company at first interpreted this to mean that the road proper would lie 50 percent on the ILA land and 50 percent on the private land, while the sloped embankment would extend eastward from the edge of the road. The private owners said, "That way you're taking more than 50 percent from us—move the road westward." For their part, the infrastructure development company and the local council said, "There is an Urban Building Plan [detailed plan], which is law, and the plan sets the place for the road." In the end, the compromise was that the infrastructure development company would build a retaining wall—to obviate the slope—and the road was built in the place set by the plan.

The events I have recounted here were among those assimilated in the narrative of Arab traditionalism and resistance to modernization as recited by Ministry of Industry and associated personnel: the Arab local authorities are not really interested in developing local industry and, rendered weak by *hamula* politics and landowner obstructionism, are unable to enforce zoning regulations or to issue expropriation orders to further such development.

The difficulties encountered in marketing the new industrial areas were another strand in that narrative. Once several of the new industrial areas in the Arab towns were ready for marketing, people connected with the project seemed to feel that there would be a rush of applicants for plots, even though one couldn't expect to see a flurry of new plants spring up overnight. Candidates had to have their applications approved by the Ministry of Industry and the ILA, and had to pay both of those bodies; after that, they needed detailed construction plans and approval by the LPBC before they could begin to build. All this would take time. Still, time was passing, and marketing and construction were not moving. One could see grass beginning to grow through the gravel surfacing of the plots in the new industrial areas. The apparent standstill was often laid at the door of the paralysis of the local authorities and the alleged nonseriousness of the local entrepreneurs: the Arabs are good suppliers of services—good middlemen and traders—but not industrialists, not manufacturers.

Now, the procedures for allocating plots lent themselves to interpretations of politics, patronage, and arbitrariness. An entrepreneur interested in a long-term lease on a plot in an industrial area would submit an application to the Development Areas Unit of the District Ministry of Industry office requesting allocation of a plot without tender.[6] He would attach to his application a recommendation from the local authority, a description of his projected enterprise, building plans and operations plans, and financial statements, together with an advance payment. The request would be sent to the appropriate Ministry of Industry economic branch section in Jerusalem for a determination as to the seriousness of the proposal. After coming back to the district, a plot allocations committee, made up of representatives from the Ministry of Industry, the ILA, and the local authority, would assign a suitable plot in the industrial area.

There were undoubtedly many would-be entrepreneurs who registered at the local authority asking for a plot recommendation, but who then fell away when they discovered that they would have to submit such-and-such documents and pay the advance payment in order for their applications to be dealt with by the Ministry of Industry. In addition, approval by the Ministry of Industry economic branch section was, by ministry guidelines, supposed to take three weeks, but in practice could take from six to nine months (Israel State Comptroller 1994: 708). It would happen that the Development Areas Unit of the ministry would move applications through the procedures only when applicants inquired as to the fate of their requests (708). Moreover, to weed out commercial as distinguished from manufacturing projects, and to eliminate an oversupply of certain products (a town needs only so many olive oil refining operations), a so-called preparatory committee (*va'ada mechina*) at the District

Office of the Ministry of Industry would winnow applications before sending them on to Jerusalem and would do so again after their return.

Following assignment of a plot in the industrial area, the applicant would sign a development agreement with the ILA (paying the leasing fee) and pay the Ministry of Industry the share of infrastructure costs that it demanded. From the time of the agreement with the ILA, the applicant would have eighteen months in which to submit detailed building plans and thirty months altogether until he would have the roof up. At that point, he would sign a forty-nine-year lease with the ILA. If the entrepreneur were to drop out at any time, he would have his infrastructure cost payment to the ministry refunded as well as his ILA fee, less 5 percent rent per year. A Ministry of Industry official put it this way: "There is a lot of room for people to get land allocated and not put it to use." This official had data revealing that up until 1992 (inclusive), only about 40 percent of approved applicants in the Development Areas actually paid; the rest dropped out. After 1992, paid applications went up to about 80 percent (apparently this was connected to the institution of the deposit requirement). Altogether, heads of local authorities might see applicants and wonder where they had disappeared to, and even serious entrepreneurs might see bureaucratic cumbersomeness and the apparently arbitrary results of bureaucratic discretion. For their part, Ministry of Industry personnel could see what they deemed the "nonseriousness" of the Arab applicants. But it should be pointed out that the ministry official's data indicating a 40 percent payment rate on approved applications in Development Areas up until 1992 must have been made up nearly exclusively of non-Arab entrepreneurs.

The mode of local authority participation in the approval process was itself problematic. The practice had been to have a local authority representative participate with official standing. The State Comptroller advised the ministry that a recommendation by the local authority was not necessary, since the local authority had its representative at the plot allocation committee (Israel State Comptroller 1994: 707). But then the ministry was told by the Comptroller (unpublished criticism) that it was not good to have the local authority participate with official standing in the committee: it would be too susceptible to alien considerations. It was enough that the local authority had its say through the issuance of a building permit by the LPBC and a business license from the municipality. With regard to "alien considerations," the State Comptroller was addressing situations that had not necessarily arisen in the Arab sector. But there were some Ministry of Industry personnel who adopted the view that this was particularly relevant to the Arab sector, arguing that it was necessary to circumvent the propensity of local officials to allow *hamula* politics to interfere in recommendations for the awarding of plots. The practice that won out was to have local authority representatives present at meetings of the plot allocation committee and to solicit the local authority's "opinion" on applications, but not to require its "recommendation." The ministry official with whom I spoke saw this as necessary to enlist support and secure cooperation.

In the case of the new industrial areas in the Arab towns, there was also the matter of applicants from outside the locality who were awarded plots, even before decisions had been made regarding local applicants. This was often made out to be an infringement of the local authority's status vis-à-vis *its* new industrial area. But Ministry of Industry officials argued that applicants could not be turned away just because they did not reside in the particular town; this was, after all, state land and government-financed development. The industrial area, though in the jurisdiction of the particular town and supposed to meet the needs of local entrepreneurs, did not *belong* to the town. It may be noted, however, that in the case of the large industrial areas in the Jewish towns or regional councils, the local authority, acting through a municipal industrial authority, did play a central role in marketing plots. The alternative way of perceiving the awarding of plots to outsiders was as the entrance/attraction of outside investors who would augment local development and contribute from the outside to local economic activity and to local tax revenue. Given the fact that, in essence, the ministry ran the allocation-of-plot process in the Arab town industrial areas as its own show ("the industrial area does not belong to the town; it is on state land and built with government money"), relegating the local authority to an advisory function only, it should cause little wonder that the role of the local authority was problematic.[7] Altogether, it emerges that the problems that arose in connection with the awarding of plots was endemic to the situation of ILA, Ministry of Industry, small local authority, and local applicant relations. These problems could be grist for the narrative of Arab traditionalism, notwithstanding the fact that they were not limited to the new industrial areas in the Arab towns.

As for the slow response when marketing of the new industrial areas began, one notes that these small areas were not designed to attract large investments from outside, but rather primarily to allow for the evacuation of public-nuisance enterprises from the residential areas of the town. But the small, local entrepreneur has to weigh multiple factors, do his own cost-benefit analysis. To move to the new industrial area, he has to pay for land and for infrastructure development, for building plans and for building—all new costs. Perhaps he or she does not pay local property tax for the enterprise in its current location next to or under his residence, but will have to do so in the new area. What does he get in return? The possibility of developing further; good transportation access; getting away from prosecution by the local authority or by the LPBC for infringement of zoning laws. These costs and benefits must be weighed; the answer is not immediate.

But there is a further point to be made. I return to the analysis by Schnell and colleagues (1995; referred to here as *AII*). The authors of *AII* refer to the elements supporting industrial entrepreneurship as "indicators of infrastructure features." They find (67) that "none of the industrial infrastructure features on its own can directly explain total investments," and furthermore, that "there are no linear relations between the infrastructure features and total investments."

The authors find that "none of the infrastructure variables on its own is a critical factor in encouraging economic growth but must work in conjunction with other features of the infrastructure" (67). Their subsequent q-analysis reveals that there is a *set* of infrastructure variables required for transition from moderate-low to moderate-high and high levels of entrepreneurship. They sum up the factors whose absence blocks higher entrepreneurship levels: "lack of approved industrial zones ... [with] physical infrastructure; limited access to investment capital;... lack of professional management with good access to information networks that provide an assessment of the state of the economy and decision-making on the national level ... [and] difficulties in breaking into Jewish and international markets" (89; see also 75, 81).

The authors of *AII* say that the absence of developed industrial areas is *one* of the primary factors impeding the rise to higher levels of entrepreneurship (81). They do *not* say that a newly available industrial area will immediately be marketed or that the plants established there will immediately reconstitute themselves with all the features of high-entrepreneurship levels. Indeed, their analysis suggests that such an expectation would be misplaced. The point is that multiple things have to ripen or become available to facilitate a jump into a new order. Bourdieu (1979) argues this in his study of Algerian peasants confronted by the colonial capitalist economic order. In the case of the Arab towns in Israel, the availability of a developed industrial area was one such element—an important one, but not the only one. Still, its very presence, there at the edge of the town's built-up area, might be expected to act as a prod, even for entrepreneurs who had not already moved there, in the direction of future development.

Toward the end of the 1990s, marketing of the new industrial areas began to move forward. The ILA's equalization of land prices in these industrial areas with those in the large neighboring industrial areas in Jewish towns and regional councils had, at the time of its enactment in 1995 (Israeli Lands Council Decision 736) set a period of two years from the time that allocation of plots began during which equal prices would be in force. If marketing was to proceed in places where it had been at a standstill, the equalization of prices had to be extended. Decision 817 of the Israel Lands Council (February 1998) did just that.

Then, in January 1999, the Ministry of Industry put someone in charge of working directly with the Arab local authorities where the new industrial areas were located and with the applicants and potential applicants for plots. The ministry took steps to reduce the fees it was charging for infrastructure development (already heavily subsidized) in the towns characterized by low socioeconomic status (high unemployment, etc.) and where marketing of the plots needed a push. I learned from a ministry official how it had also been necessary to intervene with the ILA to promote the marketing of plots: "The equalized land prices didn't get into the ILA computers automatically—one needed to press in order to get it to happen. And the ILA had been refusing to deal with applicants with whom the administration was engaged in litigation over land ownership elsewhere. Many of those who wanted to apply for an industrial plot were in that situation; we had to convince the ILA that these were separate subjects and should not be linked." It should be noted that the small Kafar Kanna industrial area (G/7088) was not one of the places where marketing had lagged. There, all the plots had been marketed without this location having been included in the ministry's special project.

By the middle of 2000, the situation of marketing the new industrial areas had progressed dramatically. Along with active problem solving with local officials and applicants, such things as intervention in the ministry itself to move the application process along, intervention with the ILA to get the equal prices into the administration's computers, and the reduction in development costs charged to the entrepreneur had, of course, a direct impact on the cost-benefit analysis of the local entrepreneurs. But all this is assimilated by officials to the narrative of Arab traditionalism. Even those in the Ministry of Industry who are connected to programs meant to advance the well-being of the Arab population and who seek to put right the falterings of the system that stand in the way of Arab participation in development do not escape the hold of the discourse on modernization and its image of Arab traditionalism. The power of the narrative continues unabated. Thus, at the time that planning for an additional new industrial area is in the works, it is possible to say "planning won't proceed unless the local authority takes steps to expropriate the land needed for an access road—there's no sense in building an industrial area that can only be accessed by helicopter." In this particular case, however, planning won't begin until the infrastructure development company working for the Ministry of Industry gets planning authorization from the ILA, and without a statutory plan, there are no grounds for expropriation from private owners, something that, in any case, the local authority has to carry out with appropriate care and consideration

The Private Landowners in Meshhed

Then there is the matter of Meshhed landowners asking that planning for an industrial area on their land be halted. What led them to do this, and what explains the apparent difference between them and Kafar Kanna landowners? One Kafar Kanna resident with whom I spoke quickly put his finger on the property tax that would be imposed if the land were rezoned for industry. But he also thought that there was a difference in experience between the people of Kafar Kanna and those of Meshhed—Meshhed, after all, had a population of only five thousand, while that of Kafar Kanna was fourteen thousand.[8] The further stimulus provided by the onset of development has had an effect in Kafar Kanna, but hasn't yet reached Meshhed, he suggested. One needs, I believe, to avoid sliding from a statement like this into an explanation in terms of "Arab traditionalism." As in the questions of land market and of marketing the new industrial areas discussed earlier, explanation is to be sought in a multifactored combination of practical cost-benefit considerations and the no less real concerns that experience brings to one's door.

Even considering that the Ministry of Industry had undertaken to pay the cost of planning for the private Meshhed land, there were still major infrastructure costs that the private owner would have to meet if he were going to develop industry there: costs associated with roads, grading, electricity, sewage, water, telephones, and so forth. The entrepreneur on ILA land paid only a fraction of these costs. The latter also had to pay a leasing fee to the ILA (also subsidized), which, of course, the private owner did not. Then again, the LPBC would impose a property improvement levy (*heteil hashbacha*) on the private owner when the value of his land went up due to development. And he would have the costs of planning and putting up his enterprise just as the entrepreneur on state land did.

Now the thing about the property tax is that the 1981 amendment to the Property Tax and Compensation Fund Law (Amendment 16, see "Legislation Cited") made only urban land (this would include land zoned for industry) that had not been built on subject to the tax. Once an owner's land had been rezoned from agriculture to industry, he or she would be required to pay the tax at an annual rate of 2.5 percent of the value of the property until he or she actually built. As an owner, you might consider developing industry on your land at some time in the future, but if you have not already been planning to do so, if you have not yet put together the wherewithal to develop industry immediately, and if you wish to avoid being pressured into selling the land, then you wouldn't want to have it rezoned for industry. The instrumental rationality of the position is manifest.[9]

There was also the matter of reparcellation and exactions for roads and other public purposes. As mentioned in chapter 3, it would seem that, unlike the situation in the Kafar Kanna area, private holdings in the Meshhed area cut across where new roads would have to go, making planning more difficult there. Moreover, very many of the private holdings were of a size far beyond what would be required for a single enterprise. Subdivision and leasing or selling would be necessary. These were options, to be sure, as demonstrated by the private owner adjacent to the Iksal industrial area. A number of owners in Kafar Kanna put together their own modest twenty-eight-dunam (gross) plan for developing industry in part of the area included in the Zipporit E plan.[10] Perhaps what made this latter plan possible was that for the time being, it took in just a piece of each of five larger parcels. In order to be entertained, such options had to appear practicable and sustainable. As in the case of Iksal, close physical proximity to an area actually being developed for industry by the government was a factor. And this was undoubtedly so for the private owners at the edge of G/7088 (the small new industrial area in Kafar Kanna) and the owners who put together the ad hoc twenty-eight-dunam plan to the north of G/7088 in Zipporit

E. It may be observed parenthetically that to develop the larger, inclusive industrial area in such circumstances would entail an overall planning and marketing challenge that would test any industrial area management.

But what of agriculture; are the people of Meshhed, and of Kafar Kanna, for that matter, not farmers? The photograph reproduced in figure 1.3 may convey a sense of the agricultural setting into which industry intrudes here. In these well-tended fields belonging to Kafar Kanna and Meshhed residents, one sees melons, watermelons, tomatoes, squash, wheat, oats, chickpeas, and olives, the latter particularly in the hillier areas ascending southward from the fertile valley. The crops are all unirrigated, but plastic cover and mulch hold in the moisture from the winter rains and from the dew. Yet, as one of my local sources explained to me, only a few families earn the main part of their livelihood from agriculture. For the others who do engage in it, farming is an auxiliary occupation, carried out perhaps by certain members of the family, while those who regularly work in other pursuits may join in work in the fields in the high season. In addition to the field crops and olive orchards, some families had some produce and fruit trees growing in their yards and kept some livestock.

All this fits with data extracted from the 20 percent sample of the 1995 Census. According to these data, only 3.2 percent of Meshhed residents who reported working *in* their locality of residence also declared that they worked in agriculture.[11] For Kafar Kanna, this figure was 0 percent. Haidar (1995: 70) describes this marginal economic role played by agriculture in Arab life today. In Majd al Kurum, one of the four towns he surveyed in great detail, he found that only 2.1 percent of those employed worked in agriculture and that there were only eleven families for whom it was the primary occupation. Yet most landowning families work their land as an ancillary activity (163).

Emanuel Marx's 1984 study of the Bedouin in Sinai is instructive here. Marx documents how that population, absorbed as wage laborers in the broader non-Bedouin economy, maintains an agricultural base. That base is merely an auxiliary project during times of prosperity, but when employment cutbacks strike, agriculture and animal husbandry back at home are ready to be expanded and able to provide economic security (see also E. Marx 1987).

There were many factors at work in the case of the Meshhed landowners who balked at having their land planned (i.e., rezoned) for industry: the new taxes to be paid; the exactions for public purposes that would diminish one's holdings; the anticipated pressure to sell, particularly if one could not immediately amass the resources for developing industry on one's own; and, in general, the loss of the land as an agricultural base. But this last, I suggest, goes well beyond the immediate cash benefit of economic security. Rather, it is also a matter of the habitus (to use Bourdieu's term) engendered by the practices encountered by the Arab townspeople, those carried out in the name of the state and those experienced in the economic domain.

The authors of *AII* devote an entire chapter (chapter 10) to presentation and discussion of material they collected in interviews with some seventy industrial entrepreneurs. Allowing the respondents to speak for themselves, the presentation of this material provides rich insights into the habitus of the Arab entrepreneurs, reflecting the experience of being confronted by closed doors, absence of job security, lack of access to information or to the centers where decisions are made. And Aziz Haidar recounted to me how he would say to Arab entrepreneurs, "such and such government programs offer you so-and-so," and how they would say to him in return, "that's not for us—they mean 'for Jews' when they say that." On the other hand, I was told how entrepreneurs in Kafar Kanna, once the new industrial area was in place, had begun to inquire into the relevance of the Encouragement of Capital Investment Law and its benefits to their project: would sales to the Palestinian Authority qualify as meeting export requirements, they wanted to know.

In the realm of state action, there were the confining, constricting effects of the statutory planning system as it was applied in the Arab localities. And there was the sense of being closed in, encircled, watched, arising from such things as the tentacled expansion of Upper Nazareth, the Jewish "outlook" settlements established on the hilltops, the new army camp established in Misgav just at the entrance to Sakhnin and less than ten meters from Sakhnin's junior high school (see, e.g., Nir, 2001), the army firing and training ranges set up on Arab agricultural land requisitioned for that purpose. There was the experience of land loss, the state's single-minded and voracious pursuit of every dunam it could possibly claim. That pursuit had made the land a matter of conflict and of principle. And there seemed to loom the constant threat of further takeover: "How, given this experience, can one trust the government?" I heard. Indeed, the municipal engineer of one Arab town recounted that "when the infrastructure development company first came to us with the Ministry of Industry plan to develop a local industrial area, we thought it was a new stratagem for confiscating our land."

Against this background, to hold onto the land, at least for the time being, could impart a sense of security, even beyond economic security, in a situation perceived as fraught with insecurity. At this point, I wish to cite again, quoted this time in full, the statement of Schnell and colleagues in *AII* (134) concerning tradition and the alleged absence of a land market:

> The traditional attitudes toward land give lower priority to the short-term economic interests of the nuclear family. This approach prevents the emergence of a sophisticated land market and limits the extent of trade in land, thus curtailing the potential land reserves available for industrial use.

I believe that this analysis must be dismissed, in the same way that Bourdieu dismisses "the ritual question of the cultural obstacles to economic development" and the concept of resistances to rational economic conduct imputed to the cultural heritage (1979: 1).[12] On this count, too, as on that of the immediately practical considerations enumerated earlier, the reluctance of Meshhed landowners to have an industrial area planned on their land may be seen to grow out of concrete experience, not out of tradition. The view from the discourse of modernization, on the other hand, abstracts the Arab landowner from the real conditions of his or her existence and attributes his or her actions to some immanent cultural essence.[13]

The Image of Arab Traditionalism and Exclusion from Development Planning

Consider now the image of traditionalism as part of the discourse of modernization. The image and the discourse are effects of power relations, and they feed back into those relations. I have discussed how they shape (at least one) scholarly study of Arab industrial entrepreneurship and have pointed to their uses in Ministry of Industry perceptions of events in the field. Beyond this, however, the discourse of modernization, as Eyal (1993) shows, is one of the mechanisms contributing to the objectification of "the Arab village." I use *objectification* here in the Foucauldian sense of producing an object, making it appear as a discrete "something" carved out of the general inchoate flux.

Now objectification implies the setting in place of a conceptual boundary around the Arab towns and villages. One effect of such imaginary boundaries is that they may make it possible to think of the village as an undisturbed entity. The village appears to exist at some ideal level, untouched by government inputs and intrusions such as land expropriation, the statutory planning system and the demolition of so-called illegal buildings, security agent surveillance. This may be thought of as the power effect of what is made to disappear from view.

But there is a further power effect to which I wish to call attention. That is the way in which these imaginary boundaries underpin and rationalize the exclusion of the Arab population in Galilee from development planning. The development of Galilee is seen as the concern of the modern population, that is, of the Jews. The Arabs, on the other hand, belong to the traditional society of their villages, and they, in good time, will come to enjoy the benefits of modernization that Israeli society is bringing to them. As Eyal puts it (1993: 44), in the discourse of modernization, the traditional Arab village is constituted (i.e., is made to come into existence) by the very cultural traits to which the barrier to development is imputed.

One functionary concerned with development programs in Galilee explained to me how Arab localities were not yet ripe for development. Then he went on:

> I told the head of the Strategic Development Unit [in one large Arab town], "develop your seventy dunam of industrial area for the local workshops and get them out from the residential area—but if you have real industry and it needs space, it should go to the large regional industrial area." In the meanwhile, we do focal points of development—and from them there is radiation; they serve as a model for imitation.

The imaginary boundary enclosing "the Arab village" made it difficult to envisage planning for a large industrial area for Kafar Kanna or for large-scale industrial development in the Arab towns alongside that of Upper Nazareth. The paradoxical result of the discourse of modernization is that for those who speak within it, the village remains always its traditional self, locked behind its imaginary boundaries, not yet ready to be an active agent of development. This discourse feeds and supports the appropriation of Arab town development needs and potential by the Jewish sector in Galilee, acting in concert with government agencies. And this, in turn, feeds back into the habitus of living in an Arab town in Galilee.

The next chapter will take up the appropriation alluded to here, while the one following it will consider the challenge and contest involved in attempts to break through Jewish-Arab boundaries in the realm of economic development.

CHAPTER 6

The Appropriation of Arab Development Needs and Potential

I turn now to the appropriation of Arab town development needs and potential by the Jewish settlements planted in the midst of Arab population centers in Galilee. I refer particularly to Upper Nazareth, established in 1957, and to Karmi'el, established in 1964, the latter located in the center of Biq'at Bet Hakerem (see figures 1.1 and 7.1). It is perhaps ironic that the themes of regional development, as distinguished from locality-specific development, and regional integration will be seen to lie at the heart of this discussion.

The Growth-Pole Approach to Regional Development in Galilee

In 1977, a Ministry of Housing planning team produced a study titled *Accelerated Urban Development in Galilee* (hereinafter *AUDG*). This document declared that

> development policy for Galilee, aiming to strengthen the Jewish hold on this region and to speed its growth [Hebrew original is unclear as to whether "Jewish hold" or "region" is the referent of "its growth"], cannot function in a vacuum. It must take into account the fact that the Galilee is settled by a large minority population. This population is developing rapidly and requires both short-term and long-term solutions in the various domains of life.... [O]nly an integrated solution for both sectors—the Arab and the Jewish—will be able to achieve the desired results for efforts at accelerated development in Galilee. (Ministry of Housing 1977: 18)

The study adopted a modified growth-pole or growth-center strategy and recommended focusing development efforts on the cities of Upper Nazareth, Zefat, and Karmi'el. It proposed that the employment needs of the Arab population be addressed through (a) the large regional industrial areas planned for

Upper Nazareth (Zipporit), near Akko, and at the western edge of Biq'at Bet Hakerem (this last later became the Bar Lev industrial area; see figure 7.1) and (b) light industry and manufacturing areas to be developed in the Arab towns themselves (*AUDG*, 76).

The *AUDG* plan had nothing to say about the possibility of cooperation between Jewish and Arab towns on joint urban development, nor could it have been expected to do so in 1977. Although it spoke in bona fide earnestness of integrating the Arab population in Galilee development, it will be suggested that this plan may have worked to hold back the relative development of the Arab towns.

In its approach to the spatial distribution of activities in Galilee, the Ministry of Housing's *AUDG* was a departure from the Ministry of Interior planning concept that had previously held sway. Rather than the balanced growth of all the existing Jewish towns in the region while preserving the rural character of Galilee, it called for focusing on and augmenting urban growth in Upper Nazareth, Zefat, and Karmi'el (cf. Czamanski and Meyer-Brodnitz 1987: 148–149). These foci of growth were selected and ranked with an eye to (a) releasing Galilee from domination by the Haifa metropolitan area (and therefore Zefat was to grow more than Upper Nazareth), and (b) developing the Akko-Zefat axis as a wedge between the Arab population mass in Lebanon and the northern border, on the one hand, and the large Arab population concentration in Nazareth and its vicinity, on the other (therefore, targeting Karmi'el and Zefat). The authors set out the growth-pole rationale quite clearly, and the present study would certainly not presume to suggest a critique of the plan on the grounds of the (modified) growth-pole strategy it adopts.[1] Nevertheless, I believe that the plan may indeed be criticized with regard to consistency with its stated aim of region-wide development. It should be noted that Baruch Kipnis, a member of the planning team that prepared *AUDG*, published an article in 1976 setting out the need for and desirability of integrating Arab development in Galilee into the general development program and setting out the principles of the approach that would be featured in *AUDG* (Kipnis 1976).

The growth-pole approach to regional development took off in many countries throughout the world during the 1960s and 1970s (Polenske 1988: 105). *AUDG* (preceded by Lichfield 1971; see preceding note) was thus part of a widespread trend. The approach was based on the growth-pole theory of economic development originated by François Perroux during the 1950s and the beginning of the 1960s. Perroux's theory holds that "economic development does not spread itself evenly throughout *space*. The mainspring of economic development is technological progress or innovation [which tend] to be concentrated in particular enterprises, the propulsive industries.... [A]ny constellation of propulsive industries is a growth pole" (Higgins 1988: 42). But Perroux's concept was not geographical. Perroux took pains to specify that although he spoke in the topological terms of poles of development, he was referring to *economic* space and not to what he called "banal geographic space." He pointed out that firms sharing the same economic space might be located on opposite sides of the globe in geographic terms (Higgins and Savoie 1988: 9). Nonetheless, those involved in practical regional planning converted Perroux's theory into something else, "into a totally different theory which treated growth poles as urban centers and spread effects as being generated in a particular geographic space, namely the region adjacent to the urban sector itself" (Higgins 1988: 44). Later, Perroux himself turned to expanding his theory in the direction of regional development in territorial space (e.g., Perroux 1988), speaking of the need for the planning of intentional development channels (63) and of transmission lines and receptors, as well as generators of growth (Higgins 1988: 44).

In keeping with the growth-pole approach, *AUDG* argued for the great advantages of the agglomeration effects that would ensue from concentrating development efforts in large urban centers (36), and went on to state that "a large urban settlement supplying a variety of quality services to its surrounding area and creating for the individual and the entrepreneur an array of possibilities for locating in the region is the engine for accelerated development in the periphery" (40).

AUDG foresaw that most employment would center in industry, and that this would mainly be located in large regional industrial areas. The size of these areas was to be calculated "on the basis of the demand for employment in the two sectors (Jewish and Arab) together, while part of the solution for employment in light industry and manufacturing [would be] developed in the Arab villages [i.e., towns] themselves" in the form of local industrial areas (11). The plan took into account the growing residential needs of the Arab population, and proposed building new housing near Makr and Shefar'am. This would solve the population problem of Nazareth and bring to a halt the Nazarene "invasion" of Upper Nazareth, while bringing the surplus Arab population closer to metropolitan Haifa, where Jews were a majority (38, 40).

Perhaps the most telling provision of the plan was its recommendation that the needs of the Arab population for commercial and professional services be taken into account in planning for the growth of those activities in the Jewish cities. Thus: "[T]he buying power in the Arab villages (each separately relatively small) will together provide the foundation for the cities' commerce and service sectors and will aid in making them poles of attraction for the Jewish population" (*AUDG*, 76–77).

It is true that *AUDG* was the first development plan for the Northern District to take into account the needs of the Arab population. In this it was a departure, as, indeed, it also was in promoting for the first time the concept of local industrial areas in the Arab towns *along with* the concentration of major industrial development in large regional interurban industrial parks.[2] One needs to credit the promulgators of *AUDG* for being able to break new ground in these regards. But one needs also, I suggest, to see the plan in the context of the perception of territorial threat posed by the Arab population and the internal contradictions growing out of that perception.

After all is said, the aim of *AUDG* was to strengthen the Jewish hold on the region, and Karmi'el and Upper Nazareth, growing Jewish centers, were to be a counterweight to the concentration of the minority population in their vicinity (e.g., p. 76). One needs to provide for the needs of the Arab population—residence, employment, and services—otherwise, there will be problems. But the sense is that for the Arabs, it doesn't matter where the latter two functions are located so long as they are available, whereas it does matter, and very much so, for the Jews. The Jewish towns are to develop into vibrant urban centers, and to that end, Arab employment needs and needs for commercial and professional services are appropriated for that development.

The plan does speak, in its final page, of the advisability of preparation of outline and development plans for the Arab localities, of a program of vocational training for the Arab population to prepare them for employment, and of developing transportation and other infrastructure to facilitate integration. But these are potential policies; they hardly qualify as "intentional development channels," whereas what the plan already accomplishes by its very organization of future policy and planning is the appropriation of Arab needs and development potential for the sake of the Jewish settlement inserted into the region.

The critics of the way in which the growth-pole concept was employed by regional planners worldwide pointed out the false sanguinity fostered by the naïve belief that the growth center would be "an engine for accelerated development in the periphery," as *AUDG* put it (Higgins 1988: 44; *AUDG*, 40). But how much more naïve and ill-founded must that promise appear in the *AUDG* case, where development and its rationale and aims are *organized* by the perception of the Jewish struggle for territorial control against the threat posed by the Arab population of Galilee.

Altogether, it would be well to recall that Karmi'el and Upper Nazareth were not spontaneous developments; rather, they had been planted in Galilee with the express intention of *thwarting* the emergence of Arab metropolitan centers there. But once they were in place, with their presence normalized, as it were, it was easy to speak of them as poles of development for the entire region. By that point, it was possible to wonder, as did one of my Jewish sources, why it was so taken for granted that development to meet Arab needs could only be accomplished by inserting and developing a Jewish town.

Throughout the 1980s and the 1990s, the appropriation of Arab employment needs in Galilee was standard practice in justifying the development of the Jewish cities' industrial areas and the expansion of their areas of jurisdiction to that end—thus, in the case of Upper Nazareth's Zipporit and in the case of Karmi'el's bid for a share in the Bar Lev industrial development and its plan for further industrial development to its east (for discussion of the Karmi'el cases, see chapter 7). The Galilee Development Authority's *Yearbook* for 1995 (448), describing Karmi'el's industrial project, had this to say: "With the growth of the city and its becoming a regional urban center—for all the localities of the area, including the Arab sector—Karmi'el has growth potential." But particularly ironic and astonishing is the following passage from an expert opinion submitted to the HCJ in support of the transfer of land to Upper Nazareth for the development of Zipporit (Frenkl 1996, 25):

> Zipporit is intended to be a large interurban employment area. As such, it will provide places of employment to meet the expected demand not only for the residents of Upper Nazareth, but also for the residents of the region, particularly from the many non-Jewish localities, in which the land reserves for the development of industry are extremely limited.

Development is thought of as pertaining to the Jewish towns, not the Arab ones (see, e.g., Alterman and Stav 2001: 93, passim). The perception, despite the "regional" vocabulary of plans such as *AUDG*, is clearly sectoral. It is this which, among other factors, enables the appropriation of the development needs and potential of the Arab towns, and is a major factor in the exclusion of the Arab towns from development.

According to the growth-pole approach, spread effects from the development pole are expected to raise the level of the entire region. But there may be the opposite effect—that of polarization between the growth center and the region's periphery. There may be development in the periphery, but overall, the region's resources and growth potential are diverted to the growth pole. Before considering this dimension of the effect of the *AUDG* approach, however, I believe it would be in place to direct some attention to two related topics: (a) the employment benefits offered to the surrounding Arab towns by the implanting of Karmi'el and Upper Nazareth, and (b) some aspects of what may be thought of as *AUDG*'s two-pronged program, according to which the Jewish towns became the location for large regional industrial areas, while small local industrial areas were developed in several of the Arab towns.

Employment Opportunities

There would seem to be little doubt that Upper Nazareth and Karmi'el, as urban centers including their industrial areas, have been a factor in providing employment for the Arab towns in their vicinity. In table 7.1, I present data extracted for the present study from the 20 percent sample enumeration of the 1995 Census. Of all who worked in Karmi'el in 1995, 13 percent lived in an Arab town in Biq'at Bet Hakerem (line B1 in table 6.1), while of all the employed residents of the Arab towns in Biq'at Bet Hakerem, 14.9 percent worked in Karmi'el (line B3). Of all who worked in Upper Nazareth, 10 percent lived in an Arab town (including Nazareth) in the vicinity of Upper Nazareth (line A1). Discrepant results were obtained for the obverse Upper Nazareth figure, however: of employed residents of Arab towns in the vicinity of Upper Nazareth (including Nazareth), only 3.5 percent worked in Upper Nazareth (line A3). This result may reflect the circumstance that Nazareth

Table 6.1 Locality of Work for Those Who Live in Arab Towns in the Vicinity of Upper Nazareth or Karmi'el; Locality of Residence for Those Who Work in Upper Nazareth or Karmi'el (1995)

Line		
A1	Percentage of workers in Upper Nazareth who live in an Arab town (including Nazareth) in the vicinity of Upper Nazareth	1205 / 11130 = 10.8%
A2	Percentage of workers in Upper Nazareth who live in any Arab town	1485 / 11130 = 13.5%
A3	Percentage of employed residents of Arab towns in vicinity of Upper Nazareth (including Nazareth) who work in Upper Nazareth	1205 / 34645 = 3.5%
A4	Percentage of workers in Upper Nazareth who live outside the Upper Nazareth natural region	1660 / 11130 = 14.9%
B1	Percentage of workers in Karmi'el who live in an Arab town in Biq'at Bet Hakerem	1510 / 11530 = 13.0%
B2	Percentage of workers in Karmi'el who live in any Arab town	2325 / 11530 = 20.2%
B3	Percentage of employed residents of Arab towns in Biq'at Bet Hakerem who work in Karmi'el	1510 / 10150 = 14.9%
B4	Percentage of workers in Karmi'el who live outside the Karmi'el natural region	2950 / 11530 = 25.6%

Notes: A1, A3: Arab towns in the vicinity of Upper Nazareth included here are Tur'an, Ein Mahel, Dabburye, Iksal, Yafi', Reine, Meshhed, Kafar Kanna, and Nazareth (see figure 1.1 and table 2.11).

B1, B3: Arab towns in Biq'at Bet Hakerem are Majd al Kurum, Bi'ne, Deir al Asad, Nahef, Sajur, and Rame (see figure 7.1 and table 2.11).

One should note the large number of "locality of work unknown" responses in the 20 percent sample enumeration of the 1995 Census from which the data presented here are drawn (see note to table 2.10).

Data supplied courtesy of the CBS.

itself is a large city and would be expected to provide employment opportunities for Nazareth residents and those of the neighboring Arab towns; investigation would require further data.

In general, the results for 1995 presented in table 6.1 are in line with those obtained in research for earlier years by other authors. Thus, Kipnis (1976: 59) found that of the employed residents of the Arab towns in Central Galilee and the Nazareth area, 15.3 percent worked in a nearby Jewish city (compare with lines A3 and B3 in table 6.1). For 1985, Rosenfeld (1988: 50) found that of the total employed in Upper Nazareth, 16.6 percent were Arab (compare with line A2 in table 6.1). For 1989, Yiftachel (1991: 173) reported that of all employed in the Karmi'el *industrial area,* 37.7 percent were Arab (compare with line B2 in table 6.1; note that data in that line refer to the entire city of Karmi'el). Yiftachel also reports (1997: 61) that in 1989, 12 percent of Majd al Kurum's labor force worked in the enterprises of the Karmi'el *industrial area,* and that Majd al

Kurum officials estimated that 25 percent of the locality's labor force worked in Karmi'el (compare both these figures with line B3 in table 6.1).

New employment opportunities go beyond direct employment in enterprises located in the Jewish towns. They include work in construction, transport services (of people and goods), building maintenance, vehicle maintenance, and so forth. Yiftachel (both citations above) describes these employment facets based on his 1989 survey of employment for residents of the towns of Biq'at Bet Hakerem in Karmi'el and its industrial area.

The former head of the Zipporit municipal industrial authority told me that

> in 2001, of the approximately 2,200 employees in Zipporit, 10 to 14 percent are Arab—from all of the towns of the area, including Nazareth. The production manager of one of the plants is an Arab; the architect of the industrial park is an Arab; there are Arab laborers and skilled workers. In addition to those employed directly in the park, there are another five hundred to one thousand people engaged as subcontractors; During periods of construction, there are more. Also, there are those engaged in transportation, shipment. Phoenicia [the factory] has an Arab subcontractor who provides all of the wood products.

One may note the point-local thoroughness of an investigation such as that carried out by Yiftachel in comparison with the generality of census data.[3] But there may also be a development effect at work that would escape even more specific surveys: as a result of increasing economic activity, one would also expect to find new enterprises in the Arab towns and employment of local residents there even where there are no unmediated links with the central town.

Yiftachel calls attention to the occupational stratification that carries over to Arab employment in the Karmi'el industrial area (see his table 7, 1991: 176). He cites Arab leaders to the effect "that while the level of education and professional qualification [has been] constantly rising in the Arab sector, professional employment opportunities have remained extremely limited" (176). An official of the Kafar Kanna local council made a similar point while speaking with me about Upper Nazareth's Zipporit: "We have engineers, technicians, professional graduates—but there is no employment for them there."

The picture painted for me by the head of the Zipporit municipal industrial authority was not checked in the field. I present it above as an individual, perhaps overly roseate, report. Obviously, his response was framed to meet the expectations that he read in my question. By his own figures, about 40 percent of the Zipporit employees come from outside the immediate area, which would include many from Haifa, the Haifa Bay area, even Karmi'el. I was told by a Phoenicia management person that while about 10 percent of the plant's employees came from the nearby Arab towns, about 37 percent were either from the former Haifa Bay plant or were engineers and executives from outside the region. This phenomenon finds expression in lines A4 and B4 in table 6.1.

The Two-Pronged Program: Large Industrial Areas for the Region and Small Local Ones for the Arab Towns

By the time *AUDG* was written, the Ministry of Industry had already taken up the large, regional industrial area approach. *AUDG* (48) cites Ministry of Industry and ILA sources identifying (i.e., locating on the map for future planning) seven such areas in the Northern District, key places among the major industrial infrastructure projects that would be developed in Galilee during the 1980s and 1990s. Such large industrial areas or parks (minimally 1,000 dunam according to *AUDG*) held out the chance to get away from the small areas located *inside* the cities, where aesthetics and upkeep had been neglected; they concentrated damage to the environment and provided better control over such damage; and they made room for agglomeration effects, an element of the growth-pole concept that Lichfield (1971) had introduced into Israeli regional planning.

The terminology was slippery. *AUDG* referred to these industrial areas as *interurban,* without regard for municipal affiliation. Thus, areas in the jurisdiction of a city or a regional council (or later, belonging jointly to a number of local authorities) were all labeled *interurban.* The meaning that emerges from the planning texts (*AUDG,* and later, *National Outline Plan 31* [*NOP 31*] and the *1992 Northern District Development Plan*) is an industrial area that would be a focal point of industrial development and would serve the employment needs of an entire region, that is, of a number of localities. But an *NOP 31* appendix on industrial development spoke of the desirability of developing large industrial complexes (*krayot*) of at least 2,000 dunam and called them *regional* (*ezoriot*) (Meir Ariav 1991). In the field, it was not unusual to hear the large industrial areas referred to alternatively, apparently at the speaker's preference, both as regional and interurban areas, without regard for the element of municipal jurisdiction. At the same time, this rather nonchalant disregard for the niceties of semantic precision became somewhat more difficult to sustain when in 1989 and 1990 two *local industrial authorities* were established by the Ministry of the Interior, a new form of local authority having only industrial and industry-related establishments in its jurisdiction and independent of any existing municipality.[4] A policy document prepared for the Ministry of Industry in 1991 extolled the virtues of this form of local authority, that is, the development of large industrial areas of 1,000 to 1,500 dunam, and defined it as truly "interurban" (Avnimelech et al. 1991: 17–21). The Ministry of the Interior and the local authorities were not kindly disposed to this municipal arrangement, however, as it deprived the neighboring local authorities of control and tax revenue; no more local industrial authorities were established after the first two. Instead, the Ministry of the Interior, and the Ministry of Industry in its wake, moved toward promoting local authority cooperation in the form of joint industrial areas. This could be a way of mobilizing large tracts of rural land for regional industrial areas; as for terminology, it tapped another sense of the term "interurban" (see, e.g., Razin et al. 1994: 20–21; Razin and Hazan 1994a: 17–27; 1994b: 40–42).

The large regional industrial areas and those being built in the Arab localities differed from one another in a number of ways. The very size of the former had implications for the size of the plots and what kind of enterprise could be induced to locate in the industrial area. Not all the parcels in Zipporit A were large, but there were enough large ones to determine the general impression made by the area. Parcels of ten, or even tens of dunam (rather than 1.8 dunam, as in the Kafar Kanna industrial area), wider roads, wider setbacks from the road, generous parking facilities, and more extensive landscaping and open public area or open private area all contributed to the ability to attract large, modern, sophisticated enterprises. Moreover, the regional industrial areas were advertising and actively seeking and wooing capital investment, often from overseas. This aggressive marketing of the industrial area was aided by collaboration between the local government and the Ministry of Industry and the Investment Center. The Jewish local authorities had the political strength and access to the centers of power that made such collaboration possible and natural, something that the Arab local authorities did not have.

On the other hand, the small local areas being built in the Arab towns were indeed a response to local need. They could improve the quality of life in these towns by getting enterprises out from under peoples' homes, and they could open up possibilities for expanding and developing. Indeed, when enterprises were located under the houses and in the narrow streets of the towns, the owners could not even begin to think of expansion. In contrast, by providing suitable physical conditions and infrastructure, the new areas could stimulate a drive for development. These areas were not geared to attract outside investors—the rationale propounded by Ministry of Industry personnel was that of clearing out nuisances from the residential areas (*pinui mitradim*). Often they were called, by officials and on the plans themselves, workshop areas (*ezorei melacha*); the reference was to marble cutting, auto repair, and carpentry or metalworking shops. The sense of disparagement of Arab readiness for industrial development connected to the image of Arab traditionalism was not far behind.

It may be noted that the dual program of large regional industrial areas and small local ones in the Arab towns contributed to the objectification of the Arab/Jewish distinction and shifted attention away from the absence of Arab town participation (as towns, not as individual entrepreneurs) in the regional areas. The *AUDG* two-pronged program opened up the space to say "small workshop areas of thirty to forty dunam for the Arab towns," and also, "not every Arab town needs an industrial area."

By 1997, the Ministry of Industry had developed fourteen large regional industrial areas in Galilee, totaling about 22,000 dunam (11,000 net for industry). This may be compared with the fourteen local areas in the Arab towns in Galilee, *totaling* about 750 dunam net. In 1996, an official of one of the infrastructure development companies at work in Galilee told me: "What the

Ministry of Industry is currently doing in Kafar Kanna—that's small peanuts (*prutot*)—a part of the program of throwing scraps to the Arab sector. But Zipporit [the Upper Nazareth part] is big, significant." It may be recalled that in 1995, 48 percent of the population of Galilee (not including the Golan) were Arabs residing in Arab towns (see table 1.3 and the notes thereto).[5] The comparative figures on industrial areas should be evaluated accordingly. Caution is required, though: employment for the Arab population provided by the regional industrial areas needs to be factored into such an evaluation.

The new local industrial areas in the Arab towns were an advance for these towns, something needed, to be sure. On the other hand, industrial development for the Jewish towns, by following the path of accelerated development through large regional industrial parks, had advanced by the end of the 1990s to a radically new, sophisticated level. This was an advance in which the Arab towns did not share, precisely by virtue of the two-pronged program first laid down by *AUDG*. The comparative figures speak for themselves, but I am making a point here beyond the figures: the effect of including the Arab towns in the two-pronged program has been to exclude them from the main thrust of Galilee development.

Polarization

In Israeli regional planning, Galilee has been considered one of the country's peripheral areas. That condition is exactly what programs like *AUDG* are designed to counter as part of achieving the dispersal of the Jewish population to such areas. And the Arab population in Galilee is perceived to be handicapped both by virtue of the region's distance from the country's core and by virtue of being themselves cut off from centers of power, information flow, and so forth (see, e.g., Schnell et al. 1995). I will have occasion to comment below on this aspect of Arab peripherality.

The question I wish to raise here, though, pertains to the possibility of the polarization of development (in the core-periphery sense) *within* Galilee—indeed within the circumscribed areas of Karmi'el and the Arab towns in Biq'at Bet Hakerem and of Upper Nazareth and the Arab towns in its vicinity.

One needs to beware of confusion in the meaning of terms stemming from the double origin of the word "pole." Perroux used it in the sense of a vector of development—a stake to which development would fasten—and he carried over this sense to his term "polarization." But other scholars writing on regional economic development at about the same time as Perroux used "polarization" in the sense of concentration about or gravitation to opposing extremes (see Hermansen 1972: 184; also Lasuén 1972: 47–48n43). Hirschman and Myrdal both dealt with polarization in the latter sense. Hirschman (1958: 187–190) used the term "trickle down effects" in the sense that growth-pole theorists spoke of "spread effects," but he pointed out that as a result of polarization, rather than benefiting from such effects, the hinterland may be drained of its resources. Myrdal (1957), speaking of "backwash effects" countering spread effects, emphasized that polarization may bring about a lasting dual society in which industrial and geographical backwardness coincide (cf. also Hermansen 1972: 184–185). Later, Friedmann (1972), writing on regional economic development, dealt at length with the connection between polarization and the ensuing emergence of core-periphery systems.[6] Friedmann took note of the hierarchical nature of spatial systems and called attention to the fact that the periphery of one system may contain within itself both core and periphery. It is this to which I attend here.

Consider the differential access to employment opportunities offered by the new regional industrial areas and the increasing gap in urban vigor opened up by *AUDG*'s two-pronged approach to the development of industrial areas. Consider also *AUDG*'s appropriating the need for services on the part of the inhabitants of the Arab towns to serve the development potential of the new Jewish localities. These create development disparities and lead to the transfer of resources from the Arab hinterland to the newly implanted Jewish towns. Recall also that the reason adduced in support of the transfer of WMS land to Upper Nazareth for the development of Zipporit A was that the land reserves for the development of industry in the Arab towns were extremely limited (Frenkl 1996: 25, cited earlier). Recall as well that the establishment of Karmi'el and Upper Nazareth had been made possible by the expropriation of Arab-owned land and the circumscription of the areas of jurisdiction of the Arab towns—surely another dimension of the transfer of resources. I suggest that beyond the positive effects that development of the Jewish towns had for the Arab population, one may also find the polarization of development at work. Indeed, Yiftachel's 1991 study addresses this question, particularly in regard to three industrial areas in Galilee, and finds that despite benefits to the Arab population, these areas "have worked to widen pre-existing economic gaps between Arabs and Jews" (177). Importantly, Yiftachel looks not only at employment opportunities created, but also at other economic linkages.

The possibility of the concatenation of development and polarization was brought home to me vividly when I visited the offices of the newly established Biq'at Bet Hakerem Local Planning and Building Commission in 1998. This commission served the six Arab towns in Biq'at Bet Hakerem, which had hitherto belonged to the ponderously slow-moving Central Galilee Planning and Building Commission together with twenty-one other localities.[7] The Biq'at Bet Hakerem commission had its offices, for whatever reason, in the Karmi'el industrial area.

The commission's engineer showed me aerial photographs of the Biq'a from about the time Karmi'el was established in 1964. "Look how small the Arab villages were then—just a few houses here and there—and see how much they've grown," he told me. Indeed, in 1962, the population of these towns was less than a third of the 37,700 they numbered in 1995, while Karmi'el by the latter date had grown to 33,100. He went on:

> Karmi'el is at the center of all this. If you live in one of these towns and want to put up a factory or find work, it's only natural to come to Karmi'el—there is a hierarchy of functions—starting from the center and going out. It's natural for a main function—like industry, like a regional health office—to be located in Karmi'el, while you would find subsidiary functions in the towns.

Karmi'el, as I have observed, had been planted here with the aim of putting a brake on what Arnon Soffer had called the metropolitanization of the Arab towns. Now, it was center—the *natural* heart and head of the functions of life in Biq'at Bet Hakerem.

"Polarization" is, of course, a way of saying that there is a growing rather than a narrowing gap between the well-being of the residents of the Arab towns and those of the Jewish towns at their center. With the intention of gaining some initial clue as to the direction of development, I looked at the socioeconomic indexes of the Arab towns in Biq'at Bet Hakerem and those of Karmi'el as measured in 1993–1994, 1995, and 1999, and similar data for Upper Nazareth and the Arab towns in its vicinity. These data are presented in table 6.2.

The socioeconomic indexes that served as the basis for compiling table 6.2 are built by factor analysis from variables having to do with demography (dependency ratio, persons per household, etc.), standard of living (per capita income and other variables), education, and employment. With the exception of Nazareth, Upper Nazareth, and Karmi'el, index values for the individual localities are not shown in table 6.2. The index values for the Arab towns as a group are an average of the values for the individual towns weighted by population. These are presented in columns 2, 4, and 6. Their divergence from the index for Upper Nazareth or for Karmi'el is shown in columns 3, 5, and 7.

One should note the different sense of the minus sign in the two sets of columns. The indexes represented in columns 2, 4, and 6 are an average, for each town, of the standard deviations of the various factors, with the deviation for each factor distributed around a mean of zero. The index goes from –2.36 to +3.71 in 1993–1994; –2.16 to +2.99 in 1995; and –2.22 to +3.01 in 1999. Thus, in column 4, for example, –0.831 is simply the lowest value, whereas +0.331 is the highest, with the others distributed between them. The minus sign is merely a part (albeit an essential part) of the designation of a particular point on the continuum. In contrast, the minus signs in columns 3, 5, and 7 indicate difference and the direction of the difference of the index of the Arab town or group of towns from either Upper Nazareth or Karmi'el. Hence, column 5, for example, shows that in 1995 the socioeconomic index for the Arab towns in Biq'at Bet Hakerem was lower by 1.162 than Karmi'el's.

It may be noted that the data for 1995 include in the per capita income variable five different welfare payments. The data for this variable for 1993–1994 did not include these welfare payments. It would be expected that their inclusion for 1995 would have raised the value of the index, particularly in the case of those

Table 6.2 Socioeconomic Index for Towns in the Biq'at Bet Hakerem and Nazareth Areas for 1993–1994, 1995, and 1999

1	2	3	4	5	6	7
	S-E index 1993–1994	Difference from Upper Nazareth/ Karmi'el	S-E index 1995	Difference from Upper Nazareth/ Karmi'el	S-E index 1999	Difference from Upper Nazareth/ Karmi'el
Towns around Nazareth	−0.837	−0.398	−0.792	−0.777	−0.857	−0.881
Nazareth	−0.563	−0.124	−0.547	−0.532	−0.586	−0.610
Total (ave.)	−0.726	−0.287	−0.693	−0.678	−0.749	−0.773
Upper Nazareth	−0.439		−0.015		+0.024	
Towns in Biq'at Bet Hakerem	−0.852	−0.725	−0.831	−1.162	−0.766	−0.973
Karmi'el	−0.127		+0.331		+0.207	

Notes: S-E index = socioeconomic index. Towns around Nazareth, other than Nazareth, are Tur'an, Ein Mahel, Dabburye, Iksal, Yafi', Reine, Meshhed, Kafar Kanna, and 'Ilut (see figure 1.1). Towns in Biq'at Bet Hakerem are Majd al Kurum, Bi'ne, Deir al Asad, Nahef, Sajur, and Rame (see figure 7.1).

Sources: Socioeconomic rank for individual localities for 1993–1994 taken from CBS n.d., Publication no. 1039; rankings for 1995 taken from CBS 1999, Publication no. 1118; rankings for 1999 are from data supplied directly by the CBS (spring 2002). Ranks of individual localities were then weighted for population of the locality and averaged for each area.

localities where conditions would warrant a higher incidence of such payments. Indeed, in the transition from 1993–1994 to 1995, the value of the socioeconomic index for most of the Arab towns represented in table 6.2 did rise, generally by very modest amounts. But for two of the Arab towns in the Nazareth area, the value of the index dropped—in the case of Tur'an by quite a bit. In the Biq'at Bet Hakerem area, the value of the index for three (half) of the Arab towns dropped considerably. At the same time, the value of the index for the two Jewish towns, Upper Nazareth and Karmi'el, rose by a considerable amount.

Altogether, there would seem to be a persisting and even *growing* difference over the course of 1993–1994 to 1995 to 1999 between the socioeconomic index for Upper Nazareth and Karmi'el and the Arab towns in their vicinity, this despite the addition of transfer payments to the index for 1995. Even in the case of Biq'at Bet Hakerem, where the difference first rose and then dropped, it was greater in 1999 than it was in 1993–1994. The differences are not extraordinarily large—Karmi'el and Upper Nazareth themselves rank only in Cluster 5 (out of ten; see table 2.1 and text at the beginning of chapter 2).[8] It may be observed that for 1995, for example, the differences ranged from one-half to over one standard deviation. The average index values for the Arab towns in

Biq'at Bet Hakerem would have put them, as a group, three clusters away from Karmi'el, while the Arab towns in the vicinity of Upper Nazareth were two clusters away from the latter town. By 1999, this situation had reversed itself: the Arab towns in Biq'at Bet Hakerem fell as a group two clusters away from Karmi'el, while the Arab towns in the vicinity of Upper Nazareth were (without the inclusion of Nazareth) three clusters away from the Jewish town.

Yiftachel's 1991 study employed a focal point–outward orientation. There is always the possibility, however, that other growth-generating forces are at work, and that these have not been caught by a study's selection of particular focal points or factors. By contrast, the look at changes in socioeconomic index and rankings that I have presented here may contribute a sense of comparative final outcomes in development.

What has been the overall effect of Karmi'el and Upper Nazareth on the Arab towns in their vicinity? There is no apparent indication that the Arab towns in those two areas have developed more than other Arab towns on average due to their proximity to Upper Nazareth or Karmi'el. Of course, a significant number of the other Arab towns are near other Jewish centers, such as Akko, the Haifa Bay area, Haifa, Hadera, Netanya, Kfar Saba. Obviously, the data I have are limited and do not allow for a strong argument on polarization. But I submit that they do allow for a weak one. By 1999, Upper Nazareth had been in place for forty-two years, Karmi'el for thirty-five years; if they were going to have any appreciable effect on accelerating development in the Arab towns toward equalization with the Jewish sector, that effect ought to be discernable by now. Even only the period of twenty-two years from the appearance of *AUDG* until 1999 ought to have been enough for that. Yet it is the gap between the Arab towns in these two areas and Upper Nazareth and Karmi'el that is plainly visible.

There is another dimension of center-periphery relations, one that goes beyond the question of polarization *within* a region. This has to do with exclusion from national centers of decision making and innovative development. Sofer and Schnell (1996) and Schnell and colleagues (1999) deal with the complex social, political, and economic factors that have contributed to the peripheralization of Arab industry in the Israeli economy, and with the attempts of Arab entrepreneurs to overcome the barriers posed by such peripheralization. The 1999 study focuses particularly on market linkages. This subject is also examined by Abo Sharkia (1998).

As the final point to be made in this discussion of polarization, I should like to call attention to a use of the concept of peripherality to which I would take strenuous objection. I have heard a prominent Israeli geographer admonish those who sought to promote industrialization in the Arab towns in Galilee, arguing that one cannot establish industry in an isolated island. His position was that Arab towns in Galilee are in the periphery, and it is therefore a matter of fighting a losing battle to try to industrialize. Why not concentrate on restaurants and bed and breakfast lodging, to exploit one's relative advantages? If you want to put up industry, he contended, go to the interurban industrial areas. I have heard the location of the Arab towns in Israel's periphery described at a public forum as a matter of God-given geography. There is a sense here in which the geographer sees "periphery" as a natural and self-evident state of affairs. Perhaps it has its conceptual antecedent in Shils (1961), who well knew, of course, that center and the inevitable periphery were social phenomena and not geographic in nature. But Shils's concern, writing in another sociological age, was with the center as the benign origin of values, authority, and social order.

"It is geography that is God-given; periphery is not," commented the sociologist Aziz Haidar in response to the suggestion of their equivalence. Just so, Sofer and Schnell (1996) and Schnell and colleagues (1999) are sensitive to the undesirable effects of peripheral subordination and the ways in which peripheralization might be challenged. And I would point out that one needs only the examples of industry in the geographically far-flung kibbutzim and the endeavors of the well-known Jewish industrialist Stef Wertheimer, who makes good use of his ability to promote his projects in the corridors of power to put to naught any peripheralization that might be expected to ensue from the geographical location of those projects. Geographic distance does not preclude access to the centers of decision making and innovation.

The Discursive Elements of AUDG: Territorial Threat and Arab Traditionalism/Jewish Development and (Dependent) Arab Integration

Before concluding the discussion of *AUDG* and its implications for the dependent integration of the Arab population in Galilee, I would like to call attention to certain reservations that must be made regarding *AUDG* as a planning document. It was produced under the aegis of the Ministry of Housing as a program; it was not a statutory planning document. When I asked in the Ministry of Industry about the origins of what I refer to here as the two-pronged approach to industrial area development, none of those with whom I spoke mentioned *AUDG;* the elements of that approach were plainly visible in current programs, yet the document itself was a thing of the past.

AUDG's population goals for Upper Nazareth, Karmi'el, and Zefat were never achieved (it foresaw 45,000, 42,000, and 65,000 in these cities, respectively, in 1992, whereas the 1995 Census found 32,000, 33,000, and 21,000). The recommended new housing developments for the Arab population near Shefar'am and Akko were never built, and it took two decades for its industrial area program, both with regard to the regional ones and the local ones in the Arab towns, to materialize.

But what *is* important about *AUDG* is, I would suggest, its discursive dimension. To begin with, *AUDG* came into being in what may be thought of as the discursive intersection of the perception of Arab town territorial threat and images of Arab traditionalism. In its turn, *AUDG* embodied discursive elements having to do with appropriation of the development needs and potential of the Arab population in Galilee, together with the integration of that population. Statements to the effect of "not every Arab town needs an industrial area" were minor statements in the discourse opened up by *AUDG*. More central ones found expression in general and specific Ministry of Interior, Ministry of Industry, and ILA programs and plans, such as those for Zipporit and those for the local industrial areas in the Arab towns. The discourse also provided space for statements that I found in the field asserting that Karmi'el's growth should be promoted to make it possible for the city to aid the growth of the other localities in the region. The appropriation of the development needs and potential of the Arab population in Galilee had, I argue, strategic consequences for the geography and topology of Jewish-Arab power relations in Galilee. One may compare the approach I adopt here to the path taken by Rabinow in his study of French urbanism. From this perspective, *AUDG* is seen here as a "strategic exemplar" whose analysis, in terms of strategic uses, transformations, and resistances, may illuminate a particular nucleus of knowledge and power (cf. Rabinow 1989: 212).

Perhaps the most cogent indication of the intimate intertwining of discourse and power is to be seen in the circumstance that the ILA plans for local industrial areas in the Arab towns, plans that had been drawn in the late 1970s and the 1980s, were not translated into action until the 1990s, when they were undertaken in tandem with the actual implementation of plans for the large regional areas and in conformity to the link embodied in the two-pronged AUDG program. I would emphasize: the programs and plans, whether general or specific, have to be understood in the context of administrative practice and political maneuver and negotiation—an approach I have used in chapter 3 and to which I return in chapter 7.

New Uses of the "Growth-Center" Concept in the 1990s

There were what may be thought of as countervailing forces acting against polarization. The first of these, of course, was inherent in the new employment opportunities that the regional industrial areas and expanding Jewish development and construction *did* offer to the Arab residents of the region. Another, undoubtedly, was the significantly increasing level of educational attainment among the Arab population. A third has to do with government programs that arose in the 1990s out of a reformulation of the implications of the growth-pole strategy for development. It will be recalled that *AUDG* had posited improvement in the situation of the Arabs in Galilee as a result of having new employment opportunities (whether in the regional or the local industrial areas) and access to professional and government services that would be located in the central Jewish towns. It suggested only in passing that it would be desirable to develop a program of occupational training for the Arab population and that steps ought to be taken to prepare development and outline plans for their towns, but beyond this, it did not consider the question of channels by which the development impulse might be transmitted to those towns.

By contrast, Bar-El and colleagues produced in 1990 (under Jewish Agency sponsorship) a document titled *Urban Growth Centers in Galilee*. Employing growth-pole terminology, this was a program calling for a high degree of integration of the urban Jewish, rural Jewish, and Arab populations in Galilee. It advocated a unified, nonsectoral approach to government intervention, joint Arab-Arab and Arab-Jewish industrial parks, and specific steps to promote economic development in the Arab towns, including the establishment of local centers for the development of entrepreneurship (*merkazei tipu'ach yazamut*), small-business loan funds, and bottom-up stimulation of skills and entrepreneurship. This approach was repeated by Bar-El in 1994, by then director-general of the Economic and National Planning Authority in the Ministry of the Economy and Planning. The proposals for stimulating entrepreneurship in the Arab towns were put into practice by the Rabin government under which Bar-El served (see, e.g., the 1995 publication of the Ministry of Industry; see also Czamanski and Khamaisi 1993; Blumenkrantz 1995). In addition, during this time there was considerable activity by the Center for Jewish-Arab Economic Development (CJAED), a nongovernment organization that sponsored courses for young Arab entrepreneurs, as well as courses and conferences for officials of the Arab towns dealing with local urban development. CJAED also instituted its own small-business loan fund (in addition to that of the government's Small Business Authority). Further, the JDC broadened its support of local "strategic planning units" to include a number of Arab localities.

Beyond mentioning them here, these moves fall outside the scope of the present study. They merit examination in their own right. Such study might address issues of neoliberalism, the conception of "development from below," and government input into such activity. Among other things, it might be argued that instruction aimed at heightening the effectiveness of the clients of the bureaucratic access system does not change the basic alignment of power. However, I believe it important to suggest here that, as usual, things cut, or can be made to cut, in two ways. Such programs did feed into new activism on the part of the Arab towns, and this is one of the developments that will be addressed in chapter 7.

CHAPTER 7

Attempts to Break Through the Boundaries

Cooperation between Local Authorities

The bid by Kafar Kanna and Meshhed to join the Zipporit industrial area was not the only move of its kind, though it is certainly the most prominent, in part by virtue of the clearly visible political maneuver mounted by the Arab towns and their leaders. Such participation might be seen as an attempt to break through the boundaries separating Jewish development from Arab development as set by *AUDG*. The Ministry of the Interior and its boundary commissions, and later, the Ministry of Industry were involved in varying degrees and ways in such moves. This chapter will take up these events. It needs to be pointed out that the Arab town activism in the Zipporit case was not the usual state of affairs in the early 1990s. Indeed, what the present chapter will argue is that there has been a discernible line of development during the past decade and a half from Arab town passivity and noninvolvement in the development planning process to clearly articulated demands for inclusion. During the course of this presentation there will be occasion to give some attention to the way in which the authorities invoked images of environmental protection and of landscape and tourism in response to Arab demands for industrial development.

As mentioned in the previous chapter, in the early 1990s, the Ministry of the Interior had come over to the idea of cooperation between local authorities in setting up joint industrial areas in general, that is, without reference to the Arab localities. The cutbacks in central government funding for the local authorities that had taken place in the mid 1980s (see table 2.3) had pushed the latter into taking an active role in promoting local economic development. Their aim was new economic activity that would provide employment for local residents and generate local property tax revenues.[1] It was the growing involvement of local authorities in local economic development that led to increased struggle over territory between urban localities and the rural authorities that bounded them, for planning logic and constraints dictated that industrial development be sited on the urban periphery. Boundary disputes led to the appointment of boundary investigation commissions by the minister of the interior. But one of the corollaries of increasing conflict was also the emergence of cooperation between local authorities for development as a rational option (see Razin and Hazan 1994a, 1994b). The conceptual model for cooperation was provided by Tzahar, an industrial park set up in 1992 by three Jewish local authorities in Galilee: Zefat, Hatzor, and Rosh Pina. The latter was able to provide land, and the first two, each in its own way, were able to mobilize the support of the central government. The industrial park was located in Rosh Pina's jurisdiction, but the three local authorities established a joint corporation to manage it. The presence of an industrial park management authority was seen as a way of ensuring that the enterprises that would locate in the area would have their needs well taken care of rather than merely being prey to municipal taxation and subsequent neglect. It should also be noted, however, that the participating local authorities remained bound by local interests, and it emerged that "joint" carries with it the ensuing potential for friction and misunderstanding.

These developments in the general local authority–central government context were what enabled Arab Kafar Kanna and Meshhed to make their bid to join Zipporit in 1992 (see chapter 3). Rassem Khamaisi and the Center for Strategic Planning in the Arab Municipalities located in Kafar Kanna, which he headed, were prime movers in the formulation of this bid. At the same time, Khamaisi cooperated with Amiram Gonen of the Floersheimer Institute in publishing a discussion of a proposal to turn a number of regional industrial areas into joint Arab and Jewish regional development centers (Gonen and Khamaisi 1992). The authors used the term "development centers" to reflect their view that these areas ought to provide room for services and tertiary economic activity rather than being restricted to manufacturing. Arab entrepreneurs, they said, would be more likely to find a place in a more broadly defined area. They also pointed out that the joint presence of Jewish and Arab firms would contribute to learning on the part of the Arab entrepreneurs, while the presence of official representatives of the Arab towns would provide needed support and reassurance for fledgling Arab industrialists.

I turn now to consideration of a number of the other actual cases in which the idea of the participation of Arab towns in neighboring regional industrial areas figured.

Majd al Kurum and the Bar Lev Industrial Area

Karmi'el had requested jurisdiction over the area, several kilometers outside its boundaries, that would eventually be developed as the Bar Lev industrial area (see figure 7.1). In its position paper submitted to the Ministry of Interior–appointed boundary commission in support of its request, Karmi'el noted that

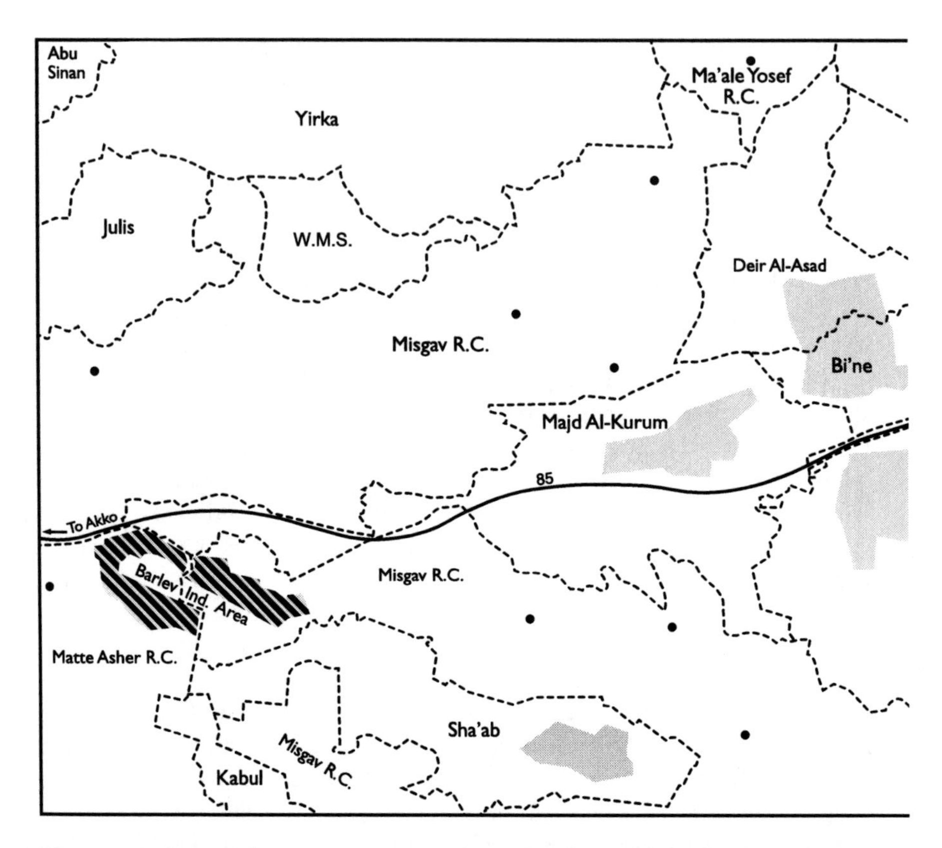

Figure 7.1 Biq'at Bet Hakerem Area. *Sources and notes:* Based on Ministry of Interior sources for boundaries of jurisdiction and on specific urban building plans, as well as municipal sources for industrial areas. Built-up areas are adapted from the 1:50,000 series of trip and paths maps

the economic success of the Jewish towns was a key to the success of the plan to Judaize Galilee and that industrialization was a basic element. The position paper went on to note that the Arab population in Biq'at Bet Hakerem was also expected to grow significantly; that that population would need to find employment mainly in industry; and that it was important for both national (read "Jewish nation") and local considerations that the industrial areas providing such employment be located in Karmi'el's jurisdiction (Karmi'el 1990; A. Soffer 1990).[2]

The boundary commission, headed by Shalom Reichman, recommended instead that a municipal union be set up to develop the industrial area. The boundary commission specified that the municipal union should include Karmi'el; the two regional councils (Misgav and Matte Asher) in whose separate jurisdictions the land lay; and Majd al Kurum and Bi'ne, the two Arab towns bordering the area. The commission's report spoke of the aim of achieving greater active involvement in the development of industry on the part of

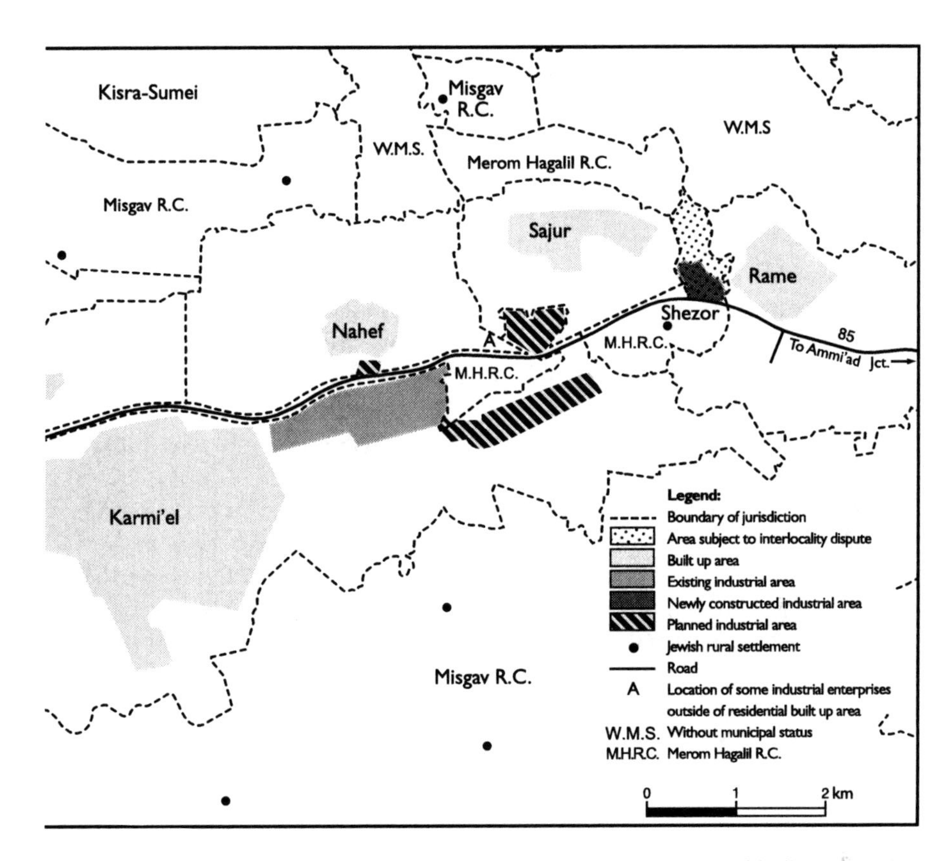

edited by Ori Dvir (printed by Survey of Israel). Except for the city of Karmi'el, all of the local authorities shown in figure 7.1 are Arab localities. Jewish rural settlements in regional councils (such settlements are localities but not local authorities) are marked by a small dot.

the local authorities situated in this geographic area (Reichman 1991). But implementation of this recommendation was not pressed. The Ministry of the Interior holds that interlocality cooperation cannot be mandated, and the Jewish localities involved were adamant in rejecting the idea.

A member of the boundary commission explained to me that commission members had seen the possible involvement of the Arab localities in development as something that should be aimed for, and this recommendation would be a precedent-setting move—justice whose time had perhaps come: "It would be right to do this." Yet Majd al Kurum and Bi'ne were not invited to testify at the commission's meetings and were not consulted; they did not know that the matter was on the agenda, nor were they informed of the commission's recommendation. "None of that was *our* job," explained the commission member with whom I spoke, "it was only later High Court of Justice decisions that made it mandatory for such commissions to actively seek out possibly interested parties." In any event, it was the two regional councils, Misgav and

Matte Asher, without Karmi'el participation, that would eventually cooperate in developing the Bar Lev industrial area.

Sajur and Karmi'el

But the young Jewish city of Karmi'el turned meanwhile to other plans, plans that brought it into contact with Sajur, its small Arab (Druze) neighbor just to its north across the Akko-Zefat road. This is the second Biq'at Bet Hakerem case to be considered here. The planned industrial area in question lay on two adjacent parcels to the north of the road that were transferred from Merom Hagalil Regional Council to Karmi'el's jurisdiction in March 1994. The area is seen on the map in figure 7.1 as the dark, striped "mushroom" shape that appears to project into Sajur's area of jurisdiction, reaching nearly to that town's built-up area.

The elders of Sajur, or their parents, say they purchased in common all the land of the village from the feudal landowner in 1944, including the two parcels now intended for the industrial area. But they could not establish the validity of the deed in the land registration court hearing in 1963, nor could they establish ownership under the Prescription Law (see chapter 4 on these topics in general), and the two parcels were registered in the name of the state, one in 1969 and the other in 1977.

The history of jurisdiction and the planning history of this area have some intricate permutations. Sajur, as a settled community, has existed at least since the sixteenth century,[3] but it was first established as an independent local authority in 1992. The late date of local authority establishment merely reflected the locality's small population. When the Merom Hagalil Regional Council was established in 1950, it included Sajur and its land. When the Sajur local authority was established in 1992, the two parcels in question remained in the regional council's jurisdiction.

Karmi'el requested that this land be transferred to its jurisdiction for the purposes of establishing an industrial area. This was in addition to a request for another approximately one thousand dunam of Merom Hagalil land south of the road for the same purpose, land that had lain within the village boundaries of Sajur during Mandatory times. The two requested additions to Karmi'el's east would double the area then in Karmi'el's jurisdiction zoned for industry. It may be noted that these two requests were separate from Karmi'el's abortive bid for control of or a share in the development of the Bar Lev industrial park several kilometers to the west.

Karmi'el's request for jurisdiction north of the road needs to be placed in the context of certain other moments in the planning history of the projected industrial area. The 1992 *Development and Outline Plan for the Northern District* (Shefer et al. 1992: 141–142), in presenting data on land reserves for industrial development, included this area in the category of reserves in *non-Jewish localities* and referred to it as the "Nahef industrial area." At about the same time, an ILA publication on land reserves for industry called it the "Nahef industrial area," but gave the name of the locality as Karmi'el (ILA, Department of Planning and Development 1991). It is clear from the coordinates of the map on page 13 of the ILA publication that the reference is to the site in Merom Hagalil to the east of Nahef, biting into Sajur's area of jurisdiction. Calling this the "Nahef industrial area" and classing it as an area in the non-Jewish sector, as the document by Shefer and colleagues did, gave rise to speculation by some over the next few years that it might be developed by and for the Arab towns of Biq'at Bet Hakerem (see Gonen and Khamaisi 1992: 21; 1993: 20–21 for internal evidence of thinking in this direction). But this was never translated into purposeful political action or concrete planning efforts.

Karmi'el's request for jurisdiction was being dealt with by a Ministry of Interior boundary commission under the chairmanship of Yigael Barzilai, appointed in 1991.[4] Karmi'el was acting here with great purpose. Both the Merom Hagalil Regional Council and Sajur (once it was constituted as a local authority in 1992) went on record before the commission to the effect that they had been planning to develop industry in this area north of the road, and at first, the commission was inclined to leave the area in the regional council's jurisdiction for development by the latter with the possible participation of Karmi'el (minutes of meeting, 13 November 1991). But Karmi'el did not relent, convincing the commission that as a dynamic urban locality, it had a better chance of developing the site than did the regional council, and that in its jurisdiction, more people would benefit from the fruits of such development (Barzilai 1993).

The commission recommended that the three local authorities (Karmi'el, Merom Hagalil, Sajur) should try to develop the area jointly, but only the chairman thought that it should be transferred immediately to the city's jurisdiction. A subsequent meeting was held at the DPBC in October 1993 in an attempt to push for the then-current Ministry of Interior policy of encouraging joint interlocality development of industry. It was at this meeting that a Karmi'el representative argued that since it was a developing city, Karmi'el's growth should be promoted to make it possible for the city to aid the growth of the other localities in the region. Some sense of Karmi'el's long-range drive may be gained from a statement by another of its representatives at this meeting to the effect that Karmi'el had assisted in getting this land north of the Akko-Zefat road transferred to the ILA (accomplished back in 1969 and 1977) with the intention of having it zoned for industry for Karmi'el. The conclusion of this meeting, although ambiguously worded, called for interlocality negotiations for joint development. But one of the planning officials present explicitly mentioned the desirability of cooperation between Karmi'el and Sajur (Minutes). In March 1994, the minister transferred the area to Karmi'el's jurisdiction.

Karmi'el did bring Sajur into the process of planning the industrial area, and there was a preliminary agreement to this effect between the two localities on 23 January 1994, an agreement that paved the way for the transfer of the land to Karmi'el's jurisdiction in March. By June 1997, a draft of a full agreement had been formulated, calling, among other things, for (a) a joint municipal industrial authority in which Sajur would have 40 percent representation and the vice-chairmanship; (b) allocation of 25 percent of the area to enterprises that Sajur would refer for approval; and (c) the division of the local taxes paid by all the occupants of the industrial area in a 30 percent to 70 percent ratio between Sajur and Karmi'el, respectively. Karmi'el submitted plans for the industrial area, and at some point, the DPBC sent them back to Karmi'el, because changes in the course of the road passing through the area to Sajur entailed changes in parcellation and because the district commission wanted full, finalized agreement on cooperation between the two local authorities.[5]

By April 1998, both conditions had been met, and the plan was ready to go back to the DPBC. The District Commission met on it in February 1999, and Karmi'el received the protocol of the meeting advising it of the commission's decision sometime at the end of March or the beginning of April. Only now, Karmi'el (and Sajur) discovered that there had been what amounted to a major shift in the commission's position, and by implication, in that of the Interior Ministry itself. I was told that the commission's answer on the industrial area was negative: the commission now thought that the land north of the Akko-Zefat road should be preserved as an open and green belt. People I spoke with expanded on this, stating that it didn't make planning sense to permit industry north of the road, that it was also a matter of the view and landscape. Karmi'el turned its attention to the major project of preparing a new outline plan for the entire area in its jurisdiction. Sajur had been finessed out of the picture.

Discourses of Environment and Landscape

Protecting the Environment

The striking turnabout in the DPBC position was hard to fathom. First, just fifteen hundred meters or so to the north lay the entire Meron mountain nature reserve—a wonderful green area that was far more extensive than any "belt"; second, the area that had been intended for industry was in any case open, stony field, not wooded or cultivated land,[6] and third, present-day planners are quite capable of producing an industrial area that blends into, preserves, and enhances the landscape rather than detracting from it. What then caused the shift in the DPBC position?

I put this question to people in the Ministry of the Environment. They pointed out that the views that prevail at a forum such as the DPBC may depend on changing political constellations—what representatives are present at the critical meeting; what the director-general of the Ministry of the Interior happens to be pushing at the time. Moreover, people find it easy to dress up "various positions" under the mantle of protecting the environment. The Ministry of Environment people with whom I was speaking went on to explain the environmental rationale for vetoing industrial development to the north of the road: there was already enough area for industry in the Northern District, they contended, and further development should be limited to expanding already existing regional industrial areas.[7] Look at Biq'at Bet Hakerem as a single metropolitan unit, they said, one that simply straddles the Akko-Zefat road. To the south of the road, there are the 33,000 residents of Karmi'el; to its north, the 37,000 of the six Arab towns. It shouldn't be necessary to create a mirror image to the north of the already existing industry to the south.

But there is definitely room to argue that there is a moral issue involved, my environmental conversants continued. Just at the juncture when developing industrial infrastructure in the Arab town seemed like an imminent possibility, environmental concerns have come to the fore and staunched such development. Then, too, one may observe that these concerns are not applied, or more accurately, do not win out uniformly; there are those who escape their limitations.

The political, power-laden nature of dealing with environmental concerns seems clear enough to me. In the case of Zipporit and the Phoenicia factory, Upper Nazareth had pushed its development into the backyard of the Arab towns, and in that case, those weaker towns had to fight to protect themselves from the dangers of pollution, while the environmental authorities were less than vigorous in establishing controls. But the Arab towns also made use of the environmental card in their maneuvers to gain entrance to the Zipporit project (see chapter 3). In the Biq'at Bet Hakerem case of industry north of the Akko-Zefat road, environmental concerns had served as the grounds for cutting off a project that would have had Sajur participating with Karmi'el in industrial development.

In their study of the way in which national, regional, and municipal plans in Israel relate to the Arab sector, Alterman and Stav (2001) find a new departure in the master plan for the Haifa metropolitan area submitted to the NBPB in 1999. The change is that, in this plan, in contrast to other plans they studied, such as earlier Northern District outline plans, "preservation of the landscape is meant to serve both sectors (Jewish and Arab) and no longer serves as a means of covering up the goal of restricting the development of the Arab sector" (112). But that relates to the text of a plan for metropolitan Haifa, and the instance of the Sajur-Karmi'el industrial area proposal took place in the Northern District where it is apparently easy, as I was told, to dress up "various positions" under the mantle of protecting the environment. Prompted by having been told that not allowing industry north of the Akko-Zefat road was not only a matter of a "green belt" but also one of view and landscape, I asked one of the Northern District Ministry of Interior planning officials whether the concern was for preserving the rural landscape associated with the Arab towns. "No," I was told indignantly, "that's a fabrication—green is green in any place—for Jews and Arabs alike!"

It is also clear to me, however, that the environmental officials with whom I spoke were genuinely exercised by the moral, social justice issues triggered by the politics of environment. They took the occasion of our somewhat rambling discussion to raise the possibility of a mechanism that would address these issues, coming back repeatedly to the idea that industrial development ought to be separated from the issue of municipal jurisdiction and that the Arab towns ought to share in the municipal revenue generated by development no matter where it was located. To my comment that the mayors and population of the Jewish towns were likely to oppose such an arrangement vigorously, they emphasized that they were referring only to *future* development as the subject of sharing. But they were speaking well outside the realm of their authority: they would never have to defend such a proposal against the objections of the Jewish local authorities. Indeed, they located their proposal in the future, never remarking that in so doing, they were postponing just that which the vetoed Sajur-Karmi'el industrial area had been designed to achieve. One may observe also that the environmentalist planning view of Biq'at Bet Hakerem as a single metropolitan unit was itself being selectively deployed, setting aside the Jewish/Arab distinction only as part of the rationale for curtailing the development of the Arab towns; it did not propose that the 33,000 residents of Karmi'el and the 37,000 of the six Arab towns ought to constitute a single municipal, or even subdistrict, electorate.

Landscape and Tourism

Now, "protecting the landscape" (*nof*) *was* one of the reasons given in explanation of why the DPBC had rejected the plan for the joint industrial area. The landscape was adduced as an aspect of a "green belt" that would somehow separate Karmi'el (its existing and growing industrial area included) from the Arab towns north of the Akko-Zefat road. Actually, four of these towns have built-up areas immediately adjacent to the road; Deir el Asad lies just to the north of Bi'ne, but is immediately contiguous with it; and thus, it is only the restriction on Sajur's development between its built-up area and the road that might be thought of in any way as preserving an open area (and not a green one, at that). But the prohibition on erecting a well-designed industrial area in that particular spot (under Karmi'el's aegis) would seem consistent with a conception of the Arab towns as traditional rural villages. The response I received to my question on this from the Ministry of Interior planner notwithstanding, I did encounter, in other official places, acknowledgment that this may have been part of the DPBC thinking. It may be suggested that there is a direct link between such a view of the Arab towns and regional plans that see them as participants in the development of tourism.

People from the Misgav Regional Council have been active in encouraging Arabs in the area to develop tourism initiatives. These include "bed and breakfast" lodgings in the Arab towns, the opening of centers to safeguard Arab folklore and Arab cultural heritage, and participating in annual nature and music festivals organized by the regional council. Misgav cites this as a program for Arab integration and Jewish-Arab cooperation in the region. Speaking of this, the Misgav master plan says: "One of the unique characteristics of the region is the 'human element'—the integration of the Arab sector with its ethnic characteristics with the Israeli pioneer spirit of the 1990s found in the rural-community settlements (Misgav) and modern urban life (Karmi'el)" (Erner et al. 1996: 69, 73).

The Galilee Development Authority's proposal for projects through the year 2020 provides another example. It speaks of industrial development geared toward both Jewish and Arab employees, and in addition, proposes building "one thousand vacation huts in small resorts and bed-and-breakfast facilities throughout the Arab sector … aimed at tourists looking for a different type of cultural experience … [these] would not compete with conventional tourist accommodations" (Shmoul 2000).

Still another case is that of the DPBC treatment of Nazareth's proposal for a new industrial area at the approach to the city from the northwest. The boundary commission that had dealt with requested boundary changes in the Upper Nazareth–Nazareth area had recommended the transfer of 550 dunam at that location for that purpose from the Emeq Yizre'el Regional Council to Nazareth, and this had indeed been done (see chapter 4). In the course of the statutory approval process, the industrial area plan was cut down to 230 dunam (110 dunam net), but it encountered opposition altogether at the DPBC. A senior district planning official reportedly stated that Nazareth, being a city of tourism, should not develop industry at the entrance to the city. The Northern District Ministry of Interior Commissioner was quoted thus in the Hebrew daily *Ha'aretz* (Algazi 2002): "The employment of Nazareth, like that of Bethlehem and other cities having a religious pilgrimage connotation, should come from tourism, hotel accommodation, restaurants, souvenir shops. These, and not factories, should be the true industry of Nazareth."

There has been a great deal of tourism-related activity in the Arab towns in Galilee. In Nazareth, this has been the case especially in connection with observance of the 2000th birthday of Jesus. Such activity has occurred in other localities as well, particularly in those towns that have associated themselves with the Misgav Regional Council tourism initiative. But the Misgav initiative has had its critics. Thus, in their 1997 publication, Hussein and Adiv present an article on the Misgav tourism programs that notes that the Arab towns derive only small benefits from them, while the Misgav settlements gain thereby "a Middle-Eastern scent." The Arabs meanwhile are cast in the role of a traditional and backward society; they provide folklore, but there is no recognition of their need for development suited to the twentieth century (1997: 17; see also Adiv and Hussein 1997).

Now, just as the Jews have done and do for themselves, the Arabs in Palestine (in Israel or not) have an interest in building and maintaining a Palestinian heritage. Moreover, this can be an economically fruitful activity. But there is a difference between the Jews and the Arabs in this endeavor, a difference built into the unequal power relations that obtain. The Jews look backward over and beyond traditional Arab society to define their past; in doing so, they define their own modernity while freezing the Arabs into a timeless, ahistorical place between past and present. One may see this in graphic vividness in the set of travel articles with their accompanying photographs in *Aretz Veteva* (Land and Nature) (Buchman and Yovel 1996) on the Sakhnin valley, showing Arab patriarchs in traditional garb sitting in "typical summer pose," reminiscing nostalgically of the days of the mule (before the automobile), and grandfathers telling their amber prayer beads, sitting, the reader is told by the accompanying text, in the same position as did their own grandfathers before them. These views of Arab life in Galilee are invoked in connection with the articles' presentation of the Misgav-Arab town tourism project.[8]

The discussion of tourism for the Arabs presented here was prompted in reference to DPBC decisions and arguments vetoing the Sajur-Karmi'el joint industrial area north of the Akko-Zefat road and holding back approval of the new Nazareth industrial area. These DPBC positions invoked the image of landscape, and, it is suggested, these positions are to be seen in the context of tourism and the image of Arab traditionalism. Among writers dealing with the political economy of tourism, Ronayne (2001: 160) observes that the creation of what she refers to as "a heritage landscape" is the "outcome of a series of changing social relations of dependency and exclusion (since those who are excluded also make a place what it is)." Selwyn (1996: 9–10) describes tourism as "one of the engines which manufacture and structure relationships between centers and peripheries." It should be noted, though, that exclusion may also be turned to advantage: in the aftermath of the Sajur-Karmi'el industrial area project, Sajur had new expectations, encouraged in the Ministry of the Interior, of having the land in question transferred to its jurisdiction and zoned for residential and commercial uses.

New Moves

The idea of interlocality cooperation in the development of joint industrial areas continued, and continues, to elicit Ministry of Interior and Ministry of Industry support. And despite the aborted cases of the 1991 boundary commission recommendation that Majd al Kurum and Bi'ne be made part of a municipal union to develop the Bar Lev industrial area and of the program for a joint Sajur-Karmi'el industrial area, the idea of Arab town participation in similar projects in Galilee continued to be promoted with unflagging enthusiasm.

In 1995, the ILA undertook a project of preparing master plans for thirty-four Arab localities.[9] These were to be development plans on which outline plans and detailed plans could be based, and this time, the local authorities themselves were involved in the planning process. It was a new departure in planning for the Arab localities (see Alterman and Stav 2001: 115–125). The plans were brought to the Biq'at Bet Hakerem Planning and Building Commission at the beginning of 2001. Of interest to the present discussion is the plan for Majd al Kurum. This revived the idea of that town adding land from its jurisdiction to the Bar Lev industrial area and sharing the development. But this time, unlike in 1991, Majd al Kurum was a party to the planning, and it was a bona fide planning *document* on the table, not sentiments expressed in boundary commission minutes. Moreover, the plan called for expanding the town's area of jurisdiction by a bit to round out the Majd al Kurum area that would enter the industrial park.

In 2000, the minister of the interior tabled a proposal for legislation that would enable him (or her) to declare an area intended for industry or commerce as an area under the joint jurisdiction of a number of local authorities. The intention was to overcome some of the legal difficulties besetting the establishment of joint industrial areas in general. The proposal itself was dropped, but new regulations were promulgated authorizing the minister to approve arrangements for the division of local taxes between local authorities (Municipalities Ordinance §9a; amendment effected by State Budgetary Arrangements Law 2000; see "Legislation Cited").

In November 2000, the director-general of the Ministry of Industry instructed the Development Areas Unit to locate areas suitable for the planning and development of regional industrial areas for the joint participation of several Arab localities (Koren 2000). Again, in January 2002, the then-minister of industry announced a policy of joining Arab towns to the municipal industrial authorities of industrial areas (Shmoul 2002a). In February 2002, the ministry announced that it was paying NIS 1.5 million (out of 2.2 million) that the Bedouin town Tuba-Zangariyye near Rosh Pina was putting into the joint industrial area Tzahar to facilitate Tuba becoming a partner (see figure 2.2). Tuba-Zangariyye was to have two directors on the board of the industrial area and 11 percent of the stock (and of future local tax revenue) (Shmoul 2002b). In March, the ministry announced that Tur'an (the Arab town to the northeast of Kafar Kanna) would become a partner in Kidmat Hagalil, the industrial area belonging jointly to Tiberias and the Galil Tahton Regional Council (Shmoul 2002c). There was talk about planning, and meetings took place regarding other sites as well. Thus, it has been reported that Sakhnin and Misgav Regional Council were preparing joint plans for industrial development, in part on Misgav land (Shmoul 2001a; Ash 2002). And the Jewish industrialist Stef Wertheimer announced plans to set up an industrial park in cooperation with Deir el Asad (Shmoul 2001b).

Now, statements regarding plans and decisions on "joint industrial areas" are, it emerges, a good thing to utter. For one thing, they forestall having to award sole control over land for development to one local authority or another, which would deprive others. Second, they nourish a sense that something is being done to correct the development gap between Arab and Jewish localities. During the course of the 1990s, the idea of joint industrial areas became the theme of one of the minor discourses that serve to organize interactions in the field: national and district outline plans such as the proposals for NOP 35 and for the Northern District (on the latter, see Shefer et al. 1992: 146) recommend large industrial areas in which there is interlocality and Jewish-Arab cooperation. The statements in these documents are general and somewhat vague, but they are there—solid elements of the discourse, available for invocation in support of particular joint projects (see, e.g., Frenkl's 1997 program in support of Zipporit D–E, the Arab town areas to be adjoined to Upper Nazareth's industrial area).

But it turns out that after the statements have been made, arrival at actual joint operation is no easy matter. Alterman and Stav (2001: 101–102) reached the conclusion that heads of Arab local authorities are wary of cooperation: "Cooperation means compromise between the interests of the different localities, and in that negotiation, it is always the stronger localities—generally the Jewish ones—that achieve their objectives." But I would suggest that the stronger local authorities are also reluctant to cooperate; for them, cooperation appears to entail sharing what otherwise would be theirs alone. As one of my sources in the planning community put it: "Localities don't cooperate—Jewish ones or Arab ones—unless they're forced to do so. You cooperate when you have something to lose if you don't. If you want interlocality cooperation, the government ministries have to make not cooperating costly."

It will be recalled (see end of chapter 3) that it was only in August 2000 that Kafar Kanna and Upper Nazareth had signed a declaration of principles regarding the establishment of a joint industrial authority, and that a meeting in June 2001 had set out the principles for the inclusion of Meshhed in the joint authority. In April 2000, shortly before the Kafar Kanna–Upper Nazareth declaration, an official of the latter town cited to me the reservations being voiced by the mayor: "Why should Upper Nazareth have to share tax revenues with Kafar Kanna—what kind of goods will they bring to the industrial area; will they bring high-level industry or only auto repair shops?" Of course, the mayor neglected to say that it ought to be the responsibility of the joint industrial authority to market the area (that is, to woo investors) for the entire area. One year later, the agreement still had to be approved by the local authorities. In Kafar Kanna, council members were saying: "Upper Nazareth will swallow us up if we are part of the same industrial area—look at the evidence—at how they jumped over our territory to grab the land of Zipporit A that should have been ours for development. Now after taking over *that* land, they will take over the industrial area inside our boundaries also" (see figure 1.1). But the head of the Kafar Kanna Local Council was pushing for ratification of the agreement on the grounds that Kafar Kanna would gain the advantages and strength of being connected with Upper Nazareth. I was told that there was a sense in Kafar Kanna that, in practice, Upper Nazareth was indeed cooperating in good faith.

In the case of the Iksal industrial area, however, located just outside Iksal's boundary in the jurisdiction of Emeq Yizre'el Regional Council (see figure 1.1), negotiations to establish a joint industrial authority were not going so well (see chapter 4 for mention of this case). In December 1992, the boundary commission had recommended that the Arab town and the regional council try to work out an agreement on joint management, but it also added that if that did not work out, the commission recommended that the area be transferred to Iksal's jurisdiction (minutes of meeting, 6 December 1992). Iksal officials claim that they did not become aware of the second part of the commission's recommendation until 1995, when they finally received a complete set of the commission's minutes as part of Emeq Yizre'el's HCJ suit against the decision to transfer land from the regional council to Upper Nazareth. In November 2001, Iksal, after what it described as exhausting and unsuccessful negotiations, applied to the Ministry of the Interior with a new request to have the area transferred to its jurisdiction. In its letter, Iksal claimed that it had expected Emeq Yizre'el, by virtue of the latter's development capabilities, to be able to attract large enterprises, but that instead, the regional council had channeled these to Alon Tavor, its large industrial area to the east. In the meanwhile, stated Iksal's letter, the town's small enterprises had moved out from the residential section into the new industrial area, and inasmuch as there they were paying municipal taxes to Emeq Yizre'el, Iksal's tax revenue situation had deteriorated (letter, 3 November 2001).

As for other places where Arab-Jewish industrial area partnership had been bruited, a year after the announcement regarding Tur'an's joining Kidmat Hagalil, there was still no agreement there; Majd al Kurum becoming part of the Bar Lev area was still far in the future; and the Sakhnin-Misgav regional council project was having ups and downs while still only a tentative program (see, e.g., Ash 2002). The first aspect of the "iffy" nature of all these initiatives was the question as to whether they would come into being at all. The second was the question as to what participation would mean: How much shared control, how much contact, how much revenue? As of the time of the conclusion of this study, these were all still unanswered questions.

One may consider also the manipulative uses of the vented Misgav partnership with its Arab neighbors, infinitely receding into the future. An official in the Arab town of Arrabe complained in 2001: "To our request for a local industrial area, the Ministry of Industry responds: 'Wait, there's a plan to do a joint industrial area with Misgav in which your town will be included.'" And Sakhnin has been answered in a similar vein. In 2004, that city submitted a request for enlarging its jurisdiction (from land currently included in Misgav's boundaries). It argued, among other things, that with the added land reserves it would be able to develop the urban functions consonant with its potential role as a true regional center. But in 2005, the boundary commission dealing with Sakhnin's request turned down most of it, including the part slated for expansion of its industrial area. Now it was Sakhnin's turn to be told, in the patronizing tone evinced by the Misgav spokesperson (press release), that it would do well to wait for the Misgav plan for a joint industrial area. But as of now, according to the regional council spokesperson, there are still no material plans for such a joint undertaking. The spokesperson describes it as "a vision" (*hazon*). Meanwhile, though, Misgav has been pushing commercial and service development in Teradyon, its large industrial area located just at the edge of Sakhnin. Misgav (via Teradyon) was on the way to appropriating a significant slice of Sakhnin's urban development potential, while Sakhnin's bid for partnership in that so-called regional industrial area (another matter and not part of Sakhnin's request for expanded jurisdiction) had been rebuffed

Razin and Hazan (1994a: 45–46, 49) mention alternative solutions for the problem of land (and other resources) for local economic development. One of these is tax-base sharing among local authorities in a region; a second is the idea of a second tier of government, that is, the creation of regional-level government. But implementation of either of these solutions would be problematic, particularly in Galilee, where they would directly engage the issue of Arab-Jewish relations and would be perceived to threaten Jewish dominance more than would a limited joint industrial area.

Altogether, Jewish and Arab town participation in joint industrial areas is beset by uncertainty and has made only halting progress thus far, but it is nonetheless something that government officials are able to talk about and something that those concerned with Arab town development might consider worth pursuing. Statements may be only statements, but once they are deployed, they take on a life of their own; someone may take hold of them and use them to promote and push; becoming part of political maneuver, they may lead to changing perceptions, changing alignments, and eventually to tangible results.

Challenging the *Normality* of Jurisdiction

The most challenging move in the direction of Arab participation in development is, in my view, Arab Nazareth's recent bid to be admitted as a partner in the Zipporit industrial area and to do so *without putting in land.* In making their case, Nazareth officials call attention to the land, population, and infrastructure development discrepancies between their city and the Jewish one inserted there to check Nazareth development. Thus, Nazareth, with a population of 51,900 in 1995, had jurisdiction over 14,400 dunam, while Upper Nazareth, with a population of 37,300, had about 28,000 dunam in its jurisdiction—and Upper Nazareth's area of jurisdiction has been expanding.[10] As for industrial infrastructure, Nazareth's existing area of 84 dunam net was poorly developed, and the new area for which it was fighting at the DPBC at the northwestern entrance to the city had been cut down to 230 dunam (110 dunam net). Upper Nazareth, with its population not quite 72 percent of that of Nazareth, had 350 dunam of industrial area within the city, another 400 dunam newly developed at Har Yona, over 1,100 dunam at Zipporit A, and another 2,700 dunam on the way for Zipporit B and C (see chapter 3 and figure 1.1). Nazareth officials argued that the city desperately needed land for residential and employment functions. A 1998 position paper examined alternatives for commercial and industrial development within the city's boundaries, and also proposed that the city become a partner in Zipporit (Sabach and Jabarin 1998; see also Czamanski 1996; Algazi 2002). The city did not have sufficient land reserves for the industrial development without which its economic situation would deteriorate, whereas joining Zipporit would mean industrial development that did not harm the city's cultural and tourism bent and would strengthen the desired aims of regional cooperation.

In a December 1998 letter addressed to the prime minister, the minister of the interior and the minister of industry explicitly focusing on Nazareth joining the Zipporit industrial area, the mayor of Nazareth raised these points and asserted that Zipporit had been established with the intention that all the localities of the region, among them Nazareth, participate in it, and that it would therefore only be right that Nazareth become an equal partner in responsibility for the area and in revenues from it. The Ministry of the Interior sent a copy on to Menachem Ariav, mayor of Upper Nazareth, asking for his comment. The Ministry of Industry answered, saying, "We explain to local authorities the great advantages of interlocality cooperation.... [I]t would be appropriate for you to bring the matter up directly with the mayor of Upper Nazareth." The prime minister's advisor on planning and development wrote, "We are investigating the proper course of action to assist in creating cooperation between Nazareth and Upper Nazareth in the Zipporit industrial area." For his part, Ariav responded, "I don't object so long as you bring land." But one Upper Nazareth person said to me with some derision in his voice, "They [Nazareth] are purveying their misery, their frustration, rather than bringing land." Nothing seemed to happen with the Nazareth request until a meeting was set in February 2003 for Nazareth officials and the district commissioner for the purpose of locating an area that could be developed for Nazareth to be joined to Zipporit.

I have chosen not to inquire into the outcome of that meeting, finding it convenient to break off the account of events at this point—a point at which possibilities for maneuver seem still open. In this, it is like the inevitably unfinished nature of all the cases I have been dealing with. At first blush, "to locate an area that could be developed for Nazareth" would appear to be a retreat from the idea of not putting in land, but reflection might reveal this to be a search for a way around the principle of bringing land to a joint industrial area and an implicit recognition of the arbitrary and politically determined nature of municipal jurisdiction. After all, boundaries of jurisdiction have been subject to change when that was deemed desirable. Upper Nazareth itself has had much land, including, of course, the land for Zipporit, added to its jurisdiction, and so have other cities. Nazareth (or, for that matter, other Arab towns in the vicinity) has just as good a claim on the land that Zipporit is on as does Upper Nazareth. To look for alternative paths to enabling the Arab towns to become part of the large "regional" industrial areas is to challenge the allocations made hitherto along Arab/Jewish lines with the aim of curtailing and controlling Arab town development. The local authority system, or "the map of local government in Israel" as it is sometimes called, stands against such challenge. But there are, it would seem, ways in which the challenge can be pursued: thus, not only the case of Majd al Kurum requesting the addition of land to its jurisdiction to round out the area that would enable it to become part of the Bar Lev industrial area, but also, along different lines, that of Tuba becoming part of the Tzahar industrial area by virtue of an investment backed up by the government.

Moves to outflank the sacrosanct *normality* of municipal jurisdiction may in the end lead to new, emergent principles. Alterman and Stav point out (2001: 121) that the steering committee accompanying the entire thirty-four-locality ILA planning project expressed for the first time the perception that development on state land could serve as a lever to promote the development of the Arab town as a whole. I would point out three implications of Arab towns becoming part, in one way or another, of the large regional industrial areas: first, this is a way of redressing the injustices entailed by the Arab loss of land and the circumscribing of Arab town areas of jurisdiction; second, and intimately associated with the first, this provides a sorely needed redefinition of the proper uses of state land. What are those proper uses? Surely, I submit, they are to serve the needs of the citizens—Arab or Jewish—and to further the development of their towns. And third, this would be a way to pursue the true growth-center strategy advanced by Bar-El and colleagues (1990) calling for policy that did not distinguish between the Arab and Jewish sectors (except for purposes of enabling the Arab population to overcome their disadvantage). For the Arab towns to be bona fide partners in the large regional industrial areas would be to set aside a large part of the Arab/Jewish distinction in the lack of local town infrastructure.

I believe it will be in place to quote at length from one of my Arab sources here:

> There has been a historical injustice in the nondevelopment of the Arab towns, discrimination in many domains, the loss of Arab lands. To become partners in the already existing large regional industrial areas would put right this historical injustice, and do it decisively.
>
> Look at the cases where boundary commissions recommend and the minister of the interior carries out transfer of land from regional councils to the lagging Jewish "development towns," or where, in such boundary disputes, the ministry pushes for cooperation in developing industrial areas jointly—that is the same kind of correction of injustice.
>
> One needs to see the industrial area as a kind of public good: the government finances the infrastructure, the land is state land, and there is government support for the investor. So far, this has involved a transfer of resources, resources to which all the citizenry has rights, to a particular segment of the population.
>
> It is true that today the Arab local authorities don't have access to national policymaking and have little influence on national policy. But, on the other hand, the change—that is, the admission of the Arab towns to joint participation—has to come from above, and precisely because this is a "public good," there are grounds for intervention from above—and *that* will come about eventually.
>
> In the end, the exclusion of the Arab towns from these regional industrial areas will not stand up to the public pressure and political demands that will be mounted by the Arabs. The injustice—the discrimination involved—will become so clear that the government will have no choice but to bring about change.

> Altogether, the regional industrial areas developed for the Jewish sector were a case of missing out on a historic opportunity—they lead to intensification of the conflict—whereas, if the Arab towns had been included, they [the areas] could have been a bridge between Arabs and Jews in Galilee.

Participation in Planning

It will be seen that the challenge to Arab town exclusion from the regional industrial areas is intimately connected with challenge to Israeli planning practices and the perceptions that inform them. I believe it fair to say that the planning conception that held sway at the time Zipporit was planned at the beginning of the 1990s was, *AUDG* notwithstanding, not true regional development but rather territorial war, the perceived need to counter what one of those involved in the planning described to me as "the entrenchment of the Arab bloc of Nazareth, Reine, Meshhed, and Kafar Kanna—this bloc was expanding and growing stronger—and it was felt necessary to curb that expansion."

I put the following (naïve) question to those who had been involved in planning Zipporit: Given that Zipporit was being planned in the backyard of these Arab towns, and given that Arab protest eventually led the authorities to undertake having Kafar Kanna and Meshhed become partners in Zipporit, wouldn't it have been a good thing to include these towns in the planning of Zipporit from the very beginning? One of my sources responded: "You have to remember that there was a lot of hostility there against Jewish planning and development programs—against the background of land confiscation for Upper Nazareth. They [the Arab towns] would only have opposed everything all the way—they would have demanded instead development for their own localities—and Zipporit wouldn't have gotten anywhere." Another of those involved in the planning responded along similar lines: "The Arabs would have said, 'what about *our* distress, *our* needs?' Planning Zipporit was a loaded subject, and had it been opened to input from the Arab localities, it would have been stalled, would never have begun."

Such were statements to give one pause. An outsider, one not caught in the discursive snare of territorial war, might find it hard to understand why Jewish planners would think it undesirable for local Arab leaders to have a chance to voice the distress of their towns and demand their development.

Now, there has been in the literature some consideration of the participation of the Arab population in Israeli planning. Alterman and Stav (2001: 99–100) note that generally the draft of a new district outline plan is opened up to public examination only when it is deposited—"by then, the decision makers are already lined up behind it, the document is fully formulated, and there is not much chance of persuading planning commissions to introduce far-reaching changes." The public, Alterman and Stav continue, is forced to assume a defensive posture, as implied by the language of the (planning) law, "to submit objections" to the plan. Amendment 9 to the Northern District Outline Plan was a departure, however, in that its planners made an attempt, in the preliminary stages of planning, "to investigate the needs of the Arab population and to hear the opinions of their leaders" (Alterman and Stav 2001: 102).

Nonetheless, I would point out that Alterman and Stav are dealing in this case with a document produced in the statutory planning system; so too do most of the public comments that are made on the subject of Arab participation in planning. They do not address the important distinction, made clearly by Yiftachel (1992: 88; see also Carmon et al. 1990: 54–56), between the statutory planning system, regulatory in nature, on the one hand, and development planning on the other. It might also be mentioned that the move to a more egalitarian approach found by Alterman and Stav lies in the realm of statutory planning. But they did not extend to the present day their examination of language and concept in the realm of development planning (their opening case was that of the plan for the *mitzpim* ["outlook"] settlements in Galilee, a development plan par excellence, after which they turned their gaze to statutory plans). A look at later development planning (such as the early planning stages of Zipporit, concurrent with the planning of DOP 2/9) or at present-day moves (plans for private ranches) would quickly reveal that the Arab population was and is still being treated by Israeli development planners as a hostile, threatening element rather than as fellow citizens.

Although national and district outline plans may chart the direction of development and set limits for it, they do not initiate development planning. Among the initiators of development planning in Israel have been various construction and industrial entrepreneurs, the Prime Minister's Office, the Ministry of Construction and Housing, the Ministry of Industry, the ILA, the Jewish Agency, the agricultural leadership, the leadership of the orthodox Jewish community, and heads of the local authorities (see, e.g., Feitelson 2001).[11] The participants in early moves on planning Zipporit, and then in the Zipporit planning team, are well covered by this list (see chapter 3). But there were no Arab local authorities among them. Altogether, the Arab local authorities, the Arab leadership, and Arab entrepreneurs have not been among these "institutional initiators of planning," as Feitelson refers to them. Unless one is properly connected, or pursues such connection actively, one does not have a place in the domain of development planning.

The distinction between initiatory development planning and statutory or regulatory planning may be brought home by the case of Karmiel and the industrial area north of the Akko-Zefat road. It will be recalled that Amendment 9 to the Northern District Outline Plan referred to this as the "Nahef industrial area," and listed it among land reserves for industry in the "non-Jewish sector." The presence of such formulations in DOP 2/9 would never make the industrial area come into being, let alone come into being as an industrial area for the Arab towns in Biq'at Bet Hakerem. At the very most, one might cite the district outline plan text as part of an attempt to win support for one's plan.

To make a plan materialize, one needed active planning, political will, and the ability to pursue collateral objectives (e.g., Karmiel's request to have the so-called Nahef area transferred to its jurisdiction).

The openly political nature of development planning will be clear. This gives rise to what might be called "the planning broth" (in Hebrew, one might say, perhaps, *belil*): a state of affairs in which various and changing actors are engaged in pursuing plans and pushing ideas, sometimes individually, sometimes in collaboration with one another. Until the situation gels, and often even after, it is open to linkage, demands, quid pro quos, and intervention. The situation is one that augurs both potential and danger.

It was this perception that lay behind the approach adopted by the then-head of the Kafar Kanna Local Council toward the end of 1992 regarding Upper Nazareth's Zipporit and the Phoenicia plant. He was advocating that rather than merely opposing the Upper Nazareth incursion, Kafar Kanna would do well to pursue plans to develop the "Australia" tract for industry (see chapter 3 and figures 1.1 and 3.1) and for joining Zipporit with this as a "dowry." The local council head explained the position to me thus:

> Look, there is a large tract of ILA land ["Australia"] in Kafar Kanna jurisdiction near where Upper Nazareth is developing industry on land recently transferred to it. The danger is that Upper Nazareth might come with a development program for the ILA tract in Kafar Kanna jurisdiction—and, in so doing, be able to mount a claim for jurisdiction. The only *good* way to resist is for Kafar Kanna to initiate its own development for that piece of land. It is the active pursuit of a program that can keep the land in Kafar Kanna jurisdiction. Passivity leaves you open to the attack of others.

One Arab planner put it this way: "'Planning' is a word with positive connotations, but the planning system is perceived by the Arabs negatively—they see planning policy as an instrument to seize land."

At some point in the process, development plans enter the channel of statutory (i.e., regulatory) approval. Here they may be held up, or often, pushed along, shepherded through the obstacles by those who stand behind them—the approval process for Zipporit A is a relevant case. But the overarching statutory plans, that is, the district and national outline plans, are in themselves only one part of a whole complex of practice, and some of this may be seen in the cases dealt with in chapter 3 and in the present chapter. Even considering only the plans themselves, there is a distinction to be made between rhetoric, on the one hand, and actual provisions and allocations embodied in the plans. Thus, where Alterman and Stav (2001) find encouraging changes in planning language, a new study by Swaid (forthcoming) shows how Amendment 9 to the Northern District Outline Plan still discriminates against the Arab local authorities.

But the point I wish to make in discussing the distinction between regulatory and development planning is this: it is *not enough* to have one's interests and needs taken into account, to have inquiries made concerning these, as evidenced in the new departure found by Alterman and Stav in the preparation of DOP 2/9, for Amendment 9 to the Northern District Outline Plan belongs to the domain of regulatory planning, and being "planned for" in this domain is not *participation* in planning. To be involved in planning, I submit, the Arab local authorities would have to be involved in the "planning broth" (the *belil*) of development planning. This would entail, of course, being active participants in the political arena in which development planning takes place. Two of my sources, one Jewish and one Arab, made this point, each in his own words, in connection with the participation of Kafar Kanna and Meshhed or of Nazareth in Zipporit: "When are Arabs involved?" they asked, and they answered, "When there is no choice/in response to the political imperative."

Now, one of the threads of development encompassed in the present study is the growing political voice of the Arab towns in Israel and the Arab leadership—from the early political response of the National Committee of Chairmen of the Arab Local Authorities in the 1970s (see chapter 2) to present-day activism. Concrete cases dealt with in the present study begin with aspects of marginality and exclusion of the Arab towns: in 1990, Majd al Kurum and Bi'ne were not invited to the Reichman boundary commission dealing with the future Bar Lev industrial area, could not articulate demands of their own there, and were not informed of the commission's recommendation, even though that recommendation had direct implications for them. But one may see a progression of involvement. For one thing, the current master plan for Majd al Kurum gives new life to the aborted Reichman recommendation and puts Majd al Kurum as a purposeful actor. Again, there is the case of Kafar Kanna and Meshhed in Zipporit, and, eventually, Nazareth's bid for inclusion in Zipporit and the clear sense that it would be legitimate to demand participation "from the beginning," without putting in land from their own jurisdiction.

Present-day activism finds expression in the activity of the Arab Center for Alternative Planning (ACAP) (located in Eilaboun), founded at the end of 2000. Among its organizational allies in the field are the Galilee Society, the Center for Strategic Planning in Kafar Kanna, as well as Strategic Planning Units in other Arab towns. ACAP addresses the issues of Arab town involvement in development planning (as well as in the formulation of National Outline Plan 35 and the Northern District Outline Plan), and it describes its stance as proactive rather than reactive.

As one might expect, one of the planks in the ACAP program calls for inclusion of the Arab towns in the large regional industrial areas in Galilee. As I have argued, such inclusion is intimately associated with the theme of development planning. Partnership of the Arab towns in the large regional industrial areas would embody the principle that these towns and through them, their residents, have a full share, by right, in national and regional development. Concomitantly, such partnership would mean that (Jewish) planners would see it not as threatening but as both proper and desirable that Arab leaders and planners participate fully in articulating not only local needs, but also the goals of national and regional development.

Conclusion

This study of practice, image, and power began in the field by looking at events that brought together two Arab towns in Galilee—Kafar Kanna and Meshhed—and their large Jewish neighbor, Upper Nazareth. Kafar Kanna was one of the places in which the Ministry of Industry was carrying out a program of establishing small, local industrial areas in Arab localities. At the same time, Upper Nazareth had reached northward and was building, with government assistance, its own large industrial park just beyond the boundaries of the two Arab towns. Arab protest, driven both by a sense of being besieged and by a desire to have a share in the fruits of development planning, and facilitated by the vulnerability of the Upper Nazareth project on environmental grounds, had resulted in proposals to expand the industrial park to include a large contiguous area in the jurisdictions of the two Arab towns and to admit them to the municipal industrial park authority as joint owners and managers.

In following these events, I came up against two at first seemingly distinct factors or moments. The first had to do with the local nature of what I was observing. There was a great deal of conflict and maneuver going on, all geographically situated even when it reached up into higher levels of the state apparatus. Moreover, I was looking at administrative practices, and one finds there the concrete, specific, and local. The second moment was the impression of the broadly defined, overall disadvantage of the Arab towns in their dealings with neighboring Jewish localities and with government agencies. The question that arose in my mind was what role to assign to this second factor, that of a hierarchical social order, in explaining local events.

Concurrently, as I sought to understand local events having to do with attempts to construct industrial infrastructure and to participate in regional development, I was led outward from the local scene to an examination of other domains. These included outline plans in the Arab localities and the disparate planning experience of Arab towns as compared with Jewish settlements; the

Jewish settlement drive in Galilee in response to the perception of the Arab population there as a territorial threat; the role of the regional council as a form of local municipal authority that would establish Jewish territorial domination; the history of Arab local government and its relations with the national government; municipal budgets in the Arab towns and the dependence on the national government; the dearth of infrastructure development in the Arab towns, including industrial infrastructure, and the consequent paucity of local economic activity and local tax revenue. Examination of these matters enabled me to present a description of the lay of the land in the sense of who were the actors involved in the events I studied and what resources they controlled.

This view of multiple domains and their multiple dimensions—geographical, historical, administrative, discursive—came together with the local nature of the events I was observing in an understanding that I could, in fact, embrace the Foucauldian move from inquiry into the *origin* of power to inquiry into *how* power works. Rather than reduction to an origin, power relations are seen to be the synergy of a multiplicity of overlapping elements producing what is discerned as the broad hierarchical order. By means of this view, one escapes essentialized perceptions of Oppressor and Victim and also structural taxonomies that short-circuit explanation by reducing everything to a single binomial principle. One gains, rather, a view of a *field* of power relations whose elements add up to a strategic disposition of forces, a particular configuration of elements at any given moment. This is the second sense in which I use the expression "the lay of the land." Note, however, that this disposition of forces may be anything but fixed on a local level: its broad, overall effect may be clear enough when seen from afar, but for its participants, engagement on this field of power may mean struggle, maneuver, and confrontation. To be sure, there may be acquiescence and submission, but these are temporary, and sooner or later, they will be confounded.

This is a view of the macro-order that diverges from the view of the local only with regard to its resolution; that is to say, only with regard to the distance of the observer from concrete, locally organized events and practices.

Administrative practice, in particular, practice having to do with bureaucratic access was one of the two major kinds of elements figuring prominently in events having to do with Upper Nazareth's large, modern industrial park and the two Arab towns in whose backyard it was situated. The second was that of discursive images—images of territorial threat and conflict, of beleaguered territory, on the one hand, and, on the other, images of Arab traditionalism and of the Zionist project as an agent of modernization vis-à-vis the Arab population.

The location of Upper Nazareth's Zipporit A was explicitly described by its planners as the result of a conception of militant Zionism establishing territorial control. In this, it was a geopolitical act. Arab protest and subsequent plans for expanding the industrial area to include Kafar Kanna and Meshhed form the main strand of events in the Zipporit case. But other threads enter into the account. There was the small industrial area (70 dunam net for industry) for

Kafar Kanna that was taken up into the then-current Ministry of Industry program for constructing local industrial areas in several Arab towns. This small area in Kafar Kanna had begun as part of the larger plan for industrial development in the Zipporit location, and it was to become an already accomplished enclave in the plans for Zipporit D–E (the area in Kafar Kanna's and Meshhed's jurisdiction). There were attempts to set up a joint industrial authority that would include Upper Nazareth and the two Arab towns, and there were the objective factors impeding progress on this—among them the circumstance that prices for ILA land in Meshhed and Kafar Kanna were over three times what they were in Zipporit A due to differential national priority region status (Upper Nazareth land enjoyed "A" status, while that of the adjacent Arab towns was only "B") and differential base prices that reflected the shortage of land for building in the Arab towns, itself an outcome of government policy.

The question of whether it would be possible to turn Zipporit into a joint industrial area by taking in the Arab towns as partners without their putting in land from their own jurisdiction arose early on. After all, Zipporit A was being established on land that had lain within Meshhed's village boundaries as set by British Survey of Palestine maps, land on which the local Arab population had grazed their livestock, and which until just months before submission of the industrial area plans had been without municipal status. But it was the mayor of Upper Nazareth who had pushed this development and who had been instrumental in attracting the anchor Phoenicia plant there. He would not relinquish any part of Upper Nazareth's hold. Moreover, he could not be seen by his own constituency to be giving away (what was now) Upper Nazareth land to the Arab towns. The question arose again when, three and a half years later, Meshhed landowners requested that planning for industry on their land be halted. Would Meshhed, even so, be allowed to be a part of the joint industrial area? Again, the Upper Nazareth municipality vetoed that possibility.

The main events dealt with here took place between 1991, when land was transferred to Upper Nazareth and plans for Zipporit A (Upper Nazareth) were formulated and submitted to the Residential and Industrial Building Commission of the Northern District, and the end of 1996, when the DPBC, before it would move ahead on the Zipporit D–E plan (the part in Kafar Kanna's and Meshhed's jurisdiction), was asking its proposers to provide material justifying the need for such a large development. Work on Zipporit A had, by contrast, begun back in April 1992, just months after the plan for it had been submitted and nearly a year before it had received final approval. Approval for the Phoenicia factory, anchor plant of the Upper Nazareth industrial area, had been handled with equal alacrity.

Now, administrative practice in the modern state and bureaucratic access systems are commonly thought to be, in principle if not always in application, even-handed, universalist in outlook, and power-neutral. But in the events of the Zipporit case, one may discern what I would describe as the power effects of bureaucratic access. Obviously, this may be seen in the wide range of discretion exercised by agencies and officials, as evidenced in the setting of national priority region status, or in ILA practices in setting the price of land, as well as in the "only-reasonable" demand by the district planner for material justifying the need for Zipporit D–E. But the effects of power run deeper than discretion. They have to do with the broader, essentially political nature of bureaucratic access, for policy and goals are embedded in the access system, and carried out through it. Once set in motion, the geostrategic aim of controlling territory through the development of Zipporit was able to shift to the ground of planning and the statutory system where bureaucratic access procedures took over. I have referred to this as the normalization effected by administrative practice. The normalization that took place in the case of Zipporit A was similar to that which took place on a wider scale when Upper Nazareth itself had been inserted into the heart of this Arab region back in 1956. Observe that only certain things and not others could happen in the domain marked out as that of the statutory planning process: Meshhed, for example, could lodge objections to the plan for Zipporit A, but could not overturn that plan by arguing that it had not participated in the plan's preparation. The weakness of the Arab towns was measured by the way in which Meshhed's objections were dealt with by the RICC, just as it was by their subsequent inability to move the plan for Zipporit D–E through the stages of statutory approval. On the other hand, the so-far qualified success in gaining admittance to the planning of a joint industrial area came as a result of public protest and demonstrative legal action that broke the boundaries of the statutory domain to reintroduce the political into the question of Zipporit. So, too, the equalization of national priority region status was an outcome of struggle waged in the political arena, while the change in ILA policy equalizing land prices was effected largely through concerted lobbying and the building of a coalition against Treasury opposition.

But the attempt to understand the Zipporit case has led me away from the immediate course of events to other, more broadly focused perspectives, perspectives in which historical and discursive elements are present in various admixtures. Thus, I argue that the experience of the state practices by which Arab land loss came about and continues to occur has led the Arab population in Galilee to a sense of constant siege and threat of dispossession. These found expression in the Arab response to the plans for Zipporit A. Part of the sense of siege and dispossession ensues from the manner in which Arab town jurisdictional boundaries have been determined. By separating the domains of municipal jurisdiction, on the one hand, and ownership, use, and the possibility of future development on the other, Ministry of Interior practices of the 1960s were able to set aside the village boundaries that had been recorded in the Mandate Survey of Palestine, leaving the land that was to become the core area of Zipporit A without municipal status. This was another expression of the weakness of the Arab towns.

I have found it relevant also to consider the image of Arab traditionalism and its uses in academic studies of Arab entrepreneurship and in Ministry of

Industry dealings with officials in the Arab local authorities and with applicants for plots in the new industrial areas in the Arab towns. I suggest that the image of Arab traditionalism is imported into academic analysis and into the Ministry of Industry narrative from the power-laden discourse in which Zionism perceives itself as the agent of modernization vis-à-vis the native Arab population. My research shows that progress in marketing the new Ministry of Industry–built industrial areas depended on overcoming barriers in the ministry itself and in the ILA and on the cost-benefit considerations of the local investors. And contrary to the image of traditional Arab landowners unwilling to develop or sell their land, I have marshaled evidence showing that when conditions are right, Arab landowners do seek both to develop their land for industry and to put it on the market.

What of the request by Meshhed landowners in the case of Zipporit D–E that planning for industry on their land be halted? A major component in landowner considerations was the property tax that would have been imposed on the land from the time it was rezoned for industry until building on it was completed—a project that would require a number of years, possibly many, and the mobilization of sufficient resources to carry it out. This, as well as other practical considerations, lay behind local Arab response to the possibility of developing their land for industry. But I suggest that this response was also anchored in the habitus (Bourdieu's concept) engendered by the practices encountered by the Arab townspeople—those carried out in the name of the state and those experienced in the economic domain. The experience of land loss is one of the important factors in that habitus. Altogether, I argue against the contention, advanced by the writers of an important recent study of Arab industrial entrepreneurship in Israel, that it is traditional attitudes toward land that holds back the emergence of a land market in the Arab towns, thereby impeding the development of industry.

Pursuant to Eyal's argument that the image of traditionalism and the discourse of modernization of which it is a part contribute to the objectification of the Arab village, I suggest that such objectification encloses the Arab towns and villages inside an imaginary boundary that underpins and rationalizes the exclusion of the Arab population in Galilee from development planning. This mechanism was at work in 1990 when the DPBC cut back the original ILA plan for developing 370 dunam net (in the 629 dunam area known as "Australia") to 90 dunam for industry; it was also at work in 1996 when the DPBC asked the planners of Zipporit D–E to demonstrate a priori that there would be demand for the new industrial area. This was a request to demonstrate demand for something that did not yet exist in the realm of perceived possibilities. The discourse of modernization is seemingly paradoxical in effect: for those who speak within it, the people of the Arab towns and villages in Galilee are not yet ready to participate in the pursuit of development.

But exclusion also leads to and is furthered by the appropriation of Arab needs and potential. Insight into this process is gained through an examination of *Accelerated Urban Development in Galilee* (*AUDG*), a major 1977 development plan that applied the growth-pole concept to regional development in Galilee. By this plan, focal Jewish towns planted in Galilee would strengthen the Jewish hold on the region and, at the same time, provide employment and services for the Arab population. Large, so-called regional industrial areas located in the jurisdiction of the Jewish municipalities would propel the growth of the Jewish towns, while the benefits of the economic activity at the centers of development were expected to radiate outward to the region as a whole. Industrial development in the Jewish towns does provide employment for the Arab population, but there is also the transfer of resources from the Arab hinterland to the implanted Jewish towns to be considered, and the possibility that the growth-center strategy may be cause for widening rather than narrowing development gaps.

The *AUDG* plan also envisaged, for the first time, the construction of small local industrial areas in some of the Arab towns. Thus, *AUDG* presented a two-pronged program: large regional industrial areas in the jurisdiction of the Jewish municipalities and small local ones in Arab localities. *AUDG* couched its proposals in the rhetoric of integrating the Arab population in planning and development. I argue, however, that the effect of *including* the Arab towns in the two-pronged program has been to *exclude* them from the main thrust of Galilee development. It is suggested that *AUDG* came into being as what may be thought of as the discursive intersection of the perception of Arab territorial threat and the image of Arab traditionalism. This, then, is the discursive context of the events of the Zipporit case. I suggest that appreciation of the discursive space embodied in *AUDG*, with its elements of Jewish development and Arab integration, even as Arab development potential is appropriated to the benefit of the implanted Jewish towns, may illuminate both the mechanisms and the logic by which development disparities between Jewish and Arab towns emerge and persist in Galilee.

I would call explicit attention to my attempts to introduce certain reservations into the conceptualization of discourse and discursive formations employed in the present study. I wrote "for those who speak within the discourse" in reference to the discourse of Zionist modernization and Arab traditionalism. My point has to do with the persisting primacy of human action. Foucault was clear enough about the role of action and practice (along with other elements) in bringing a discursive formation into being. On the other hand, he was also clear about the objective status of the discourse once it has come into being and about how the discursive formation both constrains what can be said and affords a place from which to speak. These are, I believe, useful conceptualizations. But it has also been my intention to unseat the determinism of the view that we are (only) trapped in discourse, to loosen up the rigidity that beckons, as it were, from the Foucauldian view.

As I see it, just as it is human actors and their practices that bring the discursive formation into being, so too do women and men continue to act in a world of possibilities that include various discursive elements. People speak within a discourse because that is what they know—they are caught within it—and because, for the time being and in this place, they have not yet seen the necessity or the possibility of challenging the discourse. But that is only for the time being.

Further, one may deal not with the great definitive discourse of the age but rather with the discourses and subdiscourses of the times—thus, in the present study, not the discourse of colonialism entire, but that of Zionism—and, by extension, lesser discourses too, overlapping and intersecting, growing chain-like perhaps, one from another.

On the one hand, major discourses impose themselves, even if contingently, but on the other, minor discourses offer themselves, with their apparent self-evidentialism, as places where actors may choose to stand in order to maintain or promote a congenial position. All in all, it is human action that I would privilege. From the point of view of theory, this is a matter of the use that a social anthropologist can make of the sensitivity to power in the Foucauldian view of discourse, while not allowing that view to objectify human actors.

Discursive images and discursive statements enter into the exchanges in the struggle and political maneuver that take place in the field of power. But they have a reciprocal effect: by their very deployment, they explain, rationalize, justify, and normalize; they give shape and meaning to the exchanges in the field. This may be thought of as the contextualizing effect of discursive images. Yet it is not the phenomenology of power that is my concern, but rather power's productive effects. Government programs and policies, distinguishing between Jew and Arab even as they proclaim integration, have shaped the manner in which the Arab locality is connected to industrial activity and local economic development. The Zionist images of territorial threat and Arab traditionalism enter into such programs and policies, exemplified for the purposes of this study in *AUDG*. These images establish the naturalness of the ensuing disposition of forces, the rightness, say, of planning Upper Nazareth development on the basis of the needs and potential of the Arab towns and of transferring large tracts of land to Upper Nazareth jurisdiction for that development. And that disposition of forces feeds back into the habitus of Arab life in Galilee and the truth of Arab traditionalism. Such naturalness, rightness, truth are manifestations of the truth face of power.

Now discursive elements are only one of the constituents of the field of power relations. This study has found others in state practices dividing the world into domains and distinguishing between Jew and Arab—denying, meanwhile, the legitimacy of referring to that distinction when to do so might challenge the order of things. Further, there is the experience that results from the encounter with such practices. All these are bound up with one another and with the historical, geographical, economic, and discursive elements that constitute the lay of the land in the sense of the actors and their resources. Altogether, I argue that the field of power relations on which the actors struggle and maneuver in such engagements as those dealt with in this study is a synergy of these overlapping, multidimensional factors.

To put this thesis in other words, one might call attention to the intimate connection between ontology and methodology implicit here. Starting from observation at nodes of interaction in the field, this study shifted its gaze backward to history, upward in the administrative hierarchy, and outward (or inward) to enveloping and intersecting discursive space. But it returns always to the nodes of political struggle and engagement, for these, it is argued, are the defining characteristic of the field of power relations. Altogether, it is in this manner that the present study, conceived of as an ethnography of the macro-order, seeks to take hold of that order in its complexity and multidimensionality.

In keeping with this view of the nature of the field of power relations, I return to the realm of maneuver to deal with a number of attempts in Galilee, beyond the Zipporit case, to break through the boundaries separating Jewish development from Arab development. The discourse of joint Jewish-Arab industrial areas counters the two-pronged perception of separate development set out in *AUDG*. Still, it may be remarked that the exchanges in these challenges also engaged minor discourses anchored in the broadly deployed perception of Arab territorial threat and the image of Arab traditionalism. I refer here to programs of tourism development aimed at the Arab towns and to discourses of landscape and environment. These were considered in connection with the aborted program for Sajur-Karmi'el joint development of an industrial area north of the Akko-Zefat road.

But overall, the Arab towns in Galilee have made a move, over the course of the 1990s and since, to greater activism in demanding inclusion in development and development planning. Majd al Kurum and Bi'ne were not even aware of the 1991 boundary commission recommendation (a recommendation that came to naught in the ensuing course of events) that they be made part of a municipal union to develop and manage the new Bar Lev industrial area. Today, Majd al Kurum is pushing for adding land to its jurisdiction as part of new proposals that it become a partner in that regional industrial area. Nazareth is demanding that it become a partner in the Zipporit industrial area without putting in land of its own. The Nazareth bid challenges taken-for-granted principles in the control and disposition of land—the *normality* of jurisdiction, the sense of the proper uses of state land. It is a demand for full Arab partnership in development.

This is a corollary of a move toward proactive participation in development planning. The statutory planning system has channeled what it calls "public participation" into the submitting of objections, which turns participation into an adversarial relation; it does this for both the Jewish and Arab public. But it is noteworthy that in the case of the Arabs, this meshes with the Zionist image of confrontation and territorial struggle: as a "participant," one is made to oppose development when, were Jewish-Arab relations recast, the Arab population and Arab towns could be true participants in *creating* development initiative and thrust. Planning that distinguishes between Jew and Arab in order to assure the dominance of Jewish development might give way to planning that makes that distinction in order to promote Arab equality.

There is, of course, no guarantee that struggle for change will transform the world overnight. One needs to expect that every move will be met by countermoves, by attempts to preserve power positions by shifting the ground and the terms of battle. Old dispositions of power are constantly being transformed, permuted into new ones; in the end, that is what this study has concerned itself with. But struggle for change is itself a discursive space, and one may choose to take one's stand within it: what I would present here is the challenge of an attempt to imagine a world in which Jews and Arabs, to paraphrase the prominent Israeli planner I cited near the end of chapter 1, share this land as the homeland of each.

I close with a personal note in the register of Jewish self-interest. It is my sense that, by and large, the Jewish people in Israel has, at least since the advent of the state, been embarked on a course of closing in on itself in ever narrowing circles. That way, I feel, lies not existence but eventual suffocation. Part of our constriction inheres in our attempt to exclude those others, our Palestinian fellow citizens, who, like us, may claim this land as their homeland. To share the land would mean to choose, instead, breath and life.

Chronology of Events

Note: Vertical distance does *not* represent amount of elapsed time

1974–1979	Preparation of ILA proposal for "Zippori-Meshhed" industrial area.
26 Oct. 1983	Proposed program for entire area, including 1,000 dunam for conventional industry ("a complete solution for the industrial needs of Nazareth and its satellites") and 1,400 dunam for advanced technology industry.

	Zipporit Industrial Area (Upper Nazareth)				
	Transfer of land to Upper Nazareth	**Zipporit A—the statutory plan**	**The Phoenicia factory—approval, protest, and negotiation**	**The Kafar Kanna local industrial area**	**Planning Zipporit D–E**
1982	Upper Nazareth requests 3,500 dunam for industry in the area that would eventually become Zipporit.				
1989	Glazner Boundary Commission recommends transferring 500 dunam WMS to Upper Nazareth.				
13 May 1990				Plan comprising 629 dunam (of this, 370 dunam for industry) prepared by the ILA.	

16 June 1990			LPBC (Mevo Ha'amaqim) recommends deposit in DPBC.
29 Oct. 1990			DPBC subcommittee approves for deposit of limited extent (278 dunam, with about 90 for industry) and on condition of approval by CPAL.
During 1991		Planning an Upper Nazareth residential quarter and industrial area. Mivnei Ta'asiya given responsibility for planning.	
4 Mar. 1991	Minister of the interior signs order transferring about 740dunam to Upper Nazareth jurisdiction.		
8 Apr. 1991			CPAL approves.
26 Aug. 1991		Mivnei Ta'asiya planning team decides that industrial area portion will be treated as a separate entity; UBP for industrial area will be submitted.	
15 Jan. 1992		Notices on VaLaL approval of the industrial area plan for deposit.	
30 Jan. 1992		Minister of the interior determines that plan requires his signature.	
1 Mar. 1992	Upper Nazareth submits request to have entire area (an additional 3,324 dunam) transferred to its jurisdiction (of these, an additional 541 dunam for Zipporit A).		

	Zipporit Industrial Area (Upper Nazareth)				
	Transfer of land to Upper Nazareth	**Zipporit A—the statutory plan**	**The Phoenicia factory—approval, protest, and negotiation**	**The Kafar Kanna local industrial area**	**Planning Zipporit D–E**
23 Mar. 1992		VaLaL hears objections to the industrial area plan submitted by the head of the Meshhed Local Council and others; introduces modifications in response to some of these; decides to give final approval.			
26 Apr. 1992			Phoenicia requests building permit.		
29 Apr. 1992		LPBC issues permit for earth-work (approval of UBP is still pending).			
4 June 1992			LPBC issues conditional building permit to Phoenicia (including condition that Phoenicia fulfill the requirements of the Ministry of the Environment).		
20 July 1992				Objection lodged at DPBC by the Kafar Kanna Local Council ("We were not consulted, we have other needs"); local council submits alternative plan for 157 dunam, with 70 dunam for industry.	
9 Sept. 1992	Boundary commission recommends transfer of entire area (an additional 3,324				

	dunam) for expanding the existing industrial area (Zipporit A) and for residence.			
22 Sept. 1992			Phoenicia cornerstone-laying ceremony. Protest demonstration by residents of Kafar Kanna and Meshhed.	
12 Nov. 1992		Plan referred to the minister of the interior for approval.		
13 Nov. 1992				Arab press reports that there is to be a joint industrial area and that this is supported by the Ministry of the Interior, the Ministry of Industry, and the Prime Minister's Office.
22 Nov. 1992		In light of recommendations from the Planning Administration in the Ministry of the Interior, it is decided not to approve until the plan's instructions regarding the environment are acceptably formulated.		
28 Dec. 1992			DPBC approves Phoenicia building permit (in accordance with §97a, since UBP not yet approved), subject to conditions set by the LPBC, including fulfillment of the requirements of the Ministry of the Environment.	

	Zipporit Industrial Area (Upper Nazareth)				
	Transfer of land to Upper Nazareth	**Zipporit A—the statutory plan**	**The Phoenicia factory—approval, protest, and negotiation**	**The Kafar Kanna local industrial area**	**Planning Zipporit D–E**
29 Dec. 1992			Kafar Kanna and Meshhed petition HCJ, focusing on Phoenicia and pollution.		
30 Jan. 1993			DPBC and the Ministry of the Environment respond to HCJ petition, saying that permit was issued by mistake and is not valid.		
1 Feb. 1993			Request by petitioners to cancel the petition.		
2 Feb. 1993					*Al-Ittichad* reports that HCJ petition is withdrawn. Petitioners have been convinced that this will facilitate negotiations over control of emissions, and it has been decided that the industrial area will be joint and that the three localities will share the local tax revenue.
1 Mar. 1993			New petitioners ask authorities to issue an administrative cease order on the grounds that work is being carried out without a permit.		
16 Mar. 1993			New permit issued to Phoenicia (unbeknownst to petitioners).		
18 Mar. 1993		Announcement of approval of G/IC/125 (Zipporit A).			

1 Apr. 1993	New petition submitted to HCJ attacking both easy conditions set by the Ministry of the Environment and new permit, if such has been issued.		
20 Apr. 1993	HCJ is informed that petitioners and Phoenicia are discussing practical proposals.		
May 1993			Khamaisi explains to the author in December 1993 that in May 1993 it was decided to prepare detailed plans for Zipporit D and E and go through VaLaL; the aim was to have an approved plan by November 1994.
12 May 1993		DPBC decides to accept the local authority's objection and, because of the serious change, to redeposit the plan.	
1 June 1993			Meeting of Kafar Kanna, Meshhed, and Upper Nazareth to discuss principles of the joint industrial area in pursuance of declarations of intent.
18 Aug. 1993		DPBC gives final approval to the industrial area part of the Kafar Kanna plan (70 dunam for industry) without its having been redeposited.	

	Zipporit Industrial Area (Upper Nazareth)				
	Transfer of land to Upper Nazareth	**Zipporit A—the statutory plan**	**The Phoenicia factory—approval, protest, and negotiation**	**The Kafar Kanna local industrial area**	**Planning Zipporit D–E**
15 Aug. 1993; 25 Oct. 1993	Exchange of letters between Emeq Yizre'el Regional Council and Upper Nazareth regarding new arrangements in the event that transferred land is rezoned for uses other than residential.				
1 Nov. 1993			Phoenicia furnace is fired.		
Nov. 1993				Ministry of Industry begins work on G/7088.	
21 Dec. 1993	Minister of the interior signs order transferring 173 dunam from WMS to Upper Nazareth (at southern end of the Zipporit A tract).				
11 Jan. 1994			Factory is inaugurated.		
14 Feb. 1994					HaPaT informs architect that the Ministry of Industry has authorized planning in Zipporit E on the part that is privately owned as well.
20 May 1994			Phoenicia and petitioners sign agreement (status of court judgment given to agreement 4 Aug. 1994).		

1994	Emeq Yizre'el Regional Council opposition to recommended transfer of jurisdiction, despite earlier agreement.	
May 1994		Architect begins planning; plan shows land uses in Zipporit D–E.
17 July 1994	Boundary Commission decides to uphold its earlier recommendation.	
29 Dec. 1994; 22 Jan. 1995	Emeq Yizre'el and Upper Nazareth submit opposing drafts for agreement on partnership.	
Jan. 1995	Boundary Commission submits final report.	
9 Apr. 1995	Emeq Yizre'el Regional Council decides to struggle against the recommendation "by all available means."	
5 June 1995	Minister of the interior signs order transferring area for Zipporit B and C (about 2,783 dunam) to Upper Nazareth, and for additions in the Zipporit A tract (about 368 dunam) —altogether about 2,531 dunam from Emeq Yizre'el Regional Council and 620 dunam WMS.	
27 July 1995	Emeq Yizre'el Regional Council petitions HCJ against the land transfer.	

	Zipporit Industrial Area (Upper Nazareth)				
	Transfer of land to Upper Nazareth	**Zipporit A—the statutory plan**	**The Phoenicia factory—approval, protest, and negotiation**	**The Kafar Kanna local industrial area**	**Planning Zipporit D–E**
16 Aug. 1995				National Priority Region status equalized with that of Zipporit–Upper Nazareth.	
11 Sept. 1995					Preliminary hearing in LPBC: it is decided to wait until plan is adjusted to the Kafar Kanna outline plan
28 Sept. 1995				Israel Lands Council decides to equalize land prices for industry (industrial areas in Arab localities and large neighboring [Jewish] ones) for two years from the beginning of plot allocation. Decision requires signature of the minister of finance.	
6 Feb. 1996					Conditional approval by LPBC.
19 Feb. 1996	Decision of HCJ upholding the transfer.				
17 Mar. 1996	Minister of the interior signs order transferring land to Meshhed (from WMS and in the area south of Zipporit A).				
About April 1996					Meshhed requests that planning be halted.
10 May 1996				Minister of finance signs Israel Lands Council decision to equalize land prices.	

24 Dec. 1996	DPBC meets on plan—1,961 dunam; of this, 525 for industry. Of the 1,961 dunam, 807 in Meshhed jurisdiction marked "area to be planned for industry in the future." Of the 1,961 dunam, approximately 1,053 in Kafar Kanna jurisdiction.
	Planners are asked to take out the Meshhed area; to provide tables of adjusted land rights; to provide a programmatic analysis giving the number of workers to be employed in the industrial area compared with the demographic analysis of the entire region for which the plan is relevant; to show stages of implementation in accordance with conclusions of the program; to add environmental protection provisions. Should be ready to come to DPBC for hearing by February 1997.
10 Feb. 1998	Israel Lands Council decision equalizing price of land is extended.
12 May 1999	Ministry of the Environment demands an EIA.

	Zipporit Industrial Area (Upper Nazareth)				
	Transfer of land to Upper Nazareth	**Zipporit A—the statutory plan**	**The Phoenicia factory—approval, protest, and negotiation**	**The Kafar Kanna local industrial area**	**Planning Zipporit D–E**
31 Jan. 2000					Meeting of subcommittee of DPBC: G/11414 is separated out from G/9155; separation is according to division between ILA-owned and privately owned land to enable expediting the ILA-owned part. Ministry of the Environment is willing to accept an "environmental survey" and will not insist on an EIA. It is decided to deposit both plans with conditions.
5 Sept. 2000					CPAL approves G/11414 on condition that the plan provide a satisfactory solution for preventing the seepage of pollutants into the groundwater.

Notes

Introduction

1. For various treatments of the subdiscourse on Israel as the state of the Jewish people, see Kimmerling 1985, Liebman 1988, E. Cohen 1989, Herzog 1990, Smooha 1990, Y. Peled 1992, and Handelman 1994. Kapferer (1988) and Herzfeld (1993) provide discussions in a non-Israeli setting of the nexus of nation-state and distinctions between Self and Other. The last three authors do deal with the consequences of such distinctions.

2. On Zionism and territory, see Kimmerling 1983 and Rabinowitz 1997 (76–81).

3. Adopting an actor-oriented approach for the study of development intervention, the contributors to the Norman Long and Ann Long volume referenced here (1992) put the social construction of local knowledge as a central theme of their research focus. That is not the thrust of my research. However, Andrew Long does offer conceptual observations on the uses of discursive elements that are suggestive of the approach adopted here.

4. Vulgar criticism of Zionist practices often cites the constraints placed on Arab purchase or lease of state-owned land. Except in unusual circumstances, however, state-owned land is not sold to anyone, Arab or Jew. It is the JNF charter that proscribes leasing land to non-Jews. In 1993, JNF land was about 12 percent of the total state land administered by the Israel Lands Administration (ILA 1994). There are no legal restraints on the leasing of non-JNF state land to Arabs (Kretzmer 1990).

5. Mitzpim settlements are set up by the Jewish Agency in areas having a low proportion of Jewish population with the purpose of establishing a Jewish presence in the area, establishing Jewish control over territory, and keeping a watch out for so-called illegal Arab building and for Arab incursions into state-owned land.

6. Yiftachel (1997) takes Majd al-Kurum, an Arab town in Galilee, as a case for the study of Israeli planning policy vis-à-vis the Arab population. Although the conception of a monolithic, coherent policy of control holds sway in Yiftachel's presentation and analysis, his account of local protest, political maneuver, and their results may be read in just this light of the shifting lines of battle.

7. The reader may care to compare other examples of ethnographic treatment of the macro-order such as Fischer 1980 or Rabinow 1989.

8. A *dunam* is a unit of land area equal to 1,000 square meters.

Chapter 1: The Lay of the Land (I)

1. The Phoenicia glass factory is just 1,100 meters from the westernmost dwelling in Kafar Kanna, and 900 meters from the northernmost ones in Meshhed.

2. The brief geographical discussion here draws on Kellner and Rosenau 1939; Amiran 1956; Ziv 1970; Orni and Efrat 1971; and Kliot 1983.

3. See Government Decision 21/*'Ayin-Pe*, 29 February 1976; Rokach 1982.

4. This is Isaiah 9:1 in the Revised Standard Version.

5. For statistical purposes, the Central Bureau of Statistics (CBS) divides the country into "natural regions," which it defines as "continuous areas, as homogeneous as possible in their physical structure, climate, and soil as well as in terms of the demographic, economic, and social characteristics of their population" (CBS 1998b: xxvi; see also CBS 1976 for descriptions of the natural regions). The Galilee was first divided in 1961 into fourteen such regions. Four of these were each split into two in the course of subsequent censuses. The code numbers of the natural regions were revised for the 1995 Census.

6. For a similar presentation for 1986, see also Falah 1989: 232–233.

7. The Arabs in Galilee were about one-half of all the Arabs in Israel. About one-quarter lived in the mixed cities in the rest of Israel (including East Jerusalem), and less than one-quarter lived in Arab towns (of these, 138,000 lived in the area known as the Triangle; 40,000 in a number of towns in the Carmel mountain range, along the seacoast, and at the western approach to Jerusalem; and 44,000 in the Negev). There were approximately 30,000 Bedouin residing outside of recognized localities in the Negev, and about 17,000 Druze in the Golan.

See the glossary for definitions of *locality* and related terms.

8. For the first time, the questionnaire of the 1995 Census did not ask for religion. Staff at the CBS explained to me that this was primarily the result of the antagonism the question had aroused among the Arab population in previous censuses. Also, in publications for 1995 and later, the CBS refers to the aggregate of the Arab population as "Arabs and others" rather than as "non-Jews." "Others" refers, in part, to members of other religions who once numbered only a few hundred and who in the past were included among the Druze in CBS statistics. Two relatively recent phenomena swell the ranks of this category, however: (a) tens of thousands among the immigrants from the former Soviet Union and from Ethiopia whose Jewish identity is not recognized by the Ministry of the Interior and whose religion is recorded as "unclassified" or "unknown," and (b) significant numbers of foreign workers (those who had been in the country for more than a year at the time of the census). Thus, for example, "Arabs and others" in Upper Nazareth or Karmi'el would include such persons, possibly many, as well as Arabs who had taken up residence there.

The CBS has been adding data on religion to the 1995 Census results by extracting that information for each resident of Israel from the records of the Ministry of the Interior. At the time of writing the present study, it had not yet published demographic results of the 1995 Census but furnished me, for the purposes of this study, the data needed to compile table 1.1. This data distinguished the "unclassified, alien residents, and others" as a separate category, and this is reflected in table 1.1.

Ostensibly, the category labeled "Arabs and others" goes some way to assuaging Arab indignation at being identified as "non-Jews." Given the makeup of this category, however, the implication of "Arab and others" remains "non-Jews," an ambiguous category of nonidentity and nonbelonging. For purposes of official record keeping, the

Palestinian citizens of Israel have not yet been allowed to state their identity in terms of their own choosing.

9. Unless otherwise stated, data on localities and settlement are compiled from CBS 1998b.

10. Morris cites Wallach and Lissak (1978), who show about 148 evacuated places in the same area.

11. Of the 212.2 thousand Arabs in the north in 1946, only 90.6 thousand remained after the war (Soffer 1983a). See Morris 1987 for a detailed account of the military campaigns that resulted in the destruction of the Arab localities and the widespread dislocation of the Arab population, which entailed large numbers of internal refugees, in addition to those who left.

12. I am indebted here to Sabri Jiryis, whose carefully written 1976 volume (p. 105) called my attention to this document and to the Hare'uveni newspaper article that will be cited below. These quotations suit my purpose of setting the stage for my ethnography.

13. See Falah 1989 for an analysis of Judaization policy from an Arab perspective; for the subsequent critical response and counter-response, see Soffer 1991; Yiftachel and Rumley 1991; Falah 1991. Among other things, Yiftachel and Rumley point out that Israeli policy has been marked by "fragmentation and contradiction" (289). Falah counters that his article is not based on official sources (which would show such fragmentation and contradiction), but rather is an "attempt to present empirical realities" (Falah 1991: 305). It should be noted that the concern of my own study is with ongoing local state practices and the images of the Zionist discourse, focusing on the *workings* of power rather than on its results. It might also be pointed out that the entire exchange on the Falah article provides several insights into the intimate association of power and knowledge (regardless of relative positions in the power relationship).

14. Hare'uveni puts this immediately following the word "decision" and a colon, but does not enclose the text that follows in quotation marks. The language may derive from official reports of the government proceedings. Single words enclosed here in quotation marks appear thus in the original.

15. "Outline plan" (*tochnit mit'ar*) is the Israeli term for land-use or zoning plan.

16. This is borne out by the 1976 report by the Kubersky Commission, *The Problems of Planning and Construction in the Arab Sector in the Northern District* (Kubersky 1976: 7).

17. On the Bedouin population in Galilee, see Medzini 1983 and Khamaisi 1990. The latter deals in particular with illegal building. For a vivid description of the development of one Galilean tribe, see Eloul 1984.

18. According to data extracted from the Census, the 1995 Arab population in the Northern District included about 33,300 Bedouin living in recognized Bedouin localities, and approximately 4,600 Bedouin residing outside of localities. The figure for Bedouin residing in localities does not include Bedouin in Arab towns whose population is generally non-Bedouin, nor those in mixed Jewish-Arab localities. The figure of 4,600 for Bedouin residing outside of localities is an inference from data on Muslims residing thus.

19. The ILA survey on illegal building that led to the establishment of the Kubersky Commission (included in the commission's report as Appendix 1; Kubersky Report 1976) lumps together all structures, whether permanent buildings or light, temporary ones. And it includes in the classification of state land, land whose ownership was disputed by both state and private individuals. Khamaisi (1990: 159) suggests that most of

the cases included in the ILA survey were a matter of temporary structures and land to which the Bedouin had yet-to-be adjudicated claims.

20. A quasi-government body linked to the state by a compact, the Jewish Agency carries out certain government functions. It is ultimately answerable, however, to the World Zionist Federation (i.e., to organized world Jewry) and not to the electorate of the state of Israel.

21. Carmon et al. (1990) attempt to assign realistic dimensions to the illegal building and territorial incursion. Soffer and Finkel (n.d.) show the unrealistic nature of the expectations that the settlements would exercise direct control over such building and incursion into state land.

22. Muvhar's description of the line he draws is not entirely accurate: Segev (marked on figure 1.4) had been set up in 1953 as a village of foresters and quarriers but had meanwhile been abandoned by nearly all the settlers; Yodfat (marked on figure 1.4) had been set up in 1964 and had seventy-four inhabitants in 1972. In some places Muvhar's line just barely excludes Jewish settlements established before 1975. Yet it also refrains from including two areas—one at its northeast corner, and the other at the southeast corner—in which, although there were no Jewish settlements, the jurisdictional boundaries of the Arab localities left little room free for possible settlement.

23. Information on the total area of Misgav jurisdiction varies. The *Encyclopedia of Local Government in Israel* (Huri n.d.) gives the figure of about 170,000 dunam at the time of the regional council's establishment. Orgad and Newman (1991; published by the Association of Regional Councils) give 189,000 dunam.

24. Such multiple-locality local planning and building commissions come into being when the minister of the interior sets what is known as a "local planning area" to include the areas of more than one local authority (PBL 1965: §§13, 19). The resulting PBC (planning and building commission) is "joint" in the sense that it has jurisdiction over the area of more than one local authority and includes among its members representatives nominated by some or all of those local authorities. But the chairman of the commission is directly appointed by the ministry of interior district commissioner, giving the latter considerable control. The element of domination from outside and above has undoubtedly been more salient for the Arab localities than for the Jewish ones. Also, the LPBCs for the Arab towns often had planning jurisdiction over so many localities as to make their work cumbersome and exceedingly slow. In 1996, a number of smaller (but still multiple-locality) LPBCs were established for the Arab towns in Galilee, replacing the more unwieldy ones (*KT* 5772, 11 July 1996).

25. Rural councils were subsequently renamed "regional councils." Since 1995, three of the four such councils in Israel statewide were disestablished, with some or all of their constituent localities being re-established as individual or multiple-locality local councils.

26. The Planning and Building Law provided that the preparation of local outline plans would be initiated by the LPBC, but it was amended in 1995 to allow outline plan proposals to be submitted by landowners and entrepreneurs as well (PBL, Amendment 43). Urban building plans are detailed plans whose preparation may be initiated by landowners, entrepreneurs, or the LPBC itself. Urban building plans are treated as though they were outline plan proposals when they differ from the outline plan in force or where no outline plan exists. Their preparation is more expensive, however; also, zoning changes from agricultural use require the approval of the Commission for the Preservation of Agricultural Land (CPAL), whether the change is effected by

an outline plan or a detailed plan. Preparation of an outline plan or proposed change to an outline plan would be more appropriate for long-range, extensive projects or for projects whose approval is likely to be problematic.

27. The Northern District Outline Plan that would, as of 1983, supersede the Mandatory outline scheme was then on deposit at the National Board for Planning and Building (NBPB). Strictly speaking, plans for the *mitzpim,* had they been submitted, would have had to comply with the proposed district plan then on deposit. But that plan, until it was later amended, did not provide for construction of the *mitzpim.*

28. It should be recalled that the new Bedouin towns in Galilee were recognized and built at the same time as the authorities were pressing the Bedouin relentlessly in an attempt to take over land that had been in the latter's possession, often to which they held or claimed title, since before the establishment of the state.

29. Outline plans are the only ones that follow statutory procedures in order to gain approval and, by definition, have statutory validity on approval. Master plans or development plans are not subject to such approval, although they are *adopted* by the relevant authority. They set goals and development horizons and parameters.

30. Yiftachel's data on outline plans are framed in terms of *settlements,* that is, Arab villages and towns compared with Jewish towns (a handful) and numerous rural collective, cooperative, and communal settlements. The government survey's data, as stated, are framed in terms of *local authorities.* Again, it will be recalled that the individual rural settlements that make up the regional council do not have local authority status.

31. It should be recalled that, quite naturally, the unrecognized villages do not have outline plans, and they are excluded from the domain of this statistic.

32. This change involves (a) an expected interest in community settlement on the part of settlers who will be evacuated from areas occupied by Israel in the 1967 war, and (b) areas in the vicinity of new international boundaries that will have development potential.

33. It should also be noted, however, that Alterman and Stav (2001: 91) report being told by national planners that the long delay in depositing Amendment 9 was a result of having to adapt it to the many changes in planning that took place at the national level in response to the Russian immigration of the 1990s.

34. This is the same writer cited elsewhere as Arnon Soffer. The English table of contents in this publication gives his name with a single *f.* In all other appearances in English, the name is spelled with two *f*s, and hence it is the latter spelling I have also used for publications in which his name is given only in Hebrew.

Chapter 2: The Lay of the Land (II)

1. See near the beginning of chapter 1 for figures on the Arab population throughout Israel in 1995.

2. The title of this publication, and that of its predecessor (Publication 1039 n.d.), is misleading. The data are for 1995 (as the subtitle added after publication indicates; see pp. xix–xxi, 18–19). It is likely that the use of "1999" in the main title refers to the fact that this "characterization and ranking" was prepared in 1999, to be used for calculating the year 2000 grant to the various local authorities. Similarly, Publication 1039 has "1995" in its title, but uses data from 1993 and 1994.

3. It should be noted that the set of local authorities thus ranked includes Jewish urban localities established in the various areas, including the Golan, occupied by

Israel in the 1967 war, but not Arab towns in those areas (with the exception of the Druze localities in the Golan). It does not include the regional councils (or the localities that make them up) and, of course, it does not include the unrecognized Bedouin villages or hamlets. It should also be noted that the set of local authorities ranked here are those that were in existence in 1999, not 1995. As related earlier, the Arab rural councils in Wadi 'Ara and in the Negev were subsequently broken up and reconstituted as individual or smaller multiple-locality local councils. Also, a small number of Arab localities that had been part of Jewish regional councils were recognized as independent local councils. In choosing between having socioeconomic rank based on current 1995 data or having a set of local authorities exactly equivalent to those in existence in 1995, I have opted here for the former alternative.

An earlier socioeconomic ranking, carried out for the situation in 1992 (Heimberg [Chetrit] and Dor 1994) treated the Jewish local authorities and Arab local authorities as separate groups, arriving at a slightly different set of variables for each group, with the consequence that results for the two groups could not be merged. For example, one could not say whether a low-ranking Arab locality was higher or lower in socioeconomic rank than a low-ranking Jewish locality. Starting with Publication 1039, the official statisticians were compelled to produce a single ranking when it was decided that this ranking would serve as an indicator for the distribution of budgetary grants by the Ministry of the Interior.

4. By 1992, there were sixty-five such authorities, plus the four so-called rural councils. The latter are not the same as the "village councils" established by the British (see description in chapter 1).

It should be recalled that figures for the period prior to 1948 refer to the entire area of Mandate Palestine, whereas those given here for the subsequent period refer only to the area (minus the Golan) under Israeli sovereignty.

The figures given for Israel here were extracted from CBS 1997a.

5. See Shokeid 1968 for a study of immigrant Moroccan Jews in Israel who were sent to a new settlement and were dependent on outside authorities and subject to their intervention. The ensuing local factionalism was referred to by the authorities as "*hamulot* feuding"; this was a concept imposed by the authorities themselves on village relations and not one that the immigrants had brought with them (393). The authorities fostered village organization along these lines and then attributed this to Moroccan tradition.

6. These are partial itemizations. My intention here is not to provide a complete itemization of local authority budgets, but rather the minimum detail and distinctions necessary for the discussion to follow. For a complete exposition, other sources are available, particularly CBS 1998d, Publication 1095 (or other publications in this series); and Soari 1993. In English, see Hecht 1988. The latter two sources offer good reviews of historical development.

7. It should be noted that not all investments by government or quasi-government bodies go through the municipal development budgets; hence, published municipal development budget figures are a poor indication of the actual state of affairs.

8. In addition to information on various episodes in the course of this struggle, these authors provide comparative data on Jewish and Arab current municipal budgets for the years 1970, 1975, 1982, and 1984. They also provide comparative data for 1970, 1975, and 1982 for seven Arab and seven Jewish local authorities matched for size and district.

9. In addition to one Circassian town, there were twelve local authorities that, having over 50 percent Druze in their population (with one exception), qualified for inclusion in the list of Druze and Circassian localities. Later, three towns having Druze neighborhoods were added to the list along with two Circassian localities that are part of a Jewish regional council. The five Druze localities in the Golan are not part of this group.

10. "Billion" here is consistent with American usage and refers to 10^9. Former British usage referred to that figure as "milliard," reserving "billion" for 10^{12}. Israelis commonly use the term "milliard" for 10^9, but even in Britain "billion" seems to have replaced it, and I have elected to follow American usage.

11. That is how this body translates its name, even though the Hebrew original would more accurately be translated "Bureau."

12. The wording in this sentence reflects the formulation of Razin's computations: his figures are for local authorities, that is, they are not weighted for population of the individual local authorities.

In this discussion, I use "Jewish" to stand for "Jewish and mixed"; "urban localities" stands for "cities and local councils" (as distinguished from "local authorities," which includes regional councils as well).

13. These successive agreements also made provisions for covering the deficit in the Arab local authority budgets, which had reached critical proportions each time (as was the case in some of the Jewish local authorities as well).

14. Other Ministry of Interior tables, similar in principle, are used for the *Arab*, the *Druze and Circassian*, and the regional council sectors. Officials in the Ministry of the Interior explained to me that the money available for the grant is earmarked by sector. The rate at which the current grant is increased for next year's actual grant has to work in each sector within the limits of the total funds available for that sector. But comparison between the maximum rates of increase allowed in 1999 for each sector cannot be based on immediate inspection, inasmuch as other constraints were introduced into the calculation of the maximum increase allowed in the Jewish sector for that year.

15. That is, the Soari Model is applied with the exception of certain distorting elements. For example, in computing the revenue side of the model, the minimum value allowed for property tax collection in 1999 was 482 NIS per capita, which is far beyond what the Arab localities are able to collect (see discussion below).

16. See Israel, State Comptroller 2000 (50B, 504–518) for a detailed description of the arbitrary, irregular way in which this discretion has been exercised.

17. As distinguished from Razin's data, the localities in the Arab rural councils are not included in these tables. Similarly to Razin's material, however, the figures here do not include Arab localities situated in Jewish regional councils and, of course, do not include unrecognized villages.

I call attention to the fact that government participation as a percentage of total expenditure given here differs greatly from the figures given in table 2.3, in amount but not in comparative direction. Note that the latter table is based on total revenue, not total expenditure, and this is somewhat lower. The principle source of the apparent inconsistency, however, is the fact that Razin (the source for tables 2.3 and 2.4), in keeping with the sense that the local authority is the unit of analysis, averages the individual local authority per capita values for each sectoral group. Tables 2.5, 2.6, and 2.7 take total monetary values and total population for the local authorities in each sectoral group; they are thus weighted for population, whereas Razin's are not.

18. In 1995, nine of the sixty-one Jewish localities in the lower six socioeconomic clusters collected more than 100 percent of the annual assessment, as did seven of the sixty-seven Arab localities. This represents collection of payment arrears for previous years. To avoid distortion by figures such as 137 percent or 149 percent, these were calculated as 100 percent: it was indeed 100 percent of the *current* assessment that was collected in these cases.

19. These figures are computed from CBS 1998a.

20. The conditional grant is 5 percent of the grant. The ministry stipulates that half of it will be released in return for having an approved current budget, the other half in return for achieving a minimal collection of the property tax and water rates.

21. The reference to *towns* subsumes *all* of the Arab towns *and cities*. In 1995, the population of Nazareth was close to fifty-two thousand; the six remaining Arab local authorities large enough to have been awarded the status of city ranged in size from fifteen to twenty-nine thousand.

The authors cited here mention, in passing, Rahat, a town established by the government for Bedouin settlement in the Negev. Although the Bedouin have moved to Rahat and other such towns, they are not urban centers in the sense of serving as a focus for economic and administrative activity.

See Lewin-Epstein and Semyonov 1993 and Haidar 1995 for longitudinal data on the further decline of agriculture as a source of livelihood. Haidar (69–70) observes that Arab farmers continue to cultivate their lands even though this has become economically marginal.

22. See Vanhove and Klaassen 1987 (184–186) for a European statement on the role of industry in the process of urbanization. See also writing on so-called rural industrialization, which approaches its subject in the same vein of subnational economic development: United Nations 1974; Shaw and Williams 1985; and, regarding the Israeli case, Bar-El 1987.

23. These data are based on a questionnaire administered to the owners and managers of 514 plants out of the total of 900 in the 1992 survey.

24. "Municipal industrial authority" is used as the translation of *minhelet ezor hata'asiya.* Actually, *minhelet* would be translated as "administration," and some of my informants preferred that to "authority." Other informants insisted that "municipal industrial authority" was the proper term, however, and this is the term I have adopted throughout the present work.

25. At one point, the Ministry of Industry officially defined "industrial park" as an area in which parcels (possibly in a building for rental) are owned by a single owner, with occupants subject to and served by a central park management, and having hi-tech industry (Ministry of Industry 1995: 13–14).

26. About half of the gross area would be designated for roads, infrastructure systems, public and commercial services, and open areas. The remaining 50 percent (30 dunam in this case) would be the total size of the lots available for industrial construction. See Shefer et al. 1992; see also Ministry of Interior, ILA, et al. 1989 (21–22 [table 15] and 54), according to which the lots available for industry in the Northern District averaged 51 percent of the industrial areas there. This ratio is specific to the Northern District; other regions, with different topography, exhibit other proportions. Similar data are repeated in other sources.

It may be noted that zoning regulations set the area of the lot that can be built on or what is known as land-use coverage (in percent of the lot area), but also often allow construction of more than one story.

27. See also Lewin-Epstein and Semyonov 1993 (particularly 54–59) for a sophisticated analysis of what they call "spatial mismatch," comparing occupational distribution of the population residing in the Arab localities with the occupational composition of the jobs available in those localities, and analyzing the implications of this for educational-occupational mismatch and socioeconomic inequality.

28. Bar-El does this in a preliminary, sketchy way. Also, his "work in locality" to "reside in locality" ratios do not distinguish between Arab and Jewish localities.

29. Note that census and labor force survey statistics used in dealing with the subject of labor commuting (by Khalidi, Haidar, and others, as well as in the present study) do not distinguish between the two phenomena.

30. This assertion is framed in terms of towns. It would be well to round it out by citing Lewin-Epstein and Semyonov (1993), who focus on labor force and job market characteristics. These authors find that by 1983, there were almost 50 percent more highly educated persons resident in Arab towns than there were high-status jobs available in those towns (56). They also find increasing incidence (from 1972 to 1983) of educational-occupational mismatch in the Arab labor force (such mismatch obtains when a person is employed in a job that, in the general job market, is generally filled by someone with lower training and skills than his or her own) (56–57).

31. One may refer here to Herzfeld's 1993 concept of bureaucratic indifference, to which he brings an analysis that is different from the one pursued in the present study.

Chapter 3: The Zipporit Industrial Area

1. See chapter 1 for some elaboration of the concept of development as distinguished from regulatory planning.

2. Strictly speaking, it is the state that owns the land; the ILA administers it. It is common usage to speak of ILA-owned land, however, and I follow it.

3. In documents of that period, "Nazareth" assimilates the terms of an earlier specification: "Upper Nazareth and Nazareth and its satellites." In the earlier version, "satellites" refers only to the Arab towns around Nazareth; in the assimilated version, it might include other Jewish settlements as well.

4. Correspondence (23 November 1987) and the record of an ILA meeting (26 June 1988) establish that planning was already in the works at that time.

5. The *Municipalities Ordinance* (par. 8; see in "Legislation Cited") provides that the minister of the interior may/will appoint a "commission of inquiry" to investigate proposals for the change of municipal boundaries of jurisdiction. After considering the report of the commission, the minister may "alter, extend or diminish" such boundaries at his discretion. Commissions of inquiry are also referred to as "boundary commissions," and I prefer this term.

The boundary commission in question was first appointed in 1981, with Yisrael Koenig as chairman, but due to protests by the city of Nazareth concerning the commission's composition, two of its members, including the chairman, were changed in June 1984. The commission, under Moshe Glazner, its new head, decided to begin work from scratch. The minister extended the scope of the commission's inquiry in 1985, and again in 1988.

6. No date appears in the records I was able to see; Moshe Glazner provided me with the date given here.

7. A new 1990 law, the Planning and Building Procedures Law (hereinafter PBPL), responding to the tremendous surge in immigration to Israel from the USSR, expedited the statutory approval process. To this end, the law provided for the establishment of one or more residential and industrial construction commissions (RICCs) in each district. RICC is used here for the Hebrew VaLaL, the abbreviation for Va'ada Lebniya Lemegurim uLeta'asiya. The PBPL is commonly referred to as the "VaLaL Law."

8. Of the plan's 1,340 dunam, 612 were allocated to industry (see chapter 2 for information on the average net area for industry in industrial areas in the Northern District).

9. The blue line refers to the line setting the boundary of the plan under consideration.

10. Quoted from the report of the RICC to Upper Nazareth, Mevo Ha'amaqim, and Yizre'elim LPBCs, 1 April 1992.

11. A detailed plan is often synonymously referred to in Hebrew as a *TaBa'*, an abbreviation for *Tochnit Binyan 'Arim*. Where it seems appropriate, I will use "UBP" (i.e., urban building plan) as an English equivalent. See also the discussion of outline plans and detailed plans (urban building plans) in chapter 1.

12. This is a prerogative granted to the minister by a 1988 amendment to the Planning and Building Law (§22, amending §109; see in "Legislation Cited") and adopted by the PBPL with changes in the time period allowed for action. The PBPL (§5(9)) gives the minister thirty days from the time the plan is deposited in which to rule that it will require his approval.

RICC correspondence states variously that it approved the plan for deposit on 24 November 1991 and/or on 9 December 1991. Notices were sent on 15 January 1992. The decision was published in the press on 22 January 1992 and in *Yalqut Hapirsumim* (Official gazette) 3977, 2282, 20 February 1992.

13. The title of Awawdy 1993a, "Will the Phoenicia Factory Arise on the Rotation Agreements?" bears some comment. At the end of summer 1992, there was a changeover in the chairmanship of the Meshhed Local Council, which was effected according to a coalition agreement on rotation made following the previous local elections. The issue of Phoenicia and Meshhed lands figured prominently in local politics at the time of the changeover. The rotation in the local council chairmanship appears again in the title of Bsool 1992, cited below.

14. As a matter of fact, the representative of the Infrastructure Development Company (HaPaT) which, acting for the Ministry of Industry, had engaged the earthwork firm, is on record at a meeting of 12 January 1993 in Jerusalem to the effect that all of the earthwork for the Phoenicia land parcel had already been completed (see more on this meeting below).

15. The petition was received at the HCJ on 29 December, but the deposition by at least one of the plaintiffs had been signed by 19 October.

16. Rozen does not report any elaboration by Derman on this tantalizing statement, nor does he offer any comment of his own. Following their example, I shall allow Derman's statement to stand on its own.

17. For a brief alternative account of the struggle of the Arab towns against the threat posed by Phoenicia, see Hawkins 1993. In my view, Hawkins's writing is marked by tendentiousness and certain inaccuracies and misinformation. In part, this is probably due to her desire to provide historical and political background for the immediate events despite the brevity of her treatment; in part, it would seem to be the result of the author's apparently uncritical acceptance of anything her sources

chose to tell her, even though she recognizes that the situation she deals with is highly charged politically.

18. In the very beginning, these were referred to as Zipporit B and C (*Bet* and *Gimmel*), but these labels were preempted by the westward extensions to Zipporit A planned by Upper Nazareth, and by the time of the first preliminary plan of May 1994, the Kafar Kanna–Meshhed areas were being called Zipporit D–E.

19. This plan was prepared by Yoram Fogel, architect and town planner, who was kind enough to make a copy available to me.

20. "National priority regions" were at one time referred to as "development areas," and the name of the Ministry of Industry unit was set accordingly. When the appellation changed, the ministry unit retained the original name.

21. Given the very low percentage allocated to industry, it would be in place to mention some of the other land uses (other than roads and open public areas): sport, 38 dunam; agriculture, 10 dunam; public building, 16 dunam; cemetery, 16 dunam; regional sewage-pumping facility, 51 dunam. These were all part of the original 629-dunam plan, but were, of course, not so prominent when there were 370 dunam planned for industry.

22. The project began in 1992 with just a few localities. Then, during 1992 and onward, it grew to include sixteen Arab localities in northern Israel, where work was actually completed or in process by 1996. There were another five such places in the south. Plans were being considered for other localities as well (see figure 2.2 and the notes to that figure).

23. This was a new system introduced in 1994. Up until that time, the ILA had set what it called "table prices" for industrial land in the national priority regions. These ranged from NIS 5.0 to NIS 20.0 thousand per dunam, and were only a small part of the open market price.

24. The difference might be only twice as much, once NPR status was equalized but before land prices were equalized.

25. The area transferred totaled about 3,151 dunam. Of the total, about 368 dunam would round out the area of Zipporit A.

26. Amendment 43 (1995) to the PBL augments the district planner's authority by explicitly empowering him to carry out such a preliminary examination and charging him to do so (§§62(b) and 62b in the amended law) (Sefer Hahuqim [Code of laws] 1995: 450).

27. In April 2000, the municipal engineer told me that 70 percent of the occupants of G/7088 were from outside Kafar Kanna, mostly from Nazareth.

Chapter 4: Land, Territory, and Jurisdiction

1. Peretz deals with the emergence of Israeli policy regarding refugee property. Through a step-by-step analysis drawing on records, Knesset and public debate, and government response, he is able to put the various legal instruments and the actions of state agencies into a unified perspective that I found particularly useful.

2. Cited by Peretz (1958: 180). Notwithstanding their apparent discomfort with the idea of confiscation, it was clear to Israeli lawmakers and officials that the transfer of land to the Development Authority would have the desirable effect (in their eyes) of severing the connection between that land and its original owners, a connection that

persisted so long as the land was formally in the hands of the Custodian. From then on, only compensation would be possible, when and if that were provided for by the Israelis (H. Cohen 2000: 70).

3. On the destroyed villages, see Morris 1987 and W. Khalidi 1992. The latter offers a bibliography. For an anthropological study that deals in part with the internal refugees or "present absentees" from the village of Ein Hud, see Slyomovics 1998.

4. According to Peretz (1958: 183), by 1954 over 100,000 dunam had been leased to five thousand Arab families. Cohen (2000) indicates that these figures were those cited by the Custodian in a public lecture; Cohen gives greater credence to other archival sources.

5. See Cohen 2000 (84) for a more detailed breakdown of these data.

According to Cohen (2000: 72), in 1953, the JNF held over 100,000 dunam of land in the northern part of Israel that had belonged to Arabs still present in Israel, which it had obtained via the Custodian of Absentee Property.

Peretz (1958: 183) puts the amount of land that had belonged to Arab citizens of Israel and that was being dealt with by the Land Acquisition Law at 300,000 dunam. But he adds that estimates of land taken over by the state from internal refugees/present absentees vary between 300,000 and 1 million dunam. Jiryis (1976: 131 and 267n87) gives an estimate of 768,000 dunam. He arrives at this figure by adding to a figure cited in the 1966 State Comptroller's report (350,000) an estimate of 418,000 dunam under the Absentee Property Law. The latter estimate is based on a 1964 article in the Arab press, but he notes that Tubi, the article's author, does not provide sources for his estimate. In light of Cohen's archive-based analysis, it may be suggested that Jiryis errs by simply *adding* Tubi's figures for property taken under the Absentee Property Law from those present in Israel to figures for land taken under the Land Acquisition Law.

6. Cohen suggests that much of the illegal building in the Arab towns was by internal refugees.

7. In 1969, the Ottoman Land Code was replaced by the Land Law. Paragraph 158 of the Land Law abrogated earlier Ottoman and Mandatory legislation (see "Legislation Cited").

8. These sources may, of course, be consulted for a fuller description of the land categories. They also include discussion of the Ottoman land categories not dealt with here.

9. For a clear statement using this terminology, see ILA 1965 (66).

10. Hilleli had earlier served for many years as an attorney in the Lands Division in the Ministry of Justice, engaged in settlement of title. In 1983, he was director of the Lands Department of the JNF.

11. Hilleli (1983: 587) makes much of the fact that registration of title to *miri* land now meant that the Arab villagers actually owned their land outright, particularly with the enactment of the Land Law of 1969, which did away with the legal distinction between *miri* and *mulk* land. But, as was noted above, that distinction had been for the most part a mere formality as far as actual Ottoman practice was concerned.

12. On Bedouin land loss in the Negev, see R. Shamir 1996 and E. Marx 2000.

13. This situation stands in contrast to the ability of kibbutzim and moshavim today regarding future residential and commercial development on their land.

14. See note 23 in chapter 1 on the area of Misgav jurisdiction.

15. As mentioned in chapter 3, paragraphs 188–196 of the Planning and Building Law empower the local authority to expropriate land for public purposes in accordance with a valid outline plan or detailed plan. The law provides (§190 (a)) that such

expropriation will be carried out according to the 1943 Land (Acquisition for Public Purposes) Ordinance.

16. Following the 1967 war, Israel unilaterally annexed the Golan and East Jerusalem. Official state statistics incorporate these areas (an additional 1.5 million dunam), making it difficult, in view of the insufficiency of the data generally presented in state sources, to arrive at data broken down by category of land ownership.

17. Figure on current Arab land ownership cited at Floersheim Institute for Policy Studies conference held at the Emeq Yizre'el Academic College, 27 June 2001.

18. Yiftachel's 1999a formulation includes Ashkenazi Jews, Oriental Jews, and Arabs in a three-tier set of relations. Thus, weakness is not only a matter of being an Arab in Israel (hence, the relevance of E. Marx 1976 and Shokeid 1968, studies I have cited at earlier points in this monograph).

19. In figure 1.1 current jurisdictional boundaries are shown by a dashed line, while the area within those boundaries subtended by the dotted line is that which was transferred to Meshhed in 1996; note that a small area north of Zipporit C (about 50 dunam, marked again by a dotted line) was removed from Meshhed jurisdiction at the same time.

20. These were the areas included in the jurisdictions of the two local councils as of 1996, but prior to the expansion of Meshhed jurisdiction noted earlier.

21. Cf. figure 1.1. The authors of the cited study are undoubtedly referring to the British Survey of Palestine village boundaries.

22. Data for Mandate village boundaries are from *Village Statistics* (Government of Palestine, Office of Statistics 1946). Data on area of jurisdiction are from CBS 1993. Data for Rame were updated as of 1988; data for the other two localities were updated as of 1989. The area of jurisdiction in these localities grew slightly at various times prior to these dates, but CBS publications before the one cited give only incomplete data.

The case of Rame is interesting because it is one of the local authorities first established and then disestablished by the Mandate government (see chapter 2). It was reestablished by the Israeli government in 1954.

23. Table 2.11 gives 1960 as the date Meshhed was established. This datum was taken from CBS 1998c; Ghanem (1993) gives the same date. However, the Meshhed local council was actually established as of 1 August 1958 by an order published in *KT* 816, 7 August 1958, 1723. Thus, it was not only the head of the Meshhed Local Council who was mistaken. This is not the only discrepancy in the accuracy of purportedly official data I encountered in the course of my fieldwork.

Chapter 5: The Image of Arab Traditionalism

1. This is not to be confused with the q-type principal components analysis, a multivariate statistical technique related to factor analysis.

2. At another point, the authors of *AII* refer to an entrepreneurship scale of five levels (181).

3. Q-analysis is formulated in terms of the relationships between elements of sets; these would parallel the *variables* of multivariate statistical analysis.

4. As with most Arab-owned land, this parcel too was held jointly by several owners. In this case, a principal owner had taken development in hand.

5. The photo looks southward with the right-hand edge of the page as the bottom of the photo. Thus, the parcels in question are to be seen at the left. The large trapezoidal

ungraded area at the western (right-hand) end of the industrial area was planned as a public open area and was subsequently developed and landscaped as such.

6. Regulations promulgated under the Obligatory Tenders Law 1993 (Regulation 25 §§(5)(a) and (b)) (see "Legislation Cited") authorized the ILA to lease rights to state land in national priority regions for industry or manufacture, without tender but subject to recommendation from the Ministry of Industry.

7. One is reminded of Ylana Miller's critique of the Mandatory government's failure to accord real responsibility to the local authorities it set up in Arab localities; see chapter 2 in the present study.

8. Actually, according to the 1995 Census, 5.2 and 12.8 thousand, respectively.

9. I was told that privately owned undeveloped land zoned for industry in this area would have fetched about $80,000 per dunam in 1996. The average size of privately owned parcels in the area within the Zipporit E plan in Meshhed jurisdiction was 7.07 dunam. The owner/s of an average parcel that had not been built on would have been required to pay property tax of $14,000 dollars annually. There were parcels, though, of 15, 20, or even 34 dunam involved, and the tax on these would, of course, have been correspondingly higher.

Not very long after the Meshhed landowners requested that planning be halted, the Knesset enacted Amendment 26 to the Property Tax and Compensation Fund Law (1996; see "Legislation Cited"). This amendment provided that if you (or those who had bequeathed it to you) had owned the land subject to property tax since before the establishment of the state, the value of the property for purposes of assessing the tax would be reduced by NIS 65,000 per dunam, up to a maximum reduction per taxpayer of NIS 650,000. Even if the Meshhed landowners were aware that this amendment was in the offing, it may be observed that at the average exchange rate for 1996, the new provision would reduce the value of the property by 25 percent ($20,000 per dunam), but only on the first 10 dunam. The owner/s of the average 7.07-dunam parcel would still face a yearly tax of $10,500 on the property.

In April 1999, the property tax on all land was set at 0 percent, effective as of January 2000 (Amendment 45 to the Land Improvement Tax Law, §14 (2); see "Legislation Cited"). This obviously would have been a factor in Meshhed's subsequent request that planning be resumed on the privately owned land in its jurisdiction, leading to the June 2001 meeting setting out the principles for Meshhed's inclusion in the joint Zipporit industrial authority (see end of chapter 3).

10. This particular plan was approved by the LPBC and given validity. LPBC officers explained that they would approve on an ad hoc basis local plans for industry in the area slated for Zipporit D–E so long as they were consistent with the pending Zipporit D–E plan.

11. The estimated number of such persons in Meshhed was ten.

12. Two pages after the above citation, the authors of *AII* suggest that what they refer to as "marginalization processes" have influenced Arab entrepreneurial culture. One might think for a moment that such "processes" might stand for or contain within themselves the sense of habitus, practices, and objective possibilities. But the authors' definition of marginalization process confines itself to structural economic marginalization (see, e.g., 166), and in any event, to conflate this with the Bourdieusian concept would entail repudiation of the cultural model the authors adopt.

13. See Marx 2000 for an account of the real conditions of existence of the Negev Bedouin and their relations with the state bureaucracies as these give rise "to the growth of seemingly primordial beliefs," and strengthen ostensibly traditional values.

Chapter 6: The Appropriation of Arab Development Needs and Potential

1. The growth-pole thinking with regard to Galilee is clearly set out in Lichfield 1971, particularly chapter 9, section 9.5.3 (pp. 9.10–9.14) and chapter 16 (pp. 16.22–16.24).

2. The government's 1967 development plan for the Arab towns had mentioned the absence of suitable infrastructure in those towns as an obstacle to industrial development. But such infrastructure would demand investment on a great scale, while plants set up in neighboring Jewish towns that already possessed developed industrial areas could provide employment for the Arab population in their vicinity. This, said the 1967 plan (ten years before the advent of *AUDG*), would be the preferable course of action (PMO, Bureau of the Adviser on Arab Affairs, and the Economic Planning Authority 1967: 34).

3. One may also note the large value of missing data for locality of work in the census data (see note to table 2.10).

4. These local industrial authorities were Ramat Hovav and Tefen, respectively. Since then, no additional local authorities of this sort have been established. This form of local authority should not be confused with the municipal industrial authority or administration set up by a local authority to manage an industrial area in its jurisdiction, or by a number of local authorities to manage their joint industrial area.

5. The 48 percent figure given here includes 4.6 thousand Bedouin living in unrecognized hamlets.

6. Wallerstein published his major essay on center-periphery relations and the capitalist world system shortly after (1974), yet did not cite Friedmann. But Wallerstein's was a different project.

7. Establishment of the Biq'at Bet Hakerem commission was one of several changes that the minister of the interior made in answer to long-standing Arab locality criticism of the irresponsiveness of the statutory system to their needs.

8. Computation of the socioeconomic index for each locality in the course of the CBS procedure was followed by grouping the localities by cluster analysis into ten clusters in ascending order of rank.

Chapter 7: Attempts to Break Through the Boundaries

1. For aspects of this shift in the Israeli context, see Felsenstein 1994; for the world capitalist context, see Harvey 1989.

2. This industrial area was at the time referred to as the Cyclone industrial area, after the name of the single enterprise, Cyclone Aviation Products, that was then located on the site.

The Karmi'el submission adopted verbatim the recommendation written by Arnon Soffer one month previously. Both documents are cited in the references here.

3. This is according to local history. See also Ben-Zvi 1967 on widespread Druze settlement in Galilee at that time.

4. This was different from the boundary commission under the chairmanship of Shalom Reichman that had been dealing with requests for jurisdictional changes at the Bar Lev (Cyclone) site and that submitted its final report in 1991.

5. Note that because the land was in Karmi'el's jurisdiction, it was Karmi'el that managed planning vis-à-vis the architect and contact with the DPBC.

6. Recall that in 1963 the elders of Sajur had not succeeded in establishing ownership of this land under the Prescription Law because, as stony land, it had not been cultivated at the time of the British aerial photographs. Now the planning authorities were telling them it was imperative to preserve it as a green belt, but it was still just an open stony field.

7. The development and outline plan for the Northern District submitted in 1992 (Shefer et al. 1992: 137) found that for 2005, the land reserves for industry were short by 4,100 dunam net and 8,200 dunam bruto. In his deposition to the HCJ in support of the transfer of land to Upper Nazareth from the Emeq Yizre'el Regional Council, Frenkl asserted that in planning ahead for the year 2020, the Northern District was still short between 4,300 and 7,500 dunam (minimum and maximum estimates, respectively; Frenkl 1996: 10–11). But figures could be marshaled in the opposite direction, as well. Thus, Derman, in the same case, had argued that there was a surfeit of land reserves for industry in the Nazareth area (Derman 1995: 19).

8. I note that I am indebted here to Ram's 1996 Anthropological Society Conference paper analyzing the Yigal Alon museum's treatment of Jewish pioneers and Arab townspeople.

9. The project originally referred to twenty-five localities, but the number grew to thirty-four.

10. I have found it difficult to get uniform unequivocal data: CBS 2002 gives 28,156 dunam as Upper Nazareth's area of jurisdiction for the year 2000; Algazi 2002 gives 42,000, and an Upper Nazareth official in 2002 told me it was 33,000.

11. Most of the members of the list set out here were identified by Feitelson in his 2001 paper.

Glossary

Locality and Related Terms

The CBS defines *locality* as a place that has twenty or more permanent inhabitants, has self-administration, is not within the formal boundaries of another locality, and whose establishment was authorized by planning institutions. Localities having local municipal government (i.e., they have *municipal status*) are *local authorities.* Self-administration is not in itself local municipal government: for example, the collective, cooperative, and "community" settlements (i.e., the Jewish rural localities) that make up the regional councils are not local authorities.

Regional councils are one of the three main types of local authority, the other two being local councils and cities.

Urban localities are localities with population over 2,000. Considered as local authorities, they may be *local councils* or *cities.* Status is determined by the Ministry of the Interior, and one of its dimensions is population. Local councils may have their status changed once they pass a certain population threshold. There are a small number of local councils that have populations of less than 2,000 and therefore do not fall into the category of urban locality.

While municipal status is equivalent to local authority status, I use *municipality* to refer to the local authority dimension of cities only, not of local councils. But local councils may have a *municipal industrial authority,* just as a city may.

Urban localities (and also localities with populations under 2,000 with local authority status), considered as places where people live, may be referred to as cities or towns. The word "town," as I use it, subsumes cities—all cities are towns, but not all towns are cities. At some point, villages become small towns.

A *village* is a small settled place of markedly rural character. As villages grow in size and as the local activity becomes more urban, they become small towns. It was once common among Israeli writers to refer to the Arab localities as villages; this is no longer acceptable, as these localities are today overwhelmingly and decidedly urban localities, that is, they are towns, although they may not be cities.

Some authors refer to localities as *settlements*. I prefer to reserve the word "settlement" for places where the aspect of active settling is particularly salient, such as in Jewish rural settlements or Bedouin settlements ("hit*yash*-*v*ut," as distinguished from "*yish*u*v*").

Unrecognized Arab or Bedouin villages or hamlets are obviously not localities as that term is defined by the authorities.

References

Abo Sharkia, Naief. 1998. "Small Businesses and Their Networks Among the Arab Minority in Israel" (in Hebrew). M.A. thesis at the Technion-Israel Institute of Technology, Haifa.

Abu Basel. 1992. "The Public Campaign Against Erection of the Glass Factory West of Kafar Kanna Continues" (in Arabic). *Saut Al Haqq walHurriya*, 24 July, p. 3.

Abu Raya, Issam. 1995. *The Arabs in the Regional Councils in Israel* (in Hebrew). Giv'at Haviva, Israel: Institute for Peace Research.

Adiv, Assaf, and Abed al-Majid Hussein. 1997. "Misgav and Carmiel: Judaization in the Guise of Co-existence." *Challenge*, no. 43 (May/June): 14–15.

al Haj, Majid, and Henry Rosenfeld. 1988. *Arab Local Government in Israel*. Tel Aviv: International Center for Peace in the Middle East.

Al Ittichad. 1992. "Residents of Meshhed Decide on a Public Campaign against the Polluting Factories" (in Arabic). *Al Ittichad*, 14 June.

Algazi, Joseph. 1998. "Ferment in Umm al-Fahm in the Wake of Increased Activity of the Security Forces" (in Hebrew). *Ha'aretz*, 30 November, p. A1.

______. 1999. "Head of the Hurfeish Local Council: 'There Will Be an Explosion in the Druze and Circassian Localities'" (in Hebrew). *Ha'aretz*, 19 September, p. A6.

______. 2002. "The Outline Plan Proposes That Nazareth Residents Emigrate" (in Hebrew). *Ha'aretz*, 17 February, p. B3. Hebrew.

Alterman, Rachelle. 1999. *Between Privatization and Continued National Ownership: A Future Land Policy for Israel* (in Hebrew). Jerusalem: Floersheimer Institute for Policy Studies.

Alterman, Rachelle, and Tamy Stav. 2001. *Conflict and Consensus through Language: Trends of Change toward the Arab Sector as Reflected in Urban and Regional Plans in Israel* (in Hebrew). Tel Aviv: Tami Steinmetz Center for Peace Research, Tel Aviv University.

Amiran, David H.K. 1956. "Outline of the Geomorphology of Western Palestine North of the Basin of Beersheba." In *Eretz-Israel: Archeological, Historical and Geographical Studies*, vol. 4 (in Hebrew), ed. Haim Z. Hirschberg and Benjamin Mazar, 9–24. Jerusalem: Israel Exploration Society.

Anderson, Benedict. 1991. "Census, Map, Museum." Chap. 10 in *Imagined Communities: Reflections on the Origin and Spread of Nationalism*. Rev. ed. London and New York: Verso.

Appadurai, Arjun. 1996. "Number in the Colonial Imagination." Chap. 6 in *Modernity at Large: Cultural Dimensions of Globalization*. Minneapolis: University of Minnesota Press.

Ariav, Meir. 1991. "Regional Industrial Complexes." Appendix B to the chapter "Development Strategy for Industrial Employment" in the Final Report, Stage C of *National Outline Plan 31*.

Ariel, Yehuda. 1977. "Arabs Take Over State Land in the Vicinity of Tefen and Segev by Planting Olives" (in Hebrew). *Ha'aretz*, 1 February, p. A10.

Arnon, Isaac, and Michael Raviv. 1980. *From Fellah to Farmer: A Study on Change in Arab Villages*. Rehovot, Israel: Settlement Study Center; Bet Dagan, Israel: Volcani Center.

Asad, Talal. 1975. "Anthropological Texts and Ideological Problems: An Analysis of Cohen on Arab Villages in Israel." *Economy and Society* 4: 251–282.

Ash, Uri. 2002. "Argument over Land Darkens Coexistence in Galilee" (in Hebrew). *Ha'aretz*, 12 November, p. A9.

Atrash, 'As. 1992. "Arab Industry in Israel" (in Hebrew). *Riv'on Lekalkala* [vol. 43], no. 152 (August): 112–120.

Avnimelech, Micha, Danny Ne'man, and Arnon Soffer. 1991. "Master Plan for Industrial Infrastructure in Development Areas: Final Report" (in Hebrew). Report submitted to the Ministry of Industry and Commerce and the Budget Division of the Ministry of Finance, prepared by A.B.C. Avnimelech Business Consulting, Tel Aviv.

Awawdeh, Ruwaida, and Hala Isa. 1992. "A New Industrial Area: At Our Expense and for the Benefit of Others" (in Arabic). *AsSinara*, 10 July, p. 15.

Awawdy, Wadi'. 1992. "Twin Dangers in a Single Issue: Expropriation and Environmental Pollution" (in Arabic). *Kul alArab*, 31 July, p. 2; part 2 (with same title), 7 August, p 10.

______. 1993a. "Will the Phoenicia Factory Arise on the Rotation Agreements? The Follow-up Committee and the Arab Institutions Call for Resisting the Attempt to Pollute Our Environment" (in Arabic). *Kul alArab*, 15 January, p. 8.

______. 1993b. "The Kafar Kanna and Meshhed Local Councils Suspend Legal Proceedings against the Phoenicia Factory" (in Arabic). *Kul alArab*, 5 February.

Bar-El, Rafi. 1994. *Development of Remote Regions: Regional Development in Israel*. Jerusalem: Ministry of the Economy and Planning.

Bar-El, Raphael, ed. 1987. *Rural Industrialization in Israel*. Boulder, Colo.: Westview Press.

______. 1993. *Economic Development in the Arab Sector* (in Hebrew). Herzeliyya Pitu'ach, Israel: Center for Jewish-Arab Economic Development. Hebrew.

Bar-El, Raphael, Michal Avraham, and Dafna Schwartz. 1990. *Urban Growth Centers in the Galilee: A Strategy for Aliya Absorption and Galilee Regional Development*. Rehovot, Israel: Development Study Center (sponsored by the Department for Renewal and Development of the Jewish Agency).

Bar-Gal, Yoram, and Arnon Soffer. 1976. "Changes in the Minority Villages in Israel" (in Hebrew). *Ofakim Begeographia* (Haifa University), no. 2.

______. 1981. *Geographical Changes in the Traditional Arab Villages in Northern Israel*. Durham, England: Center for Middle Eastern and Islamic Studies, University of Durham.

Barzilai, Yigael. 1993. "Report of the Commission of Inquiry on the Boundaries of Karmi'el" (in Hebrew). March. Report submitted to the Director-General of the Ministry of the Interior, Jerusalem.

Bendar, Arieh. 1994. "The New Program for the Expansion of Settlement in Galilee" (in Hebrew). *Ma'ariv*, 12 January, p. 16.

Ben Shemesh, Aaron. 1953. *The Land Laws in the State of Israel* (in Hebrew). Tel Aviv: Masada.

Ben-Zvi, Izhak. 1967. *Eretz-Israel under Ottoman Rule: Four Centuries of History* (in Hebrew). Jerusalem: Yad Yitzhak Ben Zvi.

Blumenkrantz, Zohar. 1995. "The Ministry of Industry and Commerce Will Initiate a Program for Assistance to Industry in the Arab Towns" (in Hebrew). *Ha'aretz*, 24 February, p. C2.

Bourdieu, Pierre. 1979. *Algeria 1960*. Cambridge, Cambridge University Press; Paris: Editions de la Maison des Sciences de l'Homme.

______. 1990. *The Logic of Practice*. Cambridge, U.K.: Polity Press.

Brenner, Danny. 1992. "Cornerstone for the New Phoenicia Plant Laid in Zippori" (in Hebrew). *Ma'ariv, Business*, 23 September, p. 3.

Bsool, Gassan. 1992. "The Attempt At Rotation in the Leadership of the Local Council Has Been a Resounding Failure" (in Arabic). *Kul alArab*, 3 November, p. 6. (A section of this article is captioned: "The Land of the Phoenicia Factory: A Joint Industrial Area for Meshhed, Kafar Kanna, and Upper Nazareth.")

Buchman, Yossi, and Tirza Yovel. 1996. "The Sakhnin Valley" (in Hebrew). *Aretz Veteva* 10 (5): 23–40.

Bureau of the Adviser on Arab Affairs. *See under* Israel. Prime Minister's Office (PMO).

Carmi, Shulamit, and Henry Rosenfeld. 1992. "Israel's Political Economy and the Widening Class Gap between Its Two National Groups." *Asian and African Studies* 26 (1): 15–61.

Carmon, Naomi, Hubert Law Yone, Gabriel Lifshitz, Shaul Amir, Daniel Czamanski, and Baruch Kipnis. 1990. *The New Settlement in the Galilee: An Evaluation* (in Hebrew). Haifa: Center for Urban and Regional Studies, Technion-Israel Institute of Technology.

Carmon, Naomi, Michael Meyer-Brodnitz, Jacob Yonish, and Tovi Alfandari. 1992. *Planning Housing for a Small Arab Town in Israel: A Case Study in Iksal* (in Hebrew). Haifa: Center for Urban and Regional Studies, Technion-Israel Institute of Technology.

CBS. *See* Israel. Central Bureau of Statistics.

Cohen, Abner. 1965. *Arab Border Villages in Israel: A Study of Continuity and Change in Social Organization.* Manchester: Manchester University Press.

Cohen, Erik. 1989. "The Changing Legitimations of the State of Israel." In *Israel: State and Society, 1948–1988.* Vol. 5 of *Studies in Contemporary Jewry,* ed. Peter Y. Medding. New York: Oxford University Press.

Cohen, Hillel. 2000. *The Present Absentees: The Palestinian Refugees in Israel Since 1948* (in Hebrew). Jerusalem: Institute for Israeli Arab Studies.

Colebatch, Hal K. 1987. "Recent Work on the Concept of the State." *Politics* 22 (1): 120–123.

Czamanski, Daniel. 1996. *The Needs for Industrial and Manufacturing Areas in Nazareth—1995* (in Hebrew). Haifa: Czamanski Consultants.

Czamanski, Dan, and Rassem Khamaisi. 1993. *Promoting Entrepreneurship in Arab Localities in Israel* (in Hebrew). Jerusalem: Floersheimer Institute for Policy Studies.

Czamanski, Daniel, and Michael Meyer-Brodnitz. 1987. "Industrialization in Arab Villages in Israel." In *Rural Industrialization in Israel,* ed. Raphael Bar-El, 143–168, Boulder, Colo.: Westview Press. (For Hebrew version, see entry for Meyer-Brodnitz and Czamanski below.)

Danet, Brenda. 1989. *Pulling Strings: Biculturalism in Israeli Bureaucracy.* Albany: State University of New York Press.

Dayan Center for Middle Eastern and African Studies. 1998. Conference titled "The Arab Community in Israel: Basis for Autonomy or Pattern of Integration?" Tel Aviv University, 22–23 November.

Derman, Amiram. 1995. "Changes in the Jurisdictional Boundaries of Upper Nazareth" (in Hebrew). Urban planner's expert opinion submitted to the HCJ in support of Hoshaya's petition. HCJ 4522/95. Kfar Saba, Israel: Amiram Derman, Urban and Regional Planner.

Dillon, William R., and Matthew Goldstein. 1984. *Multivariate Analysis: Methods and Applications.* New York: John Wiley and Sons.

Dominguez, Virginia R. 1987. "Of Other Peoples: Beyond the 'Salvage' Paradigm" in discussions on "The Politics of Representation." In *Discussions in Contemporary Culture,* ed. Hal Foster. Dia Art Foundation. Seattle: Bay Press.

______. 1989. *People as Subject, People as Object: Selfhood and Peoplehood in Contemporary Israel.* Madison: University of Wisconsin Press.

Doron, Yochanan. 1988. "Geographic Aspects of Jewish-Arab Relations in the Nazareth Mountains" (in Hebrew). M.A. thesis, Haifa University, Geography Department. (English title in the thesis is given thus: "Jewish-Arab Relationship [*sic*] in the Nazareth Hills: The Geographical Aspects.")

Eloul, Rohn. 1984. "'Arab al Hjerat: Adaptation of Bedouin to a Changing Environment." In *The Changing Bedouin,* ed. Emanuel Marx and Avshalom Shmueli, 157–171. New Brunswick, N.J.: Transaction Books.

Erner, Arye, Anat Carmeli, and Amnon Frenkl. 1996. "Master Plan for Development Policy for the Misgav Regional Council" (in Hebrew). Strategic Planning and Information Unit, Misgav Regional Council.

Eyal, Gil. 1993. "Between East and West: The Discourse on the 'Arab Village' in Israel." *Teoria uvikoret,* no. 3 (Winter): 39–55.
Fabian, Johannes. 1983. *Time and the Other: How Anthropology Makes Its Object.* New York: Columbia University Press.
Falah, Ghazi. 1989. "Israeli 'Judaization' Policy in Galilee and Its Impact on Local Arab Urbanization." *Political Geography Quarterly* 8 (3): 229–253.
______. 1991. "The Facts and Fictions of Judaization Policy and Its Impact on the Majority Arab Population in Galilee." *Political Geography Quarterly* 10 (3): 297–311.
______. 1992. "Land Fragmentation and Spatial Control in the Nazareth Metropolitan Area." *Professional Geographer* 44 (1): 30–44.
______. 1993. "Trends in the Urbanization of Arab Settlements in Galilee." *Urban Geography* 14 (2): 145–164.
Feitelson, Eran. 2001. "Structural Threats to the Participation of the Public in the Israeli Planning System" (in Hebrew). Paper presented at conference titled "Democratization of Planning in Israel," organized by the Laboratory for Environmental Simulation at Tel Aviv University, held at Ben Gurion University of the Negev, Be'er Sheva, 27 December.
Felsenstein, Daniel. 1994. *The Enterprising City: Promoting Economic Development at the Local Level* (in Hebrew). Jerusalem: Floersheimer Institute for Policy Studies.
Fischer, Michael M.J. 1980. *Iran: From Religious Dispute to Revolution.* Cambridge, Mass., and London: Harvard University Press.
Flapan, Simha. 1963. "Planning Arab Agriculture." *New Outlook* 6 (9): 65–73.
Foucault, Michel. 1972. *The Archaeology of Knowledge.* London: Tavistock Publications.
______. 1980. *Power/Knowledge: Selected Interviews and Other Writings, 1972–1977,* ed. Colin Gordon. New York: Pantheon Books.
______. 1981. "Questions of Method: An Interview with Michael Foucault." *Ideology and Consciousness,* no. 8 (Spring): 3–14.
______. 1982. "The Subject and Power." *Critical Inquiry* 8 (Summer): 777–795
Frenkl, Amnon. 1996. "Expert Opinion in the Matter of Changing the Jurisdictional Boundaries of Upper Nazareth" (in Hebrew). Deposition submitted to the HCJ in response to Hoshaya's suit, Bagatz 4522/95. Kiryat Bialik, Israel: MITAR-Urban and Regional Planning.
______. 1997. "Program for Stages D and E of the Zipporit Industrial Area" (in Hebrew). Report submitted to the Northern District Planning and Building Commission in support of G/9155 and G/11414.
Friedmann, John. 1972. "A General Theory of Polarized Development." In *Growth Centers in Regional Economic Development,* ed. Niles M. Hansen, 82–107. New York: The Free Press.
Gal, Sharon. 1999a. "Today the Prime Minister Will Announce a Grant to the Bedouin Localities in the North" (in Hebrew). *Ha'aretz,* 5 January, p. A4.
______. 1999b. "'My Wife Was a Neighbor of Yours' Commented the Prime Minister, and in Bet Zarzir Announced a Grant to the Bedouin" (in Hebrew). *Ha'aretz,* 6 January, p. A4.
Galilee Development Authority. 1995. *Galilee Yearbook, No. 1* (in Hebrew). Galilee Development Authority.
Gavish, Dov. 1991. *Land and Map: The Survey of Palestine, 1920–1948* (in Hebrew). Jerusalem: Yad Izhak Ben-Zvi.
Gavish, Dov, and Ruth Kark. 1993. "The Cadastral Mapping of Palestine, 1858–1928." *The Geographical Journal* 159 (1): 70–80.
Gerber, Haim. 1987. *The Social Origins of the Modern Middle East.* Boulder, Colo.: Lynne Rienner Publishers; London: Mansell Publishing.
Ghanem, As'ad. 1993. *The Arabs in Israel toward the Twenty-First Century: Survey of Basic Infrastructure* (in Hebrew). Giv'at Haviva, Israel: Institute for Peace Research.
Gilbar, Gad. 1991. "The Arabs of Israel: Consequences of Economic Integration." Paper presented at the Dayan Center conference titled "The Arab Minority in Israel: Dilemmas of Political Orientation and Social Change," Tel Aviv University, 3–4 June.

Glazner, Moshe (chairman). [1989]. "Report of the Inquiry Commission Regarding the Boundaries of Nazareth and Upper Nazareth; the Reine, Meshhed, Ein Mahel, and Dabburye Local Councils; and Emeq Yizre'el Regional Council" (in Hebrew). Ministry of Interior files.

Goadby, Frederic M., and Moses J. Doukhan. 1935. *The Land Law of Palestine.* Tel Aviv: Shoshany's Printing.

Gonen, Amiram, and Rassem Khamaisi. 1992. *Joint Arab and Jewish Regional Development Centers in Israel* (in Hebrew). Jerusalem: Floersheimer Institute for Policy Studies. (An English version of this study was published under the same title by the same publisher in 1993.)

______. 1993. *Towards a Policy of Urbanization Poles for the Arab Population in Israel.* Jerusalem: Floersheimer Institute for Policy Studies.

Gould, P. 1980. "Q-Analysis, or a Language of Structure: An Introduction for Social Scientists, Geographers and Planners." *International Journal of Man-Machine Studies* 13: 169–199.

Government of Palestine. 1946. *A Survey of Palestine.* Vol. 1. Prepared in December 1945 and January 1946 for the Anglo-American Committee of Inquiry. Palestine: Government Printer.

______. Office of Statistics. [1946?]. *Village Statistics, April 1943.* Jerusalem.

Granott, A[vraham]. 1952. *The Land System in Palestine: History and Structure.* London: Eyre and Spottiswoode.

______. 1956. *Agrarian Reform and the Record of Israel.* London: Eyre and Spottiswoode. (Translation of Avraham Granott, *Agrarian Reform in Israel and the World* [in Hebrew] [Tel Aviv: Dvir, 1955].)

Haidar, Aziz. 1985. "Patterns of Economic Initiative in the Arab Village in Israel, 1950–1980" (in Hebrew). Ph.D. dissertation, Hebrew University of Jerusalem.

______. 1995. *On the Margins: The Arab Population in the Israeli Economy.* London: Hurst, in association with the Truman Research Institute, Hebrew University, Jerusalem.

Handelman, Don. 1978. "Introduction: A Recognition of Bureaucracy." In *Bureaucracy and World View: Studies in the Logic of Official Interpretation,* ed. Don Handelman and Elliott Leyton. Social and Economic Studies, no. 22. St. John's: Institute of Social and Economic Research, Memorial University of Newfoundland.

______. 1981. "Introduction: The Idea of Bureaucratic Organization." *Social Analysis,* no. 9 (December): 5–23.

______. 1994. "Contradictions between Citizenship and Nationality: Their Consequences for Ethnicity and Inequality in Israel [1]" *International Journal of Politics, Culture and Society* 7 (3): 441–459.

Handler, Richard. 1985. "On Dialogue and Destructive Analysis: Problems in Narrating Nationalism and Ethnicity." *Journal of Anthropological Research* 41: 171–182.

Hare'uveni, Emanuel. 1965. "The Bulldozers Are Biting Into the Rocks of Galilee" (in Hebrew). *Ma'ariv,* 29 August, p. 3.

Harvey, David. 1989. "From Managerialism to Entrepreneurialism: The Transformation in Urban Governance in Late Capitalism." *Geografiska Annaler* 71B (1): 3–17.

______. 1996. *Justice, Nature, and the Geography of Difference.* Oxford: Blackwell.

Hasson, Shlomo, and Eran Razin. 1990. "What Is Hidden Behind a Municipal Boundary Conflict?" *Political Geography Quarterly* 9 (3): 267–283.

Hawkins, Julia. 1993. "The Phoenicia Glass Factory: The Politics of Pollution." *Challenge* 4 (5): 31–32.

Hecht, Arie. 1997. *Restructuring Municipal Finance in Israel* (in Hebrew). Jerusalem: Floersheimer Institute for Policy Studies.

Hecht, Arye. 1988. "The Financing of Local Authorities." In *Local Government in Israel,* ed. Daniel Elazar and Chaim Kalchheim, 263–372. Jerusalem: Jerusalem Center for Public Affairs/Center for Jewish Community Studies; Lanham, Md.: University Press of America.

Heimberg (Chetrit), Soly, and Issachar Dor. 1994. *Characterization and Ranking of Local Authorities According to the Socioeconomic Level of the Population in 1992* (in Hebrew). Jerusalem: Ministry of Construction and Housing and Ministry of the Interior.

Hermansen, Tormod. 1972. "Development Poles and Related Theories: A Synoptic Review." In *Growth Centers in Regional Economic Development*, ed. Niles M. Hansen, 160–203. New York: The Free Press.

Herzfeld, Michael. 1993. *The Social Production of Indifference: Exploring the Symbolic Roots of Western Bureaucracy*. Chicago: University of Chicago Press. Originally published by Berg, 1992.

Herzog, Hanna. 1990. "The Right To Be Included: Israeli Jewish-Arab Relations." Discussion paper no. 3-90, Pinhas Sapir Center for Development, Tel Aviv University.

Higgins, Benjamin. 1988. "François Perroux." In *Regional Economic Development: Essays in Honour of François Perroux*, ed. Benjamin Higgins and Donald J. Savoie, 31–47. Boston: Unwin Hyman.

Higgins, Benjamin, and Donald J. Savoie. 1988. "Introduction: The Economics and Politics of Regional Development." In *Regional Economic Development: Essays in Honour of François Perroux*, ed. Benjamin Higgins and Donald J. Savoie, 1–27. Boston: Unwin Hyman.

Hilleli, Avraham. 1983. "Land Rights: Historical-General Background of the Development of [Land] Title in the Land of Israel [author has simply *Ba'aretz*]." In *The Lands of Galilee* (in Hebrew), ed. Avshalom Shmueli, Arnon Soffer, and Nurit Kliot, 575–610. Haifa and Jerusalem: Society for Applied Scientific Research at Haifa University and the Ministry of Defense.

Hirschman, Albert O. 1958. *The Strategy of Economic Development*. New Haven: Yale University Press.

Hunter, David E., and Phillip Whitten. 1976. *Encyclopedia of Anthropology*. New York: Harper and Row.

Huri, Shoshan. n.d. [publication data page indicates that the first edition was published in 1990]. *The Encyclopedia of Local Government in Israel: Regional Councils, 1989–1994*. Be'er Sheva: Har Saguy.

Hussein, Abed al Majid. 1998. "Land Owners Anxious as Misgav Develops." *Challenge*, Number 34 (November–December):19.

Hussein, Abed al Majid, and Assaf Adiv. 1997. "The Misgav Master Plan Transforms the Arab Towns into Tourist Attractions" (in Arabic). In *Misgav and Karmi'el: Judaization in the Name of Coexistence* [*... Behind the Mask of Coexistence*], ed. Abed al Majid Hussein and Assaf Adiv, 15–17. Jaffa: Hanitzotz-Sharaia Publishing House.

Israel. Central Bureau of Statistics (CBS). 1973. *Vital Statistics, 1971*. Jerusalem: Central Bureau of Statistics.

______. 1976. *The Division of the State of Israel into Natural Regions for Statistical Purposes*. Population and Housing Census, 1972. Publication no. 8, Jerusalem: Central Bureau of Statistics.

______. 1993. *Local Authorities in Israel, 1991: Physical Data*. Special series no. 931. Jerusalem: Central Bureau of Statistics.

______. 1997a. *Local Authorities in Israel, 1995: Physical Data*. Publication no. 1046. Jerusalem: Central Bureau of Statistics.

______. 1997b. *Statistical Abstract of Israel, 1997*. Jerusalem: Central Bureau of Statistics.

______. 1998a. *Population in Localities with 2,000 or More Inhabitants: Selected Demographic Data from the 1995 Census of Population and Housing*. Current Briefings in Statistics no. 11. Jerusalem: Central Bureau of Statistics.

______. 1998b. *List of Localities: Geographical Characteristics and Population, 1948–1995*. Population and Housing Census 1995. Publication no. 3. Jerusalem: Central Bureau of Statistics.

______. 1998c. *Local Authorities in Israel, 1996: Physical Data* (in Hebrew). Publication no. 1082. Jerusalem: Central Bureau of Statistics.

______. 1998d. *Local Authorities in Israel 1995: Financial Data* (in Hebrew). Publication no. 1095. Jerusalem: Central Bureau of Statistics.

______. 1999. *Characterization and Ranking of Local Authorities According to the Population's Socioeconomic Level in 1999*. (The following subtitle was added by sticker to both the Hebrew and English covers, but not to the title pages: *Based on the 1995 Census of Population and Housing*. Introductory material appears in English as well as Hebrew; body of the work and tables are in Hebrew only.) Publication no. 1118. Jerusalem: Central Bureau of Statistics.

______. 2002. *Local Authorities in Israel 2000* (in Hebrew). Publication no. 1186. Jerusalem: Central Bureau of Statistics.

______. n.d. *Characterization and Ranking of Local Authorities According to the Population's Socio-economic Level in 1995.* (Introductory material appears in English as well as Hebrew; body of the work and tables are in Hebrew only.) Publication no. 1039. Jerusalem: Central Bureau of Statistics.

Israel. *Israel Government Yearbook, 1959* (in Hebrew). Jerusalem: Government Printer.

Israel. Ministry of Finance. 1991. *Budget Proposal for Fiscal Year 1992 and Explanations, 5: The Ministry of the Interior.* Submitted to the Twelfth Knesset.

______. 1994. "Review: Local Authorities in the Arab Sector" (in Hebrew). Position paper, 31 July.

Israel. Ministry of Housing. 1977. *Accelerated Urban Development in Galilee* (in Hebrew). Jerusalem: Ministry of Housing, Program Branch, Urban Planning Unit.

Israel. Ministry of Industry. 1995. *National Priority Regions—Marketing of Land for Industry and Manufacture: Procedures* (in Hebrew). May. Jerusalem: Ministry of Industry, Development Areas Unit.

______. 1997. *Information for Investors* (in Hebrew). Brochure material printed on the back of *Map of Industrial and Employment Areas;* see also the map itself. Jerusalem: Ministry of Industry, Development Areas Unit.

Israel. Ministry of Industry and Commerce. 1995. *New Initiatives for Economic and Industrial Development in the Arab Sector* (in Hebrew). Jerusalem: Ministry of Industry and Commerce, Office of the Minister.

Israel. Ministry of the Interior. 1992. *The Strategic Program of the Ministry of the Interior for the Years 1992–1996* (in Hebrew). Jerusalem: Ministry of the Interior.

______. 1997a. "Agreement with the Arab Local Authorities" (in Hebrew). January.

______. 1997b. *Audited Financial Statements of the Local Authorities for 1995* (updated edition) (in Hebrew). Jerusalem: Ministry of the Interior, Internal Office for Auditing the Local Authorities.

______. 1997c. *National Survey of Local Master, Outline, and Development Plans* (in Hebrew). February. Jerusalem: Ministry of the Interior: Planning Administration.

______. n.d. [ca. 1998]. Three directives: (a) "The 1999 Balancing Grant to Local Councils and Cities: The Method of Calculating and Allocating the Grant," (b) "The 1999 Balancing Grant to Local Councils and Cities in the Arab Sector: The Method of Calculating and Allocating the Grant," and (c) "The 1999 Balancing Grant to Druze and Circassian Local Authorities: The Method of Calculating and Allocating the Grant" (in Hebrew). Jerusalem.

Israel. Ministry of the Interior, Israel Lands Administration (ILA), Ministry of Industry and Commerce, and Industrial Buildings Corporation. 1989. *Programmatic Guidelines for Planning Industrial Areas* (in Hebrew). Jerusalem: Ministry of the Interior, ILA, Ministry of Industry and Commerce, and Industrial Buildings Corporation.

Israel. Prime Minister's Office (PMO). 1976. *Government Decision* 21/*'Ayin-Pe*, 29 February.

______. 1993. *Government Decision 721* (in Hebrew), 24 January. See also, the unpublished government manual, "National Priority Regions," in which the decision is reproduced.

______, Bureau of the Adviser on Arab Affairs, and the Economic Planning Authority. 1967. "Proposed Development Program for the Minority Population in Israel, 1967/68–1971/72" (in Hebrew). September. Jerusalem. Mimeographed.

______, Office of the Adviser for Arab Affairs. 1998. *Summary of the Government Ministries' Activities in the Non-Jewish Sector in 1997.* Jerusalem: Prime Minister's Office.

Israel. State Comptroller. 1967. *Annual Report for 1966* (in Hebrew). No 17. Jerusalem: State Comptroller.

______. 1994. *Annual Report for 1993* (in Hebrew). No 44. Jerusalem: State Comptroller.

______. 2000. *Annual Report for 1999* (in Hebrew). No. 50B. Jerusalem. State Comptroller.

Israel Lands Administration. 1962. *Report on Activities of the Israel Lands Administration for 1961/62* (in Hebrew). Jerusalem: ILA.

______. 1965. *Report on Activities of the Israel Lands Administration for 1964/65* (in Hebrew). No. 4. Jerusalem: ILA.

______. 1994. *Report on Activities of the Israel Lands Administration for 1993* (in Hebrew). No. 33. Jerusalem: ILA.

______. 2000. *Report on Activities of the Israel Lands Administration for 1999* (in Hebrew). No 39. Jerusalem: ILA.

______, Department of Planning and Development. 1991. *Land Reserves for Industry* (in Hebrew). Jerusalem: ILA, Department of Planning and Development.

Jaffa Research Center. 1991. *Arab Cities and Villages in Israel: Statistical Abstract, 1990* (in Arabic and English). Nazareth: Jaffa Research Center.

Jewish Agency for Israel. 1974. *Mountainous Galilee: Proposed Goals and Objectives for Development* (in Hebrew). Jerusalem: Jewish Agency for Israel.

______. 1975. *Proposed Development Program for the Galilee* (in Hebrew). Jerusalem: Jewish Agency for Israel.

______. 1994. *Upper Nazareth–Migdal Ha'emeq–Emeq Yizre'el: Framework Plan* (in the Partnership 2000 project) (in Hebrew). Jerusalem: Jewish Agency for Israel, Department for Development and Settlement, Galilee Region.

Jewish-Arab Center. 1998. *The Question of Land*, record of a conference in the series Minority, Majority, and the State in Israel (in Hebrew). The Jewish-Arab Center and the Gustav Heinemann Institute of Middle Eastern Studies at Haifa University and the Friedrich Ebert Foundation, 19 March

Jiryis, Sabri. 1976. *The Arabs in Israel*. New York: Monthly Review Press.

Johnson, J.H. 1983. "Hierarchical Set Definition by Q-Analysis" Part 1: "The Hierarchical Backcloth." *International Journal of Man-Machine Studies* 18: 337–359.

______. 1990. "Interpretation and Hierarchical Set Definition in Q-Analysis." *Environment and Planning B: Planning and Design* 17: 277–302.

Kano, Jacques. 1992. *The Problem of Land between Jews and Arabs (1917–1990)* (in Hebrew). Tel Aviv: Sifriat Poalim Publishing House.

Kapferer, Bruce. 1988. *Legends of People, Myths of State: Violence, Intolerance, and Political Culture in Sri Lanka and Australia*. Washington and London: Smithsonian Institute.

Kark, Ruth. 1997. "Mamluk and Ottoman Cadastral Survey and Early Mapping of Landed Properties in Palestine." *Agricultural History* 71 (1): 46–70.

Karmi'el, City of. 1990. "Memorandum of the City of Karmi'el to the Boundary Commission on Joining the Cyclone Industrial Area to the Jurisdiction of Karmi'el" (in Hebrew). 22 February.

Kedar, Alexandre (Sandy). 2001. "The Legal Transformation of Ethnic Geography: Israeli Law and the Palestinian Landholders 1948–1967." *NYU Journal of International Law and Politics* 33 (4): 923–1000.

Kedar, Sandy. 1998. "Majority Time, Minority Time: Land, Nation, and the Law of Adverse Possession in Israel" (in Hebrew). *Iyunei Mishpat* (Tel Aviv University) 21 (3): 665–746.

Kellner, D.H., and E. Rosenau. 1939. "The Geographical Regions of Palestine." *Geographical Review* 29 (1): 61–80.

Khalidi, Raja. 1988. *The Arab Economy in Israel: The Dynamics of a Region's Development*. London: Croom Helm.

Khalidi, Walid. 1992. *All That Remains: The Palestinian Villages Occupied and Depopulated by Israel in 1948*. Washington, D.C.: Institute for Palestine Studies.

Khamaisi, Rassem. 1986. "Implementation of Outline Plans in the Arab Villages" (in Hebrew). *Ofakim Begeografia*, nos. 17–18: 161–173.

______. 1990. *Planning and Housing Policy in the Arab Sector of Israel* (in Hebrew). Tel Aviv: International Center for Peace in the Middle East.

______. 1993. *From Restrictive to Developmental Planning in Arab Localities in Israel*. Jerusalem: Floersheimer Institute for Policy Studies.

______. 1994. *Toward Strengthening Local Government in Arab Localities in Israel* (in Hebrew). Jerusalem: Floersheimer Institute for Policy Studies.

Kimmerling, Baruch. 1979. *A Conceptual Framework for the Analysis of Behavior in a Territorial Conflict: The Generalization of the Israeli Case.* Jerusalem: Leonard Davis Institute for International Relations at the Hebrew University.

______. 1983. *Zionism and Territory: The Socio-Territorial Dimension of Zionist Politics.* Berkeley: University of California, Institute of International Studies.

______. 1985. "Between the Primordial and the Civil Definitions of the Collective Identity: *Eretz Israel* or the State of Israel?" In *Comparative Social Dynamics,* ed. Erik Cohen, Moshe Lissak, and Uri Almagor. Boulder, Colo.: Westview Press.

Kipnis, Baruch. 1976. "Trends of the Minority Population in the Galilee and Their Planning Implications" (in Hebrew). *Ir Ve'ezor* 3 (3) (October): 54–68.

______. 1982. "Proposal for the Municipal Organization of the New Settlement Areas in Galilee" (in Hebrew). Document prepared for the Northern District Settlement Department of the Jewish Agency.

______. 1983. "The Evaluation of the Jewish Urban Settlements in the Galilee, 1948–1980." In *The Lands of Galilee* (in Hebrew), ed. Avshalom Shmueli, Arnon Soffer, and Nurit Kliot, 723–744. Haifa and Jerusalem: Society for Applied Scientific Research at Haifa University and the Ministry of Defense.

______. 1984. "Role and Timing of Complementary Objectives of a Regional Policy: The Case of Northern Israel." *Geoforum* 15 (2): 191–200.

______. 1987. "Geopolitical Ideologies and Regional Strategies in Israel." *Tijdschrift voor Economische en Sociale Geografie* 78 (2): 125–138.

Kislev, Ran. 1976. "Land Expropriation: History of Oppression." *New Outlook* 19 (6): 23–32. (This is an English condensation of a series of six articles that appeared in the Hebrew daily *Ha'aretz* in July 1976.)

Kliot, Nurit. 1983. "The Regional Definition of Galilee: Review and Critique." In *The Lands of Galilee* (in Hebrew), ed. Avshalom Shmueli, Arnon Soffer, and Nurit Kliot, 23–36. Haifa and Jerusalem: Society for Applied Scientific Research at Haifa University and the Ministry of Defense.

Koren, Orah. 2000. "The Ministry of Industry Allocates 200 Million NIS for Industry and Commerce in the Arab Sector" (in Hebrew). *Ha'aretz,* 8 November, p. C2.

Kretzmer, David. 1990. *The Legal Status of the Arabs in Israel.* Boulder, Colo.: Westview Press.

Kubersky, Haim (chairman). 1976. *Report of the Commission on the Problems of Planning and Construction in the Arab Sector in the Northern District* (in Hebrew), (Kubersky Commission), appointed by the Prime Minister. Jerusalem.

Lahav, Hagar. 1997. "How Goodly Is Your Tent" (in Hebrew). *Ha'aretz,* 28 May, p. B3.

______. 1998. "The Ministry of Interior Promises to Halt Discrimination against the Arab Local Authorities in Financial Assistance" (in Hebrew). *Ha'aretz,* 12 February, p. A6.

Lasuén, J.R. 1972. "On Growth Poles." In *Growth Centers in Regional Economic Development,* ed. Niles M. Hansen, 20–49. New York: The Free Press.

Lehn, Walter, and Uri Davis. 1988. *The Jewish National Fund.* London: Kegan Paul International.

Lewin-Epstein, Noah, and Moshe Semyonov. 1993. *The Arab Minority in Israel's Economy: Patterns of Ethnic Inequality.* Boulder, Colo.: Westview Press.

Lichfield, Nathaniel. 1971. *Israel's New Towns: A Development Strategy.* Vol. 1. Tel Aviv: Institute for Planning and Development, Tel Aviv; Nathaniel Lichfield; London: Tavistock House South. (Title page bears the imprimatur of the Ministry of Housing.)

Liebman, Charles S. 1988. "Conceptions of 'State of Israel' in Israeli Society." *Jerusalem Quarterly,* no. 47 (Summer): 95–107.

Long, Andrew. 1992. "Goods, Knowledge and Beer: The Methodological Significance of Situational Analysis and Discourse." In *Battlefields of Knowledge: The Interlocking of Theory and Practice in Social Research and Development,* ed. Norman Long and Ann Long. London: Routledge.

Long, Norman, and Ann Long, eds. 1992. *Battlefields of Knowledge: The Interlocking of Theory and Practice in Social Research and Development.* London: Routledge.

Lustick, Ian. 1980. *Arabs in the Jewish State: Israel's Control of a National Minority.* Austin: University of Texas Press.

Marcus, George E. 1986. "Contemporary Problems of Ethnography in the Modern World System." In *Writing Culture: The Poetics and Politics of Ethnography,* ed. James Clifford and George E. Marcus. Berkeley: University of California Press.

Marcus, George E., and Michael M.J. Fischer. 1986. "Taking Account of World Historical Political Economy: Knowable Communities in Larger Systems." Chap. 4 in *Anthropology as Cultural Critique: An Experimental Moment in the Human Sciences.* Chicago: University of Chicago Press.

Marx, Emanuel. 1976. *The Social Context of Violent Behaviour: A Social Anthropological Study in an Israeli Immigrant Town.* London: Routledge and Kegan Paul.

______. 1980. "On the Anthropological Study of Nations." In *A Composite Portrait of Israel,* ed. Emanuel Marx. London: Academic Press.

______. 1984. "Economic Change among Pastoral Nomads in the Middle East." In *The Changing Bedouin,* ed. Emanuel Marx and Avshalom Shmueli. New Brunswick, N.J.: Transaction Books.

______. 1987. "Labor Migration with a Secure Base: Bedouin of South Sinai." In *Migrants, Workers, and the Social Order,* ed. Jeremy Eades. London and New York: Tavistock Publications.

______. 2000. "Land and Work: Negev Bedouin Struggle with Israeli Bureaucracies." *Nomadic Peoples* 4 (2): 106–121.

Medzini, Arnon. 1983. "Bedouin Settlement in Galilee." In *The Lands of Galilee* (in Hebrew), ed. Avshalom Shmueli, Arnon Soffer, and Nurit Kliot, 549–564. Haifa and Jerusalem: Society for Applied Scientific Research at Haifa University and the Ministry of Defense.

Meyer-Brodnitz, Michael. 1969. "Latent Urbanization in the Arab Villages" (in Hebrew). *Alon Ha'igud Letikhnun Svivati* [Bulletin of the Association for Environmental Planning], nos. 8–9: 4–12. (This publication was later superseded by the Hebrew journal *Tikhnun Svivati.)*

______. 1986. "Urbanization, Suburbanization and Regional Integration: Semantics and Planning Policy for Arab Settlements in Israel" (in Hebrew). *Ofakim Begeografia,* nos. 17–18: 105–124.

______. 1994. "Physical Planning in the Arab Settlements in Israel: Sources and Impacts." In *The Arabs in Israel: Geographical Dynamics* (in Hebrew), ed. David Grossman and Avinoam Meir, 166–177. Ramat Gan: Bar Ilan University Press; Beer-Sheva: Ben-Gurion University of the Negev Press; Jerusalem: Magnes Press, Hebrew University.

Meyer-Brodnitz, Michael, and Daniel Czamanski. 1986. "Industrialization of the Arab Villages in Israel" (in Hebrew). *Riv'on Lekalkala* [vol. 36], no. 128 (April): 533–546. (For English version, see entry for Czamanski and Meyer-Brodnitz above.)

Miller, Ylana N. 1985. *Government and Society in Rural Palestine, 1920–1948.* Austin: University of Texas Press.

Ministry of ____. *See* Israel. Ministry of _____.

Mitchell, Timothy. 1991. "The Limits of the State: Beyond Statist Approaches and Their Critics." *American Political Science Review* 85 (1): 77–96.

Mivnei Ta'asiya. 1992. "Zipporit: A Residential Quarter and Industrial Area for Upper Nazareth" (in Hebrew). May. Place not indicated.

Morris, Benny. 1987. *The Birth of the Palestinian Refugee Problem, 1947–1949.* Cambridge: Cambridge University Press.

Muvhar, Avshalom. 1983. "Rural Settlement in Mountainous Galilee, 1967–1977." In *The Lands of Galilee* (in Hebrew), ed. Avshalom Shmueli, Arnon Soffer, and Nurit Kliot, 705–716. Haifa and Jerusalem: Society for Applied Scientific Research at Haifa University and the Ministry of Defense.

Myrdal, Gunnar. 1957. *Economic Theory and Under-developed Regions.* London: Gerald Duckworth.

Nader, Laura. 1972. "Up the Anthropologist: Perspectives Gained from Studying Up." In *Reinventing Anthropology,* ed. Dell Hymes. New York: Pantheon Books.

Nakhleh, Khalil. 1975. "The Direction of Local-Level Conflict in Two Arab Villages in Israel." *American Ethnologist* 2 (3): 497–516.

New Outlook, 1962. "Five Year Program for Arab and Druze Villages." This is an unsigned report of the five-year program prepared by the Bureau of the Adviser on Arab Affairs in the Prime Minister's Office, published in *New Outlook* 5 (3): 17–21.

Newman, David. 1984. "Ideological and Political Influences on Israeli Rurban Colonization: The West Bank and Galilee Mountains." *Canadian Geographer* 28 (2): 142–155.

Nir, Ori. 2001. "The Dream of Sakhnin-Tours Fades Away" (in Hebrew). *Ha'aretz*, 8 February, p. B3.

Oded, Yitzhak. 1964. "Land Losses among Israel's Arab Villages." *New Outlook* 7 (7): 10–25.

Office of the Adviser for Arab Affairs. *See under* Israel. Prime Minister's Office (PMO).

Orgad, Avigdor, and David Newman. 1991. *Regional Councils in Israel.* Tel Aviv: Association of Regional Councils.

Organization for Economic Cooperation and Development (OECD). 1973. *Effects of Traffic and Roads on the Environment in Urban Areas.* Report Prepared by an OECD Road Research Group, July 1993. Paris: OECD.

Orni, Efraim, and Elisha Efrat. 1971. *Geography of Israel.* 3rd (rev.) ed. Jerusalem: Israel Universities Press.

Peled, Israel. 1988. "Legal Structure of the Local Authority." In *Local Government in Israel*, ed. Daniel Elazar and Chaim Kalchheim, 165–197. Jerusalem: Jerusalem Center for Public Affairs/Center for Jewish Community Studies; Lanham, Md.: University Press of America.

Peled, Yoav. 1992. "Ethnic Democracy and the Legal Construction of Citizenship: Arab Citizens of the Jewish State." *American Political Science Review* 86 (2): 432-443.

Peretz, Don. 1958. *Israel and the Palestine Arabs.* Washington, D.C.: Middle East Institute.

Perroux, François. 1988. "The Pole of Development's New Place in a General Theory of Economic Activity." In *Regional Economic Development: Essays in Honour of François Perroux*, ed. Benjamin Higgins and Donald J. Savoie, 48–76. Boston: Unwin Hyman.

Petersburg, Ofer. 1996. "The Target: 2.4 Million Jews in Galilee" (in Hebrew). *Yediot Ahronot*, 31 October, p. 6.

PMO. *See* Israel. Prime Minister's Office.

Polenske, Karen R. 1988. "Growth Pole Theory and Strategy Reconsidered: Domination, Linkages, and Distribution." In *Regional Economic Development: Essays in Honour of François Perroux*, ed. Benjamin Higgins and Donald J. Savoie, 92–111. Boston: Unwin Hyman.

Rabinow, Paul. 1989. *French Modern: Norms and Forms of the Social Environment.* Cambridge: MIT Press.

Rabinowitz, Dan. 1993. "Oriental Nostalgia: The Transformation of the Palestinians into 'Israeli Arabs'" (in Hebrew). *Teoria uvikoret*, no. 4 (Autumn): 141–151.

______. 1994. "The Original Sin" (in Hebrew). *Ha'aretz*, 3 February, p. B1.

______. 1997. *Overlooking Nazareth: The Ethnography of Exclusion in Galilee.* Cambridge: Cambridge University Press.

______. 1998. *Anthropology and the Palestinians* (in Hebrew). Israel: Institute for Israeli Arab Studies.

Ram, Uri. 1996. "Adam Begalil: 'Avar, 'Ivri Ve'aravi" [Human in Galilee: Past, Hebrew and Arab]. Paper presented at a conference of the Israeli Anthropological Society in the session titled "Ethnography of Museums," Tel Aviv University, 19 March.

Razin, Eran. 1998. *Fiscal Disparities among Local Authorities in Israel, 1972–1995* (in Hebrew). Jerusalem: Floersheimer Institute for Policy Studies.

______. 1999. *Fiscal Disparities between Small and Large Municipalities in Israel* (in Hebrew). Jerusalem: Floersheimer Institute for Policy Studies.

Razin, Eran, Shlomo Hasson, and Anna Hazan. 1994. "Struggles over Municipal Boundaries: Regional Councils and Urban Space" (in Hebrew). *Ir Ve'ezor*, no. 23 (September): 5–28.

Razin, Eran, and Anna Hazan. 1994a. *The Development of Industrial and Employment Centers: The Local Government Dimension* (in Hebrew). Jerusalem: Floersheimer Institute for Policy Studies.

______. 1994b. "The Municipal Affiliation of Industrial Areas in the Rural-Urban Fringe" (in Hebrew). *Ofakim Begeographia*, no. 39: 31–46.

______. 2001. *Municipal Boundary Changes in Arab Local Authorities* (in Hebrew). Jerusalem: Floersheimer Institute for Policy Studies.

Reichman, Shalom. 1991. "Final Report of the Commission on the Boundaries of the City of Karmi'el" (in Hebrew). 25 February.

Reuveny, Jacob. 1988. "Administrative Issues in Local Government." In *Local Government in Israel*, ed. Daniel Elazar and Chaim Kalchheim, 165–197. Jerusalem: Jerusalem Center for Public Affairs/Center for Jewish Community Studies; Lanham, Md.: University Press of America.

Rokach, Avshalom. 1982. *Development of the Galilee and Its Settlements* (in Hebrew). Jerusalem: Information Center.

Ronayne, Maggie. 2001. "The Political Economy of Landscape: Conflict and Value in a Prehistoric Landscape in the Republic of Ireland—Ways of Telling." In *Contested Landscapes: Movement, Exile and Place*, ed. Barbara Bender and Margot Winer, 149–164. Oxford: Berg.

Rosenfeld, Henry. 1978. "The Class Situation of the Arab National Minority in Israel." *Comparative Studies in Society and History* 20 (3): 374–407.

______. 1988. "Nazareth and Upper Nazareth in the Political Economy of Israel." In *Arab-Jewish Relations in Israel: A Quest in Human Understanding*, ed. John E. Hofman. Bristol, Ind.: Wyndham Hall Press.

Rosenhek, Zeev. 1995. "The Origins and Development of a Dualistic Welfare State: The Arab Population in the Israeli Welfare State" (in Hebrew). Ph.D. dissertation, Hebrew University of Jerusalem.

Rozen, Rami. 1996. "The Secret Monster" (in Hebrew). *Mussaf Ha'aretz*, 2 August, p. 18.

Sabach, Ihab, and Yousouf Jabarin. 1998. "Industrial and Manufacturing Alternatives for the City of Nazareth" (in Hebrew). Strategic Planning and Information Unit, City of Nazareth.

Sa'di, Ahmad H. 1992. "Between State Ideology and Minority National Identity: Palestinians in Israel and in Israeli Social Science Research." *Review of Middle East Studies*, no. 5: 110–130.

______. 1997. "Modernization as an Explanatory Discourse of Zionist-Palestinian Relations." *British Journal of Middle Eastern Studies* 24 (1): 25–48.

Sanjek, Roger. 1996. "Ethnography." In *Encyclopedia of Social and Cultural Anthropology*, ed. Alan Barnard and Jonathan Spenser. London and New York: Routledge.

Schaffer, Bernard B. 1977. "Official Providers: Access, Equity and Participation." Institute of Development Studies, University of Sussex, and UNESCO (United Nations Educational, Scientific, and Cultural Organization). Photocopied typescript.

______. 1980. "Insiders and Outsiders: Insidedness, Incorporation and Bureaucratic Politics." *Development and Change* 11 (2): 187–210.

Schaffer, Bernard B., and Geoff B. Lamb. 1974. "Exit, Voice and Access." *Social Science Information* 13 (6): 73–90.

Schechter, Yitzhak. 1987. "Land Registration in Eretz-Israel in the Second Half of the Nineteenth Century" (in Hebrew). *Cathedra* 45 (September): 147–160.

Schnell, Izhak, Itzhak Benenson, and Michael Sofer. 1999. "The Spatial Pattern of Arab Industrial Markets in Israel." *Annals of the Association of American Geographers* 89 (2): 312–337.

Schnell, Izhak, Michael Sofer, and Israel Drori. 1995. *Arab Industrialization in Israel: Ethnic Entrepreneurship in the Periphery*. Westport, Conn.: Praeger. (This is a translation of: Michael Sofer, Izhak Schnell, Israel Drori, and 'As Atrash, *Entrepreneurship and Industrialization in Israeli Arab Society* [in Hebrew] [Ra'anana, Israel: Institute for Israeli Arab Studies, Bet Berl, 1995].)

Selwyn, Tom. 1996. Introduction to *The Tourist Image: Myths and Myth Making in Tourism*, ed. Tom Selwyn, 1–32. Chichester, England: John Wiley and Sons.

Seymour-Smith, Charlotte. 1986. *Macmillan Dictionary of Anthropology*. London: Macmillan Press.

Shaari, Yehuda. 1963. "Co-ordinated Jewish-Arab Development of Galilee." *New Outlook* 6 (9): 60–64.

Shamir, Ronen. 1996. "Suspended in Space: Bedouin under the Law of Israel." *Law and Society Review* 30 (2): 231–257.

Shamir, Shimon. 1962. "Changes in Village Leadership." *New Outlook* 5 (3): 93–112.

Shaw, Gareth, and Allan Williams. 1985. "The Role of Industrial Estates in Peripheral Rural Areas: The Cornish Experience, 1973–1981." In *The Industrialization of the Countryside,* ed. Michael J. Healey and Brian W. Ilbery, 221–241. Norwich, England: Geo Books.

Shefer, Daniel, Shaul Amir, Amnon Frenkl, and Hubert Law Yone. 1992. *Goals, Policy, and Development Alternatives.* Vol. 1 of *Development and Outline Plan for the Northern District, Amendment 9 to District Outline Plan 2* (in Hebrew). Haifa: Center for Urban and Regional Studies, Technion. (Title page headed by the imprimatur of the National Board for Planning and Building, the Ministry of the Interior, the Ministry of Construction and Housing, Israel Lands Administration, and the Jewish Agency.)

Shehada, Amal. 1992a. "Factories That Pollute the Air ... To the Arab Region!" (in Arabic). *Al Ittichad,* 15 May, p. 3.

______. 1992b. "Arab Knesset Members Demand the Return of the Expropriated Arab Lands That Have Not Yet Been Put to Use" (in Arabic). *Al Ittichad,* 26 July, p. 1.

______. 1992c. "The Owners of the Damaged Houses in Meshhed and Kafar Kanna Apply to the Courts Demanding a Halt to the Blasting" (in Arabic). *Al Ittichad,* 31 July.

______. 1992d. "Some Nights in Kafar Kanna We Feel That We Are at the Battlefront ... and We Don't Sleep!" (in Arabic). *Al Ittichad* [July?].

______. 1992e. "The Protesting Residents: 'We Want Industry for Our Towns, But We Do Not Want Death for Our Children'" (in Arabic). *Al Ittichad,* 23 September, p. 12.

______. 1993. "Freezing of the Legal Proceedings against Establishment of the Polluting Factory on Meshhed's Lands" (in Arabic). *Al Ittichad,* 2 February, p. 5.

Shehadeh, Raja. 1982. "The Land Law of Palestine: An Analysis of the Definition of State Lands." *Journal of Palestine Studies* 11 (2): 82–99.

Shehori, Dalia. 1999a. "Suissa Will Distribute Grant Only to Authorities That Have Collected a High Percentage of the Property Tax" (in Hebrew). *Ha'aretz,* 14 January, p. A5.

______. 1999b. "'Illegal' Ranches to Block the Arabs" (in Hebrew). *Ha'aretz,* 8 December, p A5.

Shils, Edward. 1961. "Center and Periphery." In *The Logic of Personal Knowledge: Essays Presented to Michael Polanyi on His Seventieth Birthday* [no indication of editor], 117–130. London: Routledge and Kegan Paul.

Shmoul, Avi. 2000. "Galilee/21 Milliard Sheqel Development Plan Submitted for Government Approval: International Airport, Railroad, and University" (in Hebrew). *Ha'aretz,* 5 December, p. C6.

______. 2001a. "Misgav Approves Establishment of Industrial Park with Sakhnin: Will Receive Priority Area A Status" (in Hebrew). *Ha'aretz,* 26 March, p. C4.

______. 2001b. "Wertheimer Plans to Set Up Industrial Park for the Arab Sector in Deir el Asad—Near Tefen" (in Hebrew). *Ha'aretz,* 16 April, p. C6.

______. 2002a. "The Ministry of Industry Will Develop Three Thousand Dunam for Industry in the Arab Sector in the Coming Four Years" (in Hebrew). *Ha'aretz (Nadlan),* 20 January, p. 12.

______. 2002b. "Tuba-Zangariyye Has Joined the Directorate of Tzahar Following Payment of 1.5 Million NIS by the Ministry of Commerce and Industry" (in Hebrew). *Ha'aretz (Nadlan),* 24 February, p. 11.

______. 2002c. "Four Hundred and Forty-Nine Dunam for Industry Marketed in the North in 2001" (in Hebrew). *Ha'aretz (Nadlan),* 10 March, p. 12.

Shokeid (Minkowitz), Moshe. 1968. "Immigration and Factionalism: An Analysis of Factions in Rural Israeli Communities of Immigrants." *British Journal of Sociology* 19 (4): 385–406.

Sikkuy. 1996. "The Socioeconomic Level of Jewish and Arab Localities in Israel in 1995: Comparative Data" (in Hebrew). Background paper. Jerusalem: Sikkuy, Association for the Advancement of Equal Opportunity.

Slyomovics, Susan. 1998. *The Object of Memory: Arab and Jew Narrate the Palestinian Village.* Philadelphia: University of Pennsylvania Press.

Smooha, Sammy. 1990. "Minority Status in an Ethnic Democracy: The Status of the Arab Minority in Israel." *Ethnic and Racial Studies* 13 (3): 389–413.

Soari, Yitzhak (chairman). 1993. *Recommendations of the Commission on the Determination of Criteria for Allocating the "Balancing Grant" to the Local Authorities* (in Hebrew). Report submitted to the Minister of the Interior, Jerusalem.

Sofer ["Sofer" in English table of contents], Arnon. 1997. "One Hundred Years of Zionism: From 'Adding Dunam to Dunam' to 'Territory for Peace'" (in Hebrew). *Nativ* 10 (3): 26–34.

Sofer, Michael, and Izhak Schnell. 1996. "Arab Industry in the Arab Economy" (in Hebrew). *Riv'on Lekalkala*, Anno 43, no. 3 (November): 482–499.

Sofer, Michael, Izhak Schnell, Israel Drori, and 'As Atrash. 1994. "Land and Industrialization in the Arab Settlements in Israel" (in Hebrew). *Ofakim Begeografia*, no. 39: 47–58.

Soffer, Arnon. 1977. "Nazareth: The Emergence of a Galilean Conurbation" (in Hebrew). *Nofim*, nos. 9–10: 187–196.

______. 1983a. "The Arabs of the North: From the Defeat of 1948 to the Leap of the 1970s." In *The Lands of Galilee* (in Hebrew), ed. Avshalom Shmueli, Arnon Soffer, and Nurit Kliot, 763–784. Haifa and Jerusalem: Society for Applied Scientific Research at Haifa University and the Ministry of Defense.

______. 1983b. "The Changing Situation of Majority and Minority and Its Spatial Expression: The Case of the Arab Minority in Israel." In *Pluralism and Political Geography: People, Territory and State*, ed. Nurit Kliot and Stanley Waterman. London: Croom Helm.

______. 1986. "The Territorial Conflict in Eretz Israel" (in Hebrew). *Ofakim Begeografia*, nos. 17–18: 7–23.

______. 1990. "Recommendation to Place the Cyclone Industrial Area in the Jurisdiction of Karmi'el: Considerations" (in Hebrew). 18 January. (Recommendation submitted to the Ministry of Interior-appointed boundary commission.)

______. 1991. "Israeli Judaization Policy in Galilee and Its Impact on Local Arab Urbanization: A Response." *Political Geography Quarterly* 10 (3): 282–285.

______. 1998. "On the Way to Regional Autonomy in Galilee: Is Arab Separatism at the Door?" Paper presented at a conference titled "The Arab Community in Israel: Basis for Autonomy or Pattern of Integration?" Moshe Dayan Center for Middle Eastern and African Studies, Tel Aviv University, 23 November.

Soffer, Arnon, and Rachel Finkel. n.d. *The Mitzpim Project: Interim Evaluation* (in Hebrew). Rehovot, Israel: Settlement Study Center.

Sorojun, Yossi, and Yehudah Arrarat. 1993. *Proposal for the Expansion of Jewish Settlement in Galilee* (in Hebrew). Safed: The Jewish Agency, Settlement Development Department, Northern Region.

Stein, Kenneth W. 1984. *The Land Question in Palestine, 1917–1939*. Chapel Hill: University of North Carolina Press.

Swaid, Hanna. Forthcoming. *Characterization and Ranking of the Local Authorities in the Northern District According to Their Planning Situation*. Eilaboun, Israel: Arab Center for Alternative Planning.

Torgovnik, Efraim. 1990. *The Politics of Urban Planning Policy*. Jerusalem: Jerusalem Center for Public Affairs; Lanham, Md.: University Press of America.

United Nations. 1974. *Rural Industrialization: Report of the Expert Group Meeting on Rural Industrialization*. (Meeting held in Bucharest, 24 to 28 September 1973.) New York: United Nations, Department of Economic and Social Affairs.

Vanhove, Norbert, and Leo H. Klaassen. 1987. *Regional Policy: A European Approach*. 2nd ed. Aldershot, England: Avebury, Gower Publishing.

Wallach, Jehuda, and Moshe Lissak, eds. 1978. *Atlas of Israel: The First Years 1948–1961*. Jerusalem: Carta.

Wallerstein, Immanuel M. 1974. "The Rise and Future Demise of the Capitalist World System." *Comparative Studies in Society and History* 16 (4): 387–415.

Weitz, Yosef. 1969. *Yosef Nahman: Man of Galilee* (in Hebrew). Tel Aviv: Massada.

Yiftachel, Oren. 1991. "Industrial Development and Arab-Jewish Economic Gaps in the Galilee Region, Israel." *Professional Geographer* 43 (2): 163–179.

______. 1992. *Planning a Mixed Region in Israel: The Political Geography of Arab-Jewish Relations in the Galilee.* Aldershot, England: Avebury, Ashgate Publishing.

______. 1994. "Spatial Planning, Land Control, and Arab-Jewish Relations in the Galilee" (in Hebrew). *Ir Ve'ezor,* no. 23 (September): 55–97.

______. 1997. *Watching over the Vineyard: The Example of Majd al Kurum* (in Hebrew). Ra'anana, Israel: Institute for Israeli Arab Studies.

______. 1999a. "'Ethnocracy': The Politics of Judaizing Israel/Palestine." *Constellations* 6 (3): 364–390.

______. 1999b. "Land Day" (in Hebrew). *Teoria uvikoret,* nos. 12–13: 279–290. (Special issue: "Fifty to Forty-Eight: Critical Moments in the History of the State of Israel.")

Yiftachel, Oren, and Dennis Rumley. 1991. "On the Impact of Israel's Judaization Policy in the Galilee." *Political Geography Quarterly* 10 (3): 286–296.

Ziv, Yehudah. 1970. "Geographical Units of the Galilee" (in Hebrew). *Teva Va'aretz* 12 (4): 166–172.

Zukin, Sharon. 1991. *Landscapes of Power: From Detroit to Disney World.* Berkeley: University of California Press.

Zureik, Elia T. 1979. *The Palestinians in Israel: A Study in Internal Colonialism.* London: Routledge and Kegan Paul.

Legislation Cited

British Mandate Legislation

1921. Mewat Land Ordinance, 1921. *Official Gazette of the Government of Palestine,* 1 March 1921, no. 38, p. 6.
1928. Land Settlement Ordinance, 1928. *Official Gazette of the Government of Palestine,* 26 January 1928, pp. 60–74.
1943. Land Ordinance (Acquisition for Public Purposes), 1943. *Palestine Gazette,* no. 1268, 27 May 1943, pp. 463–468.
1945. Defense (Emergency) Regulations, 1945. *Palestine Gazette,* no. 1442, Supplement 2, 27 September 1945.

Israeli Legislation

1948a. Law and Administration Ordinance, 5708–1948, Emergency Regulations Concerning the Cultivation of Waste Land and the Use of Unexploited Water Resources. *Iton Rishmi* [Official gazette] 27, Supplement B, 15 October 1948, pp. 3–8.
1948b. Law and Administration Ordinance, 5708–1948, Emergency Regulations Concerning Absentee Property. *Iton Rishmi* 37, Supplement B, 12 December 1948, pp. 59–70.
1949. Emergency (Security Zones) Regulations, 5708–1948. *Kovetz HaTaqanot* [Collection of regulations] 11, 27 April 1949, p. 169.
1950a. Absentee Property Law, 5710–1950. *Sefer Hahuqim* [Code of laws] 37, 20 March 1950, pp. 86–101.
1950b. Development Authority (Transfer of Property) Law, 5710–1950. *Sefer Hahuqim* 57, 9 August 1950, pp. 278–280.
1953. Land Acquisition (Validation of Acts and Compensation) Law, 5713–1953. *Sefer Hahuqim* 122, 20 March 1953, pp. 58–60.
1958. Local Councils Ordinance (Regional Councils), 5718–1958, *Kovetz HaTaqanot* 797, 4 June 1958, p. 1259.
1958. Prescription Law, 5718–1958. *Sefer Hahuqim* 251, 6 April 1958, pp. 112–115.
1959. Encouragement of Capital Investment Law, 5719–1959. *Sefer Hahuqim* 293, 16 August 1959, pp. 234–246.
1964. Municipalities Ordinance. *Laws of the State of Israel (New Version)* 8, 9 August 1964, p. 197.
1965. Planning and Building Law, 5725–1965. *Sefer Hahuqim* 467, 12 August 1965, pp. 307–352.

1969. Land Law, 5729–1969. *Sefer Hahuqim* 575, 27 July 1969, pp. 259–283.

1973. Absentee Property (Compensation) Law, 5733–1973. *Sefer Hahuqim* 701, 6 July 1973, pp. 164–169.

1981. Property Tax and Compensation Fund Law (Amendment 16), 5741–1981. *Sefer Hahuqim* 1020, 14 April 1981, p. 200.

1988. Planning and Building Law (Amendment 26), 5748–1988. *Sefer Hahuqim* 1259, 27 July 1987, p. 147.

1990. Planning and Building Procedures (Temporary Provisions) Law, 5750–1990. *Sefer Hahuqim* 1323, 20 July 1990, p. 166.

1992. Obligatory Tenders Law, 5752–1992. *Sefer Hahuqim* 1387, 12 March 1992, p. 114.

1993. Obligatory Tenders Regulations, 5753–1993. *Kovetz HaTaqanot* 5523, 19 May 1993, p. 826.

1995. Encouragement of Capital Investment Order (Prescription of Areas for Purposes of the Schedule to the Law) (Amendment 2), 5755–1995. *Kovetz HaTaqanot* 5698, 16 August 1995, p. 1731.

1995. Encouragement of Capital Investment Order (Prescription of Areas for Purposes of the Schedule to the Law) (Amendment 3), 5755–1995. *Kovetz HaTaqanot* 5698, 16 August 1995, p. 1731.

1995. Planning and Building Law (Amendment 43), 5755–1995. *Sefer Hahuqim* 1544, 24 August 1995, p. 450.

1996. Property Tax and Compensation Fund Law (Amendment 26), 5756–1996. *Sefer Hahuqim* 1590, 10 May 1996, p. 312.

1997. State Budgetary Arrangements Regulations. *Kovetz HaTaqanot* 5863, 3 December 1997, p. 99.

1999. Land Improvement Tax Law (Amendment 45), 5759–1999. *Sefer Hahuqim* 1707, 25 April 1999, p. 130.

2000. Municipalities Ordinance, addition of §9a. Effected by §7(3) of: the State Budgetary Arrangements (Legislative Amendments for Obtaining Budget Targets and Economic Policy for the 2000 Financial Year) Law, 5760–2000. *Sefer Hahuqim* 1724, 10 January 2000, pp. 71–72.

Subject Index

Selected Author Index

STUDIES IN THE HISTORY OF CHRISTIAN THOUGHT

VOLUME LXXVIII

CHRISTOPHER B. KAISER

CREATIONAL THEOLOGY AND
THE HISTORY OF PHYSICAL SCIENCE

CREATIONAL THEOLOGY AND THE HISTORY OF PHYSICAL SCIENCE